KU-609-264

Blattella germanica (German Cockroach), showing the head
in the normal rest position.

THE RENTOKIL LIBRARY

THE
COCKROACH

VOLUME I

A Laboratory Insect and an Industrial Pest

An account of the biology of the more
common species, including details of
their structure, physiology, behaviour
and ecology.

P. B. CORNWELL

Director of Research
Rentokil Laboratories Limited

HUTCHINSON OF LONDON

HUTCHINSON & CO (*Publishers*) LTD
178–202 Great Portland Street, London W1

London Melbourne Sydney
Auckland Bombay Toronto
Johannesburg New York

★

First published 1968

20726

CLASS ....
VOL. ....\.... COPY ....\....
SUPPLIER Frobishe
REC'D 22.2.72
ACCESS K17

Assistance with illustrations from Malcolm Drake and Ron Hayward
© P. B. Cornwell 1968
Drawings © Rentokil Laboratories Ltd., 1968, unless otherwise acknowledged

*This book has been set in Times, printed in Great Britain
on Smooth Wove paper by Anchor Press, and
bound by Wm. Brendon, both of Tiptree, Essex*
09 088670 4

CITY OF LIVERPOOL
COLLEGE OF TECHNOLOGY LIBRARY

CONTENTS

Acknowledgments   *page*   8

Preface   9

1. COCKROACHES AND MAN   11
Introduction. Establishment of pest status. Historical. Common and local
names; scientific names. The scientific interest in cockroaches. Insecticide
research.

2. EVOLUTIONARY DEVELOPMENT AND
CLASSIFICATION   19
Characteristics of present-day cockroaches: lack of specialisation; areas of
modification. Fossil cockroaches; the common ancestry of cockroaches and
termites. Cockroach classification; relationships between cockroaches and
other Orthopteran-type insects. The Orders GRYLLOBLATTODEA, ORTHOP-
TERA, PHASMIDA and DICTYOPTERA. Sub-divisions of the Suborder
BLATTARIA. Evolution towards the internal incubation of eggs.

3. THE PRINCIPAL COCKROACH SPECIES   40
The origin, distribution, habitat, appearance and biology of the principal
cockroach species: I. Closely associated with man; *Blattella germanica*,
Blatta orientalis, *Periplaneta americana*, *Periplaneta australasiae*, *Periplaneta
brunnea*, *Periplaneta fuliginosa* and *Supella supellectilium*. II. Occasionally
associated with man; *Pycnoscelus surinamensis*, *Leucophaea maderae*, *Nauphoeta cinerea*, *Neostylopyga rhombifolia* and *Blaberus* spp. III. Accidental
invaders of homes; *Eurycotis floridana*, *Parcoblatta pensylvanica* and *Blattella
vaga*. IV. Outdoor species in Britain (*Ectobius* spp.), Australia (*Methana* spp.)
and the U.S.A. (*Cryptocercus punctulatus* and *Attaphila fungicola*). V. Other
species of special interest; *Gromphadorhina laevigata*. Identification key.

4. THE INTEGUMENT   101
Structure of the cuticle: pore canals; penetration of the cuticle. Thickness and
chemical composition; water- and alkali-soluble constituents. Wax layer;
hypodermis, oenocytes and wax secretion. Cement layer and dermal glands.
Pygidial glands and tergal secretions.
  Receptor organs: light receptors; contact receptors; proprioceptors; chemo-
receptors; auditory receptors.

5. ALIMENTARY CANAL AND DIGESTION   116
Basic structure: mouthparts; fore-gut and salivary glands; mid-gut; malpighian tubules; hind-gut. Speed of movement of food through the gut.
Enzymes and digestion; sites and levels of enzyme activity. Cellulase and
protozoan symbionts. The gut and feeding behaviour.

6. BLOOD CIRCULATION, RESPIRATION AND EXCRETION 134
The circulatory system: dorsal blood vessel; circulation in the wings. The haemolymph; haemolymph volume and water content; haemocyte count; division of haemocytes and haemolymph coagulation; speed of haemolymph circulation. Regulation of circulation by neuro-hormones; endocrine control and the pericardial cells; feeding and heart rate; compensating mechanisms in heart beat control. Transport of neuro-hormones.

The respiratory system: gaseous exchange; effects of temperature and differences between species. Tissue respiration; respiratory effects of hormones.

The excretory system: malpighian tubules; fat body and storage excretion; endocrine control of the fat body. Storage and excretion of uric acid by the male accessory glands. Deposition of waste products in the cuticle.

7. THE NERVOUS SYSTEM AND ENDOCRINE ACTIVITY 160
Units of nerve tissue. The central nervous system: the brain; the ganglia. The sympathetic nervous system: the stomatogastric system; functions of the stomatogastric system. Conduction of nerve impulses; neuronal pathways; reflexes; endogenous nerve activity; inhibiting centres; neuro-hormones and nerve activity. Nerve toxins. Supply of nutrients to the nervous system.

8. THE FACTORS INVOLVED IN MATING 178
Sex attractants: the volatile attractant of P. americana; endocrine control of the female sex attractant; reaction of male P. americana; sexual behaviour of B. germanica. Modifications of the terminal abdominal segments: external genitalia of the male; external genitalia of the female. Copulatory behaviour: use of the genitalia in copulation; the period in copulation; mating in other species; factors affecting receptivity of the female. Internal reproductive organs of the male: sperm formation; formation and structure of the spermatophore; insemination.

9. THE FACTORS INVOLVED IN OOTHECA PRODUCTION 198
Internal reproductive organs of the female: the ovary; oogenesis. Association of bacteroids with the ovary; appearance of bacteroids; entry into oocytes. Control of oocyte development: gonadotrophic hormone, moulting and oocyte maturation; inhibition of the hormone in cockroaches which carry the ootheca; removal of the corpora allata and implantation; inhibition of the corpora allata by the brain; artificial oothecae and severance of the nerve cord; severance of the nerve cord at different positions. Oocyte maturation and mating; oocyte maturation and enzyme activity in the gut; oocyte maturation and food. Colleterial glands and formation of the ootheca; ovulation. Fertilisation and parthenogenesis. Types of oviposition: oviparity; false ovoviviparity; false viviparity. Deposition of oothecae; structural features of the ootheca.

10. GROWTH, DEVELOPMENT AND NATURAL ENEMIES 220
Embryological development: fate of the bacteroids; incubation period of the ootheca; hatching from the ootheca. Post-embryological development: characteristics of nymphal growth; growth of the antennae; growth of the cerci; growth of the terminal abdominal sternites of the female; growth of the wings. Growth and moulting: increase in weight; increase in size; number of

moults and loss of appendages; regeneration of appendages; effects of individual and communal rearing. Effects of diet: protein requirements; vitamins. Seasonal variation in development. Inquiline cockroaches. Natural enemies of cockroaches: hymenoptera; other predators and parasites. Defence mechanisms against predators.

11. MOVEMENT   249

Voluntary movement: behaviour at rest; flight and running; articulation of the legs. Mass migration; distance of movement; effects of population pressure; influence of season. Night activity; night inspection. Measurement of the circadian rhythm; influence of temperature and food; changes in light and darkness; control mechanism of diurnal rhythm; changes in the neurosecretory cycle; reset mechanism of the neurosecretory cycle.

Involuntary movement: international dissemination; quarantine. Insects carried in aircraft; cockroaches in aircraft before World War II; cockroaches taken from aircraft in New Zealand; *P. brunnea* introduced into Britain. Cockroaches carried by ships; incidence in food storage and food handling areas of ships; incidence in ships' holds. Establishment of new infestations.

12. INFLUENCE OF THE ENVIRONMENT   278

Effects of temperature: immobilisation at low temperatures; acclimatisation; recovery from chill-coma; the cold death point; survival outdoors; the upper lethal temperature; long and short exposures to high temperatures; the temperature preferendum; preferred temperatures of different species. Response to humidity alone; desiccation in different species. Effects of air movement. Environmental factors in relation to cockroach habits. The environment of air travel: effects of low pressures; tests in jet aircraft; cockroaches in space; gaseous environments. Absence of food and water. The hatching of oothecae; water content of oothecae; loss of water from oothecae.

13. DISEASE   302

Cockroaches in sewers, latrines and cesspools. Bacteria isolated from cockroaches associated with disease outbreaks. Viruses, protozoa and parasitic worms. Experimental transmission of disease organisms. Gastroenteritis and food poisoning organisms. Vector capabilities of different species of cockroach. Typhoid. Persistence of bacteria in cockroach excrement and on utensils and food. Allergy to cockroaches. The role of cockroaches in disease transmission.

14. THE INCIDENCE OF PEST COCKROACHES IN THE
     BRITISH ISLES   315

Changes in post-war Britain. The survey. The sample: geographical distribution; types of property; age of properties in relation to distribution and type; heating. Incidence of cockroach species: infestations in different types of property; infestations and the age of properties; infestation and central heating. Locations of infestations within buildings. Geographical variation in the incidence of species; infestations in cities and large towns. Other species. Conclusions from the survey.

About Volume II   347

Bibliography   349

Subject Index   367

Author Index   388

ACKNOWLEDGMENTS

Many of my colleagues at Rentokil have helped me in the preparation of this book: especially Mr. Robin Edwards, our entomologist and photographer, for reading the text, for making many useful suggestions, and correcting the proofs. He took many of the photographs, and assisted with the layout of the illustrations. Our librarian, Mrs. Gale, has performed, with quiet efficiency, the task of obtaining most of the publications to which I have referred, returning them to outside libraries on time, and arranging for many translations. My secretary, Miss Edwards, typed the manuscript and patiently collated the information obtained from the cockroach survey. I would like to thank her for the many hours spent on this, and for arranging the bibliography.

Dr. T. G. Onions of Brunel University advised on the technical content and made a number of valued recommendations to bring the book into line with modern teaching.

The service staff of the Pest Control Division of Rentokil provided, in response to the survey questionnaire, the information on the incidence of pest cockroaches in infested premises; and, not least, I would like to thank those at Felcourt who have given me the encouragement to write this volume.

P. B. C.

PREFACE

This book, the first of two volumes about cockroaches, has been written in an effort to bring together much of the more recent knowledge which has been obtained about these insects, from laboratory studies and as pests of industry and the home. It is not intended that this volume should provide an elementary introduction to entomology, neither is it an exhaustive résumé of the wealth of information scattered through the many scientific publications of the last two decades. Rather, from this book, students of entomology, and those concerned with cockroaches as pests, may acquire a fuller appreciation of the biology, physiology and behaviour of one of the most useful insects for research, and perhaps the most maligned of insects known to man.

Four groups of people are concerned with cockroaches:
1. The pest control industry, in eradicating the pest species from infested premises, usually as part of a wider service for the control of other industrial and domestic pests.
2. Teaching establishments for which the American Cockroach provides a useful type specimen for demonstrating the external and internal features of insects.
3. The research physiologist who, because of the large size of some cockroaches, is able to use them successfully for experiments to elucidate certain internal functions of insects, and
4. The insecticide chemist who, because of the ease of rearing large numbers of cockroaches in captivity, uses them for studying the mode of action of insecticides and as test insects for evaluating the properties of promising new insecticidal compounds.

These four groups have a widely different level of scientific appreciation and it is therefore impossible in one book to provide a text which meets the demands of each. It is hoped that this volume about the insects themselves, and the second volume to follow, on insecticides and cockroach control, will provide a source of reference which will satisfy many of the demands of this heterogeneous readership.

Two previous books have been written about the cockroach: *The Structure and Life-history of the Cockroach—an Introduction to the Study of Insects* by Miall and Denny, written about the Oriental Cockroach in 1886 and now well out of print, and *The Cockroach (Periplaneta americana* L.) by Cameron, published in 1961. The first of these is a classical work based on early knowledge of entomology accumulated during the 18th and 19th centuries. The second, more recent work is designed as an introduction to entomology for students of science and medicine, with instructions for practical work. Both deal at some length with the external and internal anatomy of the species, but make only passing reference to the importance of cockroaches as pests.

The greatest single contribution to recent knowledge about cockroaches has been made by Dr. L. M. Roth and his colleagues with a series of monographs and numerous papers on various aspects of the BLATTARIA. I am grateful to him for the use of a number of photographs that appear in this book, and I have leaned heavily on his *Biotic Association of Cockroaches* and *The Medical and Veterinary Importance of Cockroaches* in preparing the chapter on disease. Other authors, too, will find that I have quoted from them, in many instances verbatim, with a view to avoiding misinterpretation.

1

COCKROACHES AND MAN

Introduction—Establishment of pest status—Historical—Common and local names; scientific names—The scientific interest in cockroaches—Insecticide research.

Introduction

The cockroach is probably the most obnoxious insect known to man. About half a dozen species of cockroaches have managed to acquire a relationship with man, rivalled perhaps only by lice and fleas. The latter are known vectors of certain rickettsial organisms (typhus) and rodent diseases (plague and murine typhus) but like the bed bug, cockroaches may be only accidental carriers of pathogens. Nevertheless there is a considerable body of evidence to incriminate a number of cockroaches as potential carriers of disease whose importance in this regard is becoming more fully recognised.

The pest status of the cockroach derives mainly from an aesthetic abhorrence of what is regarded as a loathsome intruder: its speed and unpredictable direction of movement, the enormous numbers to which populations can increase if left undisturbed, and the habit of cockroaches of tainting with a characteristic odour, and fouling with excrement all food and surfaces with which they come into contact.

Their status as pests is increased by the fact that cockroaches are usually associated with poor standards of hygiene. Thus, to the vast majority of people, cockroaches in the home and place of work are psychologically disturbing and to some can cause considerable mental distress.

Establishment of pest status

Cockroaches are an ancient group of insects which have existed on earth about 100 times longer than man. The status of a few as pests is therefore very recent. At the present time there are about 3,500 known species, mostly of tropical origin, and perhaps as many more which have not been named or described. As a group, they show considerable diversity of size, colouration and habit. Rehn[1] rightly says that 'because cockroaches are normally seen as house-haunting pests and in the majority of people cause a strong feeling of aversion, it is often difficult to convince the "doubting Thomases" that the number of species of cockroach which are domiciliary pests is greatly limited—in fact less than one per cent of all known forms. Also that cockroaches of many kinds are diurnal, with hundreds of species inhabiting tropical forests, others semi-aquatic, some living in the ground, a few wood-boring, while a dozen or so genera are found in a state of either known or suspected commensalism, in the nests of ants, wasps or termites'. To this should be added those which inhabit caves in association with bats, and others of the desert, some of which inhabit the burrows of rodents.

In the early association of cockroaches with man, outdoor living forms probably gained entry into his protective shelter. With the need for man to store food against shortage, particularly food of varied type which would appeal to omnivorous insects, it is not difficult to appreciate the beginning of the domiciliary habit. Thus whilst the great majority of cockroaches in tropical countries continue to live as scavengers outdoors, where their food consists of vegetation and organic matter, some became early co-habitants with man and have travelled with him ever since.

Today, the pest cockroaches have found our man-made environment and food highly suitable for their existence. With the increase in transport the pest species have been inadvertently carried by him to almost all parts of the world, their establishment being limited principally by temperature. The inability of domestic cockroaches to withstand unusual cold was mentioned by Marlatt[2] in connection with the freak winter in Florida in 1894 which was apparently very destructive to the citrus groves and, 'destroyed all the cockroaches even in houses, except a few unusually well protected'. Nevertheless to demonstrate the ability of cockroaches to penetrate even the polar latitudes, this same writer mentions that, 'in the far north a species occurs in the huts of Laplanders and lives on the winter stores of dried fish'.

Historical

Because of the long and close association of cockroaches with man a great deal has been written about their habits and methods of control; most of these writings undoubtedly contain an element of truth but with the passage of time it seems likely that they have been colourfully elaborated. For ex-ample, on the subject of getting rid of cockroaches, Blatchley[3] says: 'For no other insects have so many quack remedies been urged and are so many newspaper remedies published. Many of them have their good points but the majority are worthless. In fact, rather than put faith in half of those which have been established, it were better to rely on the recipe current among Mexicans: To get rid of cockroaches—catch three and put them in a bottle, and so carry them to where two roads cross. Here hold the bottle upside down, and as they fall out repeat aloud three *credos*. Then all the cockroaches in the house from which these three came will go away.'

Some of the cockroaches mentioned in this volume have long been pests of ships. Roth & Willis[4] quote a method of control adopted by the Japan-ese Navy: 'a seaman who has captured 300 cockroaches will be granted one day special shore leave. They call it "shore leave for cockroaches". The purpose is to promote extermination of cockroaches in a warship because, on the one hand, any warship suffers from numerous cockroaches, and on the other hand, any seaman likes shore leave'. These same authors have reviewed the early reports of the depredations of cockroaches on ships: the record in 1634 of Drake capturing the ship *Philip* which was overrun with cockroaches; of Bligh in 1792 disinfecting H.M.S. *Bounty* with boiling water; of Lewis in 1836 being greatly annoyed by hundreds of cockroaches in his cabin at night during a voyage from England to Van Diemen's Land and of many records reporting that cockroaches were so numerous on ships that they gnawed the skin and nails of men on board—and apparently parts of their boots.

On cockroaches attacking man, Rau[5] says that, 'one often reads of the injury done to the eyebrows of sleeping children by *P. americana* in Central and South America. The story, incredulous as it may seem, is that the roaches at night find the sleeping children and feed upon their eyebrows. From my own experience . . . I was awakened by a tickling sensation on my face only to find upon opening my eyes, a pair of long cockroach antennae playing delicately for sense impressions while the cockroach's extended mouthparts were imbibing moist nutriment from my nostrils'.

There are many reports of cockroaches being used as cures for various diseases and disorders, and of cockroaches in certain parts of the world being eaten as food. Today the domiciliary species are pests of food manufacturing industries, of food storage and food handling areas; warehouses, kitchens, hotels, restaurants; in short, **pests of poor hygiene**. Thus in more recent times, cockroaches or parts of their bodies may occasionally occur as contaminants in food, but there is reason to believe that during the earlier part of this century this was certainly more common than today. Thus Roth & Willis[6] quote Caudell (1904, *Ent. News* **15**, 62): 'Cockroaches thrive in British Columbia. . . . On this trip I had them served to me in three different styles, alive in strawberries, à la carte with fried fish and baked in biscuit', and from Blatchley[3]:

> 'On every dish the booming beetle falls
> The cockroach plays, or caterpillar crawls;
> A thousand shapes of variegated hues
> Parade the table or inspect the stews.
> When hideous insects every plate defile;
> The laugh how empty and how forced the smile.'

It is not difficult to visualise a time, probably between 1850 and 1900, when in this country both the Oriental and German Cockroaches reached a peak of co-existence with man, their presence being accepted as commonplace in homes, places of work, inns, prisons and other buildings, much in the same way that early sailing ships were invariably infested by the American Cockroach. Before 1940 and the great advances made in the development of synthetic compounds for insect control, infestations of cockroaches in buildings were difficult to eradicate. Now, however, there is no doubt that far fewer properties in Britain are infested by cockroaches than at any time since World War II. Much can be attributed to the emphasis on hygiene which has grown tremendously in the food and catering industries, and to the level of hygiene in homes which has also seen an enormous change within the present century. At the same time the control of cockroach infestations by the pest control industry has benefited greatly by the extensive armoury of available insecticides, formulations and techniques.

Wherever food is stored, manufactured, or handled, cockroaches are potentially capable of establishing an infestation. With the purchase of food by large communities from chain stores and supermarkets, any lapse in hygiene, or ignorance of the possible role of insects, such as cockroaches in the transmission of pathogenic bacteria, is surely a social offence. Similarly, with the improving standard of living of many communities the catering industry has acquired a wider clientele; schools and hospitals are served by large kitchens and many office and factory workers eat communally in large canteens. With these changes in the eating habits of the population there is an ever increasing need to ensure first-class hygiene. To harbour cockroaches in such premises at the present time is an affront to man in his endeavours to improve his living standards.

Common and local names
With the abhorrence expressed by most people towards cockroaches it is not surprising that they have become known by a variety of local names, some of which have been used as terms of abuse. The word cockroach is supposedly derived from the Spanish 'Cucaracha', but one of the earliest names given to these insects was 'lucifuga' from their habit of always shunning the light. The common English name for the Oriental Cockroach (*Blatta orientalis*) is 'black beetle' from its dark colour and the non-technical use of the word beetle to describe almost any insect that crawls. On this subject, Shipley,[7] in his book *More Minor Horrors*, quotes from *Punch* of the governess who demanding precision from her pupil says: 'And perhaps, Mabel, as they are not black and as they are not beetles you will in future call them cockroaches'. Mabel: 'Certainly, Miss Smith, although they are not cocks and neither are they roaches'. (The term cockroach, in preference to the American abbreviation 'roach', is used throughout this book.)

The Oriental Cockroach has also been referred to in Britain as the 'mill beetle' and as the 'black clock' presumably because of its regular appearance at dusk. In northern Germany, the cockroach is referred to as 'Schwabe', a term which is also applied to an inhabitant of southern Germany. In that area it is popularly known as 'Preusze' after the north Germans. In East Germany the local name is 'Russe' (or Russian Cockroach) and in West Germany 'Franzose' (or French cockroach)—these names indicating a certain national antipathy to rival countries as well as a fanciful idea as to their origin.[2] 'Spanier' dates from the time of Carlos V and 'Däne' from Denmark. The early Dutch called the cockroach 'Kakkerlak' and in the Swedish settlement they were known as 'Brotaetare' or bread eaters. Around Philadelphia in the USA, the Oriental Cockroach is locally referred to as the 'Shad roach', its abundance coinciding annually with the arrival of the Shad fish to spawn in the Delaware river.

The German Cockroach, *Blattella germanica* ('small'+*Blatta*) is also known by a variety of names: the most common is 'steam-fly' because of its association with that type of environment; 'steam-bug' was apparently at one time a local name in Lancashire and 'shiner' around Aldershot.[8] 'Water bug' is a common name used for cockroaches throughout the United States, 'Yankee settler' in Nova Scotia, and 'Croton bug' in the eastern United States because of the considerable increase in the abundance of *B. germanica* in New York City about the time of the construction of the Croton Aquaduct. The 'Bombay Canary' is a common name for the American Cockroach on ships, but the derivation of this name is obscure.

Scientific names
The scientific names given to many cockroaches have been based on less fanciful thoughts: *Periplaneta* (Gr. 'around' and 'a wanderer'); *Supella* (Gr. 'house'); *Eurycotis* (Gr. 'broad' and 'form'); *Parcoblatta* (Gr. 'frugal' and *Blatta*); *Pycnoscelus* (Gr. 'dense' and 'tarsi'); *Cryptocercus* (Gr. 'hidden' and 'cerci') and *Blaberus* (Gr. 'harmful').

One species of *Blaberus*, namely *B. craniifer*, is commonly called the 'giant death's-head cockroach' from its large size and the markings on the prothorax. As will be seen from Chapter 3 the specific names given to some of the more common pest cockroaches, e.g. *americana*, *australasiae*, *germanica* and *orientalis*, are now thought to be totally erroneous in indicating their origins.

In common with many other insects it is not surprising to find that cockroaches have been known by many different scientific names. For instance, the German Cockroach, has been given seven names during the last 300 years:

> *Blatta germanica* Linnaeus, 1767
> *Blatta obliquata* Daldorff, 1793
> *Ectobius germanicus* Stephens, 1835
> *Phyllodromia bivittata* Saussure, 1864
> *Phyllodromia germanica* Brunner von Wattenwyl, 1865
> *Ischnoptera bivittata* Thomas, 1876
> *Blattella germanica* Caudell, 1903

The same is true of the Oriental Cockroach, which until recent times was included in the genus *Periplaneta*.

The scientific interest in cockroaches

Much of our more detailed knowledge about cockroaches has been acquired relatively recently. Thirty years ago, Rau[5] wrote: 'the American cockroach (*Periplaneta americana*), even though regarded as abhorrent and loathsome, has for many years been a favourite laboratory insect for biology students and investigators. Its anatomy and physiology have been studied with some degree of thoroughness, but it is indeed surprising to find that its life-history and details of its everyday behaviour remain practically unknown. When the cockroach, steeped in alcohol, reaches the student it is quite a changed creature from what it once was—not even its odour is the same—to make no further comparison with the live, agile insect, inquisitively waving its long antennae in the air for impressions of food, mates and shelter'.

The American cockroach continues to be used widely in schools and colleges for introducing students to the subject of entomology. It is a reasonable assumption that more cockroaches have been dissected on the laboratory bench than any other insect and more cockroach mouthparts, too, have been examined and drawn under the microscope than those of any other insect. This can undoubtedly be attributed to the large size of *P. americana* and to the relative lack of specialisation in the anatomy of cockroaches as a group. It is not difficult to rear cockroaches in captivity (see Volume II) and relatively little space is required to provide sufficient numbers for class study. In any event, most commercial organisations and Government Institutions that maintain cultures of cockroaches for research are prepared to supply them for teaching purposes.

The advantages to be gained by allowing young students to rear, observe and experiment with living insects cannot be over-estimated. To observe the process of moulting alone is sufficient justification for having live insects for demonstration and there is none more suitable for this than the cockroach. The knowledge which has now been accumulated on the biology and behaviour of the different species of cockroaches has come about by introducing an eagerness for inquiry among young biologists. This, together with information on the anatomy and physiology of the cockroach, has been of considerable value in indicating the evolutionary relationships between the species, and has made a large contribution towards helping those concerned with eradicating the pest species from infested premises. Such enthusiasm for cockroaches caused one such biologist, Mr. William Bunting, who has contributed much to our knowledge of the species imported into Britain on bananas, to name his house 'Periplaneta'.

The number of contributions to the scientific literature on cockroaches has grown steadily since 1900 (Fig. 1). In this volume the reader will be introduced to only a small fraction of the many hundreds of papers which have been published concerning the structure, biology, physiology and behaviour of the principal species. As an encouragement to research workers, the eminent physiologist Dr. Scharrer[9] once wrote: 'The laboratory investigator who keeps up a battle to rid his rat colony of cock-roaches may well consider giving up the rats and working with the cock-roaches instead. From many points of view the roach is practically made to order as a laboratory subject. Here is an animal of frugal habits, tenacious of life, eager to live in the laboratory and very modest in its space requirements'. Dr. Scharrer was referring, in this instance, to her

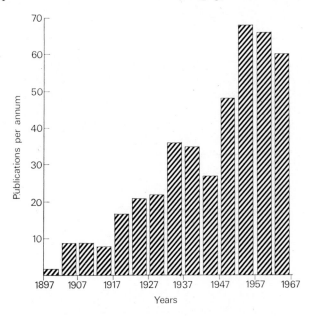

Fig. 1. Increase in the number of scientific publications during the last 70 years dealing with the biology, physiology and behaviour of cockroaches (based on the references quoted in this volume).

stock colony of the Madeira cockroach at the University of Colorado, derived from specimens which originally arrived in the U.S.A. as stow-aways in a shipment of laboratory monkeys. It was with these insects that Dr. Scharrer demonstrated the part played by hormones in the control of cockroach development, of the activity of the female reproductive organs and the incidence of tumours in the insect's alimentary canal.

Insecticide research
It is important to mention the very significant contribution which cockroaches have made to our understanding of insecticidal action and insecticide resistance, and towards the development of useful new com-pounds for insect control. These subjects are examined in some detail in Volume II, but it is relevant here to draw attention to the scientific effort

B

which has been made in this field during the last 20 years. Each year the Commonwealth Institute of Entomology publishes abstracts of scientific papers concerned with applied entomology (The Review of Applied Entomology). An analysis of reviews dealing with cockroaches and insecticides for the period 1942–66, shows the decrease in studies on inorganic insecticides and plant extracts since World War II and the con-

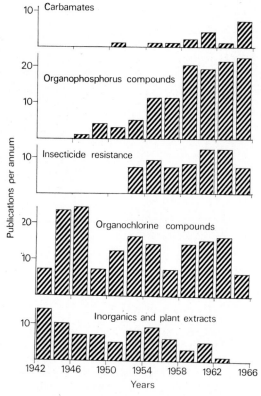

Fig. 2. Incidence of scientific papers dealing with insecticides and cockroaches during the years 1942–66.

siderable interest in organochlorine compounds immediately following the war. It also shows the development of resistance to these insecticides in 1953, and the subsequent emphasis during the last decade on organophosphorus compounds and the insecticidal carbamates (Fig. 2). Improvements in the efficacy and safety of the materials used in insect control rely on endeavours in these areas of scientific research; this effort is reflected in the range of insecticides and techniques now used to control the pest species of cockroaches.

2

EVOLUTIONARY DEVELOPMENT AND CLASSIFICATION

Characteristics of present-day cockroaches: lack of specialisation; areas of modification
—Fossil cockroaches; the common ancestry of cockroaches and termites—Cockroach
classification; relationships between cockroaches and other Orthopteran-type insects—
The Orders GRYLLOBLATTODEA, ORTHOPTERA, PHASMIDA and DICTYOPTERA—Sub-
divisions of the Suborder BLATTARIA—Evolution towards internal incubation of eggs.

Cockroaches are among the most primitive of winged insects. Their origin
dates back 250 million years to the Carboniferous period and fossil records
show that they were extremely abundant insects at that time. Other fossil
records from the Carboniferous show that this was an age in geological
history of moist conditions and high humidity which supported lush plant
growth. Tillyard[10] suggests that cockroaches probably evolved together
with the abundant flora of that time, when they became absolutely
dominant and outnumbered in individuals, if not in actual species, all
other groups of winged insects put together.

   In this chapter we are concerned with the information provided by fossil
remains, the changes which have occurred during the period of evolutionary development of cockroaches, and their affinities with other insects,
notably termites, grasshoppers and crickets, mantids, and other Orthoptera. To appreciate some of the changes which have occurred during evolutionary development, it is proposed here to give a brief description of the
characteristics of present-day cockroaches and then to point out the
primitive features which have been retained and the areas which have
become specialised.

Characteristics of present-day cockroaches
The head
The general shape of most cockroaches is oval and flattened, the head
when at rest is nearly horizontal and bent under, almost concealed by the
pronotum, and the mouth projects backwards between the bases of the
first pair of legs (Fig. 3). The whip-like antennae, inserted just below the
middle of the eyes, are often longer than the body and are composed of
very many short segments. The mouthparts serve a biting, chewing and
licking function; the mandibles are strong and toothed, the palps of the
maxillae have five segments, and those of the labium have three.

   The compound eyes are usually large with many small facets. The simple eyes (ocelli) are often present in winged forms, when they are located close to the antennal sockets, but they may be greatly reduced in size, or absent. When the forewings and hindwings are reduced, the ocelli are often represented by small pale spots (fenestrae), or lost altogether.

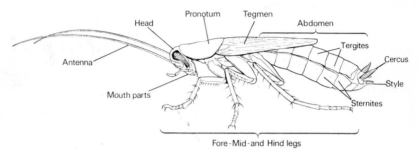

Fig. 3. An adult male *Blatta orientalis* showing the typical appearance of a present-day cockroach.

The thorax

The pronotum is large, rounded, and often projects over the head. When present, the tegmina (forewings) are usually much hardened and more or less translucent, their margins overlapping along the mid-dorsal line. The anal area of the forewing is distinctly marked off by a strong furrow.

The hindwings are membranous and delicate. They are always shorter than the tegmina, but are usually fully developed when the tegmina are long. The hindwings are always reduced if the tegmina are short, and may sometimes be rudimentary or absent.

The legs are slender, depressed beneath the body and the three pairs are almost equal in length. They are characterised by large flattened coxae, which protect the ventral surface of the thorax, and the femora are long and compressed, the lower border having two ridges, or keels, which usually bear spines varying in size and number. The tibiae are heavily spined above and beneath. The tarsi are five-jointed; the last joint has two claws with or without an arolium between, the other tarsal joints usually have a pad, or pulvillus, beneath each. The legs are developed for progression by rapid scurrying, pest cockroaches seldom using their wings to escape.

The abdomen

The abdomen is large relative to the thorax, often broad, especially in females, and composed of ten segments of which only seven or eight are visible. In some species the dorsal plates (tergites) of the first and second abdominal segments of the male are specialised or modified. The tenth abdominal tergite is known as the supra-anal plate and bears, in both sexes, a pair of jointed appendages known as cerci.

On the ventral surface of the abdomen nine plates (sternites) are visible in the male and seven in the female. The last sternite of both sexes is known as the subgenital plate. In the adult male, and nymphs of both sexes, this structure bears two unjointed appendages (styles). The tergites and sternites of the abdomen overlap each other and are capable of great extension and depression.

The cockroaches of today have no visible ovipositor as in the closely related crickets, grasshoppers and locusts. Cockroaches differ from these insects in that the eggs are not laid singly, or in pods, but in groups in a hardened capsule—the ootheca. The nymphs resemble the parents in shape but are wingless, the wing buds appearing towards the end of nymphal development.

Lack of specialisation
Comparison of the features of fossil cockroaches (Fig. 4) with their present-day descendants, shows that they have changed very little with the passage of time. They have remained relatively unspecialised insects and their

Fig. 4. *Aphthoroblattina johnsoni;* a fossil cockroach in an ironstone nodule taken from upper carboniferous rocks near Dudley in the South Stafford and Shropshire coalfield.

generalised characters still far outnumber their specialised ones; their flat bodies have enabled them to retain a cryptic habit which has undoubtedly contributed to their spread in trade, assisted in their establishment within buildings, and caused difficulties in the effective application of insecticides to control the pest species.

The records imprinted in the Carboniferous rocks show that, even as

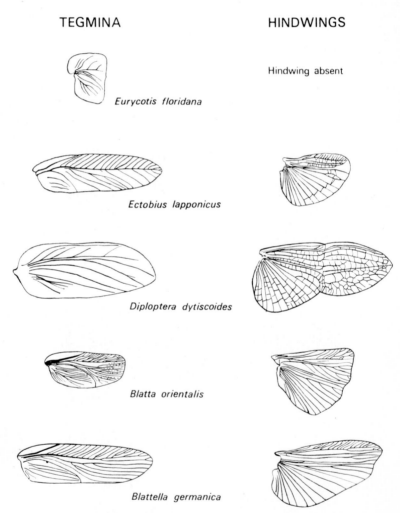

TEGMINA   HINDWINGS

Hindwing absent

Eurycotis floridana

Ectobius lapponicus

Diploptera dytiscoides

Blatta orientalis

Blattella germanica

Fig. 5. Variations in the development of tegmina and hindwings of cockroaches, demonstrating (1) wing reduction e.g. *Eurycotis* and *Blatta*, (2) reduced venation, e.g. in the tegmina of *Diploptera*, (3) increased number of minor veins, e.g. in the tegmina of *Leucophaea* and *Periplaneta*, (4) folding of the apex of the hind wing, e.g. in *Diploptera*

long ago as 250 million years, cockroaches had many of the features which allow us to distinguish present-day cockroaches from other insects. Their habitat then was much the same as most of the outdoor-living species now; 'their association with fossil plants, especially ferns, suggests that they were, as now, fond of low moist places with abundant vegetation along the banks of rivers and marshes'.[11] Some, however, have managed to accomodate much drier environments. The more recent cockroaches have,

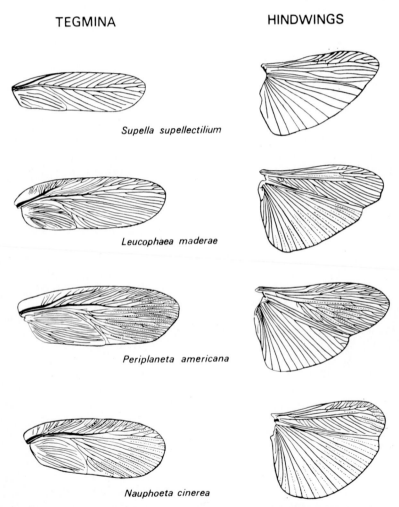

TEGMINA   HINDWINGS

Supella supellectilium

Leucophaea maderae

Periplaneta americana

Nauphoeta cinerea

and (5) increased area of the anal lobe with fan-wise folding, e.g. in *Leucophaea* and *Nauphoeta*. Wings of males illustrated in all cases except *P. americana* and *N. cinerea* (after Rehn[22]).

nevertheless, undergone some modifications, principally to the female genitalia and the wings.

Areas of modification

The female genitalia

The sword-shaped ovipositor of the female, first noticed by Brongniart[12], is one of the most striking differences between fossil and recent cockroaches. This structure has become much reduced and is no longer visible externally. It has become retracted into the body with the formation of the genital pouch. For this to have occurred, the abdomen has undergone considerable modification. The terminal segments have become retracted into the abdomen to form a cavity which holds the ootheca whilst eggs are placed into it. The eggs then develop externally in those species which retain the ootheca until hatching, or they are incubated internally (in a special brood sac) by those species which produce young alive.

Thus, the function of the ovipositor has changed. It is now to guide the eggs into the ootheca during capsule formation, rather than, as in related insects, to insert eggs into the soil or plant tissue. In this respect, Sellards[11] suggests that the crickets, grasshoppers and locusts, which retain an external ovipositor, 'present, no doubt, a closer approximation to the early condition, than do present-day cockroaches'.

The wings

Changes in the wings have involved a greater differentiation between the front and hind pair, and a reduction in size (Fig. 5). The tegmina (forewings arising on the mesothoracic segment) vary considerably in texture, form, venation and function. In early cockroaches their function was not only to assist flight, but to act as a covering for the hind (metathoracic) wings when at rest. They also gave protection to the abdomen.

In some of the most recently evolved cockroaches the use of the tegmina for flight has become more and more restricted whilst their protective value has become emphasised. In shape they are generally elongate and ovoid, but enormous variation exists; in some species the tegmina are long, extending well beyond the apex of the abdomen, but in others they have been lost altogether. There has been a tendency towards a reduction in the numbers of main veins by fusion, but this has been associated with a greater complexity of cross veins. In no species are the tegmina capable of being folded.

The hindwings, whilst less variable than the tegmina in function and texture, are more diverse in venation and show three basic methods of folding (Fig. 6). In all three, the anal area of the hindwing is bent under. In its simplest form this folded area remains flat, as a simple flap. In the more advanced forms, the anal area has become folded fanwise with alternate convex and concave folds. In the third type of folding, the anal area is folded fanwise, but in addition, the apex of the hindwing is reflexed onto its dorsal surface.

When fully developed the wings are used in flight, but when reduced they appear to be functionless. There is reason to believe that the reduction in wing size has come about in association with a burrowing habit. The need for water conservation was probably not great during the Carboniferous period but with the change in surface conditions and loss of the ideal environment, burrowing into the surface soil became essential for survival. Under these conditions wings were an encumbrance, and the eyes and ocelli, too, were of little value.

Fossil cockroaches
Some idea of the age of rocks mentioned here in connection with fossil cockroaches can be obtained from the scale of geological systems given in Table I. The literature on fossil cockroaches provides a fascinating study for the reader interested in evolutionary development. According to

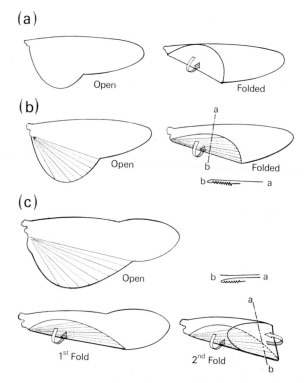

Fig. 6. Three methods of folding the hind wings in cockroaches. (a) Primitive condition. The anal lobe folded under the hindwing as a flap (similar to the termite *M. darwiniensis*). (b) Intermediate condition. The anal lobe folded under fanwise as alternate convex and concave folds. (c) Advanced condition. Combination of two foldings, the anal lobe fanwise and the apex reflexed above the wing.

THE COCKROACH

Blatchley[3] the oldest known insect is a fossil cockroach, *Palaeoblatta douvillei* Brogn., from the Silurian sandstone of France. On this subject he quotes the palaeontologist S. H. Scudder as saying: 'Of no other type of

TABLE I

GEOLOGICAL SYSTEMS

Era	System	Age in millions of years (approx.) of lowest beds of each system
CAINOZOIC	Recent	—
	Pleistocene	1
(TERTIARY)	Pliocene	15
	Miocene	25
	Oligocene	40
	Eocene	60
MESOZOIC	Cretaceous	120
	Jurassic	150
	Triassic	180
PALAEOZOIC	Permian	210
	Carboniferous	280
	Devonian	320
	Silurian	350
	Ordovician	400
	Cambrian	500
AZOIC	Pre-Cambrian	3,000

insect can it be said that it occurs at every horizon where insects have been found in any numbers; in no group whatever can the changes wrought by time be so carefully and completely studied as here; none other has furnished more important evidence concerning the phylogeny of insects'.

Fossil cockroaches are grouped under the family **Palaeoblattidae** to distinguish them from the families of the 'modern' cockroaches. These ancient insects are known mostly from the wings, particularly the tegmina, since their chitinous nature provided them with a greater chance of fossilisation than the decaying body. In common with the predators of today, those of millions of years ago probably discarded the chitinous wings in preference to the body of the insect as food, resulting in the greater chance of wings remaining for fossilisation.

The second structure which has become most often preserved is the pronotum. Portions of head among fossil cockroaches are rare, since it would seem from imprints left in Carboniferous rocks that the habit of concealing the head beneath the pronotum was already well-developed in the Palaeozoic era. Before Sellard's paper[11] on fossil cockroaches in 1904, the eyes and antennae of the Palaeoblattidae had not been observed and very few wings had been described.

The geological range of cockroaches extends from pre-carboniferous to the present day. Almost all the American fossil cockroaches which preserve the structure of the body come from two sources; the Middle or Lower Coal Measures of Illinois, and from the Upper Coal Measures in Kansas. In Europe, specimens have been taken from the coalfield at Commentry in southern France and from Westphalia in Germany. Twenty species found in Britain (Fig. 7) have been described in detail by Bolton;[13]

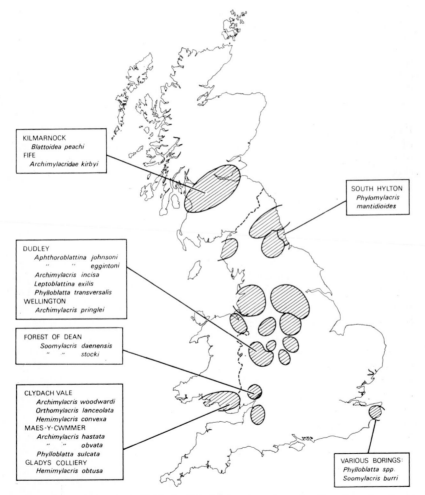

Fig. 7. Distribution of coalfields in Britain showing where fossil cockroaches have been found in shales or coal measures.

they are not restricted to one coalfield but have a wide distribution. Most have been found in ironstone nodules taken from beds of light-coloured rocks, more similar to hardened clay than normal shales and quite distinct from ordinary Coal Measure rocks. According to Bolton, these nodules occur in vast numbers ranging in size from half an inch to one foot across.

The relationships between the various fossil cockroaches of the Palaeoblattidae have been based principally on the degree of development of the wing veins. In many living insects the complex arrangement of veins makes it difficult to decipher the affinities between genera and species, but the task becomes relatively simple the further back one traces insects to their point of origin. As will be seen later in this chapter, the study of the wings of fossil cockroaches has been important in demonstrating the evolutionary link between cockroaches and termites.

Fossil cockroaches from the Palaeozoic era indicate that females at that time had probably not developed the habit of depositing eggs within an ootheca. Sellards suggests that 'many of the species doubtless deposited their eggs singly either in the ground, underneath bark of trees, or within small stems'. A fossilised ovipositor has been found on a number of rock specimens, similar in appearance to that of fossilised locusts. Certain Palaeozoic ferns in immediate association with cockroaches show a row of slits along the stem (rachis), which appear to have been made by an organ such as the ovipositor of the Palaeoblattids. Nevertheless at some stage during cockroach evolution the eggs became contained within a hardened ootheca, probably associated with the need to protect the eggs from desiccation.

Brown[14] reports finding what he believes to be a cockroach ootheca in shale of the Lower Eocene strata lying above coal measures in Wyoming. These rocks are much more recent, only 50–60 million years old. He describes this ootheca as about 3 mm long and 2 mm wide with a fluted edge along the dorsal suture, typical of oothecae of living species. It had seven vertical lines equally spaced indicating what are believed to be the internal egg chambers. Previous to this find, Brown was able to locate only five previous records of fossils purporting to be cockroach oothecae, all from the late Palaeozoic; one from Kansas,[11] two from Saxony,[15] and two from France.[16] None of these, however, appeared to Brown to be sufficiently comparable with egg cases of living cockroaches to be authentic specimens of oothecae. This view, however, is quite contrary to that of Laurentiaux[17] who is firmly of the opinion that during the Permo-Carboniferous two types of Blattidae co-existed; females with an external ovipositor which laid eggs singly, and others with a smaller internal ovipositor, laying an egg case similar to modern cockroaches.

Whether or not the evolutionary development of the ootheca occurred within the last 100 million years, or more than 200 million years ago, is of less importance than the fact that it did actually occur, since this allowed a number of modifications to take place in the method of egg incubation. These are considered later in this chapter (p. 35) in connection with the classification of cockroaches.

The common ancestry of cockroaches and termites

Termites have a close systematic relationship with cockroaches and have been found as fossils in all geological deposits from the Lower Tertiary onwards. They are more recently evolved than cockroaches and as a group are estimated to be at least 50 million years old, compared with the more ancient cockroaches with their fossil record of at least 250 million years.

According to Imms[18] there is little doubt 'that termites arose from cockroach-like forms and subsequently developed a complex social organisation'. The fossil termites are no more primitive than one of the species of termite living today. This is *Mastotermes darwiniensis* Frogg, of Australia, which has a wing structure similar to that of cockroaches as well as an egg mass (Fig. 8) similar to the cockroach ootheca. The individual eggs of this termite are firmly cemented together by a light brown gelatinous secretion which fills the interstices between the eggs.

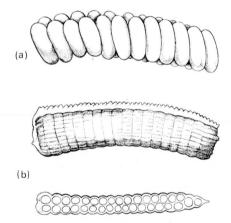

(a)

(b)

Fig. 8. The egg mass of (a) the primitive termite *Mastotermes darwiniensis* compared with that of (b) the primitive cockroach *Cryptocercus punctulatus*. The termite egg mass contains 22–24 eggs and is about 5 mm. long. That of the cockroach contains about 32 and is 8 mm. long. In both, the eggs are arranged in a double row, those of the termite held together by a gelatinous secretion and those of the cockroach in a semi-transparent ootheca.

Many writers have drawn attention to the close resemblance of winged termites with cockroaches, but not until 1937, when fossil cockroaches (of the genus *Pycnoblattina*) were discovered from the Permian system, was there rigid proof of the descent of termites from cockroaches. This critical link which associates the two groups lies in the similar folding of the hind wing of *M. darwiniensis* (the only termite which folds its wings) and the fossil genus *Pycnoblattina*. Tillyard[10] has pointed out that none of the fossil cockroaches folded their wings in the complex manner of living cockroaches, but had evolved only as far as forming a small folded area known as the anal lobe. This is exactly the type of fold found in *Mastotermes* and the fossil genus *Pycnoblattina*. (Fig. 9). As we have already seen, the more recent cockroaches have gone far beyond *Mastotermes* in the specialisation of wing folding, whereas the more recent termites have lost this feature altogether.

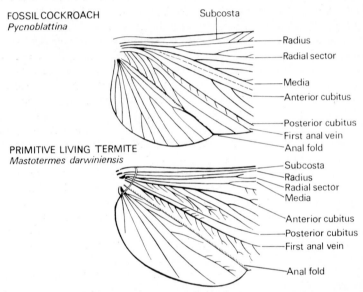

Fig. 9. A comparison of the venation and method of folding of the hindwings of the fossil cockroach, *Pycnoblattina*, and the primitive living termite *Mastotermes darwiniensis*.

Another similarity between the wings of termites and cockroaches lies in the ease with which they become broken off at the base. In the wings of some primitive cockroaches, a break occurs that is similar to the line of weakness (humeral suture) near the base of the termite wing where the wing breaks off after the colonising flight. In most termites the wings are shed easily at the humeral suture, backward pressure on the wing causing them to break off leaving only a wing stump. This feature is found in some living cockroaches which rid themselves of their wings soon after becoming adult. One genus (*Polyzosteria*) lives in rotten logs, nymphs of all stages living with the adults in the same log. Under these conditions the wings of the adult cockroach are a hindrance to it and according to Till-

in association with termites, are reduced or absent. The characters which separate the two Suborders are as follows:

Suborder **Blattaria** (cockroaches). The head is almost or completely covered by an enlarged pronotum. Occasionally two ocelli are present, but in most species they are represented by two thin areas of cuticle. The legs, including the first pair are adapted for running. The gizzard, or proventriculus, has a well-developed armature for masticating food. Most are more or less drab, brown in appearance, predominantly tropical, but some have become established in temperate zones within the artificial environments created by man, who has been largely responsible for their spread.

Suborder **Mantodea** (mantids). The head is not covered by the pronotum and one frontal and two lateral ocelli are present. The first pair of legs are toothed and developed for seizing prey (Fig. 10e). The gizzard is not so strongly developed for masticating food as in cockroaches. There are about 1,800 species of mantids which are all carnivorous, notably on other insects. Mantids are usually green and some are modified in structure to simulate their surroundings. To obtain food, mantids often sit motionless for long periods with the head erect and the legs ready to seize prey. This attitude of worship has given rise to the name 'praying mantis'. The anatomy of mantids shows that they are undoubtedly close relatives of cockroaches.

Sub-divisions of the Suborder Blattaria

Many attempts have been made to sub-divide cockroaches into families. Rehn[22] based his classification on the wings, but because many species are wingless these forms had to be excluded. Princis[38] has used a number of unrelated characters and reviewed the history of cockroach taxonomy.

Undoubtedly the best and most recent sub-division of the group is that of McKittrick.[39] Four characters are used, namely, the female genitalia and its musculature, the external male genitalia, the structure of the gizzard, or proventriculus, and ovipositional behaviour. She divides the Suborder **Blattaria** into two Superfamilies, which are further sub-divided into five Families and 20 Subfamilies. Many of the species mentioned in subsequent chapters of this book are classified according to McKittrick in Table II.

In studying the variety of forms that exist, McKittrick believes that cockroaches have evolved along two divergent lines (Fig. 11). These she uses as a basis for dividing cockroaches into the two Superfamilies, the **Blattoidea** and **Blaberoidea**. The most primitive living cockroaches are contained in two families, the Cryptocercidae, which includes the wood-eating species, *C. punctulatus* (see p. 93) and the Polyphagidae which have a simple fold to the anal lobe, resembling early termites.

TABLE II

CLASSIFICATION OF COCKROACHES—SUBORDER BLATTARIA ACCORDING TO McKITTRICK.[39]

Superfamily	Family	Subfamily	Typical species
BLATTOIDEA	Cryptocercidae	Cryptocercinae	*Cryptocercus punctulatus*
	Blattidae	Lamproblattinae	*Lamproblatta albipalpus*
		*Blattinae	*Blatta orientalis*
			Neostylopyga rhombifolia
			Periplaneta americana
			Periplaneta australasiae
			Periplaneta brunnea
			Periplaneta fuliginosa
		Polyzosteriinae	*Eurycotis floridana*
BLABEROIDEA	Polyphagidae	Polyphaginae	*Arenivaga bolliana*
		Holocompsinae	*Hypercomposa fieberi*
	Blattellidae	Anaplectinae	*Anaplecta* spp.
		*Plectopterinae	*Supella supellectilium*
		*Blattellinae	*Blattella germanica*
			Parcoblatta pensylvanica
		Ectobiinae	*Ectobius lapponicus*
			Ectobius pallidus
		Nyctiborinae	*Nyctibora noctivaga*
	Blaberidae	Zetoborinae	*Phortioca phoraspoides*
		*Blaberinae	*Blaberus discoidalis*
			Blaberus giganteus
			Byrsotria fumigata
		Panesthiinae	*Panesthia augustipennis*
		*Pycnoscelinae	*Pycnoscelus surinamensis*
		Diplopterinae	*Diploptera punctata*
		Panchlorinae	*Panchlora nivea*
		*Oxyhaloinae	*Gromphadorhina laevigata*
			Leucophaea maderae
			Nauphoeta cinerea
		Epilamprinae	*Phoraspis leucogramma*
		Perisphaeriinae	*Perisphaerus aeneus*

Asterisks indicate the Subfamilies which contain pest species.

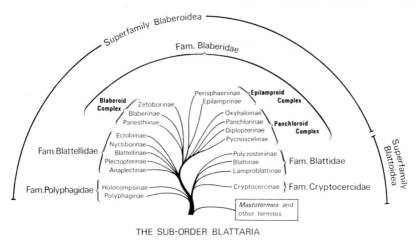

THE SUB-ORDER BLATTARIA

Fig. 11. The evolutionary development of cockroaches according to McKittrick.[39]

One of the features used by McKittrick to elucidate the lines of ancestry among the cockroaches of the **Blaberoidea** is the number of openings of the spermathecae into the genital pouch (see Chapter 8). The family Polyphagidae forms the earliest divergent line of development (with one opening) but there is evidence to show that this family and the family Blattellidae have a common ancestry, since some species of the Anaplectinae have only one opening, whilst others have two or more, as in the other Blattellidae and all members of the family Blaberidae.

Another feature used to separate cockroaches of the family Blattellidae is the ability to rotate the egg case through 90 degrees after its formation. Those species which acquired this ability are contained in the Subfamilies Ectobiinae, Nyctiborinae and Blattellinae (e.g. *Blattella germanica*), whilst those that did not, have given rise to species (e.g. *Supella supellectilium*) which comprise the Plectopterinae.

Cockroaches of the family Polyphagidae can also rotate their oothecae but the type of rotation found in these species is considered to be primitive; their oothecae have a flange by which it is held in the female's genital pouch, none of the eggs being contained within the pouch itself.[40]

The differences which occur in the genitalia of female cockroaches show that once the means to rotate the ootheca had evolved, the common stock which gave rise to these insects quickly gave rise to other forms; those which could not only rotate the ootheca, but which began to retain it, and later to retract it internally into the abdomen (the family Blaberidae). Cockroaches that do not rotate the ootheca (i.e. Superfamily **Blattoidea,** and the Subfamilies Plectopterinae and Anaplectinae) deposit them shortly after formation (see Chapter 9).

Evolution towards the internal incubation of eggs

Speculating on the possible evolutionary trend towards the internal incubation of the ootheca, Roth & Willis[41] suggest that the preliminary step, from the oviparous habit of dropping the egg case, would seem to have been for the female to retain it, clasped in the oothecal chamber, for longer and longer periods of time. To enable the ootheca to be passed back into the genital pouch it had to be rotated from the vertical to the horizontal position. McKittrick points out that rotation of the ootheca frees the keel from the ovipositor valves, which block any anterior movement of the ootheca while it is in a vertical position. This orients it so that its height lies in the horizontal plane of the cockroach, which is much greater than the insect's height. In this position it is possible for the ootheca to be shifted anteriorly beyond the bases of the valves. A logical advantage for rotating the ootheca prior to retraction suggested by Roth,[40] is that as the ootheca greatly increases in size during embryogenesis, it can be readily accommodated by lateral stretching of the abdomen, whereas there is far less room in these relatively flat insects for dorso-ventral expansion.

The primary selective pressure influencing the evolution of internal incubation was, most probably, death of the eggs due to desiccation. McKittrick believes that if this was indeed the case, 'a stage of oothecal retention such as that found in *Blattella* was undoubtedly a precursor to the gradual and progressive retraction of the egg-case inside the mother's body. The ootheca of *Blattella* remains highly permeable to water at the anterior end, where it is clasped in the genital armature, and, through this permeable area, water lost by the eggs through evaporation is replenished from the mother's body. In *Blattella*, this arrangement is evidently satisfactory, considering the success of the genus. The retention of a water-permeable ootheca would not be particularly advantageous in a damp habitat. However, under dry conditions, if water absorbed from the mother could not be replenished by her drinking, the result would be dehydration of the mother's body and eventual death of both parent and offspring. With a gradual reduction of environmental moisture, the progressive retraction of the ootheca farther anteriorly might proceed relatively rapidly, as the greater the number of eggs enclosed by the mother's body, the less the water loss, and thus, the greater chance of survival'.

To add support to these views Roth & Willis[42] point out that the time taken by those cockroaches (false ovoviviparous) to form and retract their ootheca into the abdomen is much less than that required by those (oviparous) which form and drop their oothecae. Speed is vital to the false ovoviviparous cockroaches because the oothecal wall is so thin that the egg sac loses water while exposed to the atmosphere during formation.

In addition to desiccation, the other danger which besets cockroach eggs is parasitism (see Chapter 10). The hard oothecae of cockroaches like *Periplaneta* and *Blatta* do not protect the eggs from being destroyed by parasitic wasps which can penetrate the ootheca with their ovipositors, but as far as is known, eggs which are incubated internally are not subject to attack by parasites because they are protected within the female's body.[41]

Following the development of stock which gave rise to the internal incubation of eggs three main divergencies occurred, which can be separated largely on differences in the form of the genital chamber. These three lines of evolution have given rise to what McKittrick calls the 'Blaberoid', 'Epilamproid' and 'Panchloroid' complexes.

In this chapter we have seen that cockroaches show considerable differences in ovipositional habit as well as diversity of form. Perhaps this is not surprising in a group of insects which has had 250 million years in which to evolve. The major factor which appears to have been responsible for the various modifications is the change from a hot, moist habitat to the more temperate conditions of today.

3

THE PRINCIPAL COCKROACH SPECIES

The origin, distribution, habitat, appearance and biology of the principal cockroach species: I. Closely associated with man; *Blattella germanica, Blatta orientalis, Periplaneta americana, Periplaneta australasiae, Periplaneta brunnea, Periplaneta fuliginosa* and *Supella supellectilium*—II. Occasionally associated with man; *Pycnoscelus surinamensis, Leucophaea maderae, Nauphoeta cinerea, Neostylopyga rhombifolia* and *Blaberus* spp.—III. Accidental invaders of homes; *Eurycotis floridana, Parcoblatta pensylvanica* and *Blattella vaga*—IV. Outdoor species, in Britain (*Ectobius* spp.), Australia (*Methana* spp.) and the U.S.A. (*Cryptocercus punctulatus* and *Attaphila fungicola*)—V. Other species of special interest; *Gromphadorhina laevigata*—Identification key.

Cockroaches show considerable variation in their association with buildings. Some species live entirely outdoors and are never found indoors, others occupy a high pest status, living and breeding within building structures and are rarely, if ever, encountered in their natural environments. Between these two extremes lie many species with all degrees of casual or accidental association.

Geographical location influences the dependence of any given species on man-made structures. Thus, in the tropics the majority of pest cockroaches can exist and often breed outdoors, whilst in the more northern latitudes they are dependent for survival and reproduction on the warmth of buildings. In some areas, certain of the pest cockroaches may be able to live outdoors during the warm summer months but are unable to survive the winter.

In this chapter, cockroach species are separated in groups according to their degree of association with man. In making this separation two points must be emphasised: first, the groups are without well-defined limits and second, the presence of man himself is relatively unimportant in this association.

The species included within each group differ in their geographical distribution and to some extent in their pest status. For example, it might seem incongruous to rank together the four most commonly encountered species of *Periplaneta* as all 'closely associated with man', particularly as the distribution range of *P. americana* is extremely wide, encompassing many millions of people, whereas *P. australasiae* is less tolerant of cool temperatures preferring a more tropical climate. The ranges of *P. brunnea* and *P. fuliginosa* are even more confined to tropical latitudes. Nevertheless, under the most favourable conditions within each range the degree of association of the four species with man is probably equal.

The phrase 'association with man' requires special comment. As Roth & Willis point out,[4] 'only the shelter and food that man unwittingly provides attract cockroaches to him; man's physical presence is unnecessary'. The species closely associated with man are pests of a great variety of structures, of homes, offices, shops, warehouses, ships, and aircraft, to name just a few. These species are generally described as 'domiciliary', a term used broadly to cover structures in which man lives, works, travels and stores his food, and even those for his own sanitation—toilets and sewers.

Within this chapter, extensive reference is made to the works of a number of authors, in particular to the authoritative studies of Rehn[1] on the likely origin and spread of species, of Hebard[43] and Roth & Willis[4] on the recorded distribution of cockroaches and to Willis and co-workers[44] on biology.

Concerning the probable origin and spread of cockroaches, Rehn has drawn attention to 'the erroneous assumptions often repeated in the literature, in no small measure added to by the specific names given to cockroaches by the early systematists, such as *orientalis*, *germanica*, *americana*, *australasiae*, *surinamensis* and *maderae*.' It is often not recognised that these species had most probably gone to such areas with early voyagers and thus become one of the 'first settlers'.

To determine the most likely origins of the various cockroaches, Rehn draws largely on the incidence and distribution of allied, non-domiciliary species which belong to the pest genera. This he supports with records of historical trade movements, it being certain that the spread of such pests as the German, Oriental and American Cockroaches was greatly assisted by the early maritime nations, these cockroaches now extending far outside their natural range.

Unfortunately it is not possible to provide a detailed picture of the world distribution of the common species of cockroaches. Neither is it possible at the present time to give distribution maps for particular countries. Ragge[45] has provided a recent account of the occurrence of cockroaches in Britain, but the distribution range of the most frequently encountered species in the U.S.A. is known only approximately; a detailed appraisal for all States, such as that undertaken for Texas[46] and a number of others, remains to be completed.

The number of different cockroaches found in any area is largely influenced by climate. Thus of the 57 species known to exist in the United States, almost two-thirds (32 species, including the recently established *Blattella vaga*) occur in Texas. Apart from the size of this State, Hebard suggests that the reason why such a high proportion of American species occur there, can be largely attributed to the effect of its great range of climate on the diversity of flora and ecological habitats—from the swamp forests along the eastern border with the south-eastern States, to a semi-arid area in the south-west and tropical zone on the Mexican border. Compare this with the British Isles, which have a relatively narrow range of climate, two cockroach species established in buildings, a few rare introductions which become established only occasionally and three out-door species which are confined to the southern counties.

In the following account of the principal species, the appearance of the adult is briefly described, which, together with the illustrations and key (at the end of the chapter) should enable the interested reader to identify the most frequently encountered cockroaches. Colour is not a reliable diagnostic feature; considerable variation occurs between the sexes and insects taken from different locations and therefore only a general reference to colour is given, which should not be relied upon for purposes of identification.

Brief accounts are also given of the biology of each species. Some have been studied by a number of workers, under quite different environmental conditions, with the result that marked discrepancies occur in the information reported. The best example of this is the information available on *P. americana* (Table V). It is for this reason that the data obtained by Willis *et al.*[44], at near optimal conditions for each species, is used most extensively in the following pages, so allowing a reasonably reliable comparison between the life histories and reproductive habits of the different species.

I. SPECIES CLOSELY ASSOCIATED WITH MAN

Seven domiciliary cockroaches are included under this heading. They are the ones most commonly encountered in buildings and all can legitimately be called pests. Cosmopolitan species included here are the German and Oriental cockroaches, which are the only two species of importance in Britain, and two species of *Periplaneta*—the American and Australian cockroaches.

This group also includes the Brown-banded Cockroach, which has risen to pest status in the United States, only during the last 40 years, and two other species of *Periplaneta*—the Brown Cockroach and Smoky-brown Cockroach, common in properties in the southern United States.

Blattella germanica (Linnaeus)—The German Cockroach (or 'Steamfly')
A number of Asiatic species belong to the genus *Blattella*. Fifteen occur with *B. germanica* in N.E. Africa between the great African lakes, Ethiopia and the Republic of the Sudan. It is this area of Africa[1] which is considered to be the original home of what has become one of the most widespread of the domiciliary cockroaches (Fig. 12).

From North Africa it is believed to have found its way into eastern Europe in Greek and Phoenician ships, spreading into Byzantium, Asia Minor, the Black Sea region and southern Russia. This occurred many centuries ago. It then spread slowly northward and westward across Europe, certainly more recently than the Oriental Cockroach which came to Britain by the same route.

This slow rate of spread by the German Cockroach across Europe may

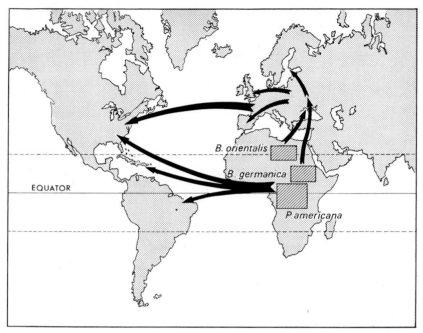

Fig. 12. Probable areas of origin and early directions of spread of *B. germanica*, *B. orientalis* and *P. americana* from Africa to the New World, as suggested by Rehn.[1]

be attributed to the very slow development of trade with Russia.[1] Once in western Europe it became distributed by commerce to virtually all parts of the world, and could best be described as the 'world's most successful commercial traveller'. The German Cockroach became established in England as recently as the middle of the last century and Miall and Denny[47] refer to its supposed establishment in Leeds by means of bread baskets carried by soldiers returning from the Crimean War.

Blattella germanica was first named *Blatta germanica* by Linnaeus[24] in 1767 from insects taken in Denmark. It is now a ubiquitous pest throughout the United States having been introduced into the New World from Europe. It reaches its greatest abundance in the Central States of North America and ranges as far north as Ontario, Manitoba and Alberta in Canada. It was first recorded in Australia in 1893.

Habitat

The German Cockroach prefers a warm, moist environment. Consequently it has become a common pest of kitchens, larders, and restaurants where food, warmth and moisture provide the necessary ecological requirements, but it is rarely found in bedrooms. The climate in Britain does not normally allow this species to survive outdoors. There is, however, a record[48] of its occurrence in considerable numbers in February within a rubbish heap, and in the temperate climate of the north-central United States the German Cockroach has occasionally been found, sometimes in large numbers outside buildings; in some areas this species has been reported living in soil under basementless properties from early summer to late autumn.[49] There are records of it occurring outdoors under rubbish and on date palms in California[50] and in large numbers in a city dump in New York.[51] The German Cockroach has also been found outdoors in other parts of the world; in woods and under moist leaves in Algeria[52] and in Formosa[53]—in environments probably resembling those of its origin. Interestingly, the German Cockroach has also been found in gold mines and caves in South Africa.[54]

In heated buildings, *B. germanica* has been able to withstand the climate of Alaska[55] and for many years this species has been the most prevalent cockroach in the galleys, store-rooms and accommodation of modern ships. The types of premises and locations in buildings most frequently infested by this cockroach in Britain are given in Chapter 14.

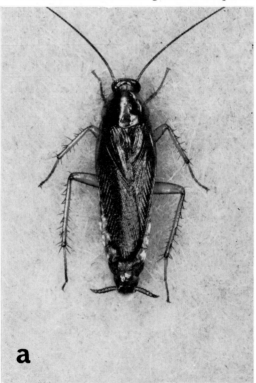

Fig. 13. Adult *Blattella germanica*, above, (a) male; opposite (b) female with ootheca. ($\times$ 5)

Appearance

Blattella germanica is a small cockroach (Fig. 13), 10–15 mm long, pale ochraceous buff to tawny in general colour, with distinct dark parallel bands running the length of the pronotum. In the nymphal stages, these

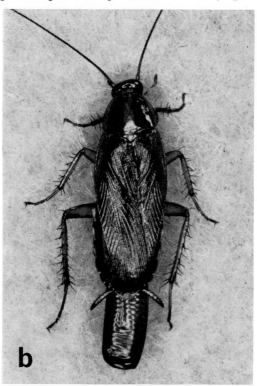

bands are normally broader and continue posteriorly onto the meso- and metanota. The sexes can be readily distinguished by the following characteristics:

Male	*Female*
Body thin, slender.	Body stout, robust.
Terminal segments of abdomen visible, just not covered by the tegmina.	Entire abdomen just covered by the tegmina.
Conspicuous depressions (gland openings) on the 7th and 8th abdominal tergites (Fig. 14).	All abdominal tergites similar, without depressions.
Cerci with eleven segments.	Cerci with twelve segments.

The ootheca is large (8 × 3 mm) relative to the size of the adult, and is carried by the female until the eggs hatch; the surface is polished with distinct divisions indicating the positions of the eggs within.

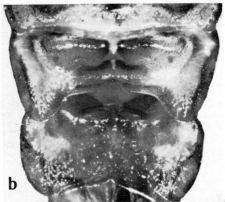

Fig. 14. The abdomen of a sexually stimulated adult male *B. germanica*, (a) with the wings displayed exposing the openings of the dorsal glands on the 7th and 8th tergites, (b) detail of gland openings.

Biology

Many laboratory studies have been made on the biology of the German Cockroach. Information on development at 30°C is given in Table III. Both sexes mature at about the same rate. Adults mate a few days after the final moult and repeated copulation by females occurs, although one mating may be sufficient to fertilise all the eggs produced during a lifetime.[56] According to Haber,[57] oothecae are produced 2–4 days after the first successful copulation, but before the ootheca is formed the abdomen of the female distends noticeably. At the beginning of ootheca formation, the external opening of the genital pouch becomes enlarged and the white, translucent tip of the ootheca is just visible. Within the same day the ootheca protrudes and is fully developed by the following day. It changes from white to pink in a few hours, then light brown and in a day or two to chestnut brown. After its appearance the ootheca is almost always rotated sideways with the keel to the left or right.

An indication of the age of the attached ootheca can be obtained from its appearance; 3 or 4 days before hatching a green band appears down each flat face of the ootheca, increasing in density until hatching occurs.

Rau[58] found that the ootheca was carried for 6–16 days with an average of 10 days, but this is much shorter than the period reported by most other workers; Gould[59] states that the incubation period of the ootheca is shortened by 1·5 days for every degree F rise in temperature. Usually it is held by the opening of the genital pouch until just before the eggs hatch. Occasionally, however, hatching occurs whilst the egg case is still attached (Fig. 98, p. 225) and it may be carried by the female for 2 days after the young have left it.

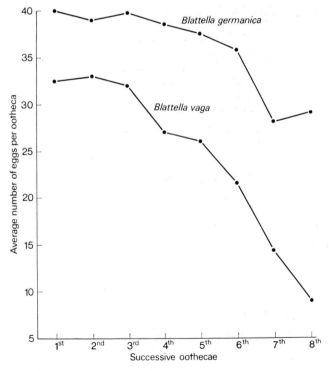

Fig. 15. The number of eggs per ootheca in relation to the sequence of ootheca formation in *B. germanica* and *B. vaga* (after Willis, *et al*,[44]).

The number of eggs in each ootheca decreases with succeeding egg cases after the production of the fourth (Fig. 15). All the eggs hatch in about five minutes. Ross[60] obtained hatching at all temperatures from 15–35°C, and from studies of many oothecae, Woodruff[56] states the average number of nymphs to emerge is 32, although the number is quite variable.

[Under optimal conditions of food and temperature, development to adult is achieved in six weeks, but in unheated buildings, where the ambient temperature may be just adequate for survival, speed of development varies with the season.] Thus in Indiana one generation is completed in 90 days for eggs produced in July and 130 days for eggs formed in September–April.[61]

The first external signs of wings occur in the penultimate nymphal stage when the posterior angles of the meso- and metanota become slightly enlarged. In the last nymphal stage these angles become conspicuous. The adult seldom flies but is capable of gliding flight. The German Cockroach runs swiftly and is generally more active than the Oriental Cockroach. It is

TABLE III

THE BIOLOGY OF *BLATTELLA GERMANICA* AND *BLATTELLA VAGA* BASED ON LABORATORY DATA (AVERAGES).
(From Willis *et al.*[44])

	B. germanica	*B. vaga*
Environmental conditions:	30°C	30–36°C
Interval between moult to adult and production of first ootheca:	8 days	8 days
Oothecae produced per female:	4–8 (average 7)	5
Interval between successive oothecae:	22 days	24 days
Incubation period of ootheca:	17 days	20 days
Eggs per ootheca:	37	28
Hatched eggs per ootheca:	28	19
Percent of hatched insects that matured:	85%	73%
Number of moults:	5–7	5–7
Period of nymphal development:		
(i) in isolation; 5 moults:	38 days (males)	36 days (males)
7 moults:	63 days (females)	93 days (males)
		84 days (females)
(ii) in groups:	40 days (males)	56 days (males)
	41 days (females)	45 days (females)
Adult life span:	128 days (males)	101 days (males)
	153 days (females)	150 days (females)

not uncommon to find one or two German Cockroaches moving during the day in infested premises whereas this is rarely so with the Oriental species.

Blatta orientalis Linnaeus—the Oriental Cockroach (or 'Black beetle')

Early literature and the name given to this cockroach suggests that it came from the East. However, when Linnaeus[23] established the genus *Blatta* in 1758, and named the species from material taken in America, Russia, Sweden and Finland, he considered that the Oriental Cockroach was a native of America and had become introduced into the East.

Evidence suggests that the assumptions of both Eastern and American origins are 'undoubtedly wrong'. Rehn[1] draws attention to the documented information which establishes the movement of *B. orientalis* westward across Europe, making its way into Holland and England by the reign of Elizabeth I. It was recorded in Holland in the early seventeenth century and in wine cellars in England in 1624.

From a study of the many species of *Blatta*, there is now reason to believe that the Oriental Cockroach was originally a native of North Africa. It travelled to eastern Europe by the same means as *B. germanica*, *via* early trading vessels in the eastern Mediterranean (Fig. 12). Once in Europe it spread northwards and westwards and its entry into Chile and Argentina, the only South American countries where it appears to have been established for many years, was doubtless by way of Spain.[1]

There is little evidence to indicate that this cockroach can establish itself in the humid tropics. As Rehn says, 'on the contrary, it would appear to have come from an area which combines summer heat and moderate winter'. This is supported by the existence of wild forms—the nearest known relatives of *B. orientalis*—in East Central Africa.

B. orientalis has become a major pest of buildings and generally distributed by commerce throughout temperate regions; it is the major domiciliary cockroach in Britain (Chapter 14), and occurs over all but the most northern parts of the United States, where, like *B. germanica*, it occurs in greatest abundance in the central latitudes. It occurs in Canada (there are records given by Hebard[43] for Toronto and Ontario in 1917) but it is apparently not common in Brisbane, Australia.[62]

Habitat

The preferred temperature range of *B. orientalis* is 20–29°C (Chapter 12). This upper limit is lower than that of *B. germanica* (33°C) and in buildings the Oriental Cockroach is therefore usually found in areas noticeably cooler than those occupied by the German Cockroach; these are typically, basements and cellars, service ducts and crawl spaces. In kitchens, harbourages occur behind radiators, ovens, hot-water pipes and under floor coverings; this species is often found in toilets, behind baths and sinks—where large numbers congregate around sources of water. The Oriental

D

Cockroach can also tolerate hot, dry locations around domestic and industrial heating appliances, provided the insects can obtain access to water at intervals.

Infestations of the Oriental Cockroach are most frequently encountered below ground level, or on the ground floor of buildings, but a greater number of reports are being received each year in the United States of insects on the second, third, fourth and even fifth floors. The number of individuals noted on upper floors is seldom large but the frequency of occurrence is much greater than reported in earlier work, varying up to 30 per cent of observations made in some areas.[49]

There are many records of this cockroach occurring outdoors: it is occasionally able to survive winter conditions in Britain and has been found under the bark of trees, sometimes far from buildings, in rubbish heaps and refuse dumps, as well as on pavements, on the outside walls of buildings and around swimming pools. In Russia it has been found in

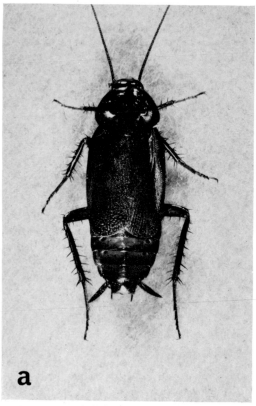

a

Fig. 16. Adult *Blatta orientalis*, above (a) male; opposite (b) female with ootheca. (× 2·5)

caves inhabited by bats but uninhabited by man.[63] In the Crimean peninsular the Oriental Cockroach has been found under stones and dead leaves, apparently breeding outdoors.

Observations reported in 1956 have pointed to an increasing incidence of the Oriental Cockroach outdoors in the temperate North Central States of America:[49] '*B. orientalis* is frequently found out of doors around homes during the summer months and can become exceptionally numerous in garbage and trash dumps. In some well-kept residential urban areas, yards of whole blocks of homes have been described as "alive" with these roaches on a warm summer night. Many observations have been reported of 25 to 30 roaches being seen on a concrete walk 25–30 feet long'.

Hebard[43] reports that in infested houses around Philadelphia, *B. orientalis* swarms during May, coinciding with the arrival of the Shad in the Delaware River (a fish which ascends the river to spawn) and in consequence is locally known as the Shad roach. Similarly, Gould[59] quotes an instance of 'migration' from a city dump to nearby houses.

b

In the United States, the Oriental Cockroach is a pest of sewers, and on ships it is associated principally with cargoes in holds (Chapter 11).

Appearance

The genus *Blatta* contains many species. In all, the sexes are dissimilar, the tegmina and wings of the male almost reach the apex of the abdomen, while the tegmina of the female are very short with the wings absent, or greatly reduced. Throughout the genus, a reduction in the organs of flight is accompanied by a broadening of the pronotum. Nymphs and adults of all species of *Blatta* are without a pad (arolium) between the claws which prevents them from climbing very smooth surfaces.

Blatta orientalis is a large cockroach (Fig. 16), about 20–24 mm long, the sexes similar in size, dark reddish-brown to black, although readily distinguished by the reduced tegmina of the female (Fig. 20), but neither sex is able to fly. The ootheca is large (10×5 mm) with feeble depressions defining the egg sacs within; it is dark reddish-brown and soft at first, intensifying in colour to black after deposition, when it becomes hard and brittle.

Biology

Early accounts of the nymphal development of *B. orientalis* suggested that the period between hatching and the final moult was about four years. This is doubtful even under the poorest conditions of food supply and low temperature. In unheated locations the ootheca may remain dormant and not hatch until the following spring and nymphal development may also cease during the winter. The maximum period of development in buildings without heat is probably two years.

The first detailed observations on the life history of this species[64] showed that the life cycle at 82°F (28°C) is completed well within a year. Gould[59] gives 533 days for nymphal development to maturity at 78°F (25°C) and 316 days at 85°F (30°C). He states that the incubation period of eggs is shortened by 2·5 days for each degree F rise in temperature.

The rate of development at 30–36°C is given in Table IV; each female produces 5–10 oothecae and at emergence the young nymph is quite unlike the active nymph; the legs, antennae and mouthparts appear soldered together. This 'pronymph' lasts for a few minutes after which the first moult occurs. At hatching the nymph is completely white except for black eye spots and three 'teeth' on the mandibles which appear brown and chitinised.

Males mature more rapidly than females, and nymphs reared in groups reach maturity sooner than those reared separately. The adult life-span varies from two months under warm conditions to nine months in cool situations. Unfertilised females are capable of producing oothecae and some of the eggs hatch, but females only are produced, few reaching maturity.

TABLE IV

THE BIOLOGY OF *B. ORIENTALIS* BASED ON LABORATORY DATA (AVERAGES).[44] TEMPERATURE 30–36°C

Duration of copulation:	40 minutes
Interval between moult to adult and production of first ootheca:	12 days
Interval between successive oothecae:*	10 days (Rau[65])
Incubation period of ootheca:	44 days
Eggs per ootheca:*	Up to 18 (Rau[65])
Hatched eggs per ootheca:	15
Percent of hatched insects that matured:	91–94%
Number of moults:	7–10
Period of nymphal development:	
7 moults:	164 days (males)
10 moults:	282 days (females)

* Not given by Willis *et al.*[44]

Periplaneta americana (Linnaeus)—The American Cockroach

The American Cockroach was first named *Blatta americana* by Linnaeus in 1758, but was referred to in 1773 as *Blatta kakerlac* when De Geer[25] described this insect. It was moved to *Periplaneta* when this genus was established by Burmeister[30] in 1838.

There is now good reason to believe that the names given to both the American and Australian cockroaches are quite erroneous in indicating their origin. Evidence points to tropical Africa as the original home of *P. americana*. A number of native non-domiciliary species of *Periplaneta* occur in many parts of tropical and southern Africa, as well as in the Far East, but throughout tropical Africa both *P. americana* and *P. australasiae* occur almost everywhere under domiciliary conditions as well as outside human habitations—more so than in most other tropical countries.[1] Rehn suggests that 'slave ships from the West African coast continuously moving for nearly two centuries, doubtless provided the means of introduction into South America, the West Indies and the southern United States' (Fig. 12).

The American Cockroach is now an outstanding pest in tropical and subtropical areas and has become distributed by commerce throughout the lower latitudes and well into the temperate regions of most of the world. It occurs throughout almost the whole of India[66] where 'it infests every dwelling house, in the store-rooms, kitchens, cupboards and libraries, etc.' In the United States it is a domiciliary species throughout the warm southern States and extends further north than any other species of *Peri-*

planeta. It has become well-established in the City of New York and has been introduced into the northern States by trade.

There are a number of known instances where the American Cockroach has become established in premises in Britain: it is readily introduced into ports on cargoes and distributed in those cargoes to inland manufacturing industries (Fig. 17). It was also once established in a number of coal mines in South Wales.[67-69]

Fig. 17. The recorded distribution of the American cockroach (*Periplaneta americana*) in Britain showing the probable ports of entry (after Ragge,[45]).

Habitat

Periplaneta americana prefers a warm moist environment. Like *B. germanica*, the upper limit of preferred temperature is 33°C (Chapter 12). In tropical and subtropical America, this cockroach is common outdoors where it is seen most often during July and August; adults and nymphs prefer to congregate where the temperature is about 28°C, but unlike the Brown-banded Cockroach (*S. supellectilium*), American Cockroaches remain active at 21°C.[59] In warm months they are abundant in dumps, outbuildings and wood piles; they have been recorded living under decaying debris in Bermuda,[70] on palm trees along the south coast of Texas where they are attracted to street lights (Gould & Deay[21]), and these same authors have observed 'alleyways and yards overrun by this species in the summer'. A recent report from Washington D.C.[71] has drawn attention to American Cockroaches feeding on the exuding sap of certain species of trees. In addition to coal mines in Britain, the American Cockroach has also been found in similar locations in India and Sumatra and in gold mines in South Africa. Specimens have also been taken in caves in India, East Africa and Madagascar.

Indoors, *P. americana* is a common pest of restaurants, bakeries, grocery stores and all premises where food is prepared and stored. It is found in basements, on the first floor and higher if food is available. In certain areas of the United States it occurs in latrines, privies and sewers. It was once common in the galleys and mess rooms of ships but in these locations the American Cockroach has been largely usurped by the German Cockroach. *P. americana* is still, however, a frequent traveller among cargoes in holds.

Appearance

A large cockroach (28–44 mm long), shining red-brown with a paler yellow area around the edge of the pronotum. The fully developed wings extend well beyond the tip of the abdomen in the male but only just over-lap the abdomen in the female (Fig. 18). These are used for flight over short distances but such flights are rare and sluggish.[61] *P. americana* may be readily distinguished from the other common species of *Periplaneta*, with the exception of *P. brunnea* from which it is more difficult to separate. (See key to species, p. 95 and Fig. 36.)

The sexes of the adult American Cockroach differ in appearance; the tip of the abdomen of the female has a ventral keel with a slit running along it. Both sexes have a pair of well-developed cerci, but the adult males only have a pair of ventral styles on the last abdominal sternite.

The first five nymphal stages are almost uniform pale brown, but a change is noticeable in the sixth, with the development of paler patches on the pronotum either side of the dorso-median line. The sexes of all the early instars can be distinguished by the posterior margin of the ninth sternite which has a sharp median notch in the female, but is smooth and only slightly indented in the male (Fig. 19).

Wing pads appear early in nymphal development during the third or fourth instar. By the last nymphal stage the tegminal pads are about 7 mm long with the venation distinct. In all the young stages styli are present on the ninth abdominal sternites of both sexes except the last nymph of the female. In the penultimate nymphal instar and the one before that, the styli in females become hidden beneath the seventh sternite.

The ootheca of *P. americana* (8 × 5 mm) is brown when freshly deposited, but turns black in one to two days. It has weak indentations between the egg sacs with usually sixteen teeth along the ridge, each tooth under magnification showing a minute opening at the apex.

Fig. 18. Adult *Periplaneta americana*, above (a) male; opposite (b) female with ootheca. (×2)

Biology

Nutrition and temperature markedly affect cockroach development and discrepancies can therefore be expected when studies are carried out under differing experimental conditions or in different environments in widely separated geographical areas. This is emphasised by the variable data summarised in Table V. In his studies on a number of cockroaches, Gould[59] found that the period of nymphal development of *P. americana* was more influenced by temperature than any other species; a reduction of three days was obtained for each degree F rise. Willis *et al*[44] observed that this species does not thrive well in isolation, more rapid development of nymphs being obtained when bred in groups.

When infestations of *P. americana* occur in unheated premises variations in the ambient temperature and humidity retard growth during the winter but maturity may be reached in any month of the year. In Pusa, India,

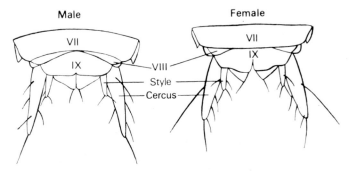

Fig. 19. Ventral view of the terminal abdominal sternites of second instar nymphs of *P. americana*.

THE COCKROACH

Table V

THE BIOLOGY OF *PERIPLANETA AMERICANA*

Interval between copulation and production of ootheca:	3–7 days[66]
Interval between moult to adult and production of first ootheca:	7–14 days;[66] 8–36 days, av. 13 days;[74] 20 days[76]
Interval between successive oothecae:	4–10 days;[66] 5–12 days;[57] av. 6 days;[74,76] av. 9 days[5]
Oothecae produced per female:	10–15 within 10 months;[66] 16–84, av. 59;[74] av. 21;[76] at least 30[75]
Period ootheca carried before deposition:	6–25 hrs;[66] <24 hrs at 25°C;[75] 24 hrs;[74] 2 days;[76] up to 3 days but occasionally longer;[5] up to 6 days[77]

	Days	°*C*	*Ref.*
Incubation period of ootheca:	24–38	30–36	44
	28	—	66
	35	30	59
	35–100	—	74
	(av. 55)		
	38	—	78
	40	29	76
	42	—	79
	45	—	5
	48	26	59
	53	17–28	76
	59	25	59

Eggs per ootheca:	6–16;[5] 14–28;[8] 16;[66] max. 18, av. 12;[76] 18–28[57]

Nigam[66] noted that the instar which falls during the cold months is exceptionally long and he refers to this period as a 'partial hibernation'. He obtained only one generation per year; oothecae were generally laid in summer (beginning in April–May) and very few during the winter.

Early records of this species[72] suggest that from four to five years is required for development from egg to adult. Perhaps this occurs under extremely adverse conditions, but more pertinent figures for the entire life

BASED ON DATA FROM VARIOUS SOURCES

Hatched eggs per ootheca:	Av. 13·6 from 511 oothecae[74]

Number of moults:	7–8;[74,66] 9–10;[75] 9–13;[44] 10[79]

	Months	Moults	Sex	°C	Ref.
Nymphal development:	Normally 4½–5, but up to 15	—	—	25–30	79
	5 13	9 13	F M	30–36	44
	6½ 17	— —	— —	28 24	59
	7	—	—	30	75
	8½ 9	— —	F M	29	73
	9½–30½	—	—	—	74
	10–15 (In India)	—	—	—	66
	11	—	—	—	2
	11½ (Puerto Rico)	—	—	—	78
	>1 year (in U.S.A.)	—	—	—	5

Adult life span:	102–588 days, av. 450, males shorter lived than females;[74] 9–12 months;[5] 200–700 days[73]

span, from egg to the natural death of adults at 29°C, under conditions simulating a well-heated building, show that life expectancy ranges over 630 days but may be as great as 1,243 days.[73]

In Gould & Deay's[74] experiments, the first three to four moults of the American Cockroach occurred at regular intervals of about a month, but thereafter the intervals varied from one to six months; variation in development occurred among cockroaches hatched from the same ootheca, adulthood being achieved by three insects in 424 to 616 days, whilst one was still in the eleventh instar at 632 days. Gier[75] using warmer conditions states that the duration of successive instars increases with stage from 18 to 50 days; if a nymph moults early in one stage it continues to moult early in succeeding instars, thus reaching maturity much earlier than average. Under these conditions some instars may be omitted.

In the studies of Gould & Deay, the maximum number of oothecae produced by one female was 90, and gave rise to 970 young. As the ootheca is formed and filled with eggs it is gradually pushed out of the genital pouch; it is white at first, but turns brown in about one hour. The complete process of ootheca formation takes three to four hours.

Among the many workers who have tried to demonstrate parthenogenesis in the American Cockroach, Nigam[66] and Gould & Deay[74] were unsuccessful. The latter showed that females can produce egg capsules without previous mating, but all were infertile. Griffiths & Tauber[76] however, found that parthenogenesis was possible but infrequent; 'it occurred among 4·5 per cent of well formed, seemingly normal capsules produced by virgin females'. Certainly the presence of males and the opportunity for mating increases the number of egg capsules and their rate of production (Chapter 9), but a fresh mating is not necessary for the production of each ootheca; Haber[57] recorded 13 oothecae laid in four months following a single mating, and Gould & Deay[74] refer to one female which lived for 232 days and produced 28 fertile capsules out of 30 (with an average of 14 young from each) after only one pre-ovipositional mating.

Periplaneta australasiae (Fabricius)—The Australian Cockroach

This species was originally named *Blatta australasiae*, when in 1775 the term 'Australasiae' probably meant not 'of Australia and New Zealand', but 'of Southern Asia'.[80] It is the most frequently encountered cockroach in houses in Brisbane,[62] reported as rare in Sydney in 1906 by Froggat,[81] and not so widespread as *P. americana* in India, where the Australian Cockroach is found mostly in the south and in Ceylon.[66]

Among species of *Periplaneta*, the Australian Cockroach is second in importance only to *P. americana* as a world-wide pest in buildings. In common with most other domiciliary cockroaches, *P. australasiae* apparently originated in the tropics or subtropics, probably in Africa, from which it 'migrated' first in association with slave labour and then through commercial channels into the warm climate of most of the inhabited world. It is now an occasional pest in the cooler areas where man has provided warm, moist, artificial environments (e.g. greenhouses) in which this insect thrives. When this cockroach has appeared in greenhouses and other artificially heated places in the colder regions of the United States, 'it breeds and increases in numbers with great rapidity, temporarily becoming a dangerous pest'.[43]

At the turn of this century, *P. australasiae* was reported as the most abundant and troublesome species in Florida[2] where it was widely estab-

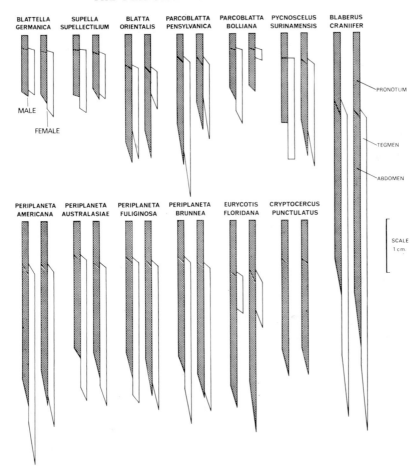

Fig. 20. Diagrammatic representation of cockroach species to show, (1) comparative size, (2) difference between males (left) and females (right), (3) degree of size variation within each sex (minimum measurement on left; maximum measurement on right) and relationship between tegmen and body length (from Hebard[43]).

Cryptocercus punctulatus is wingless; brachypterous females exist in *P. bolliana, B. orientalis* and in both sexes of *E. floridana*. *Pycnoscelus surinamensis* is parthenogenetic in America. Females produce females only. The measurements for the male are from one specimen only.

lished both in and out of doors. It does occur in the United States further north, but as it is more affected by cold than *P. americana*, it does not become a major problem in unheated buildings, such as warehouses, subject to frost.[82]

P. australasiae has now become a pest of buildings in many areas of the tropics; its domiciliary habits have been recorded as far apart as Africa, Ecuador, Puerto Rico, and the Philippine Islands. It occurs both indoors and outside in the West Indies,[83] and has been frequently imported into Britain from the West Indies and from Brazil on cargoes of bananas.

Habitat
This species is circumtropical, preferring a moist warm environment with a temperature somewhat higher than that required for the development of *P. americana*. In infested premises it occupies a similar habitat to the American Cockroach but has not, as far as is known, been taken from sewers.

Outdoors, *P. australasiae* has been found in a variety of situations: under stones in Bermuda,[84] in a field of sugar cane in the Virgin Islands,[85] under

Fig. 21. Adult *Periplaneta australasiae*, Male; opposite Female with ootheca. (×2)

leaves of coconut palms in Jamaica,[83] in bird guano in caves in Sarawak[86] and beneath logs in Florida.[3, 87] It has been taken in greenhouses in France, Italy and Britain and at one time was responsible with *B. orientalis* and *P. americana* for damage to plants in the tropical house of the Royal Botanic Gardens at Kew. Its recorded distribution in Britain is very similar to that illustrated for *P. americana* (Fig. 17).

Appearance
A large cockroach (30–35 mm), generally somewhat smaller that *P. americana*, reddish-brown with fully developed wings (which enable it to fly) overlapping the apex of the abdomen in both sexes (Fig. 20). The female has a ventral keel at the tip of the abdomen and like the previous species, the dark pronotum is surrounded at the edge by a pale ring which is more distinct in *P. australasiae* (Fig. 21). It differs from *P. americana* and

P. brunnea in having pale basal margins to the tegmina. Nymphs are strikingly marked with yellow spots on the thorax and abdomen. The ootheca (10 × 5 mm) has feeble indentations, as in *P. americana*.

Biology
Data on the reproduction of *P. australasiae* at 30–36°C is given in Table VI. Each female produces 20–30 oothecae and the rate of nymphal development is similar to *P. americana*, taking about a year. Nymphs reared collectively mature more rapidly than when alone.[44] The adult life span is four to six months. Eggs produced parthenogenetically may hatch but fail to reach maturity.

TABLE VI

THE REPRODUCTIVE ABILITY OF *PERIPLANETA AUSTRALASIAE* BASED ON LABORATORY DATA (AVERAGES)[44]. EXPERIMENTAL CONDITIONS 30–36°C

Minimum interval between moult to adult and attempted mating by males:	5 days
Interval between moult to adult and production of first ootheca:	24 days
Interval between successive oothecae:	10 days
Incubation period of oothecae:	40 days
Eggs per ootheca:	24
Hatched eggs per ootheca:	16
Percent of hatched insects that matured:	55%

Periplaneta brunnea Burmeister—The Brown Cockroach
This is another species, believed to be a native of Africa, carried around the world in commerce. Its present distribution is more confined to the tropics than *P. americana*.

The Brown Cockroach was first recorded in the United States in 1907, from the State of Illinois, subsequently in Texas in 1917 and from Chile and Guyana in 1938. It is now common in the southern United States, in Florida, North and South Carolina and from Georgia westwards to Texas. In some areas it is more common than the American Cockroach. It occurs typically in pantries, grocery stores and outbuildings and has been recorded indoors as far north as Philadelphia. It is an obnoxious household pest collected from army camps, city dumps, privies, as well as from sewers.[88]

Periplaneta brunnea has been taken on shipments of bananas arriving in Britain from Dominica.[89,90] More recently two separate infestations became established in buildings at London (Heathrow) Airport (Chapter 11), one near to an area handling baggage of passengers in transit,[91] the other in a stable of the animal transit centre.[92]

Habitat
Similar to *P. americana*.

Appearance
The colouration of this species resembles that of *P. americana*—reddish-brown with a yellow margin on the pronotum surrounding a dark central area—but it is a smaller species measuring 31–37 mm in length (Fig. 22).

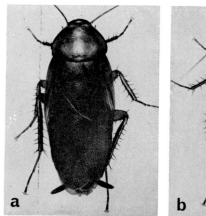

Fig. 22. (a) Adult female *Periplaneta brunnea* (×1·5); (b) adult male *Periplaneta fuliginosa* (×1·5). (Courtesy: Drs. Roth & Willis, U.S. Army Natick Laboratories.)

The paired blotches on the pronotum are usually less conspicuous; the tegmina and wings are not usually as long relative to the abdomen, and do not differ in length between the sexes quite so much as in *P. americana* (Fig. 20). *P. brunnea* is capable of gliding flight.

The most useful features which distinguish the two species are:[88]

	P. brunnea	*P. americana*
	Adult stage	
Cercus: (Fig. 36)	Stout, spindle shaped, the last segment triangular, less than twice as long as the basal width.	Stout basally, but tapers markedly, the last segment tending to be parallel sided, two or three times as long as the basal width.
Ootheca:	Large (12–16 mm long), less rounded laterally, securely glued when deposited, containing an average of 24 eggs.	Smaller (8 mm long), not so securely glued when deposited, containing an average of 16 eggs.

E

	P. brunnea	*P. americana*
	First stage nymph	
Antennae:	The first 8 and last 4 antennal segments conspicuously white, the intermediate ones brown.	Antennal segments uniformly brown.
Mesothorax:	A median translucent area allows light to pass through.	This area absent.
Abdomen:	Faint cream coloured spots on dorso-lateral margins of 1st and 2nd segments.	These segments entirely brown.
	Intermediate stage nymphs	
Abdomen:	Cream coloured spots on dorso-lateral margins extend from 2nd–6th segments.	These segments entirely brown.

Biology
Little detailed information is available on the biology of *P. brunnea*. Copulation by females occurs within a few hours of the final moult.[88] At 30°C the interval between the last moult and production of the first ootheca averages ten days.[44] This interval drops to four days between successive oothecae but increases to 13 days at the lower temperature of 24°C; the eggs hatch in 40 days at 30°C and in 81 days at 24°C. The duration of nymphal development has apparently not been recorded. Adults live 240 days (females) and 290 days (males).

In culture the ootheca is glued to the substrate by a secretion from the mouth parts which hardens to form a strong 'cement'. In the studies of Willis *et al.*[44] eggs hatched from nine per cent of oothecae produced parthenogenetically and 66 of the 208 hatched nymphs matured. All were females.

Periplaneta fuliginosa (Serville)—The Smoky-brown Cockroach
Formerly named *Kakerlac fuliginosa* by Serville,[31] this subtropical species was first recorded from North America in 1839. It is a domiciliary species found most abundantly in the southern States; it is well established in Georgia, northern Florida and westward to Texas. In the south-east it is common outdoors in garages, outbuildings, woodpiles and porches of homes where it flies to light at night.

In some parts of the southern States *P. fuliginosa* is also established inside homes. As a domiciliary pest it is second only to *B. germanica* in homes in south-west Georgia where it is the most common species in privies.[93] It has also been found on a few occasions in heated buildings further north: breeding in a greenhouse throughout the year in Indiana,[21] as far north as Chicago, Illinois[46] and as a household pest in Iowa.[94]

Appearance and biology

Periplaneta fuliginosa is similar in size to *P. brunnea* (31–35 mm long), but it is entirely shining brownish-black, almost as dark as *B. orientalis*, the only uniformly dark coloured species of *Periplaneta* found in North America (Fig. 22). The wings of both sexes cover the abdomen.

Details of the biology of the Smoky-brown Cockroach, obtained from laboratory studies, are given in Table VII. According to Gould[59] this species responds to temperature in a similar manner to *P. americana*; hatching from the ootheca occurs in 70 days at 23°C, reducing to 56 days at 25·5°C and 37 days at 30°C. Nymphal development, however, is relatively unaffected by temperature, but nymphs reared in groups mature more rapidly than those in isolation.[44] Adult males attempt to mate five days after the final moult.

TABLE VII

THE BIOLOGY OF *PERIPLANETA FULIGINOSA* BASED ON LABORATORY DATA (AVERAGES).[44] TEMPERATURE 30–36°C

Interval between moult to adult and production of first ootheca:	16 days
Interval between successive oothecae:	11 days
Eggs per ootheca:	20
Percentage of hatched insects that matured:	51%
Number of moults:	9–12
Period of nymphal development:	
(i) in isolation: 9 moults	474 days (males)
11 moults	586 days (males)
(ii) in groups:	179 days (males)
	191 days (females)

Supella supellectilium (Serville)—The Brown-banded Cockroach

This species was originally named *Blatta supellectilium* from insects taken in Mauritius in 1839. It is now known from considerable areas of the tropics and subtropics of the Old World and is distributed over much of Africa outside the forests of the West Coast. No non-domiciliary species of *Supella* is known except from Africa and it is therefore reasonable to assume that *Supella supellectilium* is of African origin.[1]

The Brown-banded Cockroach was introduced into the West Indies probably by slave ships and was first recorded in Cuba in 1862 as *Blatta cubensis*, where, according to Saussure,[95] it was very common at that time. From there it became established in Florida and was first recorded at Key

West and Miami in 1903. Shipments of fruit from Florida probably provided a ready means of spread northwards into the Southern States and by 1930 it was reported from other parts of Florida, Georgia, Alabama and Texas.

The only published account of *Supella* being troublesome in a private house in the United States before 1937 is that of Whelan[96] who recorded it in Nebraska in 1929. In 1937 Back[97] wrote: 'there is no question about its ability to maintain itself and to become a nuisance in the more southern cities of the U.S.' In that year it was recorded as far north as Chicago and Indianapolis, and Back[98] accounting for its spread, added 'it would seem that the increased travel, particularly by autoists who carry luggage to more northern parts after winter sojourns in southern Florida is responsible for the apparently recent and wide distribution of *Supella*'.

By 1940, the Brown-banded Cockroach had reached Washington D.C., Indiana, Illinois, Wisconsin, and South Dakota. By 1954 the records of the Economic Insect Survey Section of the U.S. Department of Agriculture (Fig. 23) showed that *S. supellectilium* was known from as far afield as twenty States;[82] it had become established in heated homes, apartments and hospitals where moderately high temperatures satisfied the requirements of the insect. It has now been recorded from every State of America except Vermont.

Supella supellectilium is a major domiciliary pest: an adventive from the tropics, carried around the word in trade, established notably in homes in the southern United States and has increased rapidly in abundance during the last 40 years. Such is the possible rate of development of pest status by a cockroach where conditions favour the survival and reproduction of the species. The Brown-banded Cockroach was first recorded in Queensland, Australia,[99] in 1924 where it was introduced more recently than the other domiciliary cockroaches.

Apart from two infestations of the Brown Cockroach (*P. brunnea*) found in southern England in the last two years, the Brown-banded Cockroach (*S. supellectilium*) is the most recently introduced cockroach to become established in Britain. No records of breeding colonies were recorded here before the present century and even now there are very few. According to Ragge,[45] this species has so far become established only in dwelling houses and offices, but one additional observation (unpublished) is available of it occurring at an American Air Force base in Britain, where it is thought to have been introduced with personal effects. A further infestation in London is mentioned in Chapter 14.

Habitat

Supella is recorded as the commonest cockroach in Khartoum, where some 50 years ago it was said to occur in nearly all buildings and native huts. *Supella* breeds throughout the year in the Sudan and every stage of development is seen at all seasons. It is usually nocturnal, but is occasionally

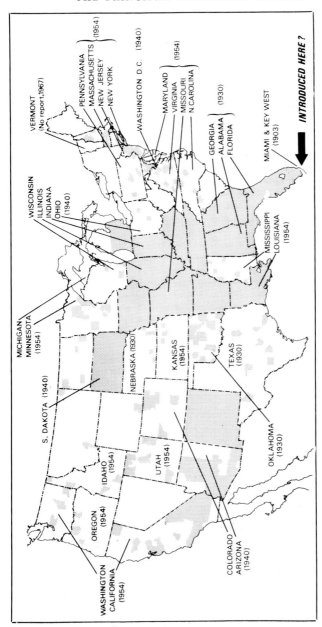

Fig. 23. Distribution (shaded areas) of the Brown-banded Cockroach (*Supella supellectilium*) compiled by the Plant Pest Survey Section of the U.S. Dept. of Agric. to September 1957. Dates within the map show the extent of spread between 1903 and 1954. This cockroach has been reported, up to 1967, from all States except Vermont, where a thorough survey would no doubt reveal its presence. (Gentry, personal communication, 1967.)

seen in the day time. It often flies around lights in houses and has also been observed flying outdoors.

Kevan & Chopard[100] refer to it as a cosmopolitan species, occurring both out of doors and as a household pest, apparently endemic to non-forested areas of Africa north of the Equator. Hafez & Afifi[101] give a number of references to its occurrence in Egypt along the Nile valley where *Supella* is found throughout the year, but not so abundantly as *B. germanica* or *P. americana*. Outside Africa and the countries mentioned above, the Brown-banded Cockroach has been recorded from Mexico,[43] Brazil,[102] Hawaii,[103] and Fiji.[104]

Unlike the German Cockroach, which is usually confined to kitchens and eating areas, the Brown-banded Cockroach spreads throughout infested premises. It prefers locations high up in heated rooms, where the temperature (in the United States), probably averaging 80°F (26·5°C) for most of the year, allows possibly two generations a year.[59]

Supella supellectilium is found in desk and bureau drawers, behind

Fig. 24. Adult *Supella supellectilium*, above, (a) male; opposite, (b) female with ootheca. (× 3·5)

pictures, on book shelves where it feeds on the gum sizing of books, behind wall paper where it feeds on the paste, beneath tables and other furniture. It is active and has a tendency to fly when disturbed. It has a preference for harbouring in furniture, bedding, cupboards and behind picture moulding, and seldom visits kitchens except in search of food.[61] Mallis,[105] commenting on the wide distribution of this cockroach throughout infested apartments, suggests that it is probably the commonest species of cockroach in bedrooms, this wide dispersal making it especially difficult to control.

Appearance

A small cockroach, similar in size to *B. germanica*, the adult male (13–14·5 mm long) is slightly larger than the female (10–12 mm); the tegmina of the male completely cover the abdomen, but rarely reach the tip of the abdomen in the female (Fig. 24). The male is extremely slender, the female broader, both generally ochraceous buff with the face and genae suffused with chestnut brown to black.

There is considerable colour variation in this species. The lateral edges of the pronotum are transparent, the remainder dark, the pronotum of the

b

adult often with a paler area in the centre. Females are usually darker than
males and in the more intensely coloured specimens the whole of the
pronotum may be dark. The basal area and posterior half of the tegmina
are chestnut coloured, fairly irridescent, giving the adult an attractive
appearance.

The nymph has two brown bands which are very distinct; one across
the posterior margin of the mesonotum, the other across the first abdominal
segment extending laterally along the next few segments. The remainder of
the mesonotum and the entire metanotum are transparent ochraceous buff.

The ootheca of *S. supellectilium* ($4 \times 2 \cdot 5$ mm) is the smallest of the more
common domiciliary cockroaches, it is reddish-brown, purse-shaped with
18–19 teeth along the seam and nine vertical furrows on each side, these
corresponding with the position of the eggs within.

Biology

Data on reproduction and the rate of development of *S. supellectilium* at
30°C (Table VIII) obtained by Willis *et al.*,[44] agree closely with the information obtained from cage experiments in Khartoum. The number of
eggs in successive oothecae remains constant at 14–17 (Fig. 25), and does
not drop so markedly as in *Blattella* (Fig. 15). The maximum egg hatch
in *Supella* is obtained from the seventh ootheca.

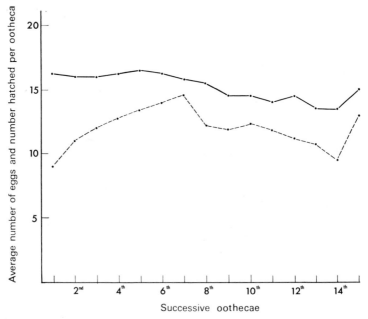

Fig. 25. The number of eggs per ootheca (solid line), and the number that hatch
(dotted line) in relation to the sequence of ootheca formation in *S. supellectilium*
(after Willis *et al*[44]).

The incubation period of oothecae at 65 per cent relative humidity falls from 74 days at 77°F to 43 days at 81°F and to 37 days at 86°F. At 77–86°F the incubation period is shortened by an average of five days for each degree F rise in temperature.[59]

Temperature also influences the rate of growth of nymphs. Development to maturity takes 164 days at 77°F, reducing to 92 days at 84°F, a shortening in development time of 11 days for each degree F rise. Both sexes mature at the same rate,[44] but adult males live longer than females. This is not supported by the findings of Hafez & Afifi[101] in Egypt, who give average life spans of 115 and 136 days for males and females, respectively, at 25°C (70 per cent relative humidity) and 87 and 104 days at 32°C (70 per cent relative humidity). Relative humidity in the range 40 per cent to 80 per cent (at 32°C) does not materially affect adult life span.

TABLE VIII

THE BIOLOGY OF *SUPELLA SUPELLECTILIUM* BASED ON LABORATORY DATA (AVERAGES).[44] EXPERIMENTAL CONDITIONS 30°C

Minimum interval between moult to adult and copulation:	3 days (females)
	5 days (males)
Period of copulation:	at least 30 minutes
Interval between moult to adult and production of first ootheca:	10 days
Interval between start of formation of ootheca and deposition:	18 hours
Oothecae produced per female:	5–18 (average 11)
Interval between successive oothecae:	6 days
Incubation period of ootheca:	40 days
Eggs per ootheca:	16
Hatched eggs per ootheca:	12
Percent of hatched insects that matured:	85%
Number of moults:	6–8
Period of nymphal development:	
(i) in isolation: 6 moults	69 days (females)
8 moults	114 days (females)
(ii) in groups:	54 days (males)
	56 days (females)
Adult life span:	90 days (females)
	115 days (males)

II. SPECIES OCCASIONALLY ASSOCIATED WITH MAN

All the species included under this heading are more likely to occur outside buildings than within. The first four species have been disseminated in trade and are capable of breeding within man-made structures. These are the Surinam Cockroach, which occurs in dwellings in various parts of the world, the Madeira Cockroach which is less widely reported as a domiciliary pest, and the Lobster Cockroach which establishes itself in buildings only occasionally. Little is known of the domiciliary habits of the fourth species, *Neostylopyga rhombifolia*, which gives rise to infestations in buildings in various parts of Asia.

Species of *Blaberus* are not usually recognised as pests of buildings, their normal habitat being the tropical rain forests of Central America. Nevertheless, breeding colonies of at least two Blaberid species have been taken from properties in the New World.

Pycnoscelus surinamensis (Linnaeus)—The Surinam Cockroach

This species, originally called *Blatta surinamensis*, was first described in 1767 from specimens taken in Surinam. Since then it has been widely distributed in trade within the humid tropics and subtropics, and is now abundant in the Florida peninsula and around Brownsville in Texas. Infestations have also been recorded in New Orleans and San Antonio.[43]

This cockroach becomes temporarily established in greenhouses artificially heated during cold weather. A few records exist of colonies confined almost entirely to these conditions in England and Scotland.[45] It has been found in greenhouses in the northern United States and in Germany where in some instances it has proved to be responsible for considerable damage to plants.

The key to the origin of this species lies in the peculiarity of parthenogenesis. As far as is known no adult male has been taken in nature in the New World and similarly none has been recorded from the British Isles. Records show that 'as far back as 1865, males were only known to the systematist Carl Brunner from the East Indies, and from Burma in 1893'.[1] Up to 1945, males had been found only in oriental collections of this insect. Other endemic species of the genus *Pycnoscelus* occur in Indo-Malaysia and these, together with the localisation of males of *P. surinamensis*, lead to the conclusion that the species is of oriental origin.

Rehn believes that *P. surinamensis* was probably introduced into Africa *via* the east coast with Arab trade across the Indian Ocean. The introduction into western Mexico is likely to have been *via* Spanish galleons from the west. Its presence on the Atlantic coast of the United States probably derived from slave ships from Africa visiting the West Indies where the species is firmly established.

Habitat

The Surinam Cockroach has been recorded as a household pest in the southern United States, the East Indian islands, Philippines, Tanzania and Trinidad. It has also been taken around chicken batteries in Hawaii. In common with many other tropical species, the distribution of *P. surinamensis* is greatly influenced by cold: in the laboratory[106] 95 per cent died at 36–40°F (2–4°C) with 100 per cent fatality overnight at 24°F (—4°C).

In tropical climates this insect is less likely to occur indoors than outdoors. The natural environment of *P. surinamensis* is under stones and loose litter where the females with young often burrow in the topsoil; they have been recorded outdoors from Egypt (in moist soil), the Virgin Islands (under rubbish), Puerto Rico (under stones), Barbados and Cuba (in sugarcane fields), Jamaica and Florida (in various situations), from Haiti (damaging potato tubers), Hawaii (feeding on pineapple roots), from Sumatra (damaging tobacco plants) and from Texas in nests of wood rats.[43]

Appearance

Pycnoscelus surinamensis is a medium-sized cockroach (18–24 mm long), shining brown to black. The tegmina and wings which are fully developed in both sexes extend considerably beyond the abdomen. The posterior margin of the pronotum is strongly sinuate (Fig. 26). In some but not all specimens the pronotum has a pale band along the anterior margin.

Fig. 26. *Pycnoscelus surinamensis*, (a) late stage nymph (× 4); (b) parthenogenetic female (macropterous adult × 3). (Courtesy: Drs. Roth & Willis, U.S. Army Natick Laboratories).

The eggs are enclosed in a transparent membrane retained within the abdomen. This egg case has the appearance of the ootheca typical of other species, but is only partially developed.

Biology

The biology of *P. surinamensis* has two features which distinguish it from the cockroaches previously described: (1) parthenogenesis (in the New World) whereby all offspring are female and (2) false ovoviviparity (Chapter 9) whereby an ootheca is produced, extruded externally and then withdrawn into the brood sac of the female where the eggs develop. This feature is also characteristic of the Madeira and Lobster Cockroaches.

TABLE IX

THE BIOLOGY OF *PYCNOSCELUS SURINAMENSIS* (PARTHENO-GENETIC STRAIN) BASED ON LABORATORY DATA (AVERAGES).[44] EXPERIMENTAL CONDITIONS 18–24°C

Interval between moult to adult and production of first ootheca:	7 days
Interval between moult to adult and hatch of first brood:	42 days
Incubation period in brood sac:	35 days
Average number of broods per female:	3
Interval between hatch of successive broods:	
1st–2nd:	48 days
3rd–4th:	82 days
Eggs per ootheca:	26
Hatched eggs (first ootheca only):	21
Percent hatched insects that matured:	86%
Number of moults:	8–10
Period of nymphal development (at 30°C):	
(i) in isolation: 8 moults:	127 days (females)
10 moults:	184 days (females)
(ii) in groups	140 days (females)
Adult life span:	307 days (females)

Leucophaea maderae (Fabricius)—The Madeira Cockroach

This species is firmly established in the West Indies where it is universally present in Cuba, Jamaica, Hispaniola, Puerto Rico and the Bahamas, often being an abundant and serious pest in homes and warehouses. It occurs in all the islands of the Greater Antilles and in some of the Lesser Antilles.

Leucophaea maderae was first reported in the United States in the early nineteenth century. In more recent years it became established in the basements of buildings in the Harlem section of New York, occupied by people from Puerto Rico. In the South American Continent, the Madeira Cockroach is found in coastal Brazil, and established colonies are known from Costa Rica, south through Panama, Colombia, Venezuela, the Guianas and from Ecuador and Argentina.

This insect was first described from the island of Madeira, in the Atlantic, about 400 miles west of Morocco. Another five species belong to the genus *Leucophaea*, which together with the Madeira Cockroach occur over most of Africa, south of the Sahara.[1] Accordingly, there is evidence to suggest that the Madeira Cockroach was originally a native of West Africa, brought across the Atlantic to the West Indies and to the coast of Brazil, probably before 1800 (Fig. 27).

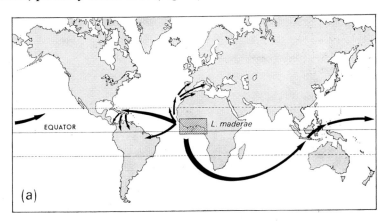

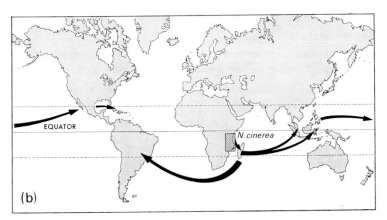

Fig. 27. Probable areas of origin and early directions of spread of (a) *L. maderae* and (b) *N. cinerea* from Africa, as suggested by Rehn[1].

Outside tropical Africa, *L. maderae* is known from the Canary Islands, Morocco, Spain and Corsica. In Asia and the Pacific, records are available for only three locations; *viz.*, Java, the Philippines and Hawaii. In the Mid-Pacific islands it was recorded in native huts as far back as 1897. As far as is known, the Madeira Cockroach does not occur in India, Australia, Southern China or the greater part of Malaysia.

Habitat

In tropical regions, this cockroach lives outdoors; it is gregarious and develops large colonies. The insect has been found in sugar-cane fields in Barbados and associated with palms, guavas and bananas in Dominica.

The banana is apparently a favourite food;[78] it is not surprising therefore that this species has been introduced on shipments into the United States and is frequently encountered at ports by quarantine inspectors. Similarly it has been brought into Britain on imports from the West Indies, Canary Islands and Cameroons[89,107] but has not succeeded in establishing itself here.

Buildings can often provide this cockroach with a suitable habitat. Outside America it is domiciliary in Madeira, the Windward Islands, Philippines and Trinidad. In Puerto Rico it is most often encountered in fruit stores, warehouses and markets, where it is especially fond of grapes.

The establishment of the Madeira Cockroach in New York in 1953 led Gurney[108] to suggest that it could become an important domestic pest in cities in well-heated buildings. He refers firstly, to the increasing pest status in the United States of the Brown-banded Cockroach (*S. supellectilium*), as an example of the potential spread of an introduced species and secondly, to the suitability of tropical Florida as a favourable habitat and point of introduction of *L. maderae* from the Bahamas and other West Indian islands. However, with the increasing importance attached to quarantine in the prevention of pest introduction the likelihood of a serious problem arising is now small.

Appearance

A large cockroach (40–50 mm long), with tegmina and wings covering the abdomen. It is pale brown to tawny olive, the tegmina marked with two dark brown lines in the basal area, and the posterior areas mottled (Fig. 28). The male has a specialised organ on the dorsum of the second abdominal segment, and the nymphs have short microscopic spines which are conspicuous along the dorsal posterior margin of each segment.

The adult is slow moving but flies actively; it is capable of producing an offensive odour when disturbed and there are reports of it being able to produce sound by stridulation, moving the posterior margin of the pronotum over the mesonotum.

Fig. 28. Adult female *Leucophaea maderae*. (×1·5) (Courtesy: Drs. Roth & Willis, U.S. Army Natick Laboratories.)

Biology
In Brazil mating occurs mainly during the warm rainy season and usually takes 20–30 minutes (Scharrer[9]). The species is false ovoviviparous (see p. 216) and according to this author the number of young produced at one time ranges from 25–32, considerably greater than the number obtained by Willis *et al.*[44] in the laboratory (Table X).

Females undergo one more moult than males and thus take longer to mature. Nevertheless, the period of nymphal development given by Willis *et al.* for the two sexes is considerably shorter than the seven to eighteen months quoted by Scharrer. She records the life span as two and a half years.

Nauphoeta cinerea (Olivier)—the Lobster Cockroach
This species gets its name from the Lobster-like design on the pronotum, but is also called the Cinereous Cockroach from its ashy colouring. It is a pest species of world-wide distribution which was first recorded in the southern United States in 1952. Occasionally, it is imported into Britain on fruit and other foodstuffs and has been recorded in England and in Germany in heated buildings.[109]

The Lobster Cockroach, originally named *Blatta cinerea* in 1789 from

THE COCKROACH

TABLE X

THE BIOLOGY OF *LEUCOPHAEA MADERAE* BASED ON LABORATORY DATA (AVERAGES).[44] TEMPERATURE 30–36°C

Minimum period between moult to adult and copulation:	11 days (females)
Interval between moult to adult and production of first ootheca:	20 days
Incubation of ootheca:	58 days
Eggs per ootheca:	34
Hatched eggs per ootheca:	18
Percentage of hatched insects that matured:	99%
Number of moults:	7–8
Period of nymphal development:	
(i) in isolation: 7 moults:	127 days (males)
8 moults:	163 days (females)
(ii) in groups:	121 days (males)
	150 days (females)

specimens taken in Mauritius, was not given its present name until 1922. It is a tropical domiciliary cockroach of the New and Old Worlds, occurring in Cuba, Hispaniola, Mexico, Brazil and the Galapagos Islands. In the East, it is widely distributed in the Philippines, Sumatra and Singapore and occurs in Australia, New Caledonia and the Hawaiian Islands. The East African records extend from Egypt through the Sudan to eastern Tanganyika (now Tanzania), the Transvaal and Natal. It also occurs in Madagascar and Mauritius.

Rehn's study[1] of the genus *Nauphoeta* indicates that the native home of *N. cinerea* is East Africa. He suggests that it spread to the Malagasy region probably through the medium of Arab trading ships, and the more distant Philippines and other Oriental centres were established through Portuguese or Spanish voyagers. The colony in western Mexico was probably established via Spanish galleons from the Philippines; that in Brazil by Portuguese traders, and the Galapagos population doubtless by tortoise-hunting seamen from ships of many nationalities. The introduction of *N. cinerea* into Cuba and Hispaniola may have come from the west in goods brought from the Philippines *via* Mexico, as the Atlantic galleons often visited the eastern Mexican coast in the sixteenth and seventeenth centuries (Fig. 27).

Habitat

Before breeding colonies were found in Florida in 1952, this cockroach was taken on products at a number of ports of entry into the United States.

With the assistance of a member of a Pest Control Company in Tampa, Florida, *N. cinerea* was found established in that area in mills producing animal feeds.[110]

The Lobster Cockroach was first recorded in Australia in 1918 where it is regarded as a 'semi-domestic' species, as it is found in out-houses and stores rather than in dwellings.[111] Nevertheless, it has been found in homes in Australia and in a hospital.[112] It is also a frequent inhabitant of native huts in the Sudan.

Illingworth[109] recorded *N. cinerea* in poultry food sheds in Honolulu. Up to 1942 this cockroach had been of somewhat rare occurrence in Hawaii but Illingworth describes it developing 'in alarming numbers in and about the feed room of a poultry plant at the University of Hawaii'. It is fond of feeds containing fish oil, and its predaceous habits extend to killing and eating the Cypress Cockroach, *Diploptera punctata*.

Appearance
A large cockroach (25–29 mm long) of ashy colouring with a lobster-like pattern on the pronotum. The wings of the male are slightly longer than those of the female and do not cover the abdomen (Fig. 29).

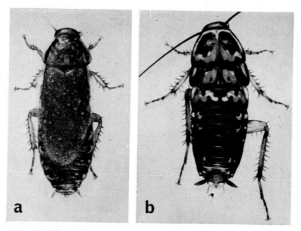

Fig. 29. (a) Adult male *Nauphoeta cinerea* (×1·5); (b) adult male *Neostylopyga rhombifolia*. (×2) (Courtesy: Drs. Roth & Willis, U.S. Army Natick Laboratories.)

Males stridulate when they court non-receptive females. The sound is produced by striae on the side and hind margins of the pronotum moving against the costal vein at the base of the tegmina.[113]

Biology
The development and reproductive characteristics of *N. cinerea* are given

F

THE COCKROACH

in Table XI. This is a false ovoviviparous species in which the oothecae contain 26–40 eggs.[114] The nymphs hatch as the female extrudes the ootheca from the brood sac; they shed their embryonic membrane as they hatch and eat both it and the ootheca. Newly hatched nymphs crawl beneath the female, even under her wings, and remain there for about an hour after hatching.[44] In the laboratory the number of nymphs hatching from oothecae increases from an average of 20 from the first egg case to about 30 from the third and decreases thereafter. Female nymphs take longer to mature than males.

TABLE XI

THE BIOLOGY OF *NAUPHOETA CINEREA* BASED ON LABORATORY DATA (AVERAGES).[44] TEMPERATURE 30°C

Minimum period between moult to adult and copulation:	6 days (in both sexes)
Interval between moult to adult and production of first ootheca:	13 days
Interval between moult to adult and hatch of first brood:	44 days
Interval between hatch of successive broods:	1st–2nd, 40 days 7th–8th, 99 days
Average broods per female:	6
Incubation period in brood sac:	36 days
Eggs per ootheca:	33
Hatched eggs per ootheca:	31
Percentage of hatched insects that matured:	99%
Number of moults:	7–8

Period of nymphal development:
    (i) in isolation: 7 moults:
                8 moults:
	73 days (males)
	94 days (females)

(ii) in groups:	72 days (males) 85 days (females)
Adult life span:	344 days (females) 365 days (males)

Neostylopyga rhombifolia (Stoll)—No common name

This cockroach is abundant throughout most of tropical Indo-Malaya, particularly in the Philippine Islands, from where it was probably introduced into Hawaii. It is also generally abundant in Madagascar, Mauritius, the Seychelles and adjacent islands. It occurs along the east coast of

Africa where distribution has followed the inland trade routes to Nyasa-
land (now Malawi), and the Zambesi valley.[1]

The Indo-Malayan region is thought to be the original home of this
species, spread from there certainly resulting from the activities of man.
The occurrence of *N. rhombifolia* in Madeira can be attributed to possible
introduction on a Portuguese ship sailing from the Indian Ocean to Europe.

Neostylopyga rhombifolia was first described in 1813, and is a domiciliary
species in areas where it occurs in large numbers. In the New World, *N.
rhombifolia* was first recorded in 1865 from Acapulco, Mexico and from
Venezuela and Argentina. Some 30 years later it was reported from Brazil.
This cockroach has been established in southern California for about 70
years—the result of spread northwards from Mexico where it has long been
established on the Mexico–Arizona boundary.[43] Rehn recalls that
Acapulco 'was the port at which the classic Spanish galleons from the
Philippines landed their cargoes for land transfer to the Atlantic side, to
be reloaded for Spain'.

Habits, Appearance and Biology

Little has been recorded of the domiciliary habits of this cockroach. It is
a medium-sized species (20–25 mm long), the males smaller than females,
the tegmina reduced in both sexes to small lobes (4 mm long). The hindwings are entirely absent. It is striking in appearance with a distinctive
colour pattern of shining brown-black, marbled with yellow (Fig. 29).
Males are said to occur less frequently than females.

Eggs produced parthenogenetically are capable of developing but do
not hatch. At 27°C and 70 per cent relative humidity, Willis *et al.*[44]
obtained an average of 22 eggs per ootheca and with nymphs reared in
groups, males took an average of 302 days to mature and females 286 days.

Blaberus spp.

A brief description must be made of the Blaberid species if only on account
of their very large size. They are almost entirely confined to the American
tropics but extend into temperate South America.

Three species, *B. atropos* (Stoll) a native of South America, *B. craniifer*
Burmeister, and *B. giganteus* (Linnaeus) (Fig. 30), have all been found in
caves, but their more normal habitat is under rotting logs and vegetation
in tropical rain forests. Both *B. atropos* and *B. boliviensis* Princis have
been found associated with bananas and *B. discoidalis* Serville has been
taken from shipments into Britain.

Blaberus craniifer is firmly established in southern Florida and is also
known as a household pest in Cuba where it has been found abundant in
houses in Santiago and Havana. It also occurs in Mexico and British
Honduras.

Blaberus discoidalis has been taken in eating places in Ecuador, in houses
in Hispaniola and Puerto Rico, as well as from fruit stores. This species is

Fig. 30. Adult *Blaberus giganteus*. (Natural size)
(Courtesy: Drs. Roth & Willis, U.S. Army
Natick Laboratories.)

also known from Cuba and Jamaica. It gets an occasional, temporary footing in the United States through introductions on tropical plants.[43]

Appearance
The head of these very large cockroaches is hidden by the extensive pronotum, which is elliptical and in *Blaberus craniifer* ornamented by a symmetrical design in the centre, resembling the human eyes, nose and mouth. The broad tegmina cover the abdomen and in some species extend well beyond. *B. craniifer* (60–70 mm long) is dark blackish-brown, with the tegmina extending by about one-third the length of the body beyond the tip of the abdomen (Fig. 20). *B. discoidalis* is a considerably smaller species in which the tegmina and wings extend only slightly beyond the end of the body.

Biology
Blaberus craniifer has been reared in the laboratory at 30°C. Under these conditions the ootheca contained 34 eggs of which 20 hatched, but only half the nymphs reached maturity. Insects which underwent 10 moults took 257 days (males) and 277 days (females) to mature. The adults were long-lived, males averaging 14 months and females 16 months.

Blaberus giganteus reared in the laboratory (at 30°C and 60 per cent relative humidity) requires 140–200 days for nymphal development and moults seven or eight times. Adults can live for as long as 20 months.[115]

III. ACCIDENTAL INVADERS OF HOMES

In tropical and subtropical countries, lights in homes at night attract a wealth of outdoor-living insects. In the United States, cockroaches which may enter properties in this way include *Eurycotis floridana*, many species of Wood Cockroaches (*Parcoblatta* spp.) and the Field Cockroach, *Blattella vaga*.

Vegetation and woodland close to homes provide breeding sites from which these species spread unassisted by man. They are not pests and do not usually breed indoors, damage property, or feed in preference on human foods. Information on these cockroaches is included here so that they may be readily distinguished from the pest species.

Eurycotis floridana (Walker)—No common name
Eurycotis includes a number of West Indian and tropical American species. *E. floridana* is found outdoors in sheltered positions; in southern Florida it occurs under the bark of dead trees, in stumps and often in cavities in the limestone rock.[43] It has also been found in dry fibre at the base of coconut palms, in leaf mould and decaying wood. Like many other cockroaches, *E. floridana* moves about at night and hides in recesses during the day. It is reported occasionally in homes.

Fig. 31. (a) Adult male *Eurycotis floridana* (×1·5); (b) adult female *Parcoblatta pensylvanica* with completely formed ootheca. (×2) (Courtesy: Drs. Roth & Willis, U.S. Army Natick Laboratories.)

Appearance

Eurycotis floridana is a large cockroach, the males (31–35 mm long) and females (30–40 mm). The tegmina are extremely small extending only just beyond the posterior margin of the mesonotum. The hindwings are absent (Fig. 31). This cockroach is rich red-brown to black, but the pro-, meso- and metanota of the late nymphal stages are often marked conspicuously with broad bands of pale yellow. The adults of both sexes emit a greasy liquid when alarmed which has a most repellent odour (see Chapter 10).

Biology

About 50–60 per cent of eggs are capable of developing parthenogeneti- cally but very few hatch. Copulation occurs about 18 days after the final moult and lasts for one to two hours. There is a lapse of 55 days between moulting to adult and production of the first ootheca; successive oothecae are produced at about eight day intervals. The egg case contains an average of 21 eggs and incubation (at 30–36°C) takes 48 days. There are six to eight moults, and the period of nymphal development (with seven moults) averages 100 days (for males) and 113 days (for females). Nymphs reared in groups mature more rapidly than isolated individuals.[44]

Parcoblatta pensylvanica (De Geer)—The Wood Cockroach

The genus *Parcoblatta* contains many species widely distributed through- out the United States. Most have females with reduced tegmina and wings. *P. pensylvanica* is among those with the least reduction, but in an allied species, *Parcoblatta bolliana* (Saussure & Zehntner), the tegmina show hardly any traces of venation and the hind wings are absent (Fig. 20).

At least a dozen species of *Parcoblatta* (Wood Cockroaches) are fortuitous intruders in homes in the United States; *P. pensylvanica* has the widest distribution, its range extending into southern Canada, but not apparently into the peninsular of Florida.

Parcoblatta pensylvanica was first recorded in 1773 as *Blatta pensylvanica* from Pennsylvania. In many rural and urban areas it invades properties from nearby woodlands and is frequently encountered by motorists driving near woods at night.[61] The long-winged males are attracted to light and are capable of flights of over 100 ft. The short-winged females may be brought indoors with firewood and groceries.[82]

Habitat

The natural environment of this cockroach is in oak, chestnut and pine forests of the east and south-east United States, where it lives under loose bark, in hollow trees, woodpiles and in the ground litter, although there are records of infestations taken in houses. An unusual infestation of *P. pensylvanica* is described by Severin[116] which occurred on the top floor of a jail in South Dakota. The building was made of brick and stone and adults and nymphs were numerous under lumber and crates on a verandah, on the roof of a verandah, as well as in living rooms and cells. Lower floors were not infested. A 60-watt lamp was left alight on the verandah from sunset until dawn which may have attracted the insects. The Wood Cockroaches are not active during the day, but will move when disturbed: 'at dusk the males search for mates, running or flying swiftly, the antennae quivering nervously as the male examines each crevice in search of a female'.[5]

Comparing the effects of temperature on many cockroach species, Gould[59] found that *P. pensylvanica* showed the least response. In its natural environment, nymphs remain active throughout the year and even at freezing temperatures this cockroach is quite active when exposed by pulling away bark.[61] Outdoors, *P. pensylvanica* has a definite seasonal cycle with one generation per year. The males are thought to overwinter as late stage nymphs, maturing to adult in early spring; flights of winged males occur in May–June, and females reach their greatest abundance in mid-July.[43] It is during these summer months that this cockroach accidentally, but frequently, infests homes. Their food in nature is unknown, but in captivity they thrive on fruits and vegetables.[5] They do not produce the repulsive odour characteristic of domestic species.

Appearance
A large, variously coloured cockroach (Fig. 31), often chestnut brown with the thorax and tegmina edged with white. The ocelli are well-defined. The males are noticeably larger (22–30 mm) than females (13–20 mm). Considerable variations occur in the appearance of this species from different locations; the tegmina of some females cover a little more than half the body but in others they extend beyond the abdomen (Fig. 20). No general description of colour is of value: 'without a large series of insects for illustration, the difficulty would be to convince even the experienced worker that insects decidedly different in appearance represent one and the same species'.[43]

Biology
The life history of *P. pensylvanica* has been studied by Rau[5]: in captivity five females produced 30 oothecae in three to four months and the period between successive oothecae averaged five to nine days. Egg cases are carried by the female for one to three days and then dropped unconcealed. At room temperatures they hatch in 32–36 days, the majority providing 24–30 nymphs. Infertile egg cases are produced in the absence of males. The total life span from hatching to death of the adult takes about a year, during which there are five to seven moults. When nymphs were caught and reared to maturity, adult females lived for 35 to 85 days but males survived for a much shorter period.

Blattella vaga Hebard—The Field Cockroach

This cockroach was first discovered in 1933 in Phoenix, Arizona, occurring along the Gila and Colorado rivers. It was later described by Hebard,[117] who considered it an 'undoubted introduction' probably of Asiatic origin since its nearest relative is found in India. In 1953, Riherd[118] also recorded *B. vaga* in Texas.

Habitat

Blattella vaga is common in most of the irrigated regions of southern Arizona. Typically it lives in irrigated fields, but it is also found in smaller numbers on dry desert. It occurs under stones and feeds on plant debris. Flock[119] found this cockroach in greatest numbers around decaying dates on the ground and reported it as capable of damaging tender plants and newly emerged seedlings, although Ball *et al.*[120] detected no damage by this insect in the field.

In dry seasons the Field Cockroach enters houses in large numbers, but whilst this is usually temporary it can, according to Flock, remain there and breed to a limited extent. Its feeding habits are said to be similar to the German Cockroach, although nymphs offered food by Riherd refused it, apparently preferring decaying organic matter.[118]

The Field Cockroach does not appear to shun artificial light; it wanders around rooms in the evening when it is easily seen and it is also common around street lights. Mulches around plants near the house tend to encourage the numbers in homes. According to Palermo,[121] *B. vaga* is gradually increasing in numbers during summer months in the southwestern part of the United States, forming an intermediate stage between the fully outdoor living and the primarily indoor species.

Appearance

The similarity in size and general colouring of *Blattella vaga* (Fig. 32) and *Blattella germanica* (Fig. 13) can lead to mis-identification. The most pronounced difference between the two species is a black line between the eyes and the mouth of the Field Cockroach, which is absent in *B. germanica*. The head of *B. vaga* is also not as elongate as that of the German Cockroach.

A close comparison of *B. vaga* and *B. germanica* shows that the Field Cockroach is very slightly smaller and more delicate in appearance: the male varies from 9·2 to 9·7 mm compared with 10·5–11·4 mm in *B. germanica*; the female is also smaller, 8·5–9·9 mm (bearing an ootheca) compared with 11·0–12·8 mm in *B. germanica*. The longitudinal bars on the pronotum of *B. vaga* are very dark and more sharply defined than is usual in the German Cockroach.

Additional differences which can be detected under the microscope include the ulnar vein of the tegmina, which is branched only once in *B. vaga*, but the best distinguishing feature lies in the male external genitalia;

the specialisation of the dorsal surface of the abdomen, the supra-anal plate and the sub-genital plate is much less intricate than in *B. germanica*. The supra-anal plate of the Field Cockroach is sclerotised and moderately produced, instead of partly sclerotised and greatly produced in *B. ger-*

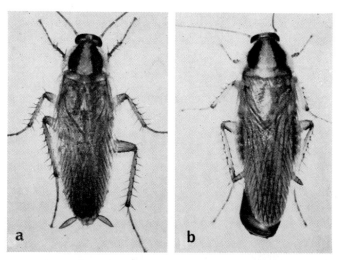

Fig. 32. Adult *Blattella vaga*, (a) male; (b) female with ootheca. (×5) (Courtesy: Drs. Roth & Willis, U.S. Army Natick Laboratories.)

manica. The sub-genital plate of *B. vaga* is also asymmetrical with small moderately elongated styles instead of being highly asymmetrical with minute, very short styles.

Biology
A comparison of the biology of the Field and German Cockroaches is given in Table III (p. 48). The ootheca of *B. vaga* contains fewer eggs, which decrease in number and in the proportion which hatch, after production of the third ootheca (Fig. 15). Unlike *B. germanica* in which the sexes mature at the same rate, female nymphs of *B. vaga* mature more rapidly than males. In the Field Cockroach the minimum period observed by Willis *et al.*[44] between the final moult and copulation was 3 days for both sexes; copulation lasted 80 minutes and the ootheca formed in 24 hours.

IV. OUTDOOR SPECIES IN BRITAIN, AUSTRALIA AND THE U.S.A.

The species included under this heading are not usually seen unless looked for in their outdoor habitats and they are in no way associated with man. Descriptions are given of the three outdoor cockroaches which occur in Britain, all members of the Ectobiinae, and brief reference is made to seven species native to Australia. Many cockroaches occur outdoors in the U.S.A., but reference is confined to two only, *Cryptocercus punctulatus*, a wood-digesting species, and *Attaphila fungicola*, which is symbiotic with ants. Place is given in this chapter to an account of outdoor species to draw attention to the range of environments occupied by non-domiciliary cockroaches.

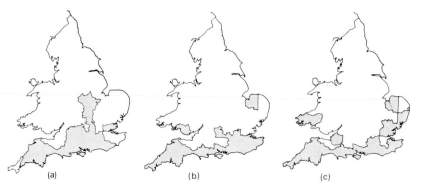

Fig. 33. Recorded distribution of (a) *Ectobius lapponicus*, (b) *E. pallidus* and (c) *E. panzeri* in southern England and Wales (after Ragge[45]).

OUTDOOR SPECIES IN BRITAIN

There are three outdoor species of cockroach in Britain. All belong to the Sub-family Ectobiinae. They are: *Ectobius lapponicus* (L.), the Dusky Cockroach; *Ectobius pallidus* (Olivier), previously known as *E. lividus* and *E. livens*, the Tawny Cockroach; and *Ectobius panzeri* Stephens, the Lesser Cockroach.

All three are actively running species, smaller than the German Cockroach. They are found in the south of England (Fig. 33) and parts of Continental Europe. None are pests. They have small dark spots on the veins of the tegmina, and the hind wings have a distinct triangular area at the tip (Fig. 34). An account of their appearance and life history is given by Ragge.[45] It is sufficient here to draw attention to the distinguishing features (Table XII), and to summarise their biology in Britain which is essentially similar for all three species.

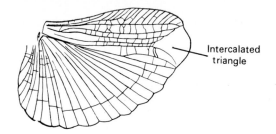

Fig. 34. Wing of *Ectobius pallidus* showing the intercalated triangle at the tip of the wing (after Gurney[108]).

Biology
Oothecae, brown and 3–4 mm long, are produced between June and September. They are rotated after formation and carried by the female for one or two days, but occasionally longer in *E. panzeri*, before being deposited on the ground where they overwinter. The nymphs hatch in the following spring and probably pass through five or six instars. The nymphs of *E. lapponicus* and *E. pallidus* hibernate in late stages of development to become adult the following May–June. Those of *E. panzeri* complete their development to adult over a period of two to three months and mature in the July of the year in which they hatched from the ootheca. The adults of all three species die in September–October.

Gurney[108] reports on the establishment of *E. pallidus* in north-eastern America. It was first discovered in 1948 on Cape Cod and has become common in some areas of south-eastern Massachusetts.[122] He referred to it as *E. livens*, giving it the common name 'Spotted Mediterranean roach' because of its appearance and region of occurrence in the Old World, and reported it as a 'potentially important cockroach' new to America. He says 'it is not likely to develop into a major pest but may be a nuisance in dwellings when attracted to light'. It does not attack household foods or goods.

The countries of Continental Europe in which *E. pallidus* occurs are Germany, Netherlands, Belgium, France, Switzerland, Italy, Portugal and Spain. It lives beneath loose lichens in woods, and among bracken and other ferns. Gurney[108] states that a good many people of Portuguese ancestry live in Massachusetts, where this cockroach is found, and visits to Portugal and the Azores are frequent. It is probable that the insect has been introduced on shipments.

OUTDOOR SPECIES IN AUSTRALIA

As far as is known, a full account of the cockroaches which occur in Australia has not been prepared. Pope[111] describes seven species native to

TABLE XII

DISTINGUISHING FEATURES OF OUTDOOR SPECIES OF
COCKROACH (ECTOBIINAE) IN BRITAIN
(From Ragge[45])

Feature	*E. lapponicus* Dusky Cockroach	*E. pallidus* Tawny Cockroach	*E. panzeri* Lesser Cockroach
Size (mm) to tips of tegmina: Males:	9·5–11·3	8·0–9·3	6·0–7·8
Females:	6·8–7·9	8·3–9·1	5·0–7·2
Development of tegmina:	Shorter in female than male, just short of tip of abdomen.	Fully developed in both sexes.	Greatly reduced in female, well developed in male.
Colour:	Generally grey-brown; male pronotum dark, female abdomen extensively dark brown beneath.	Uniform pale yellow. Female abdomen with small amount of dark brown beneath.	Pale to dark brown; legs dark brown or black. Tegmina pale yellow-brown with dark speckles.
Tubercle in glandular depression on 7th abdominal segment of male:	Tubercle with distinct median split.	Tubercle absent.	Tubercle small and hairy.
Habitat (variable in all three species):	Woodland, heath and scrubby grass-land.	Most frequently in woodland.	Preference for coastal and sandy places.
Flight in warm weather:	By males only.	By both sexes.	By males only.

Australia, which include three of *Methana* and four belonging to the sub-family Ectobiinae. The British representatives of this group have been described above.

The three species of *Methana* all occur under loose bark of trees or logs. *Methana curvigera* (Walker) is found on wattle trees and hides from sunlight in curled up leaves; it attaches its oothecae to leaves, or to the underside of loose bark. It is a pale coloured insect (20–24 mm long) with distinctive markings in black and reddish-brown. A wide, pale or transparent margin around the whole insect is a striking feature of adults and nymphs.

Methana marginalis (Saussure) is a larger cockroach (25–29 mm long), brown, with a white margin on the anterior and lateral edges of the pronotum. This species is found in Queensland and Western Australia and has sometimes been reported entering houses.

The third species, *Methana canae*, described by Pope[62] as a new species, occurs under the loose bark of trees on Fraser Island, off the east coast of Queensland. For a description and details of the biology of this cockroach, and the other species mentioned above, the reader is referred to the original account.

OUTDOOR SPECIES IN THE UNITED STATES

Reference has already been made in the introduction to this chapter to the existence of 57 known species of cockroach in the United States. One genus which contains numerous outdoor species is *Parcoblatta* and mention of two of these, *P. pensylvanica* and *P. bolliana*, has already been made on p. 86. Similarly, many of the species already described as having a close, occasional, or accidental association with man are also encountered outdoors notably in the southern States.

Space does not permit reference to all the remaining outdoor species. Information is therefore restricted to two, both with unique features: *Cryptocercus punctulatus* because of its antiquity, close relationship with termites and ability to digest cellulose, and *Attaphila fungicola* because of its association with ants.

Cryptocercus punctulatus Scudder

This cockroach occurs in two widely separated areas of the United States; in the Appalachian mountains, from Pennsylvania to northern Georgia, and on the west coast, in areas of California, Oregon and Washington State. Heavily forested areas, where the logs in which it lives are partially covered with leaves and humus, provide a suitable environment which is not subject to freezing or to temperatures exceeding 30°C.[123]

This insect is able to utilise many kinds of wood as food. Hence, it is found in decaying timber, burrowing in the sapwood of a variety of species. *Cryptocercus* is not alone in its wood-eating habit, other species belonging to the genera, *Panesthia* and *Salganea*.

Appearance

A large cockroach (23–29 mm long), shiny and almost black. It is wingless, the sexes being very similar in appearance. The eyes are much reduced and the pronotum is thickened with a wide, deep groove down the central area (Fig. 35). The anterior margin of the pronotum is raised above the head in a brief hood, presumably giving the head protection during burrowing.

Biology

The interesting feature of the biology of this species concerns the transfer

Fig. 35. (a) Adult *Cryptocercus punctulatus* (×2·5); (b) adult female
Gromphadorhina portentosa. (Natural size) (Courtesy: Drs. Roth & Willis,
U.S. Army Natick Laboratories.)

of cellulose digesting flagellates (p. 130) from parent to offspring. Cleveland
et al.[123] have made the following detailed study:

The protozoa are not found in the oothecae, and nymphs raised in
isolation never acquire the fauna which is required for them to digest
cellulose. They must be reared with other more mature nymphs which are
already infected. When these older nymphs moult, the protozoa contained
in the hind-gut withdraw their flagella and encyst. The insect ceases to feed
and no faeces are passed for two to three days before the moult. After
moulting the first faecal pellets contain large numbers of encysted protozoa,
which, when eaten by a newly hatched nymph, ensures the development
of a heavy population of flagellates within the gut in a few days.

Attaphila fungicola Wheeler

This species is the smallest of the cockroaches known in the United States.
It is 2·7 mm long and is a symbiont of the leaf-cutting ant *Atta fervens* Say,
with which it lives unmolested in large numbers in the fungus gardens and
tunnels.[43] This cockroach does not eat the fungus in the ants' nest as was
once supposed, 'but mounts the backs of soldiers and licks their surface'.[4]
It is found only in Austin, Texas.

Appearance

Apart from the minute size, this cockroach has a number of unusual features; the body is elliptical, amber-yellow with a broad pronotum, and the eyes are very small. The tegmina are much reduced, without venation, and the wings are vestigial. The antennal segments, with the exception of the 2nd and 3rd, are all longer than wide. As a result of examining a number of specimens, Wheeler[124] found that the antennae were mutilated and concluded that the ants with which this cockroach lives, crop the antennae of their guests. Four other myrmecophilous species of *Attaphila* occur in South America.

V. OTHER SPECIES OF SPECIAL INTEREST

Gromphadorhina laevigata **Sauss. & Zehntn.—No common name**
A brief description is given of this species because it is referred to in Chapter 9, as an example of false ovoviviparity among cockroaches. Other species which belong to this genus, and with the same physiology of reproduction, are *G. coguereliana* and *G. portentosa* (Schaum) (Fig. 35). All are covered with scaly granulations. *G. laevigata* is a native of Madagascar.

A description of *G. laevigata* and an account of its reproduction and behaviour are given by Chopard.[125] It is a very large cockroach (about 60 mm long) in which both sexes are wingless. The males may be distinguished by a large round tubercle on each side of the pronotum and the paired styles on the tip of the abdomen.

The ootheca (30–32 mm long) is incubated internally. It is white and very thin-walled. The eggs are incubated over a period of 70 days, and the young cockroaches are liberated over a period of two days; 32–48 young are produced. No assistance is given by the female at hatching, but the young remain grouped around her for some time during which she raises herself and protects the brood under her body.

IDENTIFICATION KEY

For keys to the identification of cockroaches of specific geographical areas, the following works should be consulted: Rehn[126] gives a concise key to the 26 known genera occurring in the United States; Rehn & Hebard[83] give keys to the 156 species (comprising 47 genera) of cockroaches of the West Indies, excluding Trinidad and Tobago. Rehn[127–129] also gives descriptions and keys to the numerous species comprising the African and Malagasy blattids, and Hebard[130] gives keys to the Malayan species.

The following key will enable the reader interested in identifying the more commonly occurring cockroaches of buildings, to distinguish and name the pest species. This key is limited to this purpose and should not be used, for example, to identify the many species introduced on imported cargoes.

KEY TO THE ADULTS OF COCKROACHES WHICH MOST COMMONLY BREED
IN, OR MAY OCCASIONALLY BE FOUND IN BUILDINGS

1. Small cockroaches, 15 mm long or less, including tegmina .. 2
— Large cockroaches, longer than 15 mm including tegmina .. 5
2. Pronotum with two longitudinal dark bars 3
— Pronotum without two longitudinal dark bars 4
3. Face with black line between eyes extending to mouth .. .. .. Field Cockroach, *Blattella vaga*

— Face without black line between eyes extending to mouth .. .. .. German Cockroach, *Blattella germanica*

4. Tegmina covering about half of abdomen; pronotum at least 6–7 mm wide Wood Cockroaches, *Parcoblatta* spp.

— Tegmina covering almost all of abdomen (female) or extending beyond abdomen (male); pronotum less than 6–7 mm wide .. .. Brown-banded Cockroach, *Supella supellectilium*

5. Large cockroaches, 15–55 mm including tegmina 6
— Very large cockroaches, greater than 55 mm including tegmina .. .. .. *Blaberus* spp.
6. Tegmina noticeably shorter than abdomen 7
— Tegmina just reaching apex of abdomen or extending beyond 12
7. Tegmina fully covering metanotum 8
— Tegmina extending beyond mesonotum but not fully covering metanotum 10
8. Pronotum with Lobster-like pattern .. Lobster Cockroach, *Nauphoeta cinerea*

— Pronotum of uniform colour, or with lateral margins only pale 9
9. Female only, pronotal margins pale .. Wood Cockroaches, *Parcoblatta* spp.

— Male only, pronotum entirely uniform in colour .. .. Oriental Cockroach, *Blatta orientalis*

10. Pro-, meso- and metanota brown-black with striking yellow pattern .. .. *Neostylopyga rhombifolia*
— Pro-, meso- and metanota not marked with yellow 11

11. Body length 25 mm or less (female only)   Oriental Cockroach,
Blatta orientalis

— Body length 30 mm or more (male or
female) ..   ..   *Eurycotis floridana*

12. Pronotum 6–7 mm wide   13

— Pronotum more than 6–7 mm wide   14

13. Hind margin of pronotum smoothly
curved   ..   ..   Wood Cockroaches,
Parcoblatta spp.

— Hind margin of pronotum strongly sinu-
ate, the posterior apex bluntly rounded   Surinam Cockroach,
Pycnoscelus surinamensis

14. Posterior half of tegmina distinctly
mottled with two pronounced dark
lines in the basal area ..   ..   ..   Madeira Cockroach,
Leucophaea maderae

— Tegmina not mottled or with dark lines
in the basal area   15

15. Base of tegmina with pale streak on
outer edges. Pronotum strikingly marked
with a dark central area and pale outer
edging (Fig. 36)   ..   ..   ..   Australian Cockroach,
Periplaneta australasiae

Base of tegmina without pale streak on
outer edges. Pronotum of uniform
colour or with pale edging only moder-
ately conspicuous   16

16. Pronotum uniformly dark in colour
(Fig. 36). Body colour very dark brown
to black   ..   ..   Smoky-brown Cockroach,
Periplaneta fuliginosa

Pronotum not entirely uniform in
colour, but with a pale edging moder-
ately conspicuous   17

17. Last segment of cercus twice as long as
wide   ..   ..   American Cockroach,
Periplaneta americana

— Last segment of cercus less than twice as
long as wide   ..   ..   Brown Cockroach,
Periplaneta brunnea

G

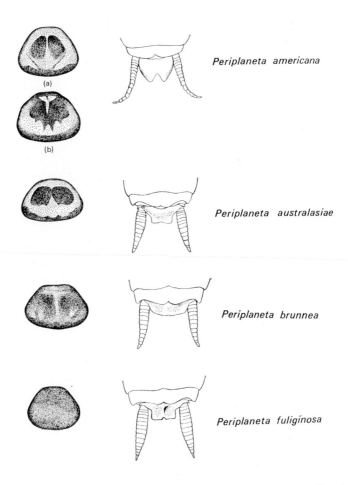

Fig. 36. Pronotal pattern and terminal abdominal segments (dorsal view) of males of four species of *Periplaneta*. (a) Normal colouration and (b) maximum intensive colouration of pronotum of *P. americana* (after Hebard[43]).

KEY TO THE OOTHECAE OF COCKROACHES MOST COMMONLY FOUND IN BUILDINGS (see Fig. 37)

1. Ootheca with obvious segmentation on ventral surface, length less than 6–7 mm   2
— Ootheca without segmentation on ventral surface, length more than 6–7 mm   3
2. With 16–20 segments, length of ootheca more than twice width ..   ..   ..   German Cockroach, *Blattella germanica*

— With 8–9 segments, length of ootheca less than twice width   ..   ..   ..   Brown-banded Cockroach, *Supella supellectilium*

3. Sides of ootheca with 8–9 raised areas just below keel   4
— Sides of ootheca with 12–13 raised areas just below keel   ..   ..   ..   Australian Cockroach, *Periplaneta australasiae* Brown Cockroach, *Periplaneta brunnea* Smoky-brown Cockroach, *Periplaneta fuliginosa*
(Oothecae of these species cannot be distinguished on external characters.)
4. Raised areas below keel nearly circular   Oriental Cockroach, *Blatta orientalis*

— Raised areas below keel elongate   ..   American Cockroach, *Periplaneta americana*

ootheca with obvious segmentation

with about 18 segments,
length more than twice width

Blattella germanica
GERMAN COCKROACH

with about 8 segments,
length less than twice width

Supella supellectilium
BROWN-BANDED COCKROACH

ootheca without obvious segmentation

8-9 raised areas below keel

areas circular

Blatta orientalis
ORIENTAL COCKROACH

areas elongate

Periplaneta americana
AMERICAN COCKROACH

12-13 raised areas below keel

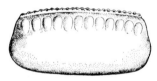

Periplaneta australasiae — AUSTRALIAN COCKROACH
Periplaneta brunnea   — BROWN COCKROACH
Periplaneta fuliginosa — SMOKY-BROWN COCKROACH

Fig. 37. Oothecae of the most common species of cockroach found in buildings.

4

THE INTEGUMENT

Structure of the cuticle: pore canals; penetration of the cuticle—Thickness and chemical composition; water- and alkali-soluble constituents—Wax layer; hypodermis, oenocytes and wax secretion—Cement layer and dermal glands—Pygidial glands and tergal secretions

Receptor organs: light receptors; contact receptors; proprioceptors; chemo-receptors; auditory receptors.

The exoskeleton of the cockroach protects it from undue loss of water, gives rigidity to the body and provides points for the attachment of muscles. The cuticle is not a uniform homogeneous piece of armour plate, as might be supposed at first sight from the external appearance of some species of cockroach, but is comprised of numerous small plates, or sclerites, joined by softer and more transparent areas, such as the inter-segmental membranes, which give the exoskeleton flexibility.

The rigidity of the cuticle controls the rate of growth; it is not sufficiently flexible to permit a gradual increase in size. Instead, development proceeds by a series of moults, or ecdyses, each preceded by active growth followed by a period during which there may be an increase in weight but no apparent increase in size. Moulting and growth in cockroaches is dealt with in detail in Chapter 10.

STRUCTURE OF THE CUTICLE

As in all insects, the cuticle of the cockroach is composed of three layers secreted by a single layer of cells, the hypodermis, resting on a thin basement membrane. In the mature cockroach the nuclei of the hypodermal cells become displaced by enlarged oenocytes which come into close contact with the cuticle (Fig. 38). The role of the oenocytes in relation to the cuticle is discussed on p. 107.

In total, the cuticle of the American Cockroach is about 40μ thick; the innermost and thickest layer, the endocuticle, is pliable and has a layered structure which is 20–30μ thick. It is overlaid by a further laminated layer the exocuticle, 10–20μ thick, which contains melanin pigment. The outer layer, or epicuticle, is extremely thin, about 2μ, and is hydrophobic.

The cuticle is a non-living membrane which covers not only the external surface of the insect, but all the ectodermal invaginations—the pharynx, foregut, hindgut, the tracheae and genital ducts. The ducts of the many

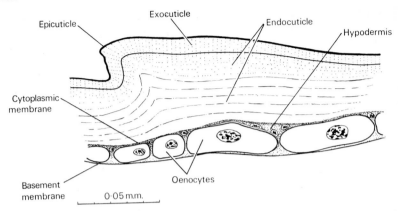

Fig. 38. Longitudinal section of a tergite of an adult *P. americana* (after Kramer & Wigglesworth[144]).

unicellular glands which open onto the surface of the cuticle are lined with epicuticle only. Thus, whilst the cuticle is primarily an exoskeleton it does provide an internal lining to certain areas. Moreover, invaginations of the cuticle, the apodemes in the thorax and abdomen and tentorium in the head, provide strength and muscle attachments, for wings, legs and certain internal organs.

In section, the endocuticle and exocuticle show striations at right angles to the surface which do not penetrate the epicuticle. These have been interpreted by some as pore canals and by others as solid rods. Richards & Anderson[132] have examined sections of cuticle of *P. americana* under the electron microscope. Because the cuticle is a non-cellular structure, hardened cuticle such as the cockroach pronotum shrinks very little, only about two per cent on drying, so that when separated from the insect little change occurs before the detailed structure can be studied.

Using sections of cuticle $0.1–0.5\mu$ thick, Richards & Anderson could distinguish five layers; the epicuticle consisting of two chemically distinct layers—an outer thin layer ($0.02–0.03\mu$), transparent, acid resistant and hydrophobic, and an inner, amber, less acid resistant layer (nearly 2μ thick). The exocuticle was seen to consist of only one layer, whilst the endocuticle again appeared as two layers—an outer pliable transparent layer and a darker inner layer.

The laminae of the endo- and exocuticles average about 3–5 per micron and appear to be strata of different molecular densities. Variation in their thickness ($0.03–0.2\mu$) occurs in both sclerites and membranes and would not therefore appear to influence the hardness of the cuticle or its flexibility.

Pore Canals
Sections of cuticle in the electron miscoscope show that for the American

Cockroach 'there can be no further question of the reality of the pore canals as hollow tubes, following a regular helicoid spiral through the endo- and exocuticles from the underlying hypodermis to, but not into, the epicuticle'. These canals have an average diameter of 0.15μ, except close to the hypodermis where suddenly for the last $4–5\mu$ of the tube their width increases to about 0.4μ. This expanded portion is straight and contrasts with the helicoid section, with its regular pitch, occupying the greater thickness of the cuticle (Fig. 39).

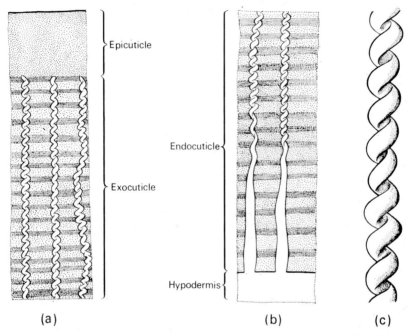

(a) (b) (c)

Fig. 39. Sections of cuticle of *P. americana* showing details of pore canals (a) outer 9μ of cuticle showing the normally straight pore canals and one drawn to show approximate extreme deviation ($\times 8500$); (b) inner 8μ of cuticle and hypodermis. The stippled areas represent laminations of the cuticle ($\times 8500$); (c) pore canal showing detail of spiral and deviation from true helix ($\times 56,000$) (after Richards & Anderson[132]).

The length of the pore canals averages twice the thickness of the cuticle; there are about 1,200,000 per square cm and they comprise 5–6 per cent of the total volume. In the cockroach, the canals are open at their inner ends and Richards & Anderson suggest that they are filled with a salt solution in ionic equilibrium with the hypodermal cells, capilliary attraction preventing any air from entering the tubes while the insect is alive. Their function is uncertain, but as they comprise such a significant proportion of the endo- and exocuticles they are thought to influence flexibility and permeability. In some insects the pore canals are thought to be responsible for the transport of cuticular wax. Richards & Anderson support the early suggestion of Leydig that the pore canals originate as protoplasmic filaments around which the cuticle is first laid down.

Penetration of the cuticle

The structure of the cuticle and its chemical composition have an important bearing on the formulation of insecticides. Liquid insecticides which become dry on treated surfaces are known to be picked up by the insect on its cuticle and ingested *via* the mouth during grooming, but certain formulations may penetrate the cuticle direct. The cuticle is not easily wetted by water-based formulations, but the more rapid action of oil sprays has been attributed in some measure to their ease of penetration of the cuticle.

In this connection, Richards & Anderson[132] have examined the possible role of the pore canals. They conclude that these canals may accelerate the diffusion of water and water-soluble substances in solution but would not appear to be penetrated by oils and oil-soluble substances, unless possibly emulsified. When mineral oil and non-volatile oils are applied to the pronota of living adult cockroaches, which are then killed 4–16 hours later, electron micrographs show that the oils, (1) do not dissolve the epicuticle, (2) do not modify the structure of the exo- or endocuticle, and (3) do not enter the pore canals. Since the cuticle of mosquito larvae lacks pore canals yet oil penetrates these insects readily, it seems likely that oil diffuses through the general matrix of the cuticle, and the pore canals (when present) play no major role in facilitating penetration.

Thickness and chemical composition

Insect cuticle is composed of carbohydrates, proteins and fatty materials. Chitin, the most characteristic component, is a nitrogenous polysaccharide which occurs in the endo- and exocuticles but not in the epicuticle. The non-chitinous material of the cuticle is composed of protein, whilst fatty materials are represented by waxes and sterols.

Dennell & Malek[133] have studied the composition of the cuticle of *P. americana* in relation to the changes which occur during development, during the hardening of the cuticle following a moult, as well as the differences between the sexes. In these studies, the abdominal tergites were analysed for all three components and for water content.

The thickness of the two inner layers of the cuticle of the American Cockroach varies during development; in the last stage nymph the exocuticle comprises only 21–24 per cent, but this increases to 51–55 per cent in the adult. The cuticle of females is thicker than males, but the cuticle of males contains slightly more water. The exception to this is in newly moulted adults when the water content of the cuticle almost doubles (Table XIII). The higher water content of male cuticle is attributed by Dennell &

Malek to the greater number of dermal glands in this sex, so that when the water content of the cuticle is reduced during tanning and hardening the male loses proportionately less. During this process the water in the exo-cuticle of females drops to about 38 per cent of the amount present in soft cuticle, compared with 52 per cent in males.

TABLE XIII

WATER CONTENT OF THE CUTICLE OF *P. AMERICANA* AT VARIOUS STAGES OF DEVELOPMENT. PERCENTAGE OF WET WEIGHT.
(From Dennell & Malek[133])

Stage	Male	Female
Cuticle of fully hardened last instar nymph:	30·1	28·0
Shed cuticle of last instar nymph (exocuticle only):	23·1	16·4
Cuticle of newly moulted adult:	43·9	44·2
Cuticle of fully hardened adult:	24·3	17·1

Water- and alkali-soluble constituents

The water-soluble constituents are amino acids, phenols and water soluble proteins. When cuticle is treated with alkali, protein is dissolved, whereas chitin is converted to the alkali-insoluble material, chitosan. Treatment of the cuticle in this way provides information on the variations that occur in the cuticular constituents during development from nymphs to adults. Marked chemical changes occur between the soft, newly formed condition just after a moult, and during the process of hardening.

Newly formed cuticle contains six to seven times more water-soluble protein and three to four times more amino acids. The fully hardened cuticle, however, contains more total protein (Table XIV). At moulting the endocuticle is eroded by moulting fluids so that the exuvium consists almost entirely of exocuticle. This, when shed by last stage nymphs con-tains almost 70 per cent protein, supporting the view that protein passes into the cuticle in preparation for hardening and accumulates in the outer layers.[134] Hardening of the cuticle also involves a substantial increase in the amounts of chitin and dihydroxyphenol. Perhaps the most surprising observation is that the cuticle of last stage nymphs and adults contains similar amounts of the two fundamental constituents chitin and protein, linked to form a chitin–protein complex, despite the considerable difference in the thickness of the exoskeletons of these two stages.

Wax layer

Wax on the surface of the cuticle fulfils the important function of water-proofing and conserving water. If the epicuticle of insects is removed by

TABLE XIV

AMINO ACID, PROTEIN AND CHITIN CONTENT OF THE CUTICLE
(AS PERCENTAGE OF DRY WEIGHT) OF *P. AMERICANA* AT
VARIOUS STAGES OF DEVELOPMENT
(From Dennell & Malek[133])

Stage	Sex	Amino acid	Di-hydroxy-phenol	Water-soluble protein	Total protein	Chitin
Cuticle of fully hardened	M	5·6	0·28	9·5	62·9	20·2
last instar nymph:	F	5·2	0·25	7·5	63·2	20·1
Shed cuticle of last instar	M	13·1	0·75	6·9	68·3	11·2
nymph (exocuticle only):	F	6·8	0·77	10·9	68·5	13·5
Cuticle of newly moulted	M	18·2	0·11	24·2	54·1	10·5
adult:	F	11·2	0·07	23·5	52·9	11·5
Cuticle of fully hardened	M	6·8	0·18	3·4	62·0	20·1
adult:	F	3·1	0·18	3·7	62·3	19·3

alkali the cuticle becomes freely permeable to water. The same is achieved by removing the wax layer by abrasive, or 'desiccant' dusts, an effect which has been exploited in cockroach control (see Volume II).

In many insects the wax is mobile when secreted but hardens in a short time to a crystalline solid. In contrast, the wax of cockroaches remains mobile throughout the insects' life.[135] If a sample of cockroach wax is extracted from the cuticle and left exposed in the air for about three months at room temperature it too becomes hard and crystalline, but when sealed against evaporation it remains unchanged. This has lead Beament[136] to suggest that the wax of the cockroach is secreted onto the surface of the cuticle in a solvent which is non-volatile and which evaporates only very slowly. Moreover, both Beament[137] and Dennell & Malek[138] believe that the wax or perhaps the solvent is secreted continuously throughout life to replace loss.

To further explore the solvents involved in wax secretion, Gilby[139] distilled the wax of *P. americana* under vacuum and examined the distillates by gas chromatography. Using this method he claimed to be able to detect volatiles, if present, in amounts less than 0·1 per cent by weight of the 0·5 mg of 'grease' present per cockroach. Gilby found that when the mouth and anal regions of the cockroach were sealed with paraffin wax, no volatile materials other than water were condensed. This happened whether he used hardened cuticle, or soft, freshly formed cuticle, a result quite unexpected in view of the suggestion by Beament[140] that volatile paraffins and alcohols are present in soft wax, which are lost on hardening.

Studies of the chemical composition of cockroach wax show that it contains saturated and unsaturated hydrocarbons, fatty acids, and a number of aldehydes. Its thickness on the epicuticle of *P. americana* ranges from 0.4μ for last instar nymphs to $1-2\mu$ for mature adults. This is not greatly different from the value of 0.6μ obtained for the wax layer on the abdomen of *B. orientalis*.[137] The amount of wax, however, is not constant; on newly moulted adults of the American Cockroach it increases considerably, especially in males, to almost 11 per cent of the total thickness of the cuticle (Table XV). Very little is extractable from the exuviae of nymphs, in which continued secretion is prevented at moulting by the separation of the cuticle from the hypodermis.

TABLE XV

THICKNESS OF THE WAX LAYER (AS PERCENTAGE OF TOTAL THICKNESS OF CUTICLE) AND LIPID CONTENT OF THE CUTICLE (AS PERCENTAGE OF DRY WEIGHT) AT VARIOUS STAGES OF DEVELOPMENT OF *P. AMERICANA*
(from Dennell & Malek,[133])

Stage	Thickness of wax layer (%)		Lipid (%)	
	Male	Female	Male	Female
Cuticle of fully hardened last instar nymph:	0·6	0·6	1·3	1·5
Shed cuticle of last instar nymph (exocuticle only):	1·2	0·4	1·7	0·8
Cuticle of newly moulted adult:	10·7	4·7	10·1	5·8
Cuticle of fully hardened adult:	2·0	1·5	3·7	3·3

The function of wax in conserving the body moisture of the cockroach cannot be overstressed. In Chapter 12 we shall see that water for drinking and water conservation are vital to survival, particularly for the German Cockroach, and that at temperatures above 30°C water is lost from the insect very rapidly. Wigglesworth[141] has shown that the approximate 'critical temperature' for the increase in transpiration through the cuticle of intact *B. germanica* is 31°C, and through a film of isolated wax[137] it is 30°C.

Hypodermis, oenocytes and wax secretion

The hypodermis serves a number of very important functions; it is responsible for secreting the cuticle, contains glands which produce the moulting hormone, possibly serves as an intermediary in the movement of wax to the surface of the cuticle and contains glands responsible for the production of cuticular cement. In addition, Winston[142] has produced evidence to suggest that the hypodermis acts as a 'cuticular water pump' and is actively involved in regulating the water relations of the insect with its environment.

Substantial changes occur in the hypodermis during nymphal development. In the Oriental Cockroach, the hypodermis of first stage nymphs consists of a single layer of cells almost equal in size, except for a few larger cells, irregular in shape, around the spiracles.[143] These larger cells are the oenocytes which in the adult become extremely abundant and conspicuous and have a secretory function as well as being concerned in fat metabolism.

As the insect grows, the oenocytes increase in number and form a second layer of cells beneath all areas of the hypodermis. At the moults, these cells again increase in number and are said to migrate into the body cavity. They are distributed below the hypodermis of the abdominal tergites and sternites, particularly over the anterior half of each segment where it is overlapped by the preceding segment. In the adult cockroach the hypodermal cells become much attenuated, and their nuclei displaced by the enlarged oenocytes which come to lie very closely beneath the inner layer of the cuticle. According to Kramer & Wigglesworth[144] direct contact is not achieved, the oenocytes remaining separated from the cuticle by an extremely thin cytoplasmic membrane.

There is reason to believe that the oenocytes of the cockroach are concerned in the production of wax. When a layer of alumina is applied to one side of the abdomen, this dust readily adsorbs the mobile soft wax and staining techniques fail to show any differences between the two sides except an increased activity of the oenocytes (Kramer & Wigglesworth[144]). These authors conclude that the oenocytes manufacture cuticular wax and that the hypodermal cells probably act as intermediaries in its transmission to the surface. Certainly the pore canals can be eliminated as a means of transfer since they do not, in the cockroach, penetrate the epicuticle, but this is not so in all insects.

As early as 1918, Dusham[145] made a study of the distribution of what he calls wax secretory glands of the German Cockroach. He describes them as so small that they can hardly be distinguished from normal hypodermal cells except for the larger nuclei. From his account it seems likely that he was referring to the oenocytes: they occur 'on the dorsal and ventral surface of each segment, scattered over each tergite and sternite and are most abundant in the median line, but not on the intersegmental membranes. The glands are most prominent on the anterior portion of each segment where they are covered by the posterior part of the preceding segment' (Fig. 40).

Dusham refers to these glands as modified hypodermal cells: 'they contain large nuclei, a nucleolus and many deeply staining chromatin

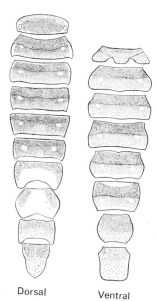

Dorsal   Ventral

Fig. 40. Wax glands (shaded) on the dorsal and ventral abdominal segments of male *B. germanica*. The highest density occurs where the sclerites are overlapped. (after Dusham[145]). The distribution of glands in the female is similar.

granules. The cytoplasm appears granular and each cell contains several vacuoles'. These secretory cells appear in the hypodermis of first stage nymphs when only two days old and by the third instar, they take on a condition similar to their appearance in the adult.

Cement layer and dermal glands

The wax secreted by cockroaches is freely exposed on the surface of the cuticle where it is probably readily removed by contact with the insect's surroundings. In most insects the wax layer is protected by a layer of 'cement' poured out by dermal glands at the time of moulting. Kramer & Wigglesworth state that there can be little doubt that a cement layer also exists in the cockroach, but the dermal glands which produce it are completely atrophied in the mature adult.

The dermal glands of insects produce a variety of secretions—wax, silk, attractant odours important to mating, moulting fluid, and compounds with irritant and repellent properties. According to Stanislavskij[143] the dermal glands of the Oriental Cockroach are of two types: (1) *simple glands* present in males only, abundant on the dorsal surface of the abdomen and sparse beneath, and (2) *alveolar glands* composed of groups of large numbers of simple glands which discharge into invaginations between the fifth and sixth abdominal tergites of both sexes. He also mentions an additional gland of this second type, in males only, which discharges into a fold beneath the sixth abdominal sternite.

In the American Cockroach, dermal glands occur in both sexes although they are far more numerous on the tergites of the male. The canals by which these glands open onto the surface of the cuticle are far larger than the pore canals of the endo- and exocuticles referred to earlier.

Pygidial glands and tergal secretions

Cockroaches possess a number of other glands in addition to those already mentioned, but their function is not precisely known. For example, on the terminal abdominal tergite of female *B. germanica* there are three groups of depressions normally hidden from view by the overlapping margin of the previous tergite (Fig. 41). Here the hypodermis is much

Fig. 41. The pygidial glands (shaded) of a female *Blattella germanica* (after Dusham[146]).

thickened and consists of several layers of cells containing reservoirs within the cytoplasm. These cells are connected to the surface by fine canals which empty the reservoirs into the depressions of the cuticle.[146] Stanislavskij describes a similar gland on the pygidium of males of the Oriental Cockroach to which he ascribes a repugnatorial function. This gland is formed as a fold of the integument and opens just over the anus. Rau[65] has observed that a viscous secretion accumulates on the terminal abdominal segments of adult females and nymphs of both sexes of *Blatta orientalis* and Stock & O'Farrel[147] have made similar observations for the cerci of nymphs of *B. germanica*. More recently Roth & Stahl[148] have found that secretions accumulate on the cerci and abdominal segments of both sexes of many oviparous cockroaches, including the common domiciliary species, particularly when isolated, or kept in small numbers. This secretion is not, however, produced by isolated nymphs of false ovoviviparous species or the false viviparous *Diploptera punctata* (see Chapter 9).

The detailed studies of Roth & Stahl with the Oriental Cockroach show that the material secreted by the cerci and produced on the sixth and seventh tergites is water soluble. It is composed of ten per cent carbohydrate, containing a polysaccharide, and 90 per cent protein, comprising a variety of amino acids. Again the function of this material is not known, nor the reason for its presence on some species but not others. It may help to keep young nymphs together[147] but this suggestion has not been supported. Roth & Stahl[148] suggest that if a type of trophallaxis (mutual exchange of nutrient in symbiosis) exists among cockroaches, whereby nymphs eat the material off each other, it is conceivable that a secretion high in protein could help to supplement food. Certainly there is evidence that the secretion produced on the abdominal tergites of male cockroaches is taken by females during copulation (see Chapter 8) and plays an important part in the mating sequence.

Finally reference must be made here to the pellets of material rich in urates produced in some species by the male colleterial glands. This material is passed into the genital pouch of the female during insemination and is thought to be a means of voiding excess waste products of metabolism (Chapters 6 & 8).

RECEPTOR ORGANS

The cuticle of the cockroach is a highly receptive area to external stimuli. It is modified to form sense organs of many different types which provide the insect with an awareness of its environment, information about both physical and chemical factors, and the insect's own movements and orientation.

Much of the information about the sensory processes of insects has been obtained by subjecting them to external stimuli, such as light, noise and odours, and measuring the degree of excitation, either as muscular activity or more simply by observing whether the insect moves towards or away from the source of stimulation.

Perhaps the biggest step forward in providing information on the nature of sensory perception has come in the last 30 years with development of techniques for detecting electrical impulses in insect nerves. This has enlarged considerably our knowledge of the functions of the many and varied types of cuticular sensory structures.

Light receptors

The largest sense organs of the cockroach are the compound eyes, composed of a number of small ommatidia, each with a biconvex lens formed from a transparent area of cuticle. As in most insects the compound eyes of the cockroach have a wide field of vision. Nevertheless, all the pest species are characterised by their avoidance of light and preference for dark situations during the day.

Cockroaches which live outdoors, have their vision supplemented by a pair of simple eyes or ocelli. The ocellus has a single lens but is not capable of perceiving form; it is simply a 'light collecting' organ which is believed to play a part in the control of circadian rhythm (Chapter 11). Ocelli have been lost in cockroaches with a burrowing habit, and in others (most of the domiciliary species) the ocelli are reduced to non-pigmented areas of cuticle known as fenestrae (see Fig. 46, p.119)

Contact receptors

The cockroach is made aware of its immediate surroundings largely by sense of touch. On the antennae, numerous tactile hairs arise from special hair-forming cells in the hypodermis. Larger structures, usually referred to as spines or setae, occur on the legs and body. All of these, like the lenses covering the compound eyes and ocelli, are shed and renewed at each moult.

The mouthparts of cockroaches play an important role in sensory perception. Their detailed structure is described in the next chapter (5), but reference is made here to one of the characteristic patterns of behaviour of cockroaches, namely the exploration of surfaces on which they walk by means of the maxillary palps.

The musculature of the five-segmented maxillary palp is shown diagrammatically in Fig. 42. The joints are formed by a thinning of the cuticle

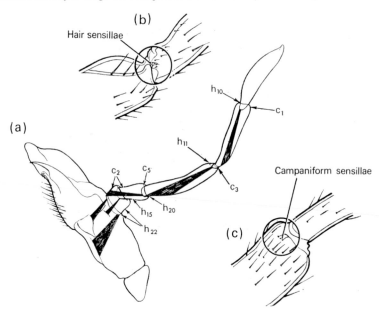

Fig. 42. (a) Left maxillary palp of *P. americana* showing muscles. Arrows show the locations of campaniform (c) and hair (h) sensillae and their numbers.
(b) Lateral view of the joint between the 3rd and 4th segments of the maxillary palp showing hair sensillae on the flexor surface.
(c) Dorsal view of the same joint showing the location of campaniform sensillae on the hinge side (after Pringle[149]).

on one side, towards which the segments can bend. The basal segment is served by two muscles which work in opposition, but each of the other segments is moved by one muscle, pull being balanced by the elasticity of the hinge. The whole of the fifth or terminal segment of the palp is covered with hairs which are sensitive to touch.

Pringle[149] has studied sensory perception in the maxillary palps of *P. americana*. To do this, fine platinum electrodes were placed on the cut maxillary nerve where it joins the suboesophageal ganglion. Impulses arising from the sense organs on the palps were passed *via* the electrodes to an amplifier and oscillograph.

The hairs on the terminal segment of the palp give a complex record of impulses due to the many active fibres. These impulses have a small amplitude and contrast with the entirely different discharge (large, rhythmic impulses of constant height), obtained with the movement of the joints of the palps.

Proprioceptors

Sensory structures at the joints of the palps (proprioceptors) perceive strains set up in the cuticle by pressure. The sensitivity of the palps varies with different areas but the joint between the third and fourth segment is by far the most reactive (Fig. 42). Considerable excitation of the palps can be obtained by applying pressure to the cuticle in this area. Here the nerve endings terminate in two types of receptor: fine hairs on the flexor surface of the joint, and mechanical receptors or campaniform sensillae on the hinge side. The sensillae are extremely small oval pits each with its own nerve fibre.

Campaniform sensillae are also present on the joints of the legs of cockroaches (Fig. 43). These perceive strains set up in the cuticle during move-

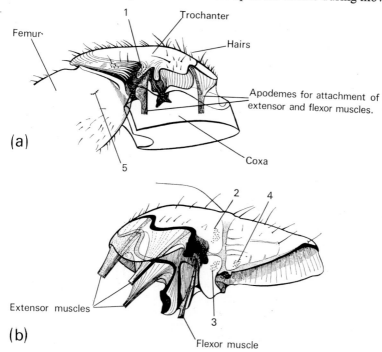

Fig. 43. Trochanter of the hind leg of *P. americana*. (a) dorsal view, (b) ventral view showing muscle attachments and groups (1–5) of campaniform sensillae (after Pringle[150]).

H

ment, whilst others provide the insect with information about its orientation. Pringle[150] describes these sensillae for *P. americana* as consisting of a fine canal penetrating the whole thickness of the cuticle, covered at the top by a domed cap. They are arranged in groups at the joints and are similar in action to those on the palps; they respond to strains in the cuticle or when artificial pressures are produced, e.g. by a glass needle on the side of the trochanter. They are so arranged as to be sensitive to forces which are set up when the insect is standing on its feet. They probably provide the insect with the sense of contact pressure and inhibit the 'righting reflex'.

Chemo-receptors

The cockroach is not highly selective in its choice of food, but the mouth-parts are well provided with receptors which enable the insect to exercise a sense of taste. Frings *et al.*[151] have undertaken tests on 23 different species of insect to discover the location of chemo-reception.

When the antennae of American and German Cockroaches are touched with a dry glass needle more than one cm from the head the insect usually withdraws. If touched within one cm of the head, the maxillary palps reach towards the source of stimulation. Because these same reactions also result with needles dipped in water, and solutions of sugar and salt, Frings *et al.* conclude that the antennae of cockroaches are not equipped with contact chemo-receptors. Tests on other parts of the body, cerci, tarsi and other sections of the legs, indicate that the chemo-receptors involved in feeding are confined to the mouth.

Detailed studies with different solutions applied to the maxillary palps show that only the ventral surface of terminal segments, near the tip, support gustatory receptors. In this area there are a number of ovoid sensillae. The tips of the labial palps also respond to solutions, but whilst other areas of the palps are well supplied with contact receptors they do not appear capable of chemo-reception. The tip of the labium and hypopharynx are sensitive to chemicals but there would appear to be no chemo-receptors within the pharynx. Frings *et al.* point out that the distribution of chemo-receptors in the cockroach differs from that of the Hemiptera, Lepidoptera and Diptera which have receptors of this type on the tarsi, and from the Hymenoptera which have antennal receptors for taste.

Auditory receptors

Sound is a series of waves involving air movements and variations in air pressure. Insects, such as grasshoppers, locusts and crickets, which produce sound as a call to one another, have well-developed tympanic organs— a thin membrane on the tibiae or tergites of the abdomen with receptive sensillae. Until recently, cockroaches were not known to produce sound, but stridulatory noise has now been recorded from the Lobster Cockroach, and similar sounds are thought to be emitted by the Madeira Cockroach.

In insects without complex tympanic organs, air movements are detected by hair sensillae. The cerci of cockroaches are clothed with receptors of this type (Fig. 44). They may also possibly respond to earthborne vibrations. Pumphrey & Rawdon-Smith[152] used platinum electrodes to show that the cerci of the American Cockroach have a partly auditory function. While there is difficulty in distinguishing between acoustic and vibratory stimuli for such an organ, it seems likely, because it is carried more or less erect in the cockroach, that its function as a 'wind gauge' may be equal in importance to its function as an acoustic organ.[153] Certainly short and gentle puffs of air on the cerci produce marked trains of electrical stimuli in the cercal nerve.

Fig. 44. The cercus of an adult male *Blatta orientalis* showing the sense organs and receptive hairs.

Rau[154] describes experiments in which observations were made on the reactions of cockroaches to sounds produced in various ways. He concludes that the Oriental Cockroach 'perceives and responds to such sounds as banging of doors, peals of thunder, blasts of dynamite and beating of metal tubs', but the response is not consistent for nymphs and adults or between the sexes. An audio-oscillator emitting up to 6,000 vibrations/second resulted in very low responses in *B. orientalis* and *P. americana*, but caused more *Parcoblatta pensylvanica* to respond. It seems probable from the information available that the cerci of the cockroach perceive stimuli, vibrations, sound or air movement, which enable the insect to initiate the escape reaction so well shown by the scurrying of the pest species when disturbed in an infested room.

5

ALIMENTARY CANAL AND DIGESTION

Basic structure: mouthparts; fore-gut and salivary glands; mid-gut; malpighian tubules; hind-gut—Speed of movement of food through the gut—Enzymes and digestion; sites and levels of enzyme activity—Cellulase and protozoan symbionts—The gut and feeding behaviour.

The simplest form of alimentary canal in insects is a straight tube from mouth to anus, but modifications to this basic structure have occurred during evolution in relation to the type of food consumed. The mouthparts, for instance, have become specialised for biting, piercing, or sucking, or they may have atrophied completely. The presence, or absence, of certain types of enzyme within the alimentary canal can be correlated with the type of food eaten. But in some insects, including cockroaches, micro-organisms in the gut assist digestion by producing enzymes not secreted, or produced only in small quantity, by the insect itself.

Cockroaches are omnivorous; almost every type of organic material is chewed, but whether or not all such material is ingested as food is questionable. Nevertheless cockroaches show preferences, as is indicated by the simple experiment in an infested room in which Oriental Cockroaches were attracted to traps baited with different foods (Table XVI). This test produced the now well-accepted conclusion that pest cockroaches prefer

TABLE XVI

THE ATTRACTIVENESS OF DIFFERENT FOODS TO *B. ORIENTALIS* AS SHOWN BY TRAPPING
(After Rau[155])

Type of food	Night on which cockroaches first entered traps	Number of cockroaches caught during 11 nights
Sugary cinnamon bun	3rd	65
White bread	3rd	44
Boiled potato	6th	22
Sliced banana, fruit and skin	8th	10
Celery	8th	2
Hard-boiled egg	10th	1
Bacon	—	0

starchy and sugary foods in preference to fruits and meats, although fresh fruits often provide a source of liquid when water is lacking.

In this chapter we shall examine the structure of the alimentary canal of the cockroach, for which *P. americana* is taken as a typical example since this species is most readily available for teaching purposes. With limited exceptions, the macroscopic appearance only is described; the reader interested in detailed cytological structure should consult the studies of Hafez & Afifi on *Supella supellectilium*[156] and of Ross on *B. germanica*[157].

In describing the various parts of the alimentary canal it is convenient to include the mouthparts, salivary glands and malpighian tubules, although these are not conventionally regarded as parts of the gut. In addition, we shall consider the movement of food through the gut, absorption, enzyme production and digestion.

Basic structure

Because cockroaches are omnivorous, their mouthparts are unspecialised; this allows them to bite and chew hard materials, consume soft foods with ease and lap up liquids. It follows that the alimentary canal is also relatively simple; it consists of a slightly coiled tube, about twice as long as the body, running from mouth to anus, but modified in different sections to fulfil specific functions. The gut is divided for convenience into three sections, the fore-, mid- and hind-gut which are easily discernible on dissection (Fig. 45).

It is perhaps necessary to emphasise here that in all insects the fore and hind sections of the gut are derived during development from the same embryonic material as the hypodermis, whereas the mid-gut is of endodermal origin, derived from the inner layer of cells which form the wall of the developing gastrula. This explains the presence of a cuticular lining to the fore- and hind-gut of the cockroach and influences the areas of the alimentary canal capable of absorbing digested food. The gut is well supplied with tracheae which hold it in place in the body cavity (the haemocoele) between the lobes of the fat body. The muscular walls of the fore-gut are innervated by the sympathetic nervous system (p. 164) and the hind-gut is served by nerves from the terminal abdominal ganglion.

Mouthparts

The mouthparts of the cockroach consist of five well-articulated structures; the labrum (upper lip or epipharynx), the strongly developed mandibles, the sensory maxillae, the hypopharynx (tongue), and the labium (lower lip). Reference has already been made to some of these structures in connection with chemo-reception and the sense organs which detect the movement of the component parts (Chapter 4).

A brief description of the relative position of the mouthparts is helpful in identifying the five structures. With the head at rest, pointing backwards, the tips of the mouthparts come into contact with the bases of the front

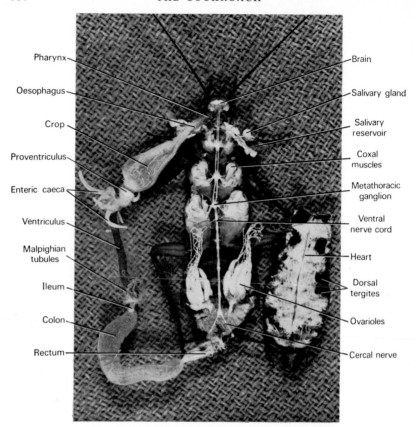

Pharynx
Oesophagus
Crop
Proventriculus
Enteric caeca
Ventriculus
Malpighian tubules
Ileum
Colon
Rectum

Brain
Salivary gland
Salivary reservoir
Coxal muscles
Metathoracic ganglion
Ventral nerve cord
Heart
Dorsal tergites
Ovarioles
Cercal nerve

Fig. 45. Dissection of an adult female American Cockroach to show the alimentary canal, with its component parts, and the central nervous system. The fat body has been removed. The dorsal tergites of the abdomen have been turned back to show the heart. Note the tracheal supply to the walls of the crop and the hind-gut. The ovarioles show developing and mature oocytes.

coxae. During feeding the head is raised and the mouthparts point vertically downwards; the labrum is clearly visible from the front attached to the lower margin of the clypeus (Fig. 46a) and forms the anterior wall of the mouth or buccal cavity. The labrum hides the toothed areas of the mandibles which are heavily sclerotised on their opposing edges; each mandible bears three well-defined denticles, which interlock when the mandibles are at rest, and a smoother 'molar' area used in mastication. During eating, the mandibles undergo a sideways movement brought about by the action of the adductor and abductor muscles (Fig. 47).

Behind the mandibles lie the paired maxillae which articulate with the posterior surface of the head (Fig. 46b). Each maxilla is composed of a number of parts; the stipes, hinged to the cardo, bears three processes, namely the lacinia (sclerotised with a pair of sharp denticles and a blunt lacinula), the galea which is not sclerotised and acts as a sheath for the lacinia, and the five-segmented maxillary palp which is sensory and does not take part in macerating food.

The labium is the most posterior of the mouthparts. It consists of the

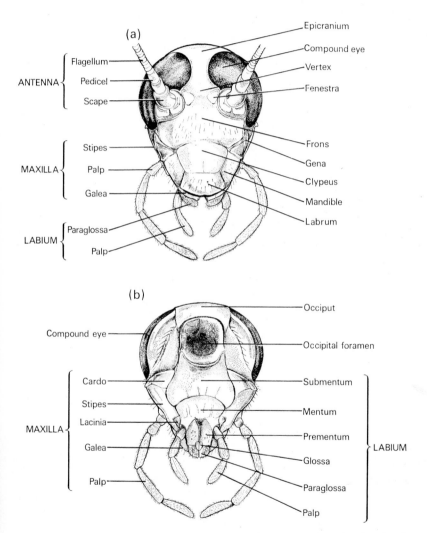

Fig. 46. Head of *P. americana* (a) anterior view, (b) posterior view showing the disposition of the mouthparts.

submentum, which borders on the occipital foramen, and the mentum which supports a paired structure, the prementum with a terminal glossa and paraglossa. The labial palps have four joints including the basal palpiger. In the middle of the buccal cavity, the hypopharynx or tongue, originates at the opening of the salivary duct.

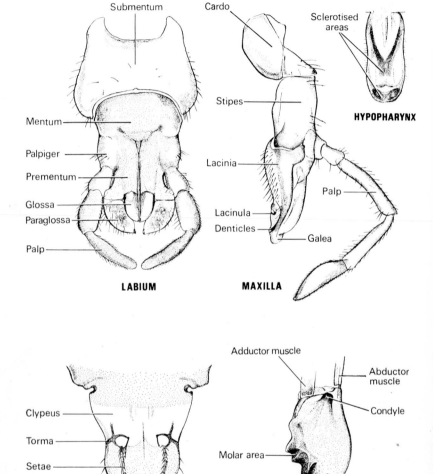

Fig. 47. Mouthparts of *P. americana* (posterior view) dissected out to show their detailed structure. (Parts drawn to same scale except hypopharynx, which is enlarged.)

Thus all components of the typical insect mouthparts are represented, and are without elaborate modifications. It is for this reason that they are invaluable for demonstrating to students the primitive condition, thus allowing a better appreciation of the evolutionary changes which have occurred to mouthparts in the higher insect Orders.

Fore-gut and salivary glands

Food is crushed in front of the hypopharynx in the region known as the cibarium; it is then passed backward into the salivarium where it is acted upon by salivary secretion and then passed into the pharynx. This is well supplied with dilator muscles, allowing it to increase in size to accommodate what is often described as the cockroach's 'voracious appetite'. Cockroaches often disgorge a clear salivary secretion onto the surfaces over which they walk, and this may be either reimbibed by the same cockroach or taken up by others. The brown smears frequently seen on cockroach infested goods are usually regarded as regurgitated, partly digested food, but observations show this liquid is of faecal origin. (Edwards & Stokes, personal communication).

Posterior to the pharynx, the fore-gut consists of, the oesophagus, crop and proventriculus (Fig. 48). The oesophagus is a straight, narrow tube which enlarges and merges into the crop, a symmetrical dilation of the hind part of the oesophagus. A pair of salivary glands (Fig. 49a) lie in the thorax on either side of the oesophagus and extend backwards along the crop. Each gland consists of a network of fine tubules (intercalary ducts) connecting secretory bodies (acini) into grape-like clusters. Associated with each gland is a salivary reservoir for the storage of saliva; the paired ducts from the salivary glands and those from the reservoirs unite in the prothorax to form the common salivary duct which opens in the salivary pocket at the base of the hypopharynx. These ducts have a stiffened spiral lining, similar to that of the tracheae, which it is thought serve to keep them open. The saliva is a clear non-viscous fluid rich in amylase, which breaks down starchy components of the food into simple sugars.

The acini of the cockroach salivary glands contain two main types of cell, described by Day[158] as zymogenic cells and ductule-containing cells (Fig. 49b). Both are responsible for the secretion of amylase as well as a mucoid substance. The zymogenic cells occur in various stages of secretory activity, except in starved cockroaches, when after 10 days without food all the cells are in the non-secretory stage. Upon feeding, secretory activity is quickly resumed.

The ductule-containing cells are innervated by the posterior part of the recurrent nerve of the stomatogastric nervous system (see Chapter 7) and it is these cells which are believed to pass the products of the zymogenic cells into the branched system of intercalary ducts. There is reason to believe, however, that the collecting ducts have more than a purely

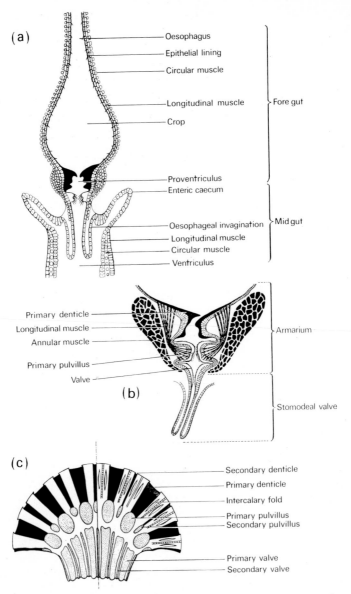

(a)

Oesophagus
Epithelial lining
Circular muscle
Longitudinal muscle
Crop
} Fore gut

Proventriculus
Enteric caecum
Oesophageal invagination
Longitudinal muscle
Circular muscle
Ventriculus
} Mid gut

Primary denticle
Longitudinal muscle
Annular muscle
Primary pulvillus
Valve

(b)

Armarium

Stomodeal valve

(c)

Secondary denticle
Primary denticle
Intercalary fold
Primary pulvillus
Secondary pulvillus
Primary valve
Secondary valve

Fig. 48 (a) Section of fore- and mid-gut of *B. orientalis*: (b) sagittal section of the proventriculus of *B. orientalis* through a primary fold, and (c) generalised cockroach proventriculus slit longitudinally and laid open (after McKittrick[39]).

mechanical function in transporting saliva from the acini to the reservoirs or mouthparts; it is thought that the ducts also play a part in the production of saliva.

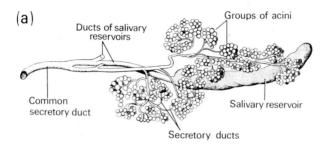

(a)

Ducts of salivary
reservoirs

Groups of acini

Common
secretory duct

Salivary reservoir

Secretory ducts

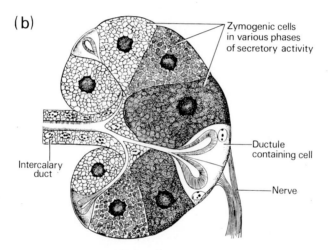

(b)

Zymogenic cells
in various phases
of secretory activity

Intercalary
duct

Ductule
containing cell

Nerve

Fig. 49. (a) Salivary gland of *P. americana*; (b) diagrammatic section of an acinus (after Day[158]).

Food may be already mixed with salivary secretion before it is taken in at the mouth. Thus the initial stages of digestion may occur before ingestion into the pharynx. Most digestion occurs in the crop where the breakdown of foods is assisted by additional secretions passed forward from the mid-gut.[159] The crop is capable of considerable distension and extends posteriorly as far as the third or fourth abdominal segment. The epithelial and cuticular lining is very much folded, practically impermeable to water and sugar solutions, but is capable of absorbing fats.

To elucidate which parts of the alimentary canal can absorb the products of digestion, studies have been made of the cuticular lining of the fore- and hind-gut. According to Eidmann[160] the cuticular lining of the crop of *B. orientalis* is three to four times thicker (5–8μ) than that of the hind-gut and to test the permeability of these linings, sections of the gut were removed and tested as semi-permeable membranes to acid and alkaline aqueous solutions. Movement through the wall of the hind-gut occurred in 10–15 minutes, but it took about 24 hours for movements to take place through that of the crop. Abbott[161] states that the crop of *P. australasiae* is capable of absorbing fat in large quantities but a minimum of eight hours is necessary to demonstrate this.

The proventriculus, or gizzard (Fig. 48b and c), is the shortest section of the fore-gut, and lies behind the crop. McKittrick[39] has made a detailed study of the proventriculus in the families of the Blattaria: it consists of an anterior armarium and a posterior stomodeal valve. The armarium is characterised by an elaborately specialised framework of 12 cuticular folds, each with an anterior sclerotised denticle, a median pulvillus clothed with hairs and a posterior valve. These 12 comprise primary and secondary structures differing in size. Cockroach species vary in the degree of specialisation of the denticles and pulvilli. Descriptions of the musculature of the proventriculus have been given by Sanford[162] for *Periplaneta*, and by Eidmann[163] for *Blatta*.

The precise function of the armarium of the proventriculus of the cockroach is uncertain; in various insects it functions as a dam, pump or triturating organ. There seems no doubt that the denticles, surrounded by the well-developed compressor muscle, serve to crush food as demonstrated by the difference in size of the particles in the fore- and mid-gut. When the teeth of the gizzard are closed they meet together so that the inward pointing denticles almost occlude the lumen. The hairs on the pulvilli act as a sphincter and may help to filter the coarse food from the fine.

Before discussing the mid-gut, there is one further structure, which belongs with the fore-gut in origin, but which extends posteriorly within the lumen of the hind-gut. This is the oesophageal invagination; it extends from the posterior end of the proventriculus and folds back on itself (Fig. 48a) and is therefore double-walled. It has a narrow lumen which directs food into the peritrophic membrane of the mid-gut.

Mid-gut

This section of the alimentary canal consists of the ventriculus (or mesenteron) with eight enteric caecae at its anterior end. The mid-gut lacks the thin cuticular lining of the fore- and hind-gut, and unlike the other regions of the alimentary canal, the haemocoelic surface of the mid-gut is served by visceral tracheae given off from each pair of abdominal spiracles. In this area there are also conspicuous anastamoses between the relatively large tracheae (see Chapter 6).

The epithelial lining of the mid-gut is composed of secretory and absorptive cells, protected from damage by food particles by the peritrophic membrane, an almost transparent tubular sheath which contains the food contents of the mid-gut and which is similar in composition to the inner layers of the cuticle. This membrane, which is constantly being regenerated, is permeable to enzymes and digested food and is separated from the inner epithelium of the mid-gut by a space filled with fluid. The epithelial cells are columnar in shape and interspersed with groups of undifferentiated replacement cells, the whole being much thicker than the epithelial lining of the fore-gut. In the absence of mucoid substances, the peritrophic membrane serves as a sleeve to protect the epithelial cells from abrasion.

The enteric caeca serve to increase the secretory and absorptive area of the mid-gut. In *P. australasiae* their combined secretory area is 1–1½ times that of the ventriculus.[161] The cells which comprise the epithelial lining of the caeca are similar to those of the ventriculus, but the lining of the caeca is very much folded to form invaginations, at the base of which nests (or nidi) of regenerative cells occur.

Malpighian tubules
The posterior end of the mid-gut is delineated by the malpighian tubules, concerned with water regulation and the ionic balance of the haemolymph. It is not usual to describe these organs in the context of the gut and

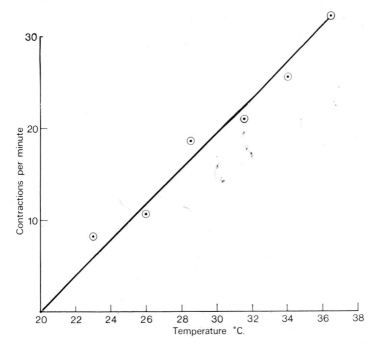

Fig. 50. Increase in contractions of the malpighian tubules of *B. orientalis* with increasing temperature (after Koller[167]).

digestion, but in *Periplaneta* the tubules have been shown to contain intracellular enzymes.[164] In most insects they are thought to have an excretory function, but in cockroaches, much waste nitrogenous matter is disposed of by storage in the fat body and by way of the male accessory glands (Chapter 8).

The number of malpighian tubules in *Periplaneta* has been variously quoted as 60–150.[165,166] They are long, slender and blind, each about 16 mm long and 0·5 mm in section. They have a surface area of about 400 sq. mm per mg of insect, and are in intimate contact with the haemolymph. The means by which waste nitrogenous matter and inorganic salts are passed from the haemolymph into the cavity of the tubule and thence to the hind-gut is not fully understood. In the cockroach, the malpighian tubules show vigorous peristaltic movements which presumably increases their contact with the haemolymph, and thus the rate of absorption of water and other materials into the hind-gut.

Studies on the movements of the malpighian tubules of *P. americana* have shown 5–15 contractions per minute at 20–25°C. The frequency of these movements increases with temperature. In *B. orientalis* regular rhythmic movements are apparent only above 20°C and reach a maximum at 35–38°C (Fig. 50). These do not appear to be under nervous control since isolated tubules retain their rhythmic mobility for an appreciable time. There is reason to believe that *in situ*, movement of tubules, best described as 'wriggling, lashing or spiralling, without detectable effect on constriction or dilation', is under hormonal control of the brain. In addition to placing the tubules in contact with the maximum possible blood volume, it is possible that these movements help to keep their liquid contents moving.[167]

Hind-gut

The principal function of the hind-gut is to remove water from digested food with the result that waste is discharged from the anus as a dry pellet. It would appear, however, that this only occurs when the cockroach is faced with a water shortage. Insects kept in the laboratory with adequate water discharge a soft, wet faecal pellet; at times a brown liquid containing a little solid waste is forcibly ejected, giving rise to the so-called 'vomit' marks of cockroaches.

The hind-gut is divided into three sections, the ileum, the colon and the rectum. As mentioned earlier, the hind-gut is derived during development from the same tissues as the fore-gut, but unlike the lining of this section the lining of the hind-gut is readily permeable to water.

The ileum, the shortest section of the gut (about 1·5 mm long), is narrower than the ventriculus of the mid-gut, and where it joins the colon there is a ring of six lobes, triangular in shape, bearing tiny spicules on the inner wall, directed towards the colon. It must be assumed that these fulfil the same function as the 'pyloric sphincter' of other insects in regulating the discharge of the mid-gut contents into the colon. The colon is easily distinguished by the irregular appearance of its wall and the darker colour of its contents.

In addition to the hind-gut being concerned with the absorption of water, it is also a site for the diffusion of certain ions. Datta[168] has studied the permeability of the isolated hind-gut of *Byrsotria fumigata* to the movement of ions and has measured the differences in electrical potential across the gut wall with different concentration gradients. Sodium moves more freely from the blood into the lumen of the colon than in the reverse direction. There is a barrier to the diffusion of potassium across the wall of the ileum, but this barrier is less marked in the colon. Chloride permeates freely through the wall of the hind-gut, but both the ileum and the colon are impermeable, or nearly so, to the movement of sulphate ions. Nitrate is thought to permeate more rapidly through the wall of the ileum than through that of the colon. It must be presumed that these variations in permeability of the ileum and colon are caused by differences in histological structure.

The rectum is oval with a number of distinct ridges. Internally there are six longitudinal thickenings in the ventral wall (the rectal pads) which are thought to absorb water from the faecal matter within the rectum. These pads are formed by development of the epithelial lining covered by a smooth layer of chitin, again readily permeable to water. They project into the lumen of the rectum and make grooves in the faecal pellets during their formation.

Speed of movement of food through the gut

Movement of food through the gut is assisted by rhythmical peristalsis, and the rate of movement varies with the type of food and whether or not the cockroach has previously fed. Soft food, such as banana paste, eaten by *P. americana* (previously starved for 48 hours), reaches the mid-gut within half an hour and small amounts are passed into the lumen of the caeca. Passage through the mid- and hind-gut is much slower. Food remains in the hind-gut for about six hours and indigestible residues remain in the rectum for 10–12 hours, but this period may extend to 20 hours,[169] the excreta then being deposited as hard, dry pellets. In Australian Cockroaches starved for one week, Abbott[161] found that a diet of fat and sugar was retained in the crop for an indefinite period varying from 30 minutes to 24 hours.

To obtain information on the speed with which food reaches various parts of the gut, German Cockroaches were fed starch paste coloured with various dyes.[170] Typical results are shown in Fig. 51 for insects starved for two days. Food is held for a short period in the crop by the proventriculus and the next delay occurs where the malpighian tubules join the gut. Once food begins to pass through the mid- and hind-gut its movement is relatively rapid.

When food is taken by a replete insect, it reaches the crop in 30 minutes but further progress is delayed. The use of dyes has shown that some mixing of successive meals can occur in the mid- and hind-gut and that after a full meal, at least three days are required for the crop to become completely empty.

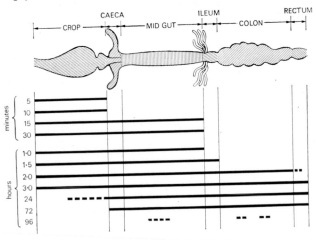

Fig. 51. Diagrammatic representation of the speed of movement of a meal through the alimentary tract of *B. germanica* after two days starvation. Dotted lines indicate the presence of traces of colouring matter from the dyed food (after Day & Powning[170]).

Enzymes and digestion

Digestion is the breakdown of complex organic compounds (carbohydrates, proteins and fats) into simpler substances, which can be readily absorbed in solution and utilised for growth and energy. The breakdown, or hydrolysis, of food constituents is brought about by the action of enzymes whose type varies with the diet of the insect. In omnivorous insects, such as the cockroach, all six of the principal types of enzyme are represented: amylase, invertase, maltase, and lactase, acting on carbohydrates, proteases which digest proteins, and lipase which acts on fats. The most comprehensive studies of the distribution of carbohydrate splitting enzymes in the different parts of the digestive tract of pest species of cockroach have been reported by Swingle,[172] Wigglesworth,[171] Schlottke[173] and Day & Powning.[170] In addition, Ehrhardt & Voss[174] have used *Blaberus discoidalis* and *Leucophaea maderae*, and Banks[175] has studied the enzyme system of *Blaberus craniifer*.

Enzymes are secreted in the cockroach by the salivary glands, the enteric caecae and the ventriculus of the mid-gut. Because starchy foods are a major constituent in the cockroach diet, amylase is exceptionally active in the saliva. Enzyme concentration increases at feeding, irrespective of the diet, and detectable levels are found in the contents of the mid-gut of *Blattella* even after three days' starvation. Because the mouthparts of cockroaches are moistened by saliva during mastication some digestion by this enzyme occurs even before the food enters the gut. Invertase is present in the saliva of *Blattella germanica*, but not in *Periplaneta*.[171]

The mid-gut secretes two proteolytic enzymes: a trypsin-like enzyme which acts on natural protein to form peptones and polypeptides; then a second group of enzymes, the peptidases, which produce the ultimate breakdown products of protein digestion, amino acids.[176] Lipase is secreted by the cells of the mid-gut which are also capable of absorbing the products of fat hydrolysis.

Sites and levels of enzyme activity

Experiments on *Blatta orientalis* have shown that the salivary glands produce only one enzyme, amylase.[172] The mid-gut caeca produce invertase, maltase, lipase and protease, and these too are produced by the ventriculus, although in smaller quantity. The hind-gut does not produce digestive enzymes. Almost the whole of digestion takes place in the crop, the enzymes passing backward from the salivary glands and forwards from the mid-gut. Swingle,[172] using extracts from washed crops showed that they contained traces of invertase, maltase and lipase, and Sanford[162] makes a similar claim for lipase. Wigglesworth,[171] however, has shown that if the gut of the living animal is washed out thoroughly by giving water only for two or three weeks, extracts of the crop are free from maltase and invertase.

Wigglesworth[171] has made a special study of the enzymes concerned in carbohydrate digestion and their activity in relation to inorganic salts and pH. To measure these effects, the various enzymes, amylase, and invertase (from the salivary glands) and invertase, maltase and lactase (from the mid-gut) were reacted with appropriate substrates and the speed of reaction measured by various techniques.

The range of activity of the four enzymes under different conditions of hydrogen ion concentration (Fig. 52) show that amylase from the salivary glands of *B. germanica* has a considerable tolerance of acid conditions, with an optimum activity at pH 5·9 and a value of 50 per cent activity at pH 4·8. Human ptyalin is completely inactivated at this pH. Invertase and maltase have an optimum range of pH 5·0–6·2, well adapted to work under the acid conditions prevailing in the crop (pH 4·4–6·2), brought about by the action of micro-organisms upon carbohydrates, and particularly yeasts upon sugar.[159] The optimal range for lactase is pH 5·0–6·4. Other studies by Wigglesworth have shown that the pH in the gut of *Blattella* varies considerably with the type of food ingested: in the crop the pH falls to 4·4 after feeding on glucose (which is broken down to lactic acid), rises to 4·8 after consuming lactose and to 6·3 after eating protein. Thus, for effective digestion the enzymes of the gut need to be

I

capable of retaining their activity over a wide range of hydrogen ion concentrations.

Studies on the effects of inorganic salts have shown that the activity of amylase from the German Cockroach, as in human ptyalin, is increased

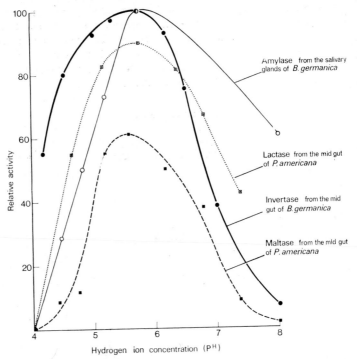

Fig. 52. Relative activity of amylase, invertase, lactase and maltase in relation to hydrogen ion concentration (pH). (From Wigglesworth[171]).

by the amount of salts in the following descending order: chlorides, bromides, iodides, nitrates, phosphates and sulphates. In contrast, low concentrations of sodium chloride have no effect upon the activity of cockroach invertase, whereas a one per cent solution has a partial inhibiting action on invertase and maltase.

Cellulase and protozoan symbionts

An account has been given in the previous pages of the alimentary canal and the enzyme production in pest species of cockroach. Mention, however, must be made of the atypical condition found in *Cryptocercus punctulatus*, for which wood is the sole diet. This is digested by cellulase-producing protozoa in the hind-gut; 12 genera, comprising 25 species of flagellate protozoa are associated with this cockroach, and their similarity with those of termites has been cited as evidence of the close relationship between the Blattaria and the Isoptera (Chapter 2). One genus of these protozoan symbionts, *Trichonympha*, occurs in both termites and *Cryptocercus*.

Barbulanympha (Fig. 53) is the most conspicuous of the flagellates in both size and abundance in *Cryptocercus*. Cleveland *et al.*[123] have found it in every one of many thousands of cockroaches examined, principally in the anterior part of the colon. These protozoa contain the enzymes cellulase and cellobiase,[177] which the cockroach itself is unable to secrete. These enzymes convert cellulose into the soluble sugar, dextrose.

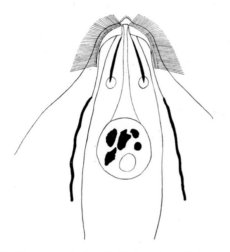

Fig. 53. Diagrammatic longitudinal section of the anterior part of *Barbulanympha* ($\times 1000$), the most abundant cellulase-producing flagellate in *Cryptocercus punctulatus* (after Cleveland *et al*[123]).

The colon of *C. punctulatus* differs from other cockroaches in that it is divided into anterior and posterior sections by a strongly developed colonic sphincter. Vigorous contractions occur three or four times per second in short bursts, forcing the contents of the colon backwards and forwards on either side of the valve. This sphincter is in addition to the iliac valve between the mid- and hind-gut and a pro-rectal valve between the colon and the rectum. The latter has thousands of projecting spines which appear to keep the protozoa in the colon. A section through the hind-gut shows that it is filled with protozoan flagellates, none occurring beyond the iliac, or pro-rectal valves. Another wood-eating cockroach which digests cellulose by means of gut protozoa is *Panesthia javanica*, but in this species the symbionts are confined to the fore-gut.

There is now evidence to suggest that some cockroaches are capable of breaking down cellulose without the assistance of intestinal symbionts, i.e. directly, by the production of an enzyme by the insect. Thus, Ehrhardt & Voss[174] claim to have demonstrated cellulase in the caeca and mid-gut of *Blaberus discoidalis* and *Leucophaea maderae*. It is also said to occur in the crop, mid-gut, hind-gut and salivary glands of *Byrsotria fumigata*.[178]

Wharton *et al.*[179] have made a detailed study of cellulase production in *P. americana* and other species, to determine its origin and concentration under different conditions. The amount of cellulase in the faeces of virgin adult females of *P. americana* increases by nine times as they grow older, from three to 12 weeks, and egg-producing females have five to seven times more in their faeces compared with virgin females. Adult males excrete 10–20 times more cellulase than virgin females of similar age. Cellulase excretion also increases with the age of nymphs, which may be correlated with a slow growth of cellulase generating organisms.

Tests on various *unwashed* tissues of the gut of *P. americana* show high cellulase activity in the salivary glands, caeca and mid-gut, but much lower activity in the proventriculus, crop and hind-gut. When, however,

TABLE XVII

CELLULASE CONTENT OF THE INTESTINAL TRACT OF DIFFERENT SPECIES OF COCKROACH, MEASURED IN CELLULASE UNITS PER INSECT. The values for 'whole intestine' include gut contents and the contribution to cellulase by gut microflora. All other tissues were washed free of contents and microflora
(From Wharton, Wharton & Lola[179])

Species	Whole intestine (unwashed)	Washed tissues					
		Salivary gland	Crop	Caecae	Mid-gut	Malpighian tubules	Hind-gut
Periplaneta americana	160	51·6	0·6	1·1	0·5	0·5	0·4
Byrsotria fumigata	162	20·8	0·4	0·6	0·5	—	0·3
ucophaea Lemaderae	140	20·4	1·0	1·8	0·6	0·4	1·0
Blaberus discoidalis	367	18·8	2·8	7·2	4·5	—	1·0
Blaberus craniifer	240	4·6	1·2	2·2	7·7	—	1·3
Blaberus giganteus	214	4·3	0·6	1·1	2·2	—	0·2

the gut is *washed*, the salivary glands are found to be the only tissue which contains significant amounts, but even these are low. Wharton *et al.* conclude that cellulase probably accumulates in the mid-gut and in the caeca of *P. americana*, but intestinal organisms in this cockroach also contribute to enzyme production.

Using the same techniques on *Byrsotria fumigata* and *Leucophaea maderae*, significant cellulase activity has again been found only in the salivary glands, and even lower levels in the glands of *Blaberus* species. Because of the much higher values obtained for cellulase in unwashed intestines of *Blaberus* species, compared with other cockroaches (Table XVII), it would appear that cellulase production in *Blaberus* is brought about mainly by intestinal symbionts and that very little is actually secreted by these insects.

The gut and feeding behaviour

In this chapter we have seen how well the structure and digestive processes of the alimentary canal suit the behaviour characteristics of pest cockroaches. The pest species feed principally at night, usually at intervals of about 24 hours; the crop is well designed to accommodate the relatively large meals taken at infrequent intervals and to act as a reservoir for the passage of food through the gut during long periods of inactivity.

With the assistance of the mandibles and the armarium of the proventriculus there seems little doubt that even very hard substrates can be readily eaten. Virtually no materials can escape the depredations of the pest species. Many different types of material are ingested; not only human food in kitchens, but the faeces of animals and man, wood, wallpaper, book-bindings, paper pastes and glues—for which the insect's alimentary canal provides a number of digestive enzymes each capable of functioning over a range of pH. The efficient absorption of water from ingested food, which results in the production of dry faecal pellets, helps the insect to conserve the maximum amount of fluid. Nevertheless water as a constituent of the diet is vital to the survival of the pest species in the premises in which cockroaches occur (Fig. 133 p. 295).

6

BLOOD CIRCULATION, RESPIRATION AND EXCRETION

The circulatory system: dorsal blood vessel; circulation in the wings—The haemolymph; haemolymph volume and water content; haemocyte count; division of haemocytes and haemolymph coagulation; speed of haemolymph circulation—Regulation of circulation by neuro-hormones; endocrine control and the pericardial cells; feeding and heart rate; compensating mechanisms in heart beat control—Transport of neuro-hormones. The respiratory system: gaseous exchange; effects of temperature and differences between species—Tissue respiration; respiratory effects of hormones
The excretory system: malpighian tubules; fat body and storage excretion; endocrine control of the fat body—Storage and excretion of uric acid by the male accessory glands—Deposition of waste products in the cuticle.

The circulatory system of the cockroach has the primary function of bathing the internal organs and tissues with blood, so conveying to them the products of digestion and, likewise, it is the means by which waste materials of metabolism are conveyed to the excretory organs. In addition, it fulfils the important functions of providing a medium for the circulation of hormones produced by the neuro-endocrine system, and the sealing of wounds after injury by coagulation. The supply of oxygen to the tissues is carried out by an entirely separate system, composed of tracheae and tracheoles which reach the tissues as minute tubes and which open to the exterior by way of the spiracles. Oxygen is conveyed through this system by diffusion, assisted by mechanical ventilation. The removal of waste is achieved by a number of different organs, including the malpighian tubules, the fat body, and in some species by the accessory glands of the male reproductive system. The excretory system regulates the water balance in the insect and the ionic balance of the haemolymph.

These three systems are dealt with together in this chapter, for convenience, rather than because they have any direct functional relationship. Nevertheless, the reader will discover that there are a number of features of the three systems by which they are inter-related.

THE CIRCULATORY SYSTEM

Blood circulation in insects consists principally of an 'open' system, whereby the circulating fluid, haemolymph, moves freely within the body cavity, the haemocoele. Movement of the haemolymph is maintained by a pulsatile 'heart' just below the dorsal surface of the integument; this movement is assisted by contractions and expansions of the abdominal sclerites during respiratory exchange, and in the cockroach by pulsatile organs at the base of the wings and antennae which assist circulation in these appendages.

The direction of movement of haemolymph within the insect is controlled by a 'one-way' flow in the heart, as well as by the dorsal and ventral diaphragms, which separate the haemocoele into the dorsal, pericardial sinus, containing the heart, the visceral sinus, containing the gut and associated organs, and the ventral, perineural sinus, containing the nerve cord. These diaphragms are composed of extremely thin connective tissue and are incomplete in the cockroach, allowing the haemolymph to pass back to the heart through a number of 'fenestrae'. The ventral diaphragm extends as septa into the legs, dividing the cavities of the joints into sinuses, thus separating the outward and return flow of blood (Fig. 54).

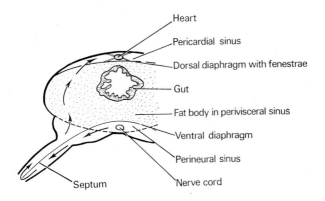

Heart

Pericardial sinus

Dorsal diaphragm with fenestrae

Gut

Fat body in perivisceral sinus

Ventral diaphragm

Perineural sinus

Septum

Nerve cord

Fig. 54. Diagrammatic section through the thorax of a cockroach showing the flow of haemolymph in the haemocoele.

Dorsal blood vessel

In the cockroach, the dorsal blood vessel is a straight tube, comprising the 'heart' in the abdominal and thoracic segments, narrowing to form the aorta in the head. The posterior end of the heart is closed and the anterior end is open. Blood from the pericardial sinus enters the heart through 12 pairs of openings, the ostia, which act as valves preventing a return flow of blood into the haemocoele when the heart contracts.

Haemolymph in the dorsal blood vessel is passed towards the head and discharged below and just in front of the brain. Here, in *Periplaneta*, lie the two small ampullae, which provide additional pumping movements to drive the blood into the antennae. Unlike the heart of most insects, that of the cockroach has a number of minute, paired segmental vessels arising from it. These were first seen in *B. orientalis* by Alexandrowicz[180] and later investigated in the American Cockroach by McIndoo;[181] there are four pairs of vessels in the abdomen (in segments three to six), and one pair each in the meso- and metathorax. They pass blood from the heart to the lateral areas of the body.

Pulsations of the heart are brought about by contractions of its muscular wall, possibly assisted by a pair of alary, fan-shaped muscles attached to the dorsal body wall of each segment. These also give the heart support in the pericardial sinus. When the heart is filled with blood, a wave of contraction passes forward along the vessel towards the head, and three phases can be distinguished (Fig. 55); contraction (systole), relaxation (diastole) and a short period of rest (diastasis). The discharge of blood into the head causes a flow backwards in the body cavity. The heart beat in *P. americana* can reverse the direction of flow of haemolymph,[182] but the conditions under which this occurs have not been documented.

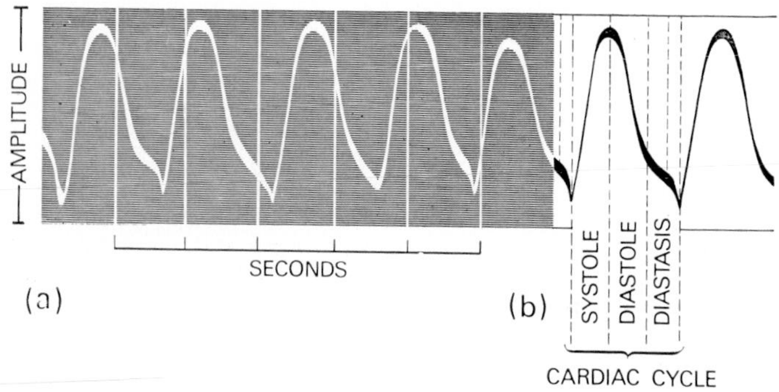

Fig. 55. A mechanocardiogram from the third abdominal segment of *P. americana*, (a) showing frequency of beats and amplitude, (b) the component parts of the cardiac cycle showing the 'presystolic notch' at the end of diastasis (after Yeager[194]).

Within the pericardial sinus are groups of large cells attached to the sides of the heart. These are the pericardial cells, concerned in the elimination of waste products and, as will be seen later, play an important role in regulating heart beat.

Circulation in the wings

The small pulsatile organs at the base of the wings of *P. americana* receive blood from the tegmina and hindwings and pass it back to the heart, but these organs occur only in adults.[182] Movement of haemolymph in the nervures of the wings can be seen if glazed paper is placed beneath them to reflect incident light; apparently, if the wings are extended from the normally disposed position into the 'flying' position, haemolymph circulation is interrupted and in some instances becomes completely inhibited.

At all stages of wing development—in the wing pads of nymphs and the fully developed tegmina and hindwings of adults—the blood is confined to the main veins and intermediates and never passes outside these channels. The normal circulation route in *P. americana* is shown in Fig. 56. If the insect remains quiet, the flow of blood is vigorous, continuous and at a constant rate; blood currents moving away from the body occur in the anterior portions of the tegmina and wings, and return to the body is in the medial and anal regions. Sometimes the circulation in one tegmen or wing is reversed, while that in the other is normal in direction.

Fig. 56. The normal direction of flow of haemolymph (indicated by arrows) in the main veins of the tegmen and hindwing of *P. americana* (after Yeager & Hendrickson[182]).

The haemolymph

The haemolymph of cockroaches has no oxygen-carrying function and therefore lacks the pigments associated with vertebrate blood, but there is reason to believe that the haemolymph may carry dissolved carbon dioxide. The blood is a clear fluid, with a high content of amino acids and uric acid; the blood of the German Cockroach normally contains 17 amino acids,[183] but the quality and concentration of these can be influenced by feeding, since certain amino acids, normally absent in the blood, can be detected if they are given to the insect in its diet.[184]

The plasma of the haemolymph contains a number of different types of cells, haemocytes, some circulating with the blood, others remaining in contact with various tissues, notably the heart. Wigglesworth[165] divides haemocytes into seven types according to their size and appearance after staining. Their primary function is to remove, by ingestion, large particles of solid matter in the body cavity. They increase by mitotic division and actively dividing cells become more abundant in the blood after moulting (see p. 139). Their scavenging activity is referred to as phagocytosis and in the cockroach, groups of phagocytes accumulate round the pericardial cells around which the blood passes on return to the dorsal vessel. Haemocytes also collect at sites of injury and take part in sealing the wound.

Haemolymph volume and water content

Many attempts have been made to measure the blood volume of cockroaches and variable results have been obtained, largely because of the use of different methods. Values are usually quoted as 'blood volume per cent', e.g. the volume in μl per 100 mg body weight. Using a dilution technique, the total amount of blood in *P. fuliginosa* is said to be 0·035 ml, i.e. a blood volume of seven per cent (or 69 mg per gram body weight).[185] The values obtained for nymphs of *P. americana* are considerably higher, ranging from 16 to 20 per cent.[186]

Wheeler[187] states that the haemolymph of *P. americana* averages about 140 μl for a cockroach weighing 800 mg (i.e. 17·5 per cent), but before the final moult there is a reduction in haemolymph volume from 17 to 14 per cent, followed by an increase during the moult to 21 per cent, and a drop again within 24 hours to 15 per cent. Withholding of food and water fails to change the blood volume;[186] and even when nymphs of *P. americana* lose 38 per cent of body weight by forced starvation over 35 days, this has no effect on the blood volume percentage.

A high proportion of the body water of cockroaches is contained in the haemolymph. Measurements of the water content of *P. americana*, as a percentage of body weight,[188] have given values of 70·4–74·8 per cent and 68·9 per cent in wild adults of mixed sexes. There is apparently no change in body water content of male *P. americana* (71·3 per cent of total weight) during the first 30 days of adult life (Wharton *et al.*[189]).

A detailed study of changes in the blood volume of male American Cockroaches in relation to body water content, has been made by injecting small amounts of radioactively labelled carboxy-inulin. This was introduced between the sixth and seventh abdominal sternites and blood samples removed from the coxae four hours later. During this period injected inulin becomes completely distributed, little accumulates in the tissues, none is lost in respiration, but a correction is necessary for eight per cent lost by excretion. In adults which have fed, the blood volume per cent, determined by this method, drops markedly from 37 per cent immediately after the moult, to 30 per cent four days later and decreases only slightly during the following four weeks. This happens despite, as mentioned earlier, no loss in body water content. Again an interdependence of haemolymph volume and body water content occurs on starvation; fed cockroaches maintain a constant water content of 70·3–71·0 per cent over a period of 12 days, whereas in starved ones it increases significantly to 74·1 per cent, whilst the blood volume decreases by about three per cent.

The observations of Wharton and co-workers on the rapid changes which occur in the blood volume of cockroaches, while the total body water remains constant, suggest that important shifts take place in the water balance of the insect. Because in starved cockroaches there is an increase in total water, but a decrease in blood volume, it is evident that food intake changes the balance, presumably by the products of metabolism causing a shift of water from the tissues to the blood; there is evidence therefore of a continuous change in water distribution as the insect eats or fasts.[189]

Haemocyte count

The total number of cells in the haemolymph of P. fuliginosa ranges from 15,000–60,000 cells per cu. mm with an average of about 30,000. This compares with 20,000 per cu. mm for Blatta orientalis.[185] By determining both the haemolymph volume and the blood cell count, Wheeler[187] has calculated the total number of haemocytes in P. americana; this procedure gives far more reliable information on changes in the numbers of haemocytes than the cell count alone because of the changes which occur in haemolymph volume. In the American Cockroach, the haemocytes account for about six per cent by volume of the haemolymph, and despite the changes which occur in blood volume during the final moult, the total number of haemocytes remains fairly constant. After the moult, however, the number of haemocytes drops from about 12 million to 9 million.

Division of haemocytes and haemolymph coagulation

During the reorganisation that occurs at moulting there is an increase in cell debris within the body cavity, requiring elimination by phagocytosis. Just before moulting, cockroaches cease to eat and become relatively inactive. This period in Blatta orientalis is associated with a drop in the number of mitotically dividing cells in the haemolymph, normally about 0·2–0·3 per cent, but three days following the moult, the number increases to a maximum and within five days of shedding the exuvium the percentage of mitotically dividing cells returns to its normal level (Fig. 57). Tauber[190] suggests that the products resulting from the breakdown of tissues, before and during moulting, may provide a stimulus to the increase in phagocytic cells.

Also at moulting, the cockroach is prone to the accidental loss of appendages—joints of the antennae and legs—and in its newly formed soft integument the insect is exceedingly susceptible to cannibalism by its colleagues, and especially in outdoor species, to predation by natural enemies.

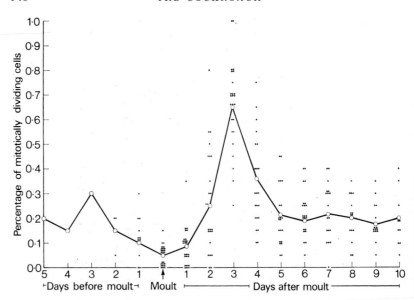

Fig. 57. Variations in the percentage of mitotically dividing cells in the haemolymph of *Blatta orientalis* before and after a moult. The curve connects average values for 25 cockroaches (after Tauber[190]).

At this time wound healing, through coagulation of the haemolymph, plays an important role in sealing the integument against excessive loss of moisture.

In the four days before the final moult and during the moult itself, there is a great increase in coagulability of the haemolymph of the American Cockroach, associated with an increase from 24 to 37 per cent of a specific type of haemolymph cell, the cystocyte or coagulocyte. The speed of coagulation of the haemolymph increases by thirteen times during this moult, but returns to normal an hour later; the number of coagulocytes drops after 24 hours.[187] The exact role of the haemocytes in causing precipitation of the blood plasma is not fully understood.

Speed of haemolymph circulation

The speed of circulation of blood in the haemocoele is controlled by the frequency of contractions of the heart. Two methods have been used to study haemolymph movement, the use of indicator dyes and observations on the movement of haemocytes.

When an aqueous solution of fluorescein is injected into the American Cockroach *via* a cercus, it is pumped forward in the dorsal vessel, and can be detected visually under ultraviolet light in successive unsclerotised areas on the ventral surface of the body (Fig. 58). The normal circulation time from injection until the appearance of fluorescein in the pulvilli of the fore-leg ranges from three to six minutes. Using this technique, Coon[191] has subjected American Cockroaches to sub-lethal exposures of a number of

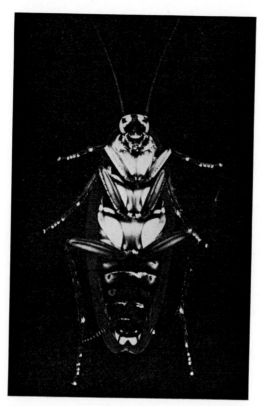

Fig. 58. The presence of fluorescein, visible especially in the compound eyes, pulvilli and coxae of the legs of *P. americana*, after injection into the left cercus to demonstrate the speed of circulation of haemolymph. The insect has been photographed under ultra violet light.

insecticides, including HCN, and examined their effect on the behaviour of the heart during paralysis; the circulation time becomes much extended (Fig. 59a) and the normal pulsation rate of the heart, 94–100 per minute, is greatly depressed (Fig. 59b).

The speed of movement of individual haemocytes and thus the rate of movement of haemolymph in the tegmina of adult *P. americana* has been measured with the aid of an ocular micrometer. Normally the blood cells are transported singly but occasionally they may clump together and become transported in groups. The rate of movement among 35 insects varied from 14 to 65 mm per minute (mean of 34 mm/min) which is not unlike the flow rate (30–50 mm/min) of corpuscles in the blood of man.[192]

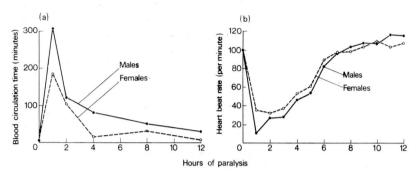

Fig. 59. (a) Increase in blood circulation time in adult *P. americana* and (b) depression in rate of heart beat, resulting from sub-lethal exposure to HCN and then recovery during a 12-hour period of paralysis (after Coon[191]).

Regulation of circulation by neuro-hormones

In Chapter 7 an account is given of the structure and activities of the sympathetic nervous system of the cockroach and mention is made of the many and varied influences of neuro-hormones in the control of body functions. Here, reference must be made to the influence of hormones in the control of blood circulation through the regulation of heart beat. In turn, mention is made in the introduction to this chapter of the function of the haemolymph in transporting hormones to the target tissues. Both these aspects have received a great deal of attention by insect physiologists.

If the dorsal sclerites of the American Cockroach are removed from the insect, with the intact heart attached, and the preparation then placed in Ringer solution, the heart continues to beat steadily for several hours. When the heart of *B. orientalis* is prepared in this way and buffered to pH 7·5, it contracts at 40–60 times per minute at temperatures between 23 and 25°C.[193] Using isolated hearts, the effects of extracts from various tissues on heart beat rate can be examined.

A method of recording photographically the frequency and amplitude of the heart beat of *P. americana* has been devised,[194] whereby the movement of the heart is transmitted by a hair to an opaque arm, interrupting a beam of light between its source and a camera. Mechanocardiograms obtained by this method are reproduced in Fig. 55 (page 136); the upward trend of the curve represents a dorsally directed movement of the dorsal diaphragm, at its point of attachment to the ventral wall of the heart, and the downward trend represents a ventrally directed movement. Following each period of rest, a 'presystolic notch' precedes the next period of contraction; it has been suggested that this is caused by pressure of haemolymph within the heart, resulting from its contraction in another region.

Endocrine control and the pericardial cells

Cameron[195] has shown that an aqueous extract from the corpora cardiaca increases the frequency of heart beat by about 50 per cent above normal and also increases the amplitude of the beat. Low concentrations of the extract increase amplitude only. By severing the nerve connections between the brain and corpora cardiaca, and waiting several days before testing their activity, proof is obtained that the corpora cardiaca, and not the neuro-secretory cells of the brain, are responsible for producing the stimulatory substance.[196]

More recent studies have shown that the corpus cardiacum is not directly responsible for exciting the heart, but does so indirectly, by causing the pericardial cells around the heart to produce a stimulatory substance.[197] Evidence for this is obtained by applying homogenates of corpora cardiaca to isolated hearts in Ringer solution: these homogenates produce the maximum stimulation in four minutes. If after three hours, when the stimulatory effect is lost, the fluid is drained off and the heart is first bathed in fresh Ringer, followed by the replacement of the same homogenate fluid, no increase in rate of heart beat occurs. Nevertheless, this same fluid is capable of producing an immediate increase in the rate of beating of another heart preparation, and demonstrates that the decrease in heart beat after three hours does not come about by destruction of the hormone by the tissues of the heart preparation. What is more, the addition of fresh hormone to the heart, after three hours, fails to elicit much of a response, even though the potency of the hormone can be demonstrated on another heart. This is not due to simple fatigue, as can be demonstrated by the use of a heart stimulant.

There appears, then, to be some substance in the tissues of the heart (believed to be an indolalkylamine)[198], which is necessary for the action of the corpus cardiacum hormone (probably a peptide or protein), but after long exposures to the hormone, the heart-substance becomes exhausted. If the heart is treated with dyes to clog the action of the pericardial cells there is no response of the heart to the corpus cardiacum hormone. Decapitation, however, proves that the corpus cardiacum is necessary for activating the pericardial cells (Fig. 60b).

Feeding and heart rate

The sequence of events outlined above does not explain what stimulates the corpora cardiaca in the first place. The more recent studies undertaken by Davey,[199] have helped to elucidate this. If an American Cockroach is fed on a ten per cent solution of glucose, the heart rate rises within four minutes to some 20 per cent above normal, and remains there for two to four hours. If the insect does not accept the food, but takes distilled water instead, the heart rate fails to rise. An increase in heart beat is not prevented by cutting the nerve cord just behind the head (after which cockroaches will still take food for up to 18 hours), and proves that the stimulus

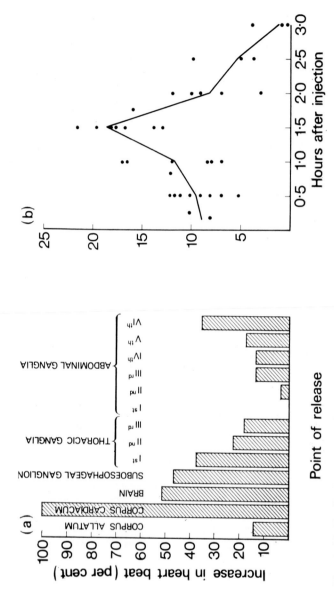

Fig. 60. (a) The distribution of cardio-accelerator hormones released by the nervous system of *P. americana*, as indicated by an increase in the beat of isolated hearts suffused with tissue extracts (after Ralph[200]).

(b) The effect on heart beat of applying homogenates of pericardial cells taken at intervals from decapitated cockroaches injected with corpus cardiacum hormone (after Davey[197]).

is not nerve conducted. Neither is it increased by damaging the corpora allata (which can again be carried out without upsetting feeding). The increase is, however, prevented by surgical removal of the corpus allatum —cardiacum complex, or by blocking the action of the pericardial cells with a dye (trypan blue).

It would appear therefore that feeding causes the release of the hormone from the corpus cardiacum which then accelerates the heart through the production of an amine by the pericardial cells. Because the increase in heart rate occurs almost immediately after feeding, it cannot result from an increase in blood sugar. A mechanism which increases blood circulation and peristaltic movements of the gut after feeding, provides an obvious advantage to the cockroach, in circulating the products of digestion as well as transporting metabolic wastes to the excretory organs.

Compensating mechanisms in heart beat control
The process of heart beat control given here is probably an oversimplification of the factors involved. The picture has been complicated by the work of Ralph[200] who has shown that there are possibly seven heart rate accelerators and five decelerators produced by various tissues. The existence of these two groups, antagonistic in action, suggests that the neuro-hormones which control muscle activity constitute a carefully balanced system. Extracts from various parts of the nervous system show that cardio-accelerators are produced by all ganglia of the nerve cord except the first abdominal ganglion. Activity varies with point of release along the nerve cord as shown in Fig. 60a.

Extracts from the thoracic muscles and testes tend to decrease heart activity and so do organic extracts (as opposed to saline extracts) from the suboesophageal ganglion.

Transport of neuro-hormones
Perhaps the best example to illustrate the part played by the blood in the transport of neuro-hormones is the movement of 'bursicon', which is responsible for the process of cuticular tanning. This is a useful example because tanning can be readily seen and measured on an arbitrary scale and the movement of bursicon in the blood can be prevented experimentally by the application of ligatures. It will be of value if we digress here for a moment to refer to the information on tanning which has been obtained from studies on flies.

The process of moulting in insects is controlled by the moulting hormone, ecdyson, and from the time that this hormone was known to cause tanning in fly puparia it was assumed that the tanning of cuticle, following a moult, was also caused by ecdyson. In 1962, Fraenkel & Hsaio[201] proved conclusively that this was not so, and in their later work[202] they pinpointed the source of secretion of the tanning hormone in the fly to two areas, the neuro-secretory cells of the *pars intercerebralis* of the brain, and to the

K

compound thoracic ganglion. Release of the hormone in the newly emerged fly is brought about by nerve impulses reaching the brain by way of the central nervous system, and extracts from the brain and thoracic ganglion of flies, taken from puparia just before emergence, are capable of producing tanning. Extracts from flies one hour old are still active, but this activity is lost one day after emergence.

Blood taken from flies 15 minutes after emergence can be diluted up to 30 times with saline and still cause full tanning in ligatured insects. Even more surprisingly, the active factor is entirely unspecific; blood extracts from flies can cause tanning in *Periplaneta* and in the mealworm, *Tenebrio*, and *vice versa*. However, the blood of fully tanned insects does not contain the tanning hormone, suggesting that an inhibitory mechanism follows soon after tanning takes place.

In the American Cockroach, the tanning hormone is released by the terminal abdominal ganglion, and as in flies, the cockroach also appears to rely on the blood system for dispersion. When ligatures are tied at various positions on the cockroach immediately after ecdysis, cuticular darkening is always confined to the posterior regions.[203] Likewise if the newly moulted cockroach is frozen, then warmed, the posterior abdominal segments tan first and darkening extends anteriorly as the hormone diffuses through the thawing insect.

When released from the terminal abdominal ganglion, the hormone is conveyed forward by the flow of blood through the heart and aorta. A ligature at the neck prevents the outflow of blood from the head and there-fore causes excessive tanning of the head sclerites (Fig. 61a). Ligatures at the neck, between the thorax and abdomen, as well as between the in-dividual thoracic segments, show that only the mesothorax fails to tan (Fig. 61b). This and other tests with ligatures (Fig. 61c and d) suggest that the mesothorax contains an inhibitory centre for the tanning hormone.[204]

Mills[205] studied the rise and fall in the level of bursicon in the blood of the cockroach and measured its activity at various intervals after ecdysis.

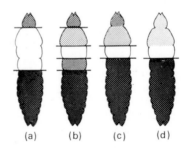

(a)   (b)   (c)   (d)

Fig. 61. The degree of cuticular tanning obtained after placing ligatures between various body segments of *P. americana*, 2–15 minutes after moulting. Note the absence of tanning of the mesothorax in all instances (after Mills[204]).

Small samples of blood (100 μl) were removed by splitting the coxae and these were tested by two methods; one, on ligated insects, and two, by incubating the extracts with isolated sections of untanned cuticle. These experiments showed that bursicon is released into the blood within 20 minutes of moulting and reaches a maximum after one and a half hours (Fig. 62); it remains high for another hour and then declines, although some tanning can still be produced by blood removed five hours after moulting. Even if the blood is diluted ten times, tanning, although much reduced, is still detectable. When, on the other hand, an *excess* of bursicon is incubated with isolated sections of cuticle, the cuticle fails to darken, suggesting the possibility of a mechanism in the intact insect for inactivating the hormone when its concentration reaches a certain level.

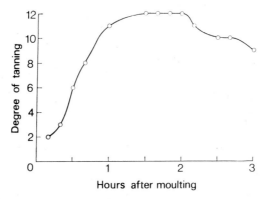

Fig. 62. The concentration of hormone (bursicon) in the blood of nymphs of *P. americana* after moulting, as measured by the degree of cuticular tanning (after Mills[205]).

THE RESPIRATORY SYSTEM

The tracheae and finer tracheoles of the respiratory system of the cockroach form a branched network of tubules lying within the haemocoele. They ramify throughout the fat body, penetrate the tissues of the body wall and viscera, and carry oxygen to all parts of the insect.

The walls of the tracheae consist of an epithelium supporting a thin layer of cuticle thrown into folds. These cuticular folds give the tube a spiral lining which helps to keep the tube open. The tracheae are formed as invaginations of the integument and the linings of the larger tracheae are shed at each moult. The walls of the tracheoles are very thin and permeable to water; in some insects the ends of the tracheoles contain fluid which moves up and down the tube in relation to the osmotic pressure of the haemolymph, but it is not known whether this is so in the cockroach.

Air enters the tracheal system of the cockroach by way of ten pairs of lateral spiracles (Fig. 63a) which have a closing device, so preventing undue loss of water; two pairs of spiracles are located in the thorax and eight in the abdomen. The first abdominal spiracle is more dorsal than the rest.

The spiracles connect to three pairs of large, parallel, tracheal trunks

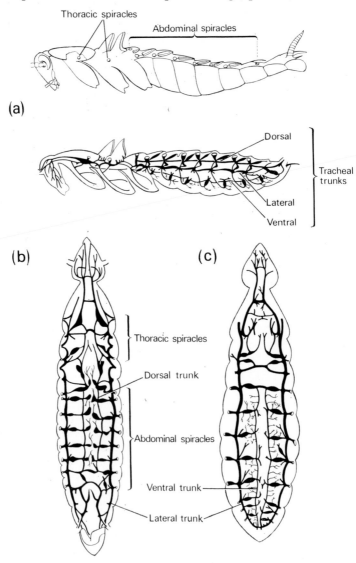

Fig. 63. The tracheal supply in *B. germanica*, (a) side view, (b) dorsal arrangement (male); (c) ventral arrangement (female) (after Haber[206]).

linked by cross commissures. Rarely are the two sides of the tracheal system of the same individual exactly symmetrical and the extent of development in different parts of the body differs between individuals.[206] The three pairs of longitudinal trunks lie laterally, dorsally and ventrally in the body; the dorsal trunks are on either side of the heart, and the ventral ones close to the abdominal nerve cord (Fig. 63b and c). Because the head is without spiracles, the tracheal supply to the anterior regions of the insect is provided by branches originating in the thorax.

Gaseous exchange
Air enters the spiracles by diffusion, assisted by mechanical ventilation brought about by contraction and relaxation of the abdominal muscles. Compression and expansion of these segments cause movements in the haemolymph which in turn influence the movement of air in the tracheal network. Oxygen reaches the tissues by diffusion through the walls of the tracheoles, and in the process of tissue respiration, carbon dioxide and water are produced. Carbon dioxide diffuses more readily than oxygen, and because of this it is thought to be eliminated through the linings of the tracheae and the integument.

Effects of temperature and differences between species
Experiments by Gunn[207] on the rate of respiration of the Oriental Cockroach show a four-fold increase in consumption of oxygen, between 20° and 36°C, resulting from increased activity of the insect as well as an in, crease in its metabolism (Fig. 64). The change in respiratory mechanism-

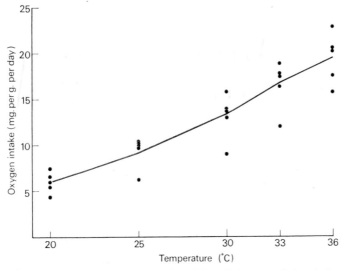

Fig. 64. The consumption of oxygen by adult male *B. orientalis* in relation to temperature (after Gunn[207]).

from diffusion regulation to ventilation regulation occurs at about 30°C. This same species can remain alive for a number of hours in the complete absence of oxygen and with all the spiracles blocked. On its release from an atmosphere of nitrogen, the insect consumes an excess of oxygen equal to the amount from which it has been deprived.

There are notable differences in the oxygen requirements of *B. germanica*, *B. orientalis* and *P. americana*. The oxygen consumption of the German Cockroach at 30°C (24 mg/g/day) is almost twice that of *P. americana*. However, when account is taken of the differences between species, in the ratio of surface area to weight, the German Cockroach consumes less oxygen (1·1 mg per cm² of cuticle per gram body weight) compared with 1·5 mg by *B. orientalis* and 1·6 mg by *P. americana* (Table XXXI, p. 289).

Tissue respiration

The end use of oxygen passed to the tissues by the tracheoles, referred to as tissue respiration, is the oxidation of organic substrates, i.e. breakdown products of carbohydrates, fats and proteins carried to the cells by the haemolymph. This releases energy for flight, running and body metabolism, and produces carbon dioxide and water. The oxidation of organic materials requires that they are first acted upon by an enzyme, dehydrogenase, and from then on the process involves a long and complex series of steps requiring the presence of certain 'carriers' and additional enzymes depending on the type of substrate being oxidised. It is not proposed to discuss the complex biochemistry of biological oxidation, except to mention that the final step is referred to as the tricarboxylic acid (Kreb's) cycle, details of which are given in most advanced text books on insect physiology.

The entry of oxygen into, and the exit of carbon dioxide from tissues is referred to as oxidative metabolism. As the ratios of carbon, hydrogen and oxygen vary widely in the range of organic materials available for oxidation, the ratio of carbon dioxide released, to the amount of oxygen used, (the respiratory quotient), varies with the type of substrate acted upon. It is 1·0 for carbohydrates, 0·7 for fatty acids, and a value between these two for proteins. The tissues which have been used most extensively to study tissue respiration in insects are muscle and fat body. There is evidence to suggest that the release of energy through oxidation comes about by the same process in both.

The tissue in insects which expends most energy in the performance of its activities is flight muscle. Because flight is rarely encountered in the Blattaria, the tissue which consumes most energy in the cockroach is probably leg muscle; in *P. americana* there is a two-fold difference at 25°C between the uptake of oxygen by males (5 cu. mm per mg of muscle dry weight per hour) and females (2·6 cu. mm).[208] Not surprisingly the leg muscle of the male has a large quantity of substrate (glycogen) for oxidation (11–15 mg/g of fresh tissue), which is six times higher than in females

(2·1–2·4 mg/g). In contrast, the oxygen uptake by thoracic muscle of *Leucophaea maderae* is the same for both sexes, 3·3 cu. mm/mg dry weight/hour.[209]

The respiratory quotient of the leg muscle of the American Cockroach is close to unity; the uptake of oxygen by males and females is 5·1 and 3·6 cu. mm/mg dry weight of muscle/hour, respectively (equal to the oxygen uptake of pigeon breast muscle); 4·9 cu. mm and 3·6 cu. mm of carbon dioxide is produced by muscle tissue of male and female cockroaches, respectively.

Respiratory effects of hormones

Because of the considerable interest shown during the last ten years in research into the effects of insect hormones, it is not surprising that studies have been made of the effects of neuro-endocrine secretions on tissue respiration. It must be mentioned here, however, that the effects observed in different insects have been far from consistent.

The early work of Samuels[209] showed a significant increase in the endogenous consumption of oxygen in both sexes of *L. maderae*, two to three months after surgical removal of the corpora allata. This result suggested that allatectomy may lead to an increase, either (1) in the concentration of substrate (glucose and glycogen) in the tissue of the muscle, or (2) in the level of some oxidative enzymes.

In one important regard the false ovoviviparous cockroach, *Leucophaea maderae* is more suitable than *P. americana* for studying the effects of the corpora allata on respiration, since in *Leucophaea* these glands vary in size, and thus in secretory activity, in relation to the maturation of eggs. This allows changes in oxygen consumption to be studied in relation to the reproductive cycle, and Sägesser[210] has found that the maximum oxygen consumption occurs during the phase of most rapid increase in volume of the gland (Fig. 65). The normal rhythm of the endocrine cycle can be changed by removing the ootheca from a pregnant female, when the corpora allata are stimulated into re-activity and oxygen consumption increases concurrently. Experiments in which active and inactive glands have been implanted into females, with the reproductive organs removed, confirm that active corpora allata stimulate respiratory metabolism, independently of their effect on the development of oocytes, whilst inactive glands have no effect.

Ralph & Matta[211] have investigated the effects of a number of components of the endocrine and neuro-endocrine complex on the respiratory behaviour of the thoracic muscles and abdominal fat body of cockroaches. These tissues were taken from normal cockroaches, to which extracts of the endocrine organs were added, and from insects operated upon for their removal. Results point to the conclusion that the sub-oesophageal ganglion is particularly influential in altering the activities of enzymes concerned in tissue oxidation, and that the neural connections (the *nervi corporis allati*

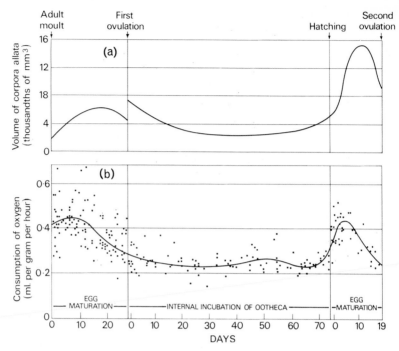

Fig. 65. Relationship between (a) the size of the corpora allata of *Leucophaea maderae* during the first 18 weeks of adult life and (b) changes in oxygen consumption (after Sägesser[210]).

—see Fig. 70, p. 163) between the sub-oesophageal ganglion and the corpora allata are of primary importance to the joint functioning of these two organs in regulating tissue respiration. There is reason to believe that the same applies to the hormonal control of egg production[212] and to locomotor activity.[213]

THE EXCRETORY SYSTEM

The products of digestion conveyed by the haemolymph to the body tissues provide the insect with materials for cell repair, growth and energy. There, various chemical reactions take place and the haemolymph once more becomes concerned as a transport system in conveying the waste products of these reactions to the excretory organs.

Excretion is a regulatory mechanism whereby the amounts of nitrogenous materials, inorganic salts and water in the haemolymph are maintained in satisfactory equilibrium, thus ensuring a stable ionic composition and osmotic pressure. The most important end-product of metabolism, provided in excess by proteins in the food, is nitrogen, and its removal, principally as uric acid, is the primary function of the insect excretory system.

There are four sites in the cockroach involved in excretory regulation: (1) the malpighian tubules (see Chapter 5), which in conjunction with the hind-gut are responsible for the elimination of waste *via* the anus, (2) certain cells of the fat body which are capable of 'locking up' nitrogen in a process referred to as 'storage excretion', (3) uricose glands, special tubules of the accessory glands of males of certain species of cockroach, which discharge urates in association with the spermatophore during copulation, and (4) the cuticle, into which waste materials may be deposited and thus eliminated during moulting. It is not possible to say which of these sites is primarily responsible for waste regulation in the Blattaria, except to emphasise that the malpighian tubules of the cockroach have not been found to contain uric acid and as this is the principal end-product of excretion in insects, the fat body would appear to take a major role in waste regulation.

Malpighian tubules

These long, slender tubes, arranged in six groups, lie freely in the haemolymph of the body cavity, and are attached to the alimentary canal at the junction of the mid-gut and hind-gut (Fig. 45, p. 118). They are closed at their free ends and contain a narrow lumen. It seems probable that waste materials passed from the haemolymph to the tubules are taken up through their walls and then secreted into the lumen by the epithelial lining.

In insects which feed on blood and plant sap a high proportion of the diet consists of fluid and the conservation of water by such insects is not a serious problem. They may in fact have an abundance of water for elimination with the result that the waste products of these insects can be excreted in solution. This is not so in the cockroach which under dry conditions, can ill-afford to lose water as an excretory product. In this insect the fluid which is passed from the malpighian tubules into the hind-gut is resorbed in the colon and rectum with the result that any waste products of metabolism, which are excreted by the malpighian tubules, are passed out as dry material in the faeces. When water is abundant, however, waste products may be excreted in a liquid or semi-dry condition.

The efficiency of excretion in the American Cockroach has been studied by recording the rate of elimination of injected dyes. When an aqueous solution of indigo carmine (2·5 per cent) is injected into the pericardial cavity of last stage nymphs, about 90 per cent is removed within five hours. The rate of excretion in the American Cockroach increases with temperature up to 35°C (Fig. 66), but falls as the temperature is raised higher. The withholding of food and water, or the injection of water (at 10–20 per cent of blood volume) have no effects. The technique of dye elimination has been used to examine the effects of sub-lethal doses of insecticides on

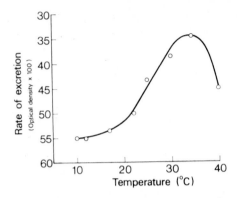

Fig. 66. The effect of temperature on the rate of excretion (clearance of dye from the blood) in last stage nymphs of *P. americana*, as measured by the optical density of samples taken from cut antennae. Dye injected 60 minutes before test (after Patton, Gardner & Anderson[214]).

excretion. When injected 24 hours before measuring the rate of dye elimination, the organochlorine compounds, heptachlor and dieldrin (3–4·5 μg) and isodrin and endrin (15μg) were found to inhibit excretion, the latter virtually stopping excretory activity completely.[214]

Fat body and storage excretion

If the dorsal sclerites of the cockroach are removed, one of the most conspicuous organs immediately apparent is the fat body, occupying a large part of the body cavity, principally in the abdomen, but extending also between the muscles of the thorax (Fig. 67). This organ is seen as compact lobes, which on more detailed inspection are found to be surrounded by a membrane of connective tissue. The fat body contains a number of different types of cells of which the more important are: trophocytes, mycetocytes, oenocytes, and the urate cells.

The fat body cells proper, the trophocytes, which function as a depot for reserves of fat, glycogen (carbohydrate reserve) and protein, increase in size during development of the insect so that eventually they contain some of the largest cells in the insect's body. The size of the fat body and thus its content of reserves, notably of glycogen, varies with the level of nutrition and the stage in the developmental cycle. There is no doubt that the ability of the cockroach to survive long periods without food (see Fig. 133) can be largely attributed to this reserve; lipid in the fat body can be rapidly mobilised during starvation to sustain continuous muscular activity and the fat body also contains labile protein which accumulates during periods of feeding and disappears on starvation.[215]

In addition to providing the insect with a site for the deposition of reserves, the fat body is also a site for intermediary metabolism: in the

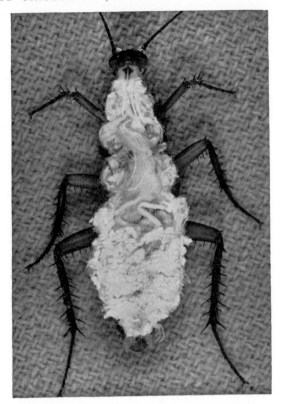

Fig. 67. Dissection of a female American cockroach showing the mass of fat body surrounding the internal organs.

cockroach and in many other insects the fat body is packed with intracellular bacteria (bacteroids) usually confined to certain cells, the mycetocytes. These symbionts contribute to the synthesis of amino acids as illustrated by the studies of Henry & Block.[216] When German Cockroaches are fed radioactive glucose and vitamins, the radioactive 'label' becomes combined into 14 amino acids, but when the symbionts are destroyed by aureomycin, six of the amino acids are lacking.

Enzyme systems enable the fat body to manufacture complex materials from smaller molecules brought by the haemolymph, and with the contribution of the bacteroids, the fat body is capable of synthesising several vitamins (ascorbic, folic and pantothenic acids).[217] It provides a mechanism for regulating substances, such as glucose in the blood, after a meal of carbohydrate, by rapid conversion to glycogen. In addition certain cells, the oenocytes, are believed to be concerned in the production of lipoprotein, required for the formation of the new epicuticle at moulting (see Chapter 10).

In addition to all these functions, this mass of white amorphous tissue is capable of taking up, producing and storing uric acid. The fat body of the cockroach contains urate cells, distinct in appearance from the ordinary cells of the fat body (Fig. 68), which originate in the embryo and accumulate uric acid, apparently harmlessly, throughout the insect's life.

Nevertheless there is some evidence to suggest that the storage of waste materials in the fat body may involve the cockroach in difficulties especially when the diet is high in protein. If the American Cockroach is given a low protein diet (less than 11 per cent), the fat body is almost absent. Development is normal on a diet of 22–24 per cent protein, but 79–91 per cent protein results in a greatly enlarged fat body, which completely fills the abdominal cavity;[218] white deposits of uric acid occur almost everywhere in the insect and its life span is reduced. When such insects are transferred to a normal diet, much of the accumulated uric acid disappears and there is a loss in body weight of up to 23 per cent. It appears likely that the fat body is the actual site of uric acid formation and the work of Keller[219] suggests that the intracellular symbionts of the cockroach are able to utilise the uric acid for remobilising the nitrogen locked up in it. Moreover, if under conditions of poor nutrition the products formed by the breakdown of uric acid can be utilised, then 'storage excretion' in the fat body may be of considerable advantage to the cockroach.

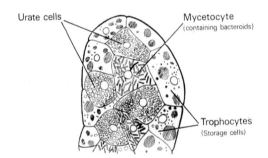

Fig. 68. Lobe of fat body in *Blatta orientalis*, showing mycetocytes, urate cells and fat storage cells (after Gier[272]).

Endocrine control of the fat body

Urates appear in the fat body of *P. americana* as granular concretions of various sizes, closely packed together, and normally present in abundance. Removal of the endocrine glands, the corpora allata and cardiaca, causes the disappearance of almost all the urates throughout the fat body of the insect. If, however, only the corpora allata are removed, large amounts of urate remain in the fat body for at least six weeks. Thus, because urates are breakdown products of digested protein, there is evidence to suggest that protein metabolism, or perhaps the mobilisation of urates, is under hormonal control.

This conclusion is supported by experiments in which corpora cardiaca have been re-transplanted into cockroaches. If this is done with insects from which both the corpora allata and cardiaca have previously been removed, urates become re-deposited. In certain experiments extreme starvation of cockroaches from which both glands have been removed, can also result in recovery in deposition of urates.[220]

Further evidence that the corpora cardiaca exercise control over the fat body is that allatectomy increases the amount of fat in the American Cockroach from 63 per cent (dry weight) in normal insects, to 77 per cent in operated insects.[220] It is convenient here to refer to the more detailed work of Vroman et al.,[221] on the effect of allatectomy on lipids. These workers have shown that the corpora allata influence the utilisation of stored fat by increasing the amount of triglyceride, the major storage form of fatty acids. Like many recent biochemical investigations, this study involved the use of a radiotracer technique, in this instance the injection of ^{14}C-labelled sodium acetate. It was introduced into allatectomised and normal cockroaches to provide a qualitative and quantitative estimate of the increase in fat (Table XVIII).

TABLE XVIII

COMPOSITION OF COCKROACH LIPID WITH AND WITHOUT
ALLATECTOMY
(Data from Vroman, Kaplanis & Robbins[221])

Lipid fraction	Control		Allatectomised	
	Mg/roach	% of total lipid	Mg/roach	% of total lipid
Triglyceride	32·5	52	69·6	68
Phospholipid	20·5	32	18·5	18
Hydrocarbon	5·3	8	5·6	5
Other lipids	4·5	8	9·3	9
Total	62·8		103·0	

The normal cockroach lays down lipid in the oocytes as they mature, but in allatectomised cockroaches, oocytes never mature and this results in a lower utilisation of triglyceride. Thus, in the American Cockroach the corpora allata regulate the turnover of lipid by controlling one of the mechanisms responsible for its use. The accumulation of triglycerides in the absence of hormonal regulation can be related to failure in the development of the ovaries where 70 per cent of lipid appears to be triglyceride.

Storage and excretion of uric acid by the male accessory glands

The accessory, or mushroom gland, of the male reproductive organs of the cockroach is responsible for the formation of the spermatophore. This gland consists of a number of blind tubules of which the longer ones, arising on the periphery of the gland, are referred to as the *utriculi majores*. They occur at the junction of the vasa deferentia and the ejaculatory duct (Fig. 82, p. 187). In 1964, Roth & Dateo[222] identified uric acid in the *utriculi majores* of the accessory glands of *B. germanica*, and subsequently they examined these glands in 40 species of cockroach.[223] The presence of uric acid was detected by chromatography, and the amount present estimated by spectrophotometry. Of the 40 species examined, uric acid was found in the glands of eight species only, including *B. germanica* and *B. vaga*, but excluding all other common species. Uricose glands are not found in males of other orthopteroid insects (Mantidae, Phasmidae, Acarididae, Gryllidae and Tettigoniidae).[223]

Uric acid is restricted to the *utriculi majores*, and when present causes the tubules to become greatly enlarged. The amount of acid which accumulates in the glands varies considerably (13–47 mg/g live weight in four species) and is influenced largely by frequency of mating, since during mating these glands are almost emptied.[224] In one species (*Onychostylus notulatus*) the male is said to pass so much uric acid during copulation that the female's genital segments gape open and cannot be closed because of it.

Earlier work by Khalifa[225] indicated that the secretion of the *utriculi majores* of the German Cockroach passes into the spermatophore during its formation. Analysis of spermatophores by Roth & Dateo showed that uric acid does indeed occur on the outside of the sperm capsule, but none can be detected within it. They conclude that 'the *utriculi majores* may be considered as storage excretory organs of uric acid between matings and as active excretory organs during copulation when the waste product is poured over the spermatophore. Since males can eliminate the uric acid by way of the *utriculi majores* it would appear that this is a more effective excretory device than fat body storage and that mating may be an important excretory function of the male'. Referring to the findings of Haydak,[218] mentioned on p. 156, that a very high protein intake and a consequent high urate content of fat body can reduce longevity, Roth & Dateo[223] raise the interesting questions, (a) whether excessive accumulation of uric acid in the *utriculi majores* is harmful when males are prevented from mating, and (b) which of the two methods of excretion is more important, fat body storage or elimination by way of copulation? These questions have still to be answered. Whether or not the presence of uric acid around the spermatophore serves any protective function is not known. Roth[226] suggests that uric acid, when poured over the spermatophore, may have some evolutionary significance in protecting the spermatophore from being eaten by the female cockroach or by other insects.

Deposition of waste products in the cuticle

With the shedding of the cuticle at each moult there is good reason to believe that the exo- and epicuticle of insects might provide them with a relatively efficient method of disposing of unwanted metabolic products at regular intervals. Reference has already been made in Chapter 4 to the considerable changes which occur in the composition of the cockroach cuticle, between its soft, newly formed condition, and during the process of hardening. The epicuticle of last stage nymphs of *P. americana* contains 70 per cent protein compared with just over 50 per cent in the whole of the cuticle of the newly moulted adult, and it seems possible that the loss of this nitrogenous component by way of the exuvium could provide yet an additional means of excretory regulation.

In this chapter we have considered the systems of blood circulation, respiration and excretion in the cockroach, more or less as separate entities. In the living insect there is clearly an interplay of function between these three systems, as there is also with the gut, nervous and reproductive systems, discussed in other chapters. In this regard, one should recognise the haemolymph as the 'universal' transport system for all materials outside the gut, nervous and reproductive tissues; it is the medium for the transport of digestive products, regulatory substances, dissolved carbon dioxide, urates, salts and of cells with a multiplicity of function. It influences the movement of air in the tracheoles and contains the major proportions of the insect's body water. Maintenance of its chemical composition is essential for the normal functioning of all the organs and tissues that are bathed in it.

Little has been said here of the biochemical processes involved in blood circulation, respiration and excretion. The advanced student interested in the processes of osmotic and ionic regulation of the haemolymph should refer to the review by Shaw & Stobbart.[227] The biochemistry of tissue respiration and energy metabolism is the subject of a book, 'The Metabolism of Insects',[228] by Gilmour and the biochemistry of the insect fat body has been reviewed by Kilby.[215]

7

THE NERVOUS SYSTEM AND ENDOCRINE ACTIVITY

Units of nerve tissue—The central nervous system: the brain; the ganglia—The sympathetic nervous system: the stomatogastric system; functions of the stomatogastric system—Conduction of nerve impulses; neuronal pathways; reflexes; endogenous nerve activity; inhibiting centres; neuro-hormones and nerve activity—Nerve toxins— Supply of nutrients to the nervous system.

This chapter is concerned with the means by which external stimuli, perceived by sense organs on the cuticle (Chapter 4), cause the cockroach to avoid unfavourable situations in its environment and react positively towards favourable conditions. It is also concerned with the means by which the various body functions of the cockroach are maintained. Two processes are involved: first electrical conduction, in the form of nerve impulses which cause the cockroach to run when disturbed, take food to its liking or display sexual behaviour in the presence of a mate; second, chemical conduction of physiologically active compounds, neuro-hormones or endocrine secretions, carried principally in the haemolymph and responsible for the internal co-ordination of organ function and activity cycles.

Because the cockroach is a relatively unspecialised insect its nervous system conforms with the generalised pattern of a typical insect. When we use the term 'nervous system' it should be recognised that three systems are in fact involved, each serving different parts of the insect body (Fig. 69). The most obvious of these, seen on dissection of the cockroach, is the central nervous system (the somatic system of Willey[229]), which consists of the brain, the ventral nerve cord and its ganglia (Fig. 45). The others are the peripheral and the sympathetic (or visceral) nervous systems. Some have suggested the existence of a fourth, 'autonomic nervous system' which is self-regulatory and independent of the others, but at present there is little evidence for its existence. Of the three systems, only the central and sympathetic nervous systems will be considered in detail. First, however, we shall examine the composition of nervous tissue.

Units of nerve tissue
The smallest unit of the nervous system is the neurone, a nerve cell body with short fibrils, or dendrites, which receive nerve impulses, and a long filament, or axon, which transmits impulses away from the nerve cell. The

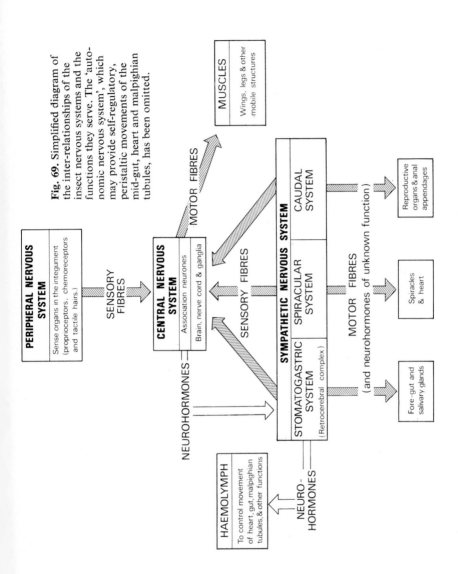

Fig. 69. Simplified diagram of the inter-relationships of the insect nervous systems and the functions they serve. The 'autonomic nervous system', which may provide self-regulatory, peristaltic movements of the mid-gut, heart and malpighian tubules, has been omitted.

intimate association of the branched ends of the axon of one neurone, with the dendrites of another, is called a synapse.

The majority of neurones are massed together to form the segmental ganglia of the central nervous system. Their axons constitute the nerves which arise from the ganglia, and the connectives which link the ganglia together. Other neurones are located in the integument and in the tissues of various organs.

These nerve cells, or neurones, are of three types: first, the sensory or afferent neurones, which convey impulses away from the sensory areas, (e.g. receptors in the cuticle), and have their cell bodies close to the area where impulses arise. Sensory neurones are associated with the hypodermis, and comprise the peripheral nervous system. The axons of sensory neurones connect to the ganglia of the central nervous system. Sensory neurones are also associated with the muscular wall of the alimentary canal and other body organs, and form part of the sympathetic nervous system.

The second type of neurone is the motor or efferent neurone which conveys impulses away from the central nerve cord. Impulses conveyed by motor neurones to the muscles of the leg, for instance, result in the insect reacting to a stimulus. The cells bodies of these neurones are located in the ganglia and connect to the inner mass of nerve tissue in the ventral cord, the neuropile. Axons of both afferent and efferent neurones are present within a given nerve so that it has both sensory and motor functions.

The third type of nerve cell is the association neurone. These are intermediate in position between the afferent and efferent neurones and link the sensory and motor impulses within the nervous system. Association neurones are situated in the lateral areas of the ganglia and comprise large areas of the brain.

The central nervous system

In all insects, the greatest proportion of nerve tissue combines to form the central nervous system. This, as we have seen, consists of the brain, the ventral nerve cord and ganglia, as well as the nerves which arise from the ganglia. The brain (sometimes called the supraoesophageal ganglion) lies in the head above the oesophagus. In the cockroach, the ventral nerve cord is composed of ten ganglia linked by paired connectives; one ganglion lies in the head below the oesophagus (the suboesophageal ganglion), three are located in the thorax, which are large and conspicuous, and six in the abdomen of which the terminal one is larger than the preceding five. The paired connectives which link the brain to the suboesophageal ganglion are called the circumoesophageal commissures.

The brain

The brain (Fig. 70) comprises three fused ganglia of the head and is divided into three regions, of which the most dorsal is the protocerebrum, representing the fused ganglia of the optic segment. The protocerebrum is divided into two protocerebral hemispheres, each with a lateral optic lobe, connected by retinal fibres from the eyes. The second region, the deutocerebrum, lies ventral to the protocerebrum and represents the fused ganglia of the antennal segment. It consists of a pair of antennary lobes each with a nerve to the antenna. These, in common with other nerves contain both afferent and efferent neurones and therefore receive impulses from the antennae as well as supplying motor impulses for their movement. The third, most ventral and smallest part of the brain is the tritocerebrum. This is formed from the ganglia of the third segment of the head and lies lateral to the gut. It supplies nerves to the frons and the labrum and provides the origin of the circum-oesophageal commissures to the suboesophageal ganglion.

For a detailed account of the anatomy of the brain the reader should consult the work of Willey[229] on *Periplaneta americana* and of Willey & Chapman[230] on *Blaberus craniifer*. The brain together with the suboesophageal ganglion have both nervous and neuro-endocrine functions.

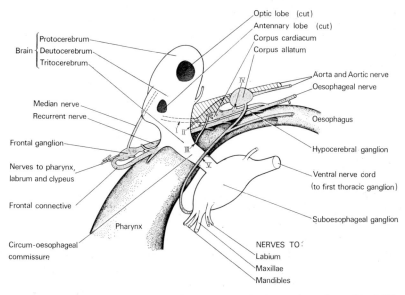

Fig. 70. Diagrammatic representation of the brain and suboesophageal ganglion (of the central nervous system) and the anterior part of the stomatogastric nervous system in relation to the gut and aorta. (From left hand side). Nerves I, II and III (the *nervi corporis cardiaci*) connect the corpora cardiaca to the brain. Nerves IV and V (the *nervi corporis allati*) connect the corpora allata to the corpora cardiaca and to the sub-oesophageal ganglion, respectively (modified from Willey[229]).

The ganglia

The ganglia of the remaining three segments of the head are fused to form the suboesophageal ganglion, which is posterior to the brain and, as its name implies, lies below the oesophagus. Three main pairs of nerves arise from this ganglion, to the mandibles, maxillae and to the labium.

The three thoracic ganglia are prominent and well-spaced, one in each thoracic segment. The first, or prothoracic ganglion, is joined to the suboesophageal ganglion by a pair of connectives in the same way that the remaining thoracic and abdominal ganglia are linked to form a chain on the ventral body wall. Nerves from the thoracic ganglia innervate the muscles of the thorax, notably those of the wings and legs.

There are six ganglia in the abdomen which are much smaller than those of the thorax, except the terminal one. A pair of nerves arise on each side of the first five abdominal ganglia to supply the dorsal and ventral muscles of the body wall; they also innervate the spiracles and the dorsal heart as part of the sympathetic nervous system. The terminal ganglion is noticeably larger than the rest because it comprises the fused nerve tissue of a number of terminal segments. It supplies nerves to the muscles of the last three abdominal segments, to the reproductive organs, copulatory appendages and to the cerci, as the 'caudal' part of the sympathetic nervous system.

A section through one of the ganglia shows the cell bodies of the motor and association neurones in the outer areas, supported by non-nervous tissue, the neuroglia, within which there is a central area, the neuropile, consisting mainly of nerve fibres. The whole is surrounded by a protective sheath, the neural lamella. A section through the connectives of the nerve cord shows that each contains two or three giant fibres, about $40-45\mu$ in diameter, four or five of $20-40\mu$ and a group of six or eight of $10-20\mu$. Collectively, these giant fibres are readily distinguished from the mass of smaller and more numerous sensory fibres, and pass forwards from the last abdominal ganglion reducing in diameter towards the head. There appears to be no synaptic interruption in the giant fibres between the last abdominal ganglion and the metathoracic ganglion but there are synapses in each of the thoracic ganglia, where most of the fibres terminate in association with motor neurones.

The sympathetic or visceral nervous system

This system exhibits both nervous and endocrine (hormonal) activity and is also composed of sensory, motor and association neurones. It consists of three parts: first, the stomatogastric system (or stomodeal system of Willey[229]) which comprises the ganglia and nerves serving the anterior part of the gut; secondly, nerves which arise from the ventral nerve cord, innervate and interconnect the spiracles (spiracular system); thirdly, the caudal system (or proctodeal system of Willey[229]) which consists of nerves arising from the terminal abdominal ganglion to serve the posterior part of the gut, reproductive organs and anal appendages, Willey has given a detailed account of the gross anatomy of the stomatogastric system in *P. americana*, *Blaberus craniifer* and *Blaberus giganteus*. The summarised account given here applies to *P. americana*.

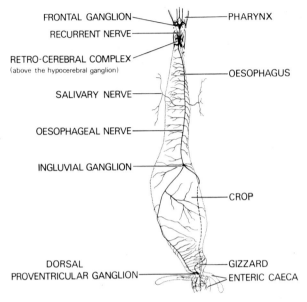

FRONTAL GANGLION
PHARYNX
RECURRENT NERVE
RETRO-CEREBRAL COMPLEX
(above the hypocerebral ganglion)
OESOPHAGUS
SALIVARY NERVE
OESOPHAGEAL NERVE
INGLUVIAL GANGLION
CROP
DORSAL
PROVENTRICULAR GANGLION
GIZZARD
ENTERIC CAECA

Fig. 71. The stomodeal nervous system (dorsal view) of *Periplaneta americana*. The fore-gut is in dotted lines (after Willey[229]).

The stomatogastric system

The stomatogastric system (Fig. 71) consists of four ganglia and the retro-cerebral complex. The frontal ganglion lies anterior to the brain just above the pharynx; small nerves pass forwards from this ganglion to innervate the pharynx, the clypeus and the muscles of the labrum. The frontal ganglion is linked with the protocerebrum of the brain by a thin median nerve (the *nervus connectivus*) and is also linked to each lobe of the trito-cerebrum by a pair of thick nerves (the frontal connectives). An unpaired nerve, the recurrent nerve, passes backwards from the frontal ganglion along the dorsal surface of the pharynx, beneath the brain, to form the second ganglion. This is the diffuse, hypocerebral ganglion from which arises, posteriorly, the single oesophageal nerve with smaller lateral nerves to the salivary glands and ducts. The oesophageal nerve forks about half way along the crop at the third ganglion (the ingluvial ganglion), where the branches continue posteriorly, one dorsal and the other ventral to the crop, to terminate in the fourth paired ganglia on the surface of the proventri-culus.

By far the greater part of the stomatogastric system consists of the 'retrocerebral complex' (Fig. 72), which is made up of the paired corpora cardiaca and corpora allata, and related connectives. Willey has observed that the corpora cardiaca contain nerve cell bodies, but the corpora allata are glands of non-nervous origin.

The corpora cardiaca are connected ventrally by three pairs of short nerves to the hypocerebral ganglion; three pairs of nerves (the *nervi corporis cardiaci*) connect the copora cardiaca to the posterior surface of the brain, in an area of dense neurones known as the *pars intercerebralis*. The paired corpora cardiaca are joined by a well-developed 'bridge' of nerve tissue (the *commissurus corporis cardiaci*) which also forms the ventral and lateral walls of the aorta.

The paired corpora allata are attached as two lobes to the posterior ends of the corpora cardiaca (by the *nervi corporis allati*) and are also joined across the mid-line (by the *commissurus corporis allati*). In addition, each corpus allatum is connected by a long slender nerve to the suboesophageal ganglion. From studies on *Leucophaea maderae*, Engelmann[212] has sug-

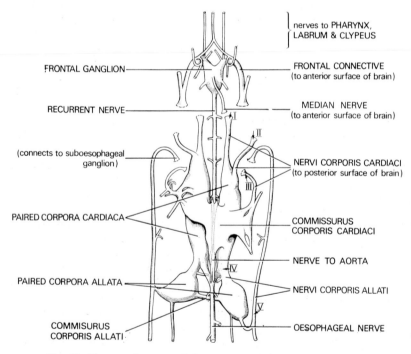

Fig. 72. The anterior part of the stomatogastric nervous system of *P. americana*, dorsal view, with the brain and aorta removed (after Willey[229]).

gested that this nerve conducts inhibitory impulses from the suboesophageal ganglion to the corpora allata.

Functions of the stomatogastric system

The primary function of the stomatogastric system is to innervate the foregut. The corpora cardiaca have two known functions: the storage and release of secretory products of the brain, and the production of their own secretory substances. A multiplicity of function has been attributed to these secretions in different species of insects. The corpora allata have also had many functions attributed to them, including the production of the juvenile hormone which maintains the immature characteristics of the growing insect and the production of the gonadotrophic hormone which influences the development of oocytes.

A great many studies have been undertaken to determine the functions of the corpora cardiaca and corpora allata of cockroaches. Extracts of the corpus cardiacum have been shown to increase the frequency and amplitude of the heart beat of *P. americana*[195,197] (Chapter 6). They also increase the rate of peristalsis of the hind-gut, but inhibit peristalsis of the fore-gut.[195] The corpus allatum controls the production of a volatile sex attractant in *Byrsotria fumigata*[231] as well as promoting the maturation of oocytes and the production of accessory gland secretion (Chapter 9). Removal of the corpora allata and cardiaca from *P. americana* causes the disappearance of urates from the cells of the fat body, which reappear when the glands are re-transplanted.[220] In addition, the corpora allata of the American Cockroach influence the synthesis and turnover of lipids in the body[221] (Chapter 6).

Severance of the recurrent nerve in *Leucophaea maderae* causes the development of tumours in the anterior part of the mid-gut,[232] but this does not occur in *P. americana*.[233] Tumours can also be induced in the mid-gut of American Cockroaches by implanting fresh oesophageal ganglia.[234] The ability of the corpora allata to bring about normal ovarian development in *Leucophaea* occurs only when the nerve connecting them with the suboesophageal ganglion remains intact.[212]

The suboesophageal ganglion and other parts of the central nervous system are also directly or indirectly responsible for regulating a number of body functions. The suboesophageal ganglion appears to be a primary source of a hormone which stimulates respiration;[211] it also plays a major role in the control of circadian rhythms[213] (Chapter 11). The brain of *P. americana* initiates the release of a hormone, bursicon, from the last abdominal ganglion, prior to moulting, which is responsible for cuticular tanning.

These and many other endocrine functions of the central and sympathetic nervous systems are discussed in greater detail in the chapters dealing with the physiology of the various organs.

Conduction of nerve impulses

Three types of nerve activity can be distinguished in the cockroach: first, impulses which pass to the ventral nerve cord, to the thoracic ganglia, and sometimes to the brain, which result in stimulation of a motor fibre at some point distant from the sensory, input; secondly, conduction referred to as the 'reflex arc', usually involving the sensory and motor fibres of one ganglion only, but perhaps also those in front and behind; thirdly, endogenous or spontaneous activity, which is normally suppressed by the suboesophageal and the thoracic ganglia.

The phenomena of excitation and conduction of impulses in nerves has been studied by causing artificial stimuli in motor nerves supplying muscles. The excitation of a muscle through its nerve involves three stages: first, excitation of the nerve, i.e. the initiation of some local change at the point of application of the stimulus, second, conduction in the nerve, i.e. the propagation of an electrical disturbance along the nerve fibre, and third, reaction, i.e. the production of some change at the junction between the nerve and a muscle.

Present evidence suggests that electrical discharges do not cross the synapse between adjacent neurones. The transmission of an electrical disturbance across a synapse is probably brought about by the liberation of a chemical substance, possibly acetylcholine, which sets off a new electrical disturbance in a succeeding neurone. The importance of acetylcholine in the conduction of nerve impulses will be better appreciated when we come, in Volume II, to consider the available evidence to explain the poisoning of cockroaches by certain groups of insecticides.

Neuronal pathways

The conduction of nerve impulses along a nerve can be recorded on an oscilloscope, the strength of the wave varying with the strength of the stimulus. Variations in the frequency of the electrical discharge cause muscle tissue to contract and relax.

Many of the experiments to obtain an understanding of nerve conduction in the cockroach have involved recording impulses at different points along the ventral nerve cord. Most frequently studied, have been the impulses which arise after the cerci are stimulated by a puff of air or by sound. [235-237] Each cercus (Fig. 44, p. 115) bears many hundreds of receptors, slender, chitinous hairs, about 0·5 mm long and 0·005 mm in diameter, articulated with the exoskeleton and innervated by a single afferent fibre. Air movements within a foot of the cerci result in bursts of electrical activity in the central nervous system.

The last (sixth) abdominal ganglion contains synapses between sensory fibres from the cerci and the large motor fibres of the nerve cord. There are also 'through' fibres which transmit stimuli from the cerci, forward along the nerve cord without synapsing in the terminal ganglion (Fig. 73). Stimulation of the cercus produces, first, a small response, probably conveyed by the 'through' fibres, as well as a much greater response, of large spike potentials, transmitted by the giant fibres.[236]

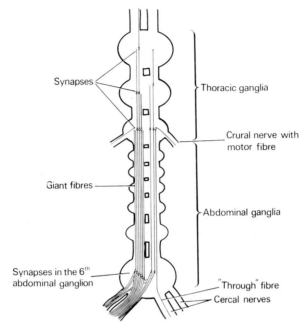

Fig. 73. Schematic diagram of the ascending pathways involved in the evasion response. The cercal nerves are shown entering the 6th abdominal ganglion. The crural nerves leaving the metathoracic ganglion are included to represent motor connections. Not shown are the reinforcing connections of the motor centres with the head ganglia (after Roeder[238] and Pumphrey & Rawdon-Smith[236]).

By using fine, tapered, silver electrodes to detect impulses in the nerve cord, Roeder and co-workers[237] have studied transmission across the synaptic origins of the giant fibres in the last abdominal ganglion. These synapses conduct synchronously up to 400 stimuli per second with a delay of 0·6–1·6 milliseconds. Stimuli between 400 and 800 cycles per second produce partially synchronised responses and the higher the stimulus frequency above 800 cycles per second, the more asynchronous the responses become.

Most of the impulses which are passed forward in the giant fibres synapse with motor neurones in the thoracic ganglia and increase the speed of locomotion; analysis of cine film suggests that all the legs are excited equally.[239] Once the muscles have become excited, rhythmic movements of the legs persist because of the feed-back to the thoracic ganglia of local reflexes (Fig. 74).

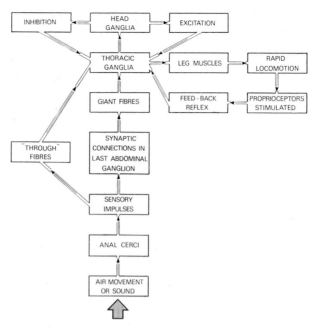

Fig. 74. Flow diagram showing the sequence of events leading to the evasion response in the cockroach.

Some of the impulses in the nerve cord are, however, passed to the brain, but because the brain is lacking in motor neurones it is not in direct control of body appendages. Its main function is to receive information, coordinate and regulate body activity by means of its great mass of association neurones. There is some evidence of descending nerve pathways from the head of the cockroach to the thoracic ganglia which may have an inhibitory rather than excitatory function. In contrast to the regulatory function of the brain, the suboesophageal ganglion directly controls feeding, influences locomotion, and has endocrine control over various body functions.

Reflexes

The type of stimulus/response mechanism outlined above illustrates the way in which nerve reflexes, initiated by proprioceptors on the legs (Chapter 4) play a part in cockroach locomotion. The reflex arc is perhaps the most primitive connection between neurones, and in its simplest form consists of the passage of impulses between a sensory and motor neurone within the ganglion of one segment. Hughes[239] has commented, however, that at the present time there is no information concerning the mechanism of transmission within the ganglion during these reflexes, and it is not known how many synapses may be involved. He says that 'in addition to evidence for purely segmental reflexes, there is a growing body of knowledge which emphasises the importance of intersegmental relationships between ganglia. It has been shown, for example, that sensory neurones entering an abdominal ganglion may ascend to at least the next anterior ganglion and in some cases such fibres also have connections in the ganglion they enter and in the one posterior to it'. In the cockroach, axons of motor fibres are also known to descend from one ganglion to the one behind, before emerging in a segmental nerve (Fig. 75).

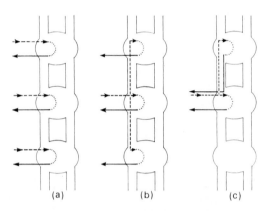

Fig. 75. Diagrams to illustrate the paths of reflexes in the ventral nerve cord. Dashed lines show sensory fibres; continuous lines indicate motor fibres; dotted lines indicate synapses. (a) Reflexes involving single segmented ganglia, (b) the sensory axon branches to ascend and descend the nerve cord to synaptic regions in three successive ganglia, (c) the sensory axon ascends the nerve cord and the motor neurone with which it synapses descends before leaving in the same segment as the sensory fibre entered (after Hughes[239]).

Endogenous or spontaneous nerve activity

Most studies to investigate the physiology of the insect nervous system have involved an examination of stimulus/response relations. Roeder *et al.*[240] suggest, however, that the assumption that the insect is a stimulus/response system ignores the possibility that endogenous nervous activity may be responsible for certain behaviour patterns. They cite the example that if a male mantis is decapitated, it continues to make co-ordinated movements of the legs, abdomen and phallomeres for many days, which can lead to effective copulation if the male encounters a female.

To examine the existence of endogenous or spontaneous nerve activity in the cockroach, Roeder and co-workers used electrical detection equipment on insects in which all sensory connections were eliminated. Male *P. americana* were pinned to restrain them and the abdominal ganglia and nerves exposed and immersed in saline. Elimination of sensory input to the last abdominal ganglion was achieved by cutting all the nerves arising from it except the motor nerves serving segments nine and ten. Hooked silver electrodes were placed under these nerves and changes in electrical discharge observed.

When the nerves to the cerci were cut a small but consistent increase in discharge was obtained in the dorsal branch of the tenth nerve (Fig. 76a), but complete neural isolation of the last abdominal segments, by cutting the abdominal connectives joining the terminal ganglion to the rest of the nerve cord, resulted in a marked and sustained increase in motor activity (Fig. 76b). This increase usually occurred within five minutes after cutting the nerve cord and spontaneous activity usually reached its peak in a

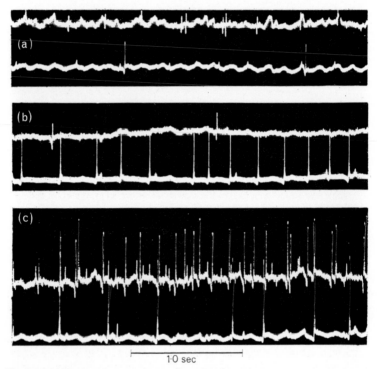

1·0 sec

Fig. 76. Oscilloscope traces of nerve impulses in male *P. americana*. (a) motor impulses in the nerves to abdominal segment IX (upper trace) and the phallic branch of X (lower trace) with the abdominal connectives of the nerve cord intact; (b) endogenous nerve activity in the form of spikes in the phallic nerve, four minutes after cutting the nerve cord. No increase in impulses has occurred in the IXth nerve at this stage, (c) the same, 10 minutes after cutting the nerve cord showing increased endogenous activity in the IXth nerve (after Roeder et al.[240]).

further ten minutes, continuing in most preparations for several hours (Fig. 76c). Cutting of only one of the paired abdominal connectives usually caused an increase in efferent activity in nerves on both sides of the ganglion. These bursts of motor impulses produce an ordered pattern of movement of the phallomeres, similar to those which occur during copulation.

Inhibiting centres

Studies to locate the centres in the intact insect which inhibit endogenous nerve activity show that removal of the compound eyes, ocelli and antennae of the cockroach causes no permanent increase in the output of motor impulses from the abdominal ganglion. Removal of the brain results in only a slight increase in electrical activity, but decapitation, or cutting of the nerve cord connectives in the neck, produces a more pronounced increase, similar to that obtained by cutting the abdominal nerve cord. It would appear, therefore, that the suboesophageal ganglion is the main source of inhibition of spontaneous nerve activity, although Roeder et al.[240] found that in some instances, cutting the abdominal nerve cord, subsequent to decapitation, brought about a small additional increase. This suggests that the thoracic ganglia may also contribute in small measure to the suppression of efferent activity.

Neuro-hormones and nerve activity

Because of the long delay between removal of the inhibiting centre (caused by cutting the nerve cord) and the onset of spontaneous motor activity from the last abdominal ganglion, Roeder has suggested that inhibition of spontaneous nerve activity in the cockroach is exerted by agents other than nerve impulses, and that neuro-hormones may be involved.

Indeed, the later work of Milburn & Roeder,[241] has shown that extracts of corpora cardiaca applied to the uninjured nerve cord can produce phallic nerve activity similar to that released by decapitation. Moreover, the more recent studies of Strejčková and colleagues,[242] have shown that extracts from both the brain and corpora cardiaca cause a temporary increase in the amplitude of spontaneous nerve activity when applied to the suboesophageal and first thoracic ganglia. The effects of these neuro-hormones on the suboesophageal ganglion depends on their concentration and on the ratio of concentrations one to the other. Their effects when applied separately to the prothoracic ganglion are quite different: the extract from the corpora cardiaca induces a rhythmic activity with spikes of high amplitude, whereas that from the brain has no excitatory effect unless the ganglion is first showing spontaneous activity.

Nerve toxins

It is not intended to give here an account of the physiology involved in the poisoning of cockroaches by insecticides (see Vol. II), but as an example of toxins which can be produced by the insect itself, mention must be made of the action of DDT.

When a cockroach is poisoned by DDT, paralysis and death are preceded by a period of stimulated nervous activity causing excitable behaviour. It has been suggested that the quantity of DDT required to bring about this modification in behaviour is so small as to indicate that DDT causes the insect to manufacture toxins, and it is these which are the eventual cause of death. Support for this suggestion is given by the work of Kearns[243] which has shown that DDT poisoned cockroaches contain in their blood a material, which is not DDT, but which on injection into normal cockroaches can be lethal. Beament[244] has attempted to reproduce this condition without the aid of DDT. He produced a situation whereby cockroaches were induced to struggle; the movement of nymphs of *P. americana* was restrained by confining them for three to four days on wax blocks, a treatment which had no adverse effects on respiration or blood circulation. After the cockroaches were released, they failed to recover their normal movements; they became incapable of righting themselves and were unable to walk in a co-ordinated fashion. Some survived in this state of partial paralysis for several days. The tests showed that the chance of paralysis occurring was more likely the more the insect was impeded and the greater it struggled: it occurred more readily when all the legs were fixed than when they were not. A similar state of paralysis can be induced, in a shorter time, by direct stimulation of the insect by mechanical or electrical means.

These experiments suggest that hyperactivity of the cockroach promotes the production of a nerve toxin which can lead to paralysis and the condition usually referred to in insecticide studies as 'knockdown'. Beament concludes that 'hyper-stimulation of the nervous system regardless of whether it is produced by chemical stimulation, mechanical or electrical stimulation of the animal, or self-promoted activity through imprisonment, can all give rise to autocatalytic metabolites which cause paralysis and death'.

Supply of nutrients to the nervous system

One of the problems which has confronted physiologists concerned with the insect nervous system is the means by which it is supplied with nutrients. Most organs and tissues of insects are composed of single layers of cells which can be readily supplied with nutrients by the blood; the connective tissue surrounding them is sufficiently thin to allow nutrients to penetrate easily. The ganglia, however, are covered by a tough fibrous sheath, penetrated by tracheoles supplying oxygen, but there is no provision for the circulation of haemolymph. This problem, as posed by Wigglesworth,[245] led him to surmise that nutrients must also enter the ganglia by diffusion if they are to reach the neurones within.

A detailed study of the structure of a nerve ganglion (Fig. 77) shows that beneath the outer sheath (the neural lamella) and the perineurium cells within, there is a matrix of glial cells which are penetrated by tracheoles. The glial layer is heavily vacuolated (the glial lacunae) which Wigglesworth suggests may serve as a pool into which nutrients are discharged, and from which they can be drawn by those cells—the nerve cells and their axons—which require them. The nerve cells are deeply penetrated by the glial cytoplasm and this appears to be the mechanism by which the glial cells provide nerve cells with nutrients.

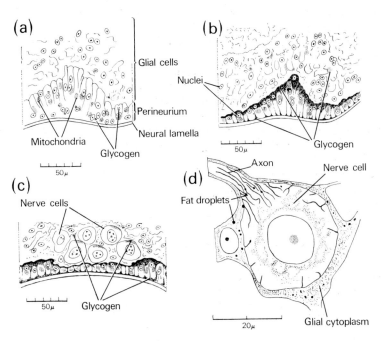

Fig. 77. Sections through the terminal ganglion of the cockroach: (a) horizontal section of the anterior end just above the connectives; cockroach starved for three weeks. The section has been stained to show the traces of glycogen in the perineurium; (b) the same in a starved cockroach three hours after feeding on honey. Much glycogen appears in the perineurium and traces in the glial cells; (c) the same but the ganglion is sectioned at the posterior end to show glycogen in the nerve cells and glial cytoplasm; (d) a nerve cell surrounded by glial cytoplasm stained to show fat droplets in the glia and in the invaginations at the base of the axon (after Wigglesworth[245]).

This conclusion was reached after injecting ganglia with dyes, and studying the movement of carbohydrate and fat in the nerve cord of fed, and starved, cockroaches. Contrary to previous views, the injection of dyes shows that the neural lamella is freely permeable to quite large molecules, but the underlying perineurium resists the entry of substances into the glial cells beneath. Staining techniques show that in cockroaches that are well-fed, glycogen is abundant in the perineurium cells but only traces occur in the glial cells (Fig. 77b). No visible deposits of fat occur in the perineurium, but the underlying glial cells contain numerous small droplets. The picture in starved cockroaches is quite different. If the cockroach is without food for three to four weeks, glycogen practically disappears from the ganglia. It is, however, quickly restored to the perineurium, the glial cells and the nerve cells, three to six hours after a meal of honey.

This demonstrates that the various cell layers of the ganglion play a major part in regulating the penetration of nutrients: the perineurium is responsible for storing glycogen, and the glial cells for transferring both glycogen and fat to the nerve cells by way of their thin cytoplasmic invaginations into the nerve cells (Fig. 77c). These reserves, particularly glycogen, become concentrated in the nerve cell at the base of the axons (Fig. 77d).

Support to this conclusion has been given by studies using radioactive glucose,[246] which becomes rapidly converted to trehalose in the haemolymph. Both glucose and trehalose penetrate the nerve cord but the smaller glucose molecules penetrate about two and a half times faster than the larger trehalose molecules (Fig. 78). About half the radioactivity in the nerve cord appears as glutamic acid and glutamine, indicating that a very reactive amino acid is important in the metabolism of the central nervous system and that there is a linkage of carbohydrate and amino acid metabolism in the nervous system of the cockroach.

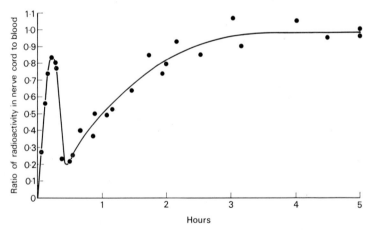

Fig. 78. The appearance of radioactivity in the nerve cord of *P. americana*, following injection of ^{14}C-labelled glucose into the haemolymph, expressed as a ratio of the radioactivity in the nerve cord to that in the blood. The first peak represents the penetration of labelled glucose and the second, slower rise, the accumulation of labelled trehalose, to which glucose is rapidly converted (after Treherne[246]).

This chapter has done little more than outline the structure and functions of the various parts of the cockroach nervous system; it may be adequate as a general introduction for the student of biology, but for those requiring more detailed information, reference should be made to the collection of papers, 'The Physiology of the Insect Central Nervous System' edited by Treherne & Beament.[247] These papers reveal the rapid increase in knowledge obtained from studies in insect neurophysiology in recent years, due to the variety of laboratory techniques which have become available. But as Hughes[239] has rightly commented 'despite a long history of histological work, there is still a surprising lack of information about the functional anatomy of insect neurones and there is a danger that advances in this whole field may be held up because of insufficient knowledge about neuronal architecture'.

M

8

THE FACTORS INVOLVED IN MATING

Sex attractants: the volatile attractant of *P. americana*; endocrine control of the female
sex attractant; reaction of male *P. americana*; sexual behaviour of *B. germanica*—
Modifications of the terminal abdominal segments: external genitalia of the male;
external genitalia of the female
Copulatory behaviour: use of the genitalia in copulation; the period in copulation;
mating in other species; factors affecting receptivity of the female
Internal reproductive organs of the male: sperm formation; formation and structure of
the spermatophore; insemination.

In any large laboratory culture of cockroaches, a number of pairs may be
seen in copulation, occasionally the male below the female, but more often
the two sexes end to end. This chapter is concerned with the factors which
bring the sexes together and the sequence of events which take place before
and during mating. Also described here are the external male and female
genitalia; the external structures of the female are designed to receive those
of the male during mating and to provide a chamber for the formation of
an egg case or ootheca. The external genitalia of the male are designed to
keep the sexes together during the copulatory period and for the transfer
of sperm. Towards the end of the chapter a description is given of the
internal reproductive organs of the male and the formation of the spermatophore, the tiny capsule of sperm, which is passed to the female during
copulation.

Sex attractants
Much effort has been made in recent years to discover the mechanisms
which bring the sexes of insects together for mating, and it is now known
that females of many species produce sex attractants or pheromones.[248]
Volatile sex attractants are produced by virgin females of at least seven
species of cockroach,[231] including *P. americana*. When these substances are
perceived by the chemoreceptors of males, they are attracted from a
distance and then follows a characteristic pattern of behaviour.

The volatile sex attractants of certain insects have been identified and
synthesised, providing a new tool in insect control: extremely small
amounts of sex attractant are required to stimulate males, and if these
substances are used in traps, the male population can be depleted. Alter-
natively, if these materials are released into the environment of a pest, the
effect might be so confusing to the males that they would be incapable of
finding a mate. Moreover, if other substances could be found which mask

178

the attractant odours of insects, these too might be used in preventing insects from 'courting' each other, thus reducing the possibility of successful copulation.

In the German Cockroach, recognition of the female by the male, and the 'release' of male courting activity is brought about by physical contact between the sexes. In this instance, a non-volatile sex attractant is produced on the integument of the female[224] and 'sparring' of the antennae between male and female is necessary before courtship is initiated (Fig. 79a). During this process the male becomes contaminated with the attractant from the female by direct contact with her cuticle.

In studying the attraction of the sexes, efforts have been made to find the part of the insect's body that produces the sex pheromone. This has been successful with females of certain Lepidoptera,[249] but the glands in cockroaches which produce active attractants have not so far been located. The chemical composition of the female sex attractant has been established for certain insects including the American Cockroach.[250,251]

Virgin females of P. americana produce a highly potent sex attractant (2,2,-dimethyl-3-isopropylidene-cyclopropyl proprionate), which brings about intense excitement among males and elicits the wing-raising posture characteristic of the stimulated male (Fig. 79b). The tegmina are raised to an angle of 45–90° and the hindwings are vibrated rapidly. The receptors for detecting the female sex odour are located on the male's antennae. Vision appears to play no part in sex recognition, or in the mating sequence.

It is also known that males of about 50 species of insect produce pheromones to attract the female, but none of these compounds have yet been chemically identified. Isolation and identification of male pheromones might also have considerable practical significance in insect control. Among cockroaches, the behaviour displayed by some 25 species shows that females which are ready to mate are drawn to the dorsal tergites of the male by some attractive substance.[252] This, as we shall see later, assists in positioning the two insects so that the male can make connection with the female's genitalia.

The volatile attractant of P. americana

It was Roth & Willis in 1952, who first showed that female American Cockroaches emit a specific odorous attractant and that this substance adheres to paper and other surfaces with which females come into contact.[224] They showed, too, that the response of the male to paper contaminated with attractant, is identical in every way with his response in the presence of a female.

The attractant is produced chiefly by virgin females and is not normally produced by nymphs, at least not in any detectable quantity. At the last moult the newly emerged adult female produces very little attractant, but it increases to a maximum during the second week after moulting, and then decreases as more and more oothecae are produced.[253]

Large amounts of the attractant of the American Cockroach have been obtained by passing air continuously over large numbers of virgin females and condensing the vapours over ice.[251] About 10,000 females 'milked' continuously for a period of nine months were required to produce 12 mg of pure attractant, a yellow liquid with a characteristic odour. Yamatoto[254] has described the method for obtaining the attractant and it is of interest that live male cockroaches were used to detect any leakage from the equipment; males are so responsive that less than $10^{-14}\,\mu g$ of the material is sufficient to bring about a stimulatory reaction.

Biochemical studies have shown that in addition to producing an attractant, female cockroaches also produce 'activity-masking' compounds, which nullify its stimulatory effect.[255] Thus when crude extracts of the bodies of virgin females are made in organic solvents, none of these extracts evokes a sexual response in males. When, however, the extracts are split into various components, one fraction has been found to produce a strong sexual response, but when remixed with the other inactive components the response is completely lost. The chemical composition of these masking agents has not so far been determined.

Endocrine control of the female sex attractant
In addition to the American and German Cockroaches, several others produce attractant substances which bring about a pattern of behaviour leading to copulation. Engelmann[256] first showed with the Madeira Cockroach (*L. maderae*), that quite a significant proportion of females of this species fail to mate if deprived of their corpora allata soon after becoming adult. These glands (Chapter 7) form an integral part of the neuroendocrine complex and Engelmann found that mating could be induced if females were implanted with glands from last stage nymphs. This suggested to Barth[257] the possibility that failure of allatectomised females to mate might be caused by their failure to produce the sex attractant and this he demonstrated in the Cuban Burrowing Cockroach (*Byrsotria fumigata*): 90 per cent of females in which the corpora allata were left intact produced the attractant, whereas only 14 per cent did so after the corpora allata were removed.

Subsequently, Barth was able to demonstrate a high correlation between production of the attractant and successful mating, as indicated by the presence of inseminated spermatophores. Females of *Byrsotria* begin to produce sex attractant between 10 and 30 days after the final moult, but production of the pheromone gradually decreases if females are allowed to mate and is almost completely eliminated in those carrying an ootheca.

These studies demonstrated for the first time that the *stimulus* to mating in insects is under endocrine control. According to Barth[231] it is only the production of the sex attractant, and no other feature of the female's sexual behaviour, which is influenced by neuro-endocrine secretion. This is not to be confused with the known effects which the endocrine system has in controlling the maturation of eggs (p. 202), and in stimulating the production of secretion in the female accessory glands. He says, 'it seems quite appropriate that the same endocrine organ which controls egg maturation, should also be involved in informing the male of the female's readiness to mate'. Removal of corpora allata appears to have no effect on the reproductive behaviour of the male, and removal of gonads from both sexes is also without effect on mating hehaviour.

Reaction of male *P. americana*

It is now well-established that the raised tegmina and wing fluttering of the male cockroach is the surest visible sign that he has been sexually stimulated. This is a clear indication that he has recognised the attractant odour of a female, and if the concentration of the attractant is increased his intensity of stimulation is also increased: the percentage of males which respond to the attractant is proportional to the logarithm of the concentration.[258] Males in isolation sometimes fail to respond but invariably do so when put together in groups. It is believed that this may in some way be associated with the normal gregarious habit of the American Cockroach.

The ability of the male of this species to respond to the sex attractant of the female, varies at different times; he may be highly sensitive for a few days, or even for many months, but then gradually, or even suddenly, becomes quiescent. The reasons for this are not known. There is evidence that males can become adapted (habituated) to the olfactory stimulus, involving a 'blockage' of the normal reaction, particularly in the presence of very small doses of the attractant, and it may be this which is partly responsible for the variation in the male's sensitivity.

Sexual behaviour of *B. germanica*

Raising of the wings is also a sure indication of stimulated sexual activity among males of the German Cockroach, but in this species, wing-raising exposes the openings of two pairs of glands on the dorsal surface of the seventh and eighth abdominal segments (Fig. 14, p. 46). The areas around these glands become moistened with secretion which is eaten by the female (Fig. 79c). It is clear that this secretion cannot become available to the female when the male is at rest, as the openings of the glands are covered by both the wings and the margins of the preceding abdominal segments, so that wing-raising and the extension of the abdomen form an essential prelude to the mating sequence.

From some 6,000 observations on German Cockroaches, Roth & Willis[224] have detailed the factors which influence the male's mating response: a good appreciation has been obtained of the sequence of events and the importance of each in getting the male and female into copulation. The following is a summary of these findings.

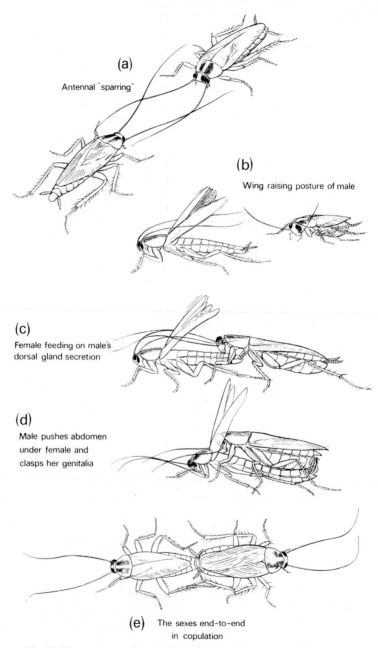

(a)
Antennal "sparring"

(b)
Wing raising posture of male

(c)
Female feeding on male's
dorsal gland secretion

(d)
Male pushes abdomen
under female and
clasps her genitalia

(e) The sexes end-to-end
in copulation

Fig. 79. The sequence of courtship and mating in the German cockroach.

Male German Cockroaches which are sexually mature, are able to distinguish between adult males and females, since males fail to 'court' others of the same sex. As the first essential step to mating, the male must establish physical contact with a female before making a courting response. The female German Cockroach cannot provide any 'distance attraction' for the male, as in *P. americana*, and even close promixity of the male and female is not enough. Moreover there is no evidence to suggest that the female may be attracted from a distance to the male.

Physical contact, initially with the antennae, is therefore necessary to begin courting behaviour of the male. When he comes into contact with another German Cockroach he investigates it with his antennae and if the other insect is a female they rapidly stroke each other's antennae. During this process a substance from the female is transferred to the male, which also makes him sexually stimulating to other males. The male can become stimulated sexually, even within five minutes of moulting, and by a female carrying an ootheca, although it is, of course, physically impossible for her to copulate. It is presumed that the substance acquired from the female is contained in her cuticular wax.

Normally the courting of a female leads to the male twitching the end of his abdomen several times, extending it and then turning his terminal segments towards her, with his tegmina and hindwings raised, exposing the dorsal surface of his abdomen. Sometimes a male may become stimu-lated into sexual activity by another, because of the latter's previous contact with a female, when he will also feed on the dorsal gland secretion of the courting male. Courting behaviour, however, is not self-propagating; one male courting a female, in the presence of other males, does not induce in them the courting reaction.

'Sparring' with the antennae between males and females, and active movement by the female, are both important factors in getting the female to take the dorsal gland secretion. Nevertheless, males will court females from which the antennae have been removed, so that mutual 'sparring' is not vital for the induction of courtship; males will also court a dead female, but will not copulate with her, indicating the importance of feeding by the female on the male's dorsal glands if the male is to grasp her genitalia. Removal of the male's antennae markedly reduces his response.

Because contact between the antennae is, under normal circumstances, the preliminary step which stimulates the male, Roth & Willis did some experiments to find out what would happen if the antennae were taken from males and females and then used experimentally, to stimulate males. Cockroaches could distinguish the sex from which the antennae had come, but antennae taken from females lost their ability to stimulate males after three days. Males, however, which had been isolated from females for as long as 100 days, were still capable of discriminating between freshly removed antennae of the sexes.

Evidence that the attractant of the German Cockroach is non-volatile comes from experiments in which the antennae of a male were used mechanically to stimulate another male, with a female held close by, but not touching. No courting response was elicited. Isolated parts of the female's body, other than the antennae, also stimulate males, if brought in contact with the male's antennae, but they produce a smaller response.

With this information, Roth & Willis then postulated that perhaps the salivary secretion of the female plays a part in male stimulation. It is customary for both sexes to clean their antennae by passing the flagellum through the mouthparts and perhaps in this way the active material might be transferred. Antennae were thus removed from females just emerging from the last moult, and which had not had the opportunity to clean their antennae with their mouthparts. These proved positive without contact with salivary secretion, as incidentally, did the antennae of a newly emerged male, and the antennae of a male which had been moistened with saliva from an adult female. Also, surprisingly, the sexual response of the male German Cockroach can be stimulated by the antennae of nymphs of both sexes of the German Cockroach, and by the antennae of adult males and females and full grown nymphs of *B. orientalis*, and to a lesser extent by those of *P. americana*.

These studies by Roth & Willis point to the conclusion that the ability of the male German Cockroach to discriminate between the sexes and the stimulus to sexual behaviour are brought about by contact chemoreception.

Modifications of the terminal abdominal segments
The external genitalia of male and female cockroaches are characterised by the formation of a genital pouch, containing the dorsal anus and the ventral genital opening. In the adult male, ten dorsal tergites and nine ventral sternites are visible externally, but only seven sternites are visible in the female. The reduction in the female comes about during nymphal development by retraction of some of the sclerites into the abdominal segments to form the genital pouch (Figs. 83 and 101). This contains various sclerotised structures, which in the male become extended during copulation and assist in grasping the female, whilst in the female they provide a means for passing eggs into the ootheca and in those species which incubate their eggs internally, for manipulating the ootheca into a brood sac.

External genitalia of the male
The ninth tergite of the male Oriental Cockroach is fused to the tenth, to form the supra-anal plate or epiproct, a median notched extension of the tenth tergite (Fig. 80a, c). The area beneath the supra-anal plate is referred to as the proctiger which bears the cerci. There are two lateral structures, the paraprocts, on either side of the anus, believed to be derived from the 11th sternite. This also forms the sub-genital plate which bears the anal styles on its posterior margin (Fig. 80b, c).

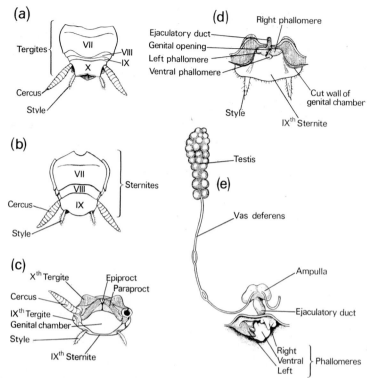

Fig. 80. The terminal abdominal segments of an adult male *Blatta orientalis* and the nymphal development of the external and internal genitalia. (a) Dorsal view of end of abdomen of adult, (b) ventral view, (c) posterior view, (d) genital chamber of young nymph, exposed from above, showing three simple phallomeres around the genital opening, (e) later stages of development showing also the internal genitalia of a nymph (after Snodgrass[259]).

The phallic organs of the male arise as outgrowths of the anterior membranous wall of the genital pouch. They appear as small lobes in the nymph (Figs. 80d and 81b) and become the variously shaped phallomeres of the mature adult. These are partly sclerotised and associated with the opening of the ejaculatory duct, although they are concealed by the ninth sternite.

Cockroaches can be divided into two groups according to the number of phallomeres. A left and right phallomere is present in all cockroaches, but in some there is a third, the ventral phallomere, which is found below the opening of the ejaculatory duct. This condition occurs in the super-family **Blattoidea** (which includes all species of *Periplaneta* and *B. orientalis*: see Table II) and the family Polyphagidae of the **Blaberoidea**. In some species of the family Blattellidae (including *B. germanica*), there is a retractile penis between the left and right phallomere, formed by a posterior continuation of the ejaculatory duct.

One of the most complete descriptions of the external genitalia of the male cockroach has been given for *B. germanica*.[259] The phallomeres, when retracted, are contained in separate pouches; the left phallomere is hooked,

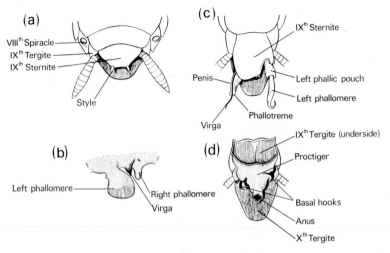

Fig. 81. The external genitalia of male *B. germanica*: (a) end of abdomen of nymph (ventral view) showing the symmetrical IXth sternite, (b) the same with the IXth sternite removed to show the developing phallomeres and virga, (c) end of abdomen of an adult (ventral view) with the left phallomere and penis extended, (d) the same, with the sternites and phallomeres removed to show the basal hooks on each side of the anus (after Snodgrass[259]).

and protrudes during mating from the left side of the asymmetrical ninth sternite (Fig. 81c), whilst the right phallomere is more membranous, and is boat-shaped with a chitinised area along one side. There is also a 'cresentic sclerite' associated with the right phallomere about half way along its length (Fig. 82).

The penis lies between the phallomeres and is a conical membranous lobe, which has a structure called the phallotreme on its ventral surface. This is possibly the equivalent of the ventral phallomere of other species. At the apex of the penis is a free spine, or virga, from which a long slender apodeme runs forwards through the dorsal wall of the endophallus and projects anteriorly with muscles attached. On either side of the penis and arising close to the base of the cerci are two small curved and forked basal hooks, sclerotised at their ends (Fig. 81d).

External genitalia of the female
The female has a large genital pouch to receive the external genitalia of the

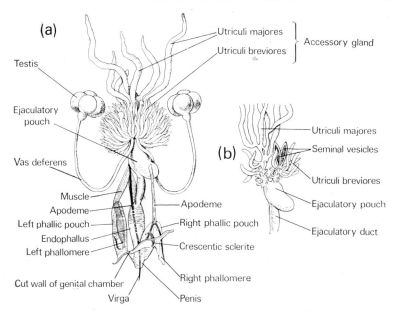

Fig. 82. (a) The internal and external genitalia of an adult male *B. germanica*; (b) most of the utriculi breviores removed to show the seminal vesicles (after Snodgrass[259]).

male, and to hold the egg case, or ootheca, as it is being formed. The sternite of the seventh abdominal segment of the female is expanded posteriorly to form the floor of the pouch, which is roofed over by the sternites of segments eight and nine, and in some species by the sternite of segment ten. These segments are completely telescoped into, and hidden by, the seventh. The pouch is divided into two communicating chambers, the large posterior vestibulum which is to contain the ootheca, and the smaller, anterior genital chamber which receives the ducts from the ovaries and spermathecae (Fig. 83a). In cockroaches of the family Blaberidae, which incubate their oothecae internally, there is a large and highly distensible brood sac at the anterior end of the vestibulum and beneath the genital chamber (Fig. 83b). It is here that the ootheca is retained during gestation (Fig. 83c).

The external genitalia of the female consist of three pairs of small ovipositor valves, various sclerites and the openings of several ducts: these are the common oviduct, the ducts of the spermatheca and spermathecal gland, and the paired ducts of the accessory glands. All are concealed within the female's genital pouch. The posterior and lateral membranes of its floor are expanded into a pair of extensive intersternal folds which grip the ootheca as it is produced. The ovipositor valves are attached to the roof of the vestibulum and these guide the eggs into the ootheca during its formation; they are thought to be responsible for moulding the crenulated edge of the ootheca while still soft. The ovipositor valves take no part in copulation, except to provide an anchorage for the external genitalia of the male.

Mention has already been made of the blaberoid cockroaches in connec-

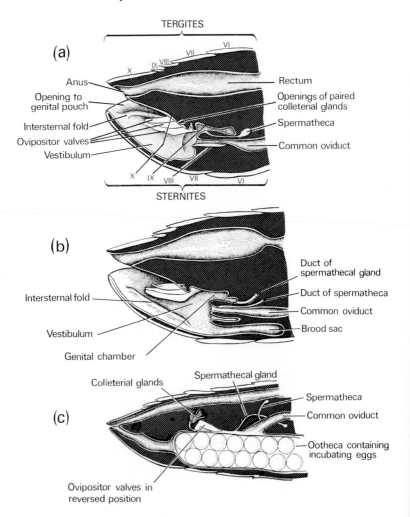

Fig. 83. Sagittal sections of the terminal abdominal segments of female cockroaches, (a) as in the Blattellidae (e.g. *B. germanica*), (b) as in the Blaberidae (e.g. *L. maderae*), (c) as in the Blaberidae with the ootheca being incubated in the brood sac (after McKittrick[39]).

tion with internal incubation. The ovipositor valves of these are relatively unsclerotised and are capable of being reversed in direction, as the ootheca is passed into the brood sac, allowing them to become squeezed between the retracted ootheca and the roof of the genital chamber (Fig. 83c). The intersternal folds of the Blaberidae are also greatly reduced, since these have no great function to perform as in cockroaches which expel and retain the ootheca externally.

Copulatory behaviour

We can now return to the sequence of events which bring the male and female cockroach into copulation. Once the male of the German Cockroach has raised his tegmina and wings and the secretion from his dorsal glands becomes available for the female to feed from, he stands in front of her and depresses his abdomen with the cerci reaching under the female's thorax. The feeding of the female on the dorsal secretion then appears to serve as a stimulus for the male to push his abdomen still further under the female in an attempt to clasp her genitalia (Fig. 79d). For copulation to occur the female must acquiesce; she must remain above the male long enough for connection to be made.

Again from observations on considerable numbers of German Cockroaches, it is clear that some females may be unresponsive to the male at mating, and not in every case can she be induced to feed on the dorsal gland secretion. Likewise males are not always ready to mate; copulation appears to occur more readily in the dark, but males can be stimulated to produce a courting response in both dark and light. With the cerci so well equipped with sensory receptors it seems anomalous that neither the cerci of males or females appear to be involved in normal mating behaviour; this at least is so in the American Cockroach although the male cerci of some species are able to respond to stimuli from the female.[260]

Use of the genitalia in copulation

As the male German Cockroach pushes his abdomen backwards under the female, the left, hooked phallomere becomes fully extended, directed upwards, and inserted into the female's genital chamber. Here it clasps a small sclerite in front of the ovipositor (Fig. 84a). If the male has been successful in grasping the female's genitalia, he moves from beneath her and by twisting his abdomen they assume an end-to-end position (Fig. 79e).

Once this position has been reached it allows the male to obtain a hold on the ovipositor with his forked basal hooks (Fig. 84b). Then the small crescentic sclerite located about half way along the male's right phallomere provides a further firm grip across the female's ovipositor from beneath (Fig. 84c). At this stage the male manufactures a spermatophore, a tiny capsule of sperm, in the pouch of the ejaculatory duct. When this is fully formed, the large endophallus is evaginated and the spermatophore passed from the male to the female and deposited within her genital pouch, close

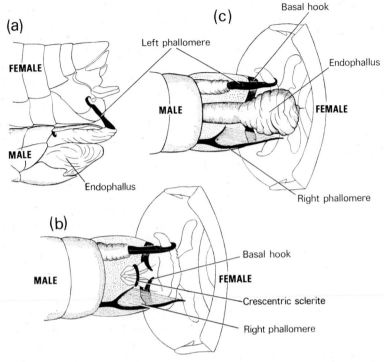

Fig. 84. The part played by the external genitalia of *B. germanica* during copulation (diagrammatic). (a) Side view with female in superior pose. The left phallomere is fully extended and inserted into the female's genital chamber. (b) The end-to-end position in ventral view. The basal hooks hold the ovipositor from both sides and the crescentic sclerite, from the ventral side. The last sternites of both insects and the endophallus have been removed. (c) The endophallus is much evaginated when the spermatophore is fully developed and ready to be pushed out (after Khalifa[225]).

to the spermathecal duct. The structure of the spermatophore is described on p. 194.

The period in copulation

Copulations are of two types: short, of a few seconds, during which no spermatophore is passed, and long, of an hour or more, which results in about 90 per cent of females producing an ootheca of which 85 per cent are fertile.[224] Females which separate from the male after successful copulation are immediately capable of stimulating other males.

Mating in other species

The sequence of mating in German, Oriental and American Cockroaches is essentially similar, but there are one or two differences. The wing-raising response appears to be characteristic of all male cockroaches that have wings, but, as emphasised in the early part of this chapter, the male of the American Cockroach is stimulated into sexual activity by a volatile pheromone and it is not essential for the male, as in *B. germanica*, to make physical contact with the female to initiate the wing-raising response. No dorsal secretion is produced on the abdominal tergites of male Oriental Cockroaches, but the female nevertheless moves her mouthparts actively over the male's dorsum. Males, females and nymphs of the Oriental Cockroach have tergal glands, but these do not appear to be connected with sexual behaviour.

In contrast to the behaviour of *B. germanica*, the male American Cockroach attempts to copulate without the stimulus of the female's mouthparts on his abdomen and the volatile attractant appears to be the only mechanism involved in releasing the responses of the male: he is much more direct in his approach and the female appears to be relatively passive, although Rau[5] noted that only 1 in 20 attempted matings appeared to be successful. All species in which copulation has been observed mate with the female initially above the male, and eventually gain the end-to-end position. Sperm is always passed in a spermatophore.

Males of other species perform different types of body movement. For example, the Madeira Cockroach, as part of his courting behaviour, stands near the female and moves his body up and down; this consists of small vertical jerks of the body, the abdomen moving down as the head and thorax move up.[260] *Blaberus craniifer* raises his body on his legs and makes trembling movements;[261] the wingless male of *Eurycotis floridana* stands close to the female, vibrates his body repeatedly from side to side, and extends his abdomen so revealing the light coloured intersegmental membranes. Species of *Gromphadorhina* produce loud hissing sounds by expelling air through the second abdominal spiracles.

The male of *Nauphoeta cinerea* stridulates during courtship. If the female happens to be receptive mating proceeds quickly, but if she does not respond by palpating on his dorsal tergites, or he fails to grasp her genitalia, he stands about an inch away and produces a series of courting chirps. This noise is produced by striations on the upper surface of the costal veins of the tegmina engaging striations on the posterolateral corners of the pronotum. The tegmina are raised and rotated slightly so that the two surfaces are adjacent and the male begins to tremble. He produces the courting sounds by minute movements of the pronotum over the vein, but only if the female is quiescent; if she moves, he usually turns away from her and raises his tegmina and hindwings.

The sound consists of short 'phrases' of five to ten seconds linked to form sentences lasting for about three minutes. Hartman & Roth[262] compare this noise with the rubbing together of two finely ridged files. These workers have been unable to observe a response by the female to this stridulation but suggest that it may influence her behaviour only if she is exposed to it at a brief critical time as she approaches receptivity.[113] The female also has the same stridulatory mechanism, but appears to use it only 'in protest' when captured.

Factors affecting receptivity of the female

Little is known from pest species of cockroaches of the factors which affect the receptivity of the female for the male. Females of many species mate again very soon after successful copulation but this contrasts markedly with the behaviour displayed, for example, by *Nauphoeta cinerea*. Virgin females of this species, once mated, become unreceptive and do not mate again before the first ootheca is produced. There is evidence to suggest that the presence of the spermatophore within the female's genital pouch in- hibits the female's sexual feeding response on the male's dorsal ter- gites.[263,264] *Nauphoeta cinerea* is one of the species which incubates its oothecae internally within a brood sac (p. 216); the female remains un- receptive to the male during the period of gestation, when the mechanical presence of the ootheca in the brood sac is also believed to be responsible for inhibiting receptivity.

Receptivity of female *Nauphoeta* for the male can be correlated with the time of maturation of her oocytes. As will be seen later, (p. 202), maturation of the egg cells in cockroaches involves the deposition of yolk which is dependent upon the activity of the corpora allata. Nevertheless, removal of the corpus allatum from females still leaves them capable of mating.[265] Roth[266] concludes that 'receptivity is determined by some event, presumably in the brain, which occurs at the same time as the onset of activity of the corpora allata'.

Another factor which is known to influence the reaction of female cock- roaches to males is the availability of food. Female *Nauphoeta* for example, become receptive and mate usually within a few days of becoming adult and this occurs irrespective of food availability. This is not so, however, with females of the Madeira Cockroach (*L. maderae*); when these have been without food since becoming adult, only about half will mate, indi- cating that their receptivity is greatly reduced. Englemann[267] has shown that mating of female *Leucophaea* is partly controlled by the corpora allata and suggests that the hormone secreted by this gland may act in the female by lowering the threshold for the perception of male odour.

The mechanisms which control the formation of sex attractants of male cockroaches are unknown. The male Lobster Cockroach produces a highly active sex attractant (seducin) which acts from a short distance, and arrests the receptive female sufficiently long, usually about six seconds, for the male to make connection with his external genitalia. The sexual activity of male cockroaches is not cyclical, as in females, and repeated mating does not interfere with production of the male's pheromone.[252]

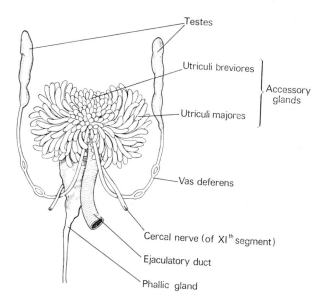

Fig. 85. Internal genitalia of adult male *B. orientalis*, dorsal view (after Snodgrass[259]).

Internal reproductive organs of the male

These consist of a pair of testes, genital ducts (vasa deferentia), accessory glands (often called the 'mushroom' gland), seminal vesicles and phallic gland. The paired testes vary in appearance in different species. Those of *B. orientalis* become fully mature in the final nymph, when each consists of a mass of rounded sacs around a central duct, the vas deferens (Fig. 80). They develop continuously throughout nymphal development and reach their maximum size in the sixth instar, becoming smaller in the adult with the collapse of the follicle cells (Fig. 85). Qadri,[64] suggests that this deterioration is related to the large number of seminal vesicles in the Oriental Cockroach which provide storage for the mature sperm. Each testis of the German Cockroach consists of four round sacs arranged radially around the end of the vas deferens (Fig. 82).

The paired vasa deferentia, one from each testis, run posteriorly beneath the cercal nerves and then change course to enter the ejaculatory duct. Here arise the ducts of the accessory glands which in some cockroaches may be involved in excretion (Chapter 6). The vasa deferentia of nymphs of Oriental Cockroaches terminate in a pair of small ampullae associated with the ejaculatory duct and it is these which give rise to the accessory glands of the adult.

These glands of the German Cockroach consist of a mass of tubules arranged in three groups (Fig. 82): firstly, the *utriculi majores*, long slender

N

tubes arising from the anterior end, which sometimes extend well into the anterior segments of the abdomen; secondly, the *utriculi breviores* (1 mm long) which make up the major portion of the gland, and thirdly, a central group (1·3 mm long), hiding the seminal vesicles which arise from the surface of the ejaculatory duct. In *B. germanica* the seminal vesicles consist of two small oval sacs at the anterior end of the ejaculatory duct (Fig. 82), whereas in *Blatta* and *Periplaneta* they consist of two groups of numerous small sacs on the ventral surface of the duct.

The ejaculatory duct is a muscular tube which opens at the base of the three phallomeres in *Periplaneta* and *Blatta*, or into the endophallus of *Blattella*. In the German Cockroach, the anterior part of the ejaculatory duct is enlarged into a pouch (the ejaculatory pouch) situated at the base of the accessory gland.

Finally, there is a large gland (the phallic gland) of unknown function which lies beneath the accessory glands and ejaculatory duct. This gland varies in form in different species: in *Blatta* it is an elongate sac which tapers posteriorly and ends in a duct on the left phallomere; in *Periplaneta* it is subdivided into several lobes and in *Blattella* it consists of a mass of coiled tubules.

Sperm formation

Amerson & Hays[268] have made a study of spermatogenesis in the German Cockroach, from hatching of the first stage nymph through the nymphal instars to maturity of the adult. The testes of first instars are embedded in a matrix of fat cells and are already spherical and divided into compartments. In the second instar, the testes contain numerous spermatogonia (primordial germ cells), and in the third, the testes increase in size. By the fourth instar (19 days at 27°C), the spermatogonia have undergone mitotic division and by 23 days reduction division (meiosis) has begun: the testes then contain primary and secondary spermatocytes, spermatids, nurse cells, and mature sperm. In the last nymphal stage, mature sperm are abundant and the testes are divided into a zone in which sperm are forming and maturing and another containing fully mature sperm. The testes of the adult contain an abundance of mature sperm, but spermatogonial cells also present in some areas of the testes are greatly reduced.

Formation and structure of the spermatophore

The formation and structure of the spermatophore has been described for *B. orientalis*,[269] and *P. americana*,[64,270] whilst the following description is that for the German Cockroach.[225]

During copulation secretions from the male accessory glands are passed into the ejaculatory pouch. A 'milky substance' from the *utriculi majores* is secreted first, which is then slowly surrounded by secretion from the *utriculi breviores* and the third group of tubules. Sperm flows from each of the two seminal vesicles into the middle milky layer. Each of the two sperm masses forms a separate sac and when the spermatophore is complete, the pouch is fully extended. The two sperm sacs lie flattened, close to each other within the spermatophore, each with its own duct to the outside (Fig. 86a). When finally formed the spermatophore is tough, oval and flattened, milky in appearance and about 2 mm long and 1 mm wide.

The spermatophore of the German Cockroach differs in many details from that of the American Cockroach as described by Gupta.[270] In the latter it is pear-shaped with only one opening for the exit of sperm and is said to be composed of three layers containing the sperm floating in a thin, clear fluid (Fig. 86b). The spermatophore eventually occupies half the length of the ejaculatory duct and is said to take six days to form. This period is now known to be erroneous and present evidence shows that the spermatophore of both the German and American species is formed only during the act of copulation, which explains why very short matings are always infertile.

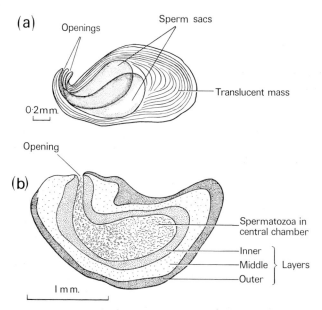

Fig. 86. Spermatophore of (a) *B. germanica* (after Khalifa[225]) and (b) *P. americana* (after Gupta[270]).

Insemination

The spermatophore descends the ejaculatory duct to be introduced into the genital pouch of the female. At the same time a considerable amount of secretion, in the form of urates, is poured out onto the spermatophore of the German Cockroach and onto the sclerites within the female genital pouch. When ejected, the spermatophore is elongate and the end bearing the two openings of the sperm sacs emerges first. During copulation, however, the endophallus of the male secures the spermatophore onto the sclerites within the female's genital pouch flattening the capsule in the process.

Each female can be inseminated with a number of spermatophores during adult life: sperm remain in the capsule for some hours and observations show that if a spermatophore is removed from the female's genital pouch soon after mating and placed in saline, sperm flow out from the tip and move actively in the solution. Inside the genital pouch the tip of the spermatophore, which bears the openings of the sperm sac, lies close to the paired openings of the spermathecae. Khalifa[225] suggests that the two large spermathecal glands of the female German Cockroach are responsible for liberating a substance which activates the sperm to leave the spermatophore. If a spermatophore is removed from the female some 25 minutes after copulation a thin thread of spermatozoa, hair-like in appearance, may extend from the female's spermathecal opening.[224]

Spermatozoa held in the spermatheca can be stored by females for long periods of time. One female American Cockroach observed by Griffiths & Tauber[76] which was associated with males from the final moult to the formation of the first ootheca (i.e. about 17 days), produced fertile eggs for just short of a year; 13–15 nymphs per egg case hatched during the first eight months and six to seven during the remaining four months. This provides clear evidence of the highly favourable conditions for sperm storage in the spermatheca of the female and highlights the problem, all too familiar with pest species of cockroach, of the apparent ease with which one fertilised female can establish a new infestation.

The spermatophore remains in place in the genital pouch of the female German Cockroach for about 12 hours and then shrinks. Twenty-four hours after successful mating the dried, shrunken and empty spermatophore is released by the female. In other species, the spermatophore may be retained by the female for two to three days (*Blatta orientalis*[269]), or for as long as five days (*Blaberus craniifer*[261]). Very often after mating, a white substance, urates from the *utriculi majores* of the accessory gland (see p.193), adheres to the terminal segments of the male German Cockroach, especially if he has been isolated from females for more than a week. This substance soon dries and flakes off as the male cleans itself with its hind legs.

The task for which the male was attracted to the female is now over. Following copulation the production of fertile eggs (described in the next chapter) and the protection of those eggs against parasites, predators and loss of water is the responsibility of the female. Thus far we have seen that the coming together of males and females for copulation is anything but a haphazard process. There is a rationalised sequence of events through which the sexes must pass if the two are to mate. It is clear from the variation in external genitalia of different species of cockroach, notably those of the male, that successful copulation between the male of one species and a female of another is prevented. The possibility of cross fertilisation between species is also prevented by differences in the number of chromosomes in the germ cells. The diploid number determined during spermogenesis is 24 in *B. germanica*, 28 in *P. australasiae*, 34 in *P. americana* and 48 in *B. orientalis*.[42] There seems no doubt that given time, we shall find that even the attractant compounds which play a major role in bringing the sexes together are also peculiar, chemically, to individual species.

9

THE FACTORS INVOLVED IN OOTHECA PRODUCTION

Internal reproductive organs of the female: the ovary; oogenesis—Association of bacteroids with the ovary; appearance of bacteroids; entry into oocytes
Control of oocyte development: gonadotrophic hormone, moulting and oocyte
maturation; inhibition of the hormone in cockroaches which carry the ootheca; removal
of the corpora allata and implantation; inhibition of the corpora allata by the brain;
artificial oothecae and severance of the nerve cord; severance of the nerve cord at
different positions—Oocyte maturation and mating; oocyte maturation and enzyme
activity in the gut; oocyte maturation and food—Colleterial glands and formation
of the ootheca; ovulation—Fertilisation and parthenogenesis
Types of oviposition: oviparity; false ovoviviparity; false viviparity—Deposition of
oothecae; structural features of the ootheca.

Oviposition in cockroaches is characterised by the formation of an ootheca.
To those familiar only with the pest species of cockroach, *B. germanica*,
B. orientalis and species of *Periplaneta*, it may seem anomalous that the
female German Cockroach should carry its ootheca, held by the end of the
abdomen until, or shortly before, the nymphs hatch, whilst others deposit
the ootheca soon after formation. From this has come the suggestion that
the German Cockroach exercises a protective, or 'parental' care over its
eggs, which is lacking in other species. If parental care is interpreted to
mean that the eggs of *B. germanica* are prevented from becoming desiccated, and that retention by the female is necessary for her to supply water
for the development of the embryos, this understanding is correct. It has,
of course, come about through evolution as a means to survival.

The carrying of the egg case by one species and not by others is better
understood by studying oviposition in cockroaches as a group. Then it
will be seen that there are not two types of ovipositional behaviour but a
gradation of many stages, from the dropping of the egg case soon after
it is formed, to its retention internally, the eggs hatching within the female's
body and the extrusion of live nymphs.

This chapter is concerned with the events which take place after copulation. Production of young by the female involves five processes: (1) the
formation of oocytes in the ovary and the control of egg maturation,
(2) ovulation, i.e. the release of eggs into the genital pouch and their
fertilisation by sperm released from the spermatheca, and (3) oviposition,
i.e. the enclosure of the eggs in an ootheca and its extrusion. In those
species of cockroach which produce live young there are two further

processes: (4) the retraction of the ootheca into the genital pouch and its incubation in a brood sac (gestation) and (5) the release of young live nymphs from the female (or parturition). Before examining each of these aspects, it will first be necessary to describe the internal reproductive organs of the female. We can then proceed to examine the differences between species in their ovipositional behaviour.

Internal reproductive organs of the female

These consist of paired ovaries, oviducts, colleterial (accessory) glands, and spermathecae, although in some species there is only one spermatheca. Each ovary consists of a number of ovarioles connected by short pedicels to the oviducts, the junction of these pedicels being referred to as the calyx. The paired oviducts unite to form a common oviduct which opens into the genital chamber close to the opening of the spermatheca, where, in the American Cockroach, there is also an opening to a spermathecal gland. The paired colleterial glands open by separate ducts into the vestibulum of the genital pouch at the base of the ovipositor valves (Fig. 83, p. 188).

The ovary

The ovaries of the cockroach are surrounded by fat body and lie on either side of the alimentary canal occupying all but the last two or three segments of the abdomen.

In the American Cockroach, each ovary is composed of eight ovarioles (Fig. 45) each consisting of an anterior germarium, containing cells at an early stage of oocyte formation (or differentiation) and a posterior vitellarium containing oocytes in various stages of growth (maturation). The anterior end of each ovariole is extended to form a terminal filament which unites with others at a common point of anchorage on the body wall (Fig. 87). The ovarioles are of the paniostic type in which nutritive, or nurse cells, are wanting. Each ovariole is little more than an elongate tube within which developing eggs are arranged one behind the other, the youngest lying in the tapering anterior end and the oldest situated at the base. The release of a mature egg into the oviduct (ovulation) is prevented by an epithelial plug.

In most cockroaches one mature egg is present at the base of each ovariole and the remaining oocytes are in various stages of growth. Exceptions are found in *Cryptocercus punctulatus*, in which each ovariole may contain three or four oocytes as large as those deposited in the ootheca, and in *S. supellectilium* in which the basal oocyte is not well-developed at the time of oviposition.[271]

Each ovariole is enclosed in a tough non-cellular membrane, the tunica propria, covered by a thin layer of connective tissue, the peritoneal coat. The germarium contains oogonia, the primordial germ cells, which undergo division to form the primary and secondary oocytes. The vitellarium forms the major portion of the ovariole and its wall closely surrounds each developing egg, enclosing it in an egg chamber. As the egg matures it becomes surrounded by a layer of follicular cells which secrete materials for the formation of yolk and the 'egg shell' or chorion.

Oogenesis

The development of oocytes has been studied throughout the nymphal development of the German Cockroach by Amerson & Hays.[268] The ovarioles of the first stage nymph are distinct and embedded in fat cells; the primordial germ cells are present but no divisions occur during the first four nymphal stages. At the fourth instar, the ovarioles increase in size, relative to the other abdominal organs, but not until the fifth nymphal stage are primary and secondary oocytes developed. Both mitotic and meiotic divisions then occur but the gametes are still immature. In their description of oogenesis, Amerson & Hays mention the presence of 'nurse cells' in the last stage nymph, but this presumably refers to the follicle cells which ultimately form the follicular epithelium.

Mature eggs are present in the adult soon after the final moult. In the American Cockroach the oocyte at the base of each ovariole measures 0·7 mm before the final moult, increases to 2 mm after the moult and reaches its full size, 3 mm, eight days after copulation.[272]

Association of bacteroids with the ovary

It is convenient here to digress for a moment from the fate of the developing eggs to consider the transmission of bacteroids from parent to offspring. Bacteroids in the cockroach have been mentioned in connection with the fat body (p. 155) occurring as bacteria-like bodies in the mycetocytes (Fig. 68). Cockroaches were among the first insects found to harbour these organisms,[273] and they are now known to occur in all individuals of a host species. The physiology of these bodies is not precisely known: their relationship with the insect has been described as one of symbiosis, in that they may provide additional food factors such as vitamins, of commensalism ('feeding at the same table'), the one organism not benefiting from the other, or of parasitism, since in some species (see p. 202) the bacteroids may destroy some of the developing egg cells. Bacteroids are transmitted from parent to offspring *via* the egg and their entry into the developing oocytes of *P. americana* has been studied by Gier.[272]

Appearance of bacteroids

Under the microscope the bacteroids of the American Cockroach appear as slightly curved rods, about one micron in diameter, and $1·5$ to $6·5\mu$ long. They have rounded or slightly pointed ends and appear either solid or with alternate dark and light bands (Fig. 87a), differing in shape and size in different species of cockroach. They increase by transverse division, the constriction occurring between two dark bands, thus dividing the bacteroid sometimes into equal, but often into unequal parts. In species of *Parco-blatta*, the divided parts of the bacteroid may remain attached forming a chain; they are non-motile and in living tissue can readily be seen under the microscope without the aid of stains.

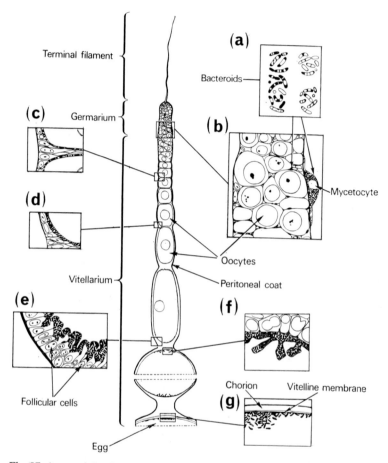

Fig. 87. An ovariole of *P. americana* showing the introduction of bacteroids into the egg during growth of the oocyte. For explanation of a-g, see text.

Entry into oocytes

The covering of connective tissue around both the testes and ovaries of cockroaches contains mycetocytes, but bacteroids are found only within the gonads of the female (Fig. 87b). It is not clear from the description given by Gier whether the bacteroids penetrate the wall of the ovariole, or whether they find their way into the mass of ovarian cells and become incorporated into the primitive germ cells during early development of the ovary. In the mature female, bacteroids occur both in the mycetocytes outside the ovary, and in the germarium of the ovariole, where they become tightly pressed between the oocytes and the follicular epithelium forming a layer around each oocyte (Fig. 87c). The increase in number to form a compact layer one bacteroid thick (Fig. 87d), and still increasing in number, eventually form an irregular pallisade projecting into the cytoplasm of the oocyte (Fig. 87e). During the final stages of oocyte maturation the layer of bacteroids becomes broken into small clumps, eventually to form a disc-shaped mass at each pole of the egg (Fig. 87f).

Throughout development of the oocyte, the bacteroids are located between the oocyte membrane and the follicle cells and are never found within the follicle cells themselves. Shortly before the egg is oviposited and soon after the first appearance of the chorion, the oocyte membrane disappears and a new membrane (the vitelline membrane) forms between the bacteroids and the chorion (Fig. 87g); the bacteroids, formerly limited to definite ridges, then disperse throughout the cytoplasm between the vitelline membrane and the yolk so that 36 hours after oviposition there is a compact mass of bacteroids at each pole and numerous isolated clumps around the periphery of each egg.

It is of interest that in *Cryptocercus punctulatus*, about 10 per cent of the young oocytes are destroyed by the bacteroids;[272] they penetrate the oocyte membrane at an early stage of development and increase within the yolk until the whole oocyte becomes a mass of bacteroids. A similar condition is occasionally found in *Blatta orientalis* and rarely in *P. americana*. We will return to the fate of the bacteroids within the egg when we consider embryological development (Chapter 10).

Control of oocyte development

Our knowledge of the factors responsible for the maturation of eggs in insects dates back to 1936 when Wigglesworth first showed, in the bug, *Rhodnius*, that deposition of yolk in the oocytes is regulated by a hormone produced by the corpora allata. This substance is now known as the gonadotrophic hormone and since this original discovery, extensive studies on its production in insects have been carried out.

A great deal has been written about the control of egg production in cockroaches, including many controversial views on the precise mechanisms involved. It will be sufficient in the next few pages to summarise the principal findings and provide the reader with adequate references to the literature.

Gonadotrophic hormone, moulting and oocyte maturation

In all cockroaches studied, the development of the oocytes is under the control of the gonadotrophic hormone, and in 1955 Lüscher & Engelmann[274] showed that the periodic change in activity of the corpus allatum of the Madeira Cockroach parallels oocyte maturation. Since then, these observations have been confirmed in this and in many other species.[212,275,276] Elucidation of the mechanisms involved has required the measurement of the basal oocytes in the ovarioles and the removal and implantation of the corpora allata.

In the American Cockroach growth of the oocytes during nymphal development is continuous but slow, and this same rate of growth continues during the first five days of adult life. Between the sixth and twelfth days, the oocytes grow rapidly and by the end of this period reach their maximum size (Fig. 88). At the peak of reproductive performance the

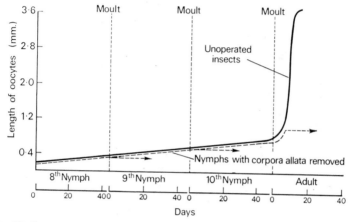

Fig. 88. Growth of oocytes in *P. americana*; normal (unoperated) insects, and various nymphal stages from which the corpora allata have been removed (after Girardie[277]).

female produces about eight oothecae per month and because this cockroach drops the ootheca soon after it is formed there appears at this stage, in the normal insect, to be very little interruption of oocyte development.

Experiments in which the corpora allata have been removed from the last nymphal stage show that this endocrine gland has no effect on the growth of oocytes before the final moult, or during the first five days of adult life. After the sixth day, however, growth of the oocytes is inhibited, coinciding with the time at which yolk is normally deposited in the oocyte.[277] Removal of the corpora allata from earlier nymphs (long before the deposition of yolk) allows the oocytes to grow until the next moult and for a few days after, but then again their growth is stopped. It would appear therefore that the ovaries are insensitive to the gonadotrophic hormone until after a moult has occurred, and that inhibition of oocyte growth can occur in *P. americana* well before yolk is normally deposited.

Inhibition of the hormone in cockroaches which carry the ootheca

The German Cockroach carries the ootheca until, or almost until the young hatch, this usually taking about 30 days. Another ten days is then required before the next ootheca is fully formed. The maturation of eggs and the formation of the next ootheca are therefore governed by the hatching of the previous ootheca.

Whilst the egg case is being carried, the basal oocytes in the ovary increase only slightly in size from 0·3 to 0·5 mm and the secretory activity of the colleterial glands is inhibited. During the following 10 days while the next ootheca is being formed, the oocytes increase rapidly to 2·6 mm (Fig. 89a). If an egg case is removed from a female before it is due to

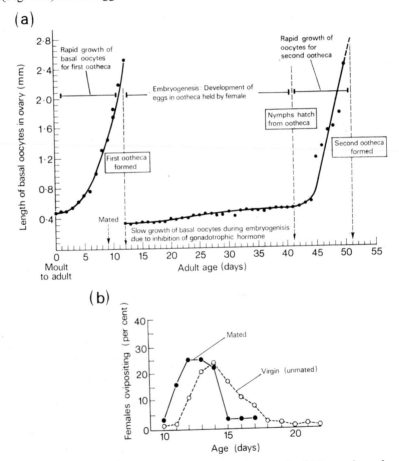

Fig. 89. Oocyte growth and ootheca formation in *B. germanica*: (a) the ovarian cycle in females mated when 9 days old, (b) the effect of mating on time of formation of the first ootheca (females mated when 8–14 days old) (after Roth & Stay[271]).

hatch, the production of oocytes is accelerated,[278] and a new ootheca is produced much earlier than if the original ootheca had been left attached. The older the ootheca at the time of removal, the larger the oocytes in the ovary and the shorter the time required for them to mature for the next ootheca.[271] While an ootheca remains attached to the abdomen it inhibits the release of the gonadotrophic hormone; when the ootheca hatches, or is experimentally removed, oocyte development is quickly reinstated through the activity of the corpora allata.

Removal of the corpora allata and implantation
Removal of the corpora allata inhibits oocyte development in mated females. Unmated females of *B. germanica* are as capable of producing oothecae (Fig. 89b), but the infertile egg case is usually retained for a little longer.[271] If these are operated upon for removal of the corpora allata they too are prevented from maturing their eggs, and the colleterial glands fail to secrete. If corpora allata are then implanted into these insects the oocytes mature and an ootheca is produced in the period which normally elapses between successive oothecae. Dissection of the insect shows that

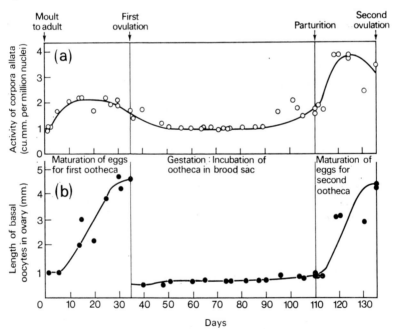

Fig. 90. Correlation between (a) activity of the corpora allata and (b) the growth of basal oocytes in the ovary following moulting to adult of *Leucophaea maderae*. Ovulation refers to the release of eggs from the oviducts at formation of the ootheca. Parturition refers to the hatching of the ootheca and the release of live nymphs (after Engelmann[256]).

any oocytes which are mature before removal of the corpora allata are resorbed, but any secretion present in the colleterial glands is maintained.

Inhibition of the corpora allata by the brain

Many species of cockroach incubate their oothecae in a brood sac. During 'gestation' no yolk is deposited in the oocytes, but after the nymphs hatch, the ovaries again become active and yolk is deposited.

Lüscher & Engelmann[274] and Engelmann[212] suggest that eggs in the brood sac of *L. maderae* release a substance which causes the brain to inhibit secretion of the gonadotrophic hormone by the corpora allata (Fig. 90). If ova are implanted into the body cavity of the cockroach, the corpora allata are inhibited almost as effectively as when the eggs are undergoing embryological development in the genital pouch.

Engelmann[212] concludes that during 'pregnancy' the corpora allata are inhibited through the protocerebrum of the brain and *via* the *nervi corporis allati*. 'The corpora allata must be properly innervated by the brain to ensure their cyclic activity (with the brood sac) at the "right time".' Severence of the *nervi corporis allati* results in sustained activity of the corpora allata, causing several successive batches of eggs to mature.[279] Engelmann also concludes that the nerve connection between the suboesophageal ganglion and the corpora allata must remain intact for activation of the endocrine gland, this nerve apparently carrying stimulatory impulses (Fig. 91).

Artificial oothecae and severance of the nerve cord

The presence of an ootheca attached to the abdomen of a female German Cockroach inhibits the development of eggs in the ovary and so too does the replacement of a real ootheca by a glass bead, or an empty case filled with wax. Under these circumstances oocytes develop only after the nerve cord has been cut in the anterior region of the abdomen. The same applies following severance of the nerve cord of a female carrying a normal ootheca; under these circumstances a German Cockroach may produce a succession of new oothecae at very short intervals. A third ootheca can be formed while the previous two are still being carried. The colleterial glands are also continuously stimulated to produce the excess of secretion required for rapid ootheca formation. In all species in which the ventral nerve cord has been cut during 'pregnancy' the corpora allata have been activated, followed by egg maturation.

Roth & Stay[280] conclude that prevention of oocyte development in the German Cockroach whilst an ootheca is being carried, is due to nervous stimuli resulting from pressure of the ootheca on the genital pouch. They suggest the existence of 'stretch receptors', which respond to the increasing size of the ootheca as it absorbs water from the female. When the nerve cord is cut, these impulses are prevented from reaching the brain and the corpora allata remain active.

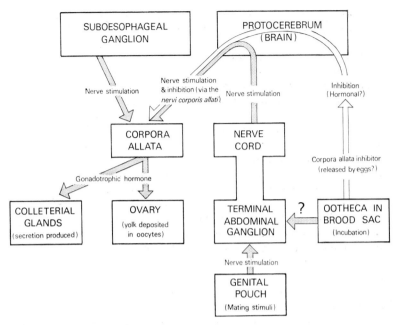

Fig. 91. Diagram of the control of oocyte development in the Madeira Cockroach (*L. maderae*) as postulated by Engelmann[212,275]. There may be nervous or hormonal connection between the brood sac and the terminal abdominal ganglion leading to inhibition of the corpora allata *via* the brain.

Similar conclusions arise from studies on cockroaches which incubate their oothecae internally. 'Pregnancy' in the Surinam Cockroach inhibits oocyte development; the normal period of 'gestation' is eight weeks (at 25°C) during which the oocytes grow only slightly from 0·6 to 0·8 mm. Two weeks after the nymphs hatch a new ootheca is produced when the oocytes measure 3·2 mm. Accordingly there is usually a period of about ten weeks between the formation of successive oothecae. If the ootheca is removed from the brood sac within a week of its formation, the period before formation of the next ootheca is reduced from ten to four weeks. A wax ootheca, substituted in the brood sac for a real one inhibits oocyte development, but females in which the nerve cord is cut within four days of forming a normal ootheca have well-developed oocytes (2·7 mm long) and full colleterial glands about 30 days after the operation. Whether a wax ootheca, or a real one, is present in the brood sac, oocytes develop only after severance of the nerve cord and there is no indication that any substance is released by the eggs or the ootheca which act *via* the brain to inhibit secretion of the corpora allata as reported for *L. maderae*.[280]

Severance of the nerve cord at different positions

Doubt has been thrown on the view that inhibition of the corpora allata is brought about by eggs in the brood sac activating 'stretch receptors', causing impulses to be transmitted by the ventral nerve cord to the brain. Engelmann[281] argues that if the ventral nerve cord is responsible for transmitting these impulses, then severance of the nerves of segments seven to nine, which originate from near the brood sac, should also activate the corpora allata during 'pregnancy'. In fact, they do not.

To obtain detailed information on the mechanism involved, Engelmann cut the ventral nerve cord at different levels: severance between the second and third abdominal ganglia resulted in rapid egg maturation in 88 per cent of females, but when severed between the fifth and sixth ganglia maturation occurred in only 33 per cent. The more posteriorly the nerve cord was cut the lower was the percentage of cockroaches with fully developed eggs.

There is as yet no morphological proof of the existence of the 'stretch receptors' postulated by Roth & Stay.[271,280] Inhibition of oocyte development is thus considered by Engelmann,[281] to be caused most probably by an agent, released by the egg case or brood sac, to which neurones in the nerve cord are sensitive. These may be located in the terminal abdominal ganglion. It seems probable that both nervous and chemical inhibition are involved, the contribution of the two factors varying in different species.

Oocyte maturation and mating

Mildly active corpora allata stimulate female *Leucophaea* to accept a courting male, but in *Diploptera* mating occurs without the intervention of the corpora allata. In both species, the stimuli provided by mating, (presumably the presence of a spermatophore), when received by the brain, counteract its inhibitory influence over the corpora allata; the glands are then free from the restraining influence of the brain and release the gonadotrophic hormone which induces maturation of the eggs and activates the accessory glands.

It is essential for female *Diploptera* which have not previously borne young to be mated before the normal rate of egg maturation occurs,[279] but after parturition oocytes mature without the further stimulus of copulation.[256] In *Periplaneta* also, (Table XIX), mating accelerates egg maturation.[73,282] In *Pycnoscelus*, however, mating of the parthenogenetic strain is unnecessary for egg maturation. Between these two extremes, of *Diploptera* and *Pycnoscelus*, other species of cockroach show varying degrees of dependence on the stimulus of mating to overcome inhibition, and to stimulate secretion of the corpora allata.[271]

Oocyte maturation and enzyme activity in the gut

The synthesis of proteins in the ovaries of the mature female is directed principally towards the maturation of eggs. With the demand for yolk, the enzymes responsible for supplying materials for the synthesis of protein show much greater activity. There is evidence from studies on locusts that a hormone, produced by the neurosecretory cells of the brain, is released into the blood shortly before the ovaries begin to develop; this continues until yolk is deposited in the oocytes.[283] Also, the concentration of protein in the blood of the locust is correlated exactly with the release of this hormone.[284]

TABLE XIX

EFFECTS OF THE PRESENCE OF MALES ON THE PRODUCTION OF
OOTHECAE BY FEMALE *P. AMERICANA*
(From Griffiths & Tauber[73])

Males present	*Egg capsules per female*	*Days between ootheca formation*
Throughout female's life:	20·1	7·7
During first 4 weeks of female's life:	26·0	8·0
Between final moult of female and formation of first ootheca:	16·7	13·4
With virgin females only in latter part of life:	4·4*	27·3*
Absent from virgin females throughout life:	9·7	24·7

* Data for period before introduction of males.

The enzyme, trypsin, is of primary importance for the breakdown of ingested protein. Rao & Fisk[285] have shown that the concentration of trypsin in the mid-gut of *Nauphoeta* increases simultaneously with the development of the ovary, but is markedly reduced following ovulation, when the basal eggs have been released for inclusion into an ootheca (Fig. 92). In unmated females trypsin activity also increases with the development of the oocytes but is maintained at a high level for a further six weeks: Rao & Fisk suggest that in unmated females secretion of the neuro-hormone controlling trypsin activity may not cease so abruptly as in fertilised cockroaches, but maintains a high level of trypsin activity while the unfertilised eggs degenerate.

There is at present some evidence to suggest an inter-relationship between the five factors, fertilisation, active neurosecretion, oocyte development, high trypsin activity in the gut and high protein levels in the blood, but proof of this in cockroaches is not so far available.

Oocyte maturation and food

An ample diet, high in protein, is required for maximum oocyte development and reproductive performance of most insects, and in Chapter 10 an account is given of the effects of diet on the growth of the three common

o

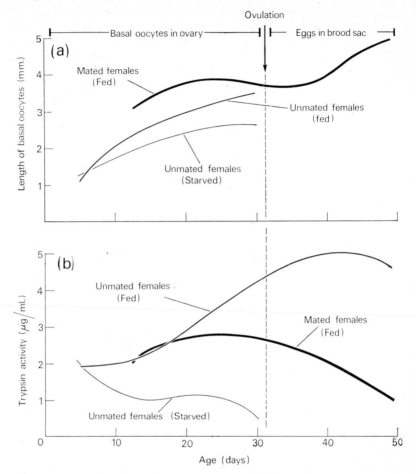

Fig. 92. Relationship between (a) rate of growth of basal oocytes in the ovary and (b) activity of trypsin in the mid-gut, in mated and unmated females of *Nauphoeta cinerea* and the effects of food (after Rao & Fisk[285]). The slight reduction in length of oocytes in mated females which occurs at ovulation is associated with an increase in their width.

pest cockroaches. Detailed studies on food availability in relation to the activity of the corpora allata and oocyte growth, have been made principally on cockroaches which incubate their eggs internally. Roth & Stay[271] have arranged cockroaches in a series, from those demonstrating complete dependence upon food for oocyte development (*Blattella germanica*, *B. vaga*, and *Leucophaea*) to those which show complete independence (*Pycnoscelus surinamensis* and *Diploptera*).

A good example of dependence on food is demonstrated by *L. maderae*: if an egg case is removed from the brood sac of a well-fed female the corpora allata soon become active with the result that the basal oocyte in each ovariole quickly matures. If the female is starving, the corpora allata remain inactive or become only feebly active.[212]

In certain species, notably *Nauphoeta cinerea* and *L. maderae*, there appears, according to Roth,[264] 'to be a synergistic action of nutrition and mating stimuli in controlling the rate of oocyte development, since both stimuli are usually required for activating the corpora allata to enable oocytes to mature at the maximum rate'.

Colleterial glands and formation of the ootheca

The ootheca of cockroaches varies in shape, size, texture, colour, permeability to water and completeness of formation in different species. The material of the ootheca is secreted by the female's paired colleterial glands, which in the Oriental Cockroach consist of a large number of branching tubules which open into a common duct. The ducts from the two glands remain separate and open close together into the genital pouch. The tubules of the left gland are much longer than those of the right and completely surround it.

The glands of different species of cockroach vary in size at different periods of their secretory cycle; in species which incubate their eggs internally, or carry them in an attached ootheca, the colleterial glands are inactive and small while the ootheca is being carried. They become active again during maturation of the next batch of basal oocytes.[286]

The composition of the secretions of the two glands and the way in which they react to produce a hard rigid structure has been determined by Pryor for the Oriental Cockroach.[287-289] The milky white secretion of the left gland is composed of a water soluble protein and an oxidising enzyme. It also contains calcium oxalate, probably present as an excretory product, crystals of which become embedded in the wall of the ootheca. The clear watery secretion of the right gland has very little protein but contains an ortho-dihydroxy phenol (protocatechuic acid), secreted initially as a β-glucoside (Brunet & Kent[290]). It should be mentioned that these latter workers are not entirely in agreement with Pryor on which of the two glands secretes the polyphenol.

The ootheca is formed from the interaction of these two secretions; according to Pryor, the phenol of the right gland is oxidised to form a quinone which acts as a tanning agent. This then combines and reacts with the protein of the left gland to form a rigid structure, very resistant to chemical reagents and enzymes. The protein of the mature ootheca is a scleroprotein (as is found in cuticle) for which Pryor[287] has proposed the name 'sclerotin'. The wall of the ootheca resembles cuticle in appearance, but is completely lacking in chitin.[291]

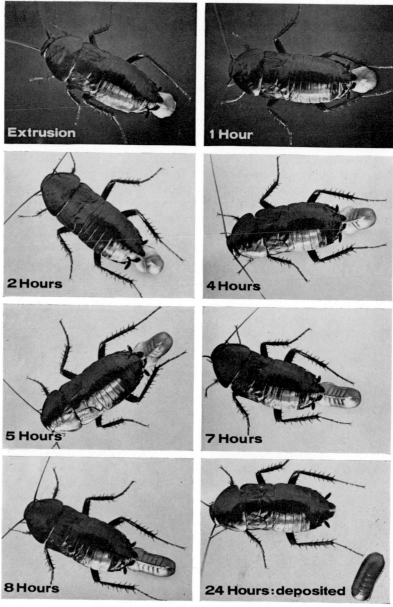

Fig. 93. Formation of an ootheca by *Blatta orientalis*. (Courtesy: Drs. Roth & Willis, U.S. Army Natick Laboratories).

The production of an ootheca by the Oriental Cockroach takes about 24 hours during which more and more secretion is laid down in the genital pouch until the ootheca is complete. In this species the ootheca remains white for three to four hours as it is extruded, and gradually changes through pink to chestnut (Fig. 93). After it is dropped, the ootheca continues to darken and becomes almost black in three weeks. At the same time it becomes progressively harder and more brittle.

In cockroaches which deposit the egg case, or retain it attached to the abdomen outside the body, the ootheca is fully formed and completely envelops the eggs (Fig. 37, p. 100). In species which incubate the ootheca internally it may be incomplete, covering only half the eggs, as in *Diploptera punctata*.[292] In these species too, the wall of the ootheca is relatively thin, membranous and quite often pale in colour. Sometimes the egg mass of the American Cockroach may be deposited without an ootheca,[42] presumably because of a deficiency of secretion from the colleterial glands. The egg case of different species also varies in porosity to water, which, together with the other characteristics mentioned above, imply differences in the chemical nature of the secretions of the colleterial glands.

Ovulation
During formation of an ootheca the secretion of the colleterial glands forms a layer over the inner surface of the vestibulum. This becomes filled with eggs, one passing into the developing ootheca from each ovariole. Eggs from the right ovary are said to pass into the left side of the ootheca and *vice versa*. As the eggs are introduced they move posteriorly and the ootheca is extruded; it is compressed by the walls of the genital chamber thus giving the posterior end of the egg case a characteristic shape. The anterior end within the abdomen remains open until all the eggs are included and the intersternal folds form a collar around the ootheca as it slowly emerges. The eggs are manipulated into position in a double row by the ovipositor valves so that the micropylar ends (and subsequently the heads of the developing embryos) come to lie uppermost beneath the keel, the eggs of one row resting against the interstices between the eggs of the other row. Should the eggs be placed upside down they will develop, but the nymphs have little chance of emerging. When all the eggs are in the ootheca, the ovipositor valves are withdrawn and the anterior end is sealed. The full compliment of eggs is thus determined by the number of ovarioles, and it is for this reason that the number of eggs remains reasonably constant for each species. Thus, if an oocyte has matured in each ovariole of *P. americana* the full compliment is 16, but it is very often less than this because of failure in one or more ovarioles. Among 534 oothecae examined by Gould & Deay[21] the number of hatched nymphs averaged 13·6 and among a further 100 egg cases, only three contained more than 16 eggs.

Fertilisation and parthenogenesis

With one or two exceptions, fertilisation—the fusion of sperm and egg nuclei—is necessary for the production of viable young. In the normal sequence of events, sperm stored in the spermatheca fertilise the eggs as they pass from the common oviduct into the vestibulum for inclusion in the ootheca. Females of many species are capable of producing oothecae in the absence of males, but far fewer unmated females are capable of producing eggs which hatch. In these instances, females only are produced.

The best example of parthenogenesis in cockroaches is that shown by *Pycnoscelus surinamensis*. Males and females of this species exist in Indo-Malaya, but a parthenogenetic form only is found in North America and Europe (see p. 74). Unfertilised eggs of the Brown-banded and German Cockroaches may undergo partial embryological development in the ootheca, but fail to hatch. This is also true of *B. vaga*, *E. floridana* and *N. rhombifolia*.[44] Some unfertilised eggs of *B. orientalis*, *P. americana*, *P. australasiae* and *P. brunnea* may hatch and of these, all but *P. australasiae* have been reared to maturity.[42,44]

Types of oviposition

A classification has been suggested for embryological development in cockroaches based on the two inter-related factors, ovipositional behaviour and the water relationships of eggs.[293] This classification distinguishes the habits of the different species and divides them into three groups: *viz.* those showing oviparity, false ovoviviparity and false viviparity. The following description of the different types of egg development that occurs after ovulation in cockroaches will provide an understanding of what is meant by these terms.

GROUP I. OVIPARITY

This term is applied to conditions where eggs, or offspring, are surrounded at 'birth' by an egg shell or chorion. An oviparous cockroach is one in which the eggs develop outside the body of the female. This is the normal condition in most insects, but there are notable exceptions, such as aphids, and tsetse flies which nourish the eggs and produce young alive, referred to as viviparity. Three types of oviparity can be distinguished among cockroaches.

Type (1). *Species in which the ootheca is deposited long before the eggs hatch and in which the ootheca and eggs contain sufficient water for embryological development*

This group includes the pest species, *B. orientalis*, *S. supellectilium* and all species of *Periplaneta*. The ootheca is so constructed as to prevent loss of water after deposition and the eggs can develop at low relative humidities. Adequate water is present in the ootheca at the time of its formation and this is taken up from within the egg case by the developing embryos. This group also includes the non-pest species, *Eurycotis floridana* and *Neostylopyga rhombifolia*.

Type (2). Species in which the ootheca is deposited long before the eggs hatch, but in which the ootheca and eggs do not contain sufficient water for embryological development, but can acquire it if the egg case is deposited in a humid environment

This group includes the non-pest species of Europe and Southern England, namely, *Ectobius pallidus* and the outdoor species of *Parcoblatta* common in the U.S.A. Water can be absorbed through the oothecal wall if the egg case is laid on a damp substrate, but in a dry environment water is lost rapidly and the eggs desiccate. This group also includes *Ectobius panzeri* and *E. lapponicus* which may carry the ootheca for ten days or more before deposition. The egg case may then over-winter before hatching.

Type (3). Species in which the ootheca is not deposited soon after formation but is carried externally by the female until, or shortly before, the young hatch

This group includes the German Cockroach and the Field Cockroach, *Blattella vaga*. The wall of the ootheca is noticeably thinner than that of species in Type (1) and is less-heavily tanned. The embryos rely for their development on water provided by the female through the soft permeable end of the ootheca held in the genital pouch. The water relations of the ootheca and the effects of removing it from the female German Cockroach at various stages of embryological development are discussed on page 299.

Apart from water regulation, two other features distinguish the oviparous cockroaches of Types (1) and (2) from Type (3). Species which drop their oothecae soon after formation can, and usually do, form another a few days later; the interval between successive oothecae is short and usually much less than the period required for hatching. This contrasts with cockroaches which carry the oothecae until hatching; these are unable to form another until the empty case is dropped and the interval between successive oothecae must therefore be somewhat longer than the period of incubation.[44] Nevertheless, under experimental conditions, instances have been recorded of female *B. germanica* carrying two oothecae attached end-to-end.

The second distinguishing feature of cockroaches which carry oothecae during embryological development is that the egg case whilst held by the abdomen, is rotated through 90° soon after its formation, with the result that the dorsal keel comes to lie on one side. Roth[40] suggests that rotation—to the left or the right—is a genetic trait but this has yet to be proved. The reason for rotation will be readily understood if one takes account of the problem confronted by species (in Groups II and III below) which incubate their oothecae internally; for internal incubation, the ootheca is retracted back into the abdomen, which is of course wider laterally than dorso-ventrally. Thus the German Cockroach provides an example of an intermediate condition in ovipositional behaviour, between those which deposit the ootheca and those which retract it. Rotation also facilitates the carrying of the ootheca if its widest dimension lies in the same plane as the greatest dimension of the parent. Carrying the ootheca throughout the entire period of egg development is considered to be the most advanced type of ovipositional behaviour among oviparous cockroaches and rotation of the ootheca, whilst it is held, may be considered as a pre-adaptation for the evolution of internal incubation.[40]

GROUP II. FALSE OVOVIVIPARITY

Viviparity, as defined by Hagan[292] is the birth of young without an enveloping chorion, but has come to be used to describe conditions involving the birth of young in some pre-adult stage other than the egg. In ovoviviparity there are two birth products, first the production of an ootheca, containing eggs each surrounded by a chorion, and secondly the production of live nymphs after the eggs are incubated internally. The term 'false ovoviviparity' is used by Roth & Willis[293] to describe egg development in cockroaches which *first extrude* the ootheca from the abdomen, rotate it and then retract it for incubation within the brood sac, where the eggs remain until, or just before, hatching.

This group includes cockroaches in which the ootheca usually encloses 25 eggs or more and which contain sufficient yolk to complete their development. Water only is provided by the female resulting in a loss in dry weight of the ootheca during development of the embryos. The group is subdivided, arbitrarily, according to the thickness and colouration of the ootheca:

Type (1): in which the ootheca is thick and dark, e.g. species of *Blaberus* and *Byrsotria fumigata*.

Type (2): in which the ootheca is relatively thin and amber to colourless, e.g. *Nauphoeta cinerea*, *Leucophaea maderae* and *Pycnoscelus surinamensis*. Also included is *Gromphadorhina laevigata*, the species for which Chopard[125] first recorded the extrusion and retraction of the ootheca.

GROUP III. FALSE VIVIPARITY

This group contains only one cockroach, *Diploptera punctata*, about which there has been some controversy concerning its ovipositional habit.[42] This cockroach is now known to extrude the ootheca and retract it into a brood sac in a similar manner to the false ovoviviparous species[293] and not to pass the eggs directly from the oviduct into the brood sac as was once suggested. It differs from the false ovoviviparous cockroaches in that the eggs, usually 12 in number, gain both water and solids from the female during embryological development, and the ootheca is incomplete and never covers more than half of each egg.[292] As far as is known there is no true viviparity in cockroaches involving incubation in the oviduct.

Deposition of oothecae

Many authors who have reared cockroaches for research have made observations on the behaviour of cockroaches which deposit their oothecae. Haber[77] in particular has set down his observations on *P. americana* made throughout the night: at the beginning of egg-laying the female first roughened the surface of a piece of paste-board with her mandibles and chewed it until there was an appreciable groove. The pieces were not dropped, but were mixed with secretion from the mouth until they were damp and then stuck as a mass onto the surface of the paste-board. Half an hour later she crawled forward over the groove with the abdomen bent anteriorly and downwards, probing about with the protruding ootheca until she located the groove. Then she dropped the ootheca into it, but as the groove was too shallow the ootheca rolled out and fell to the floor of the cage. The female turned about and with her palpi sought for the ootheca; 'finding it missing, immediately she ran down the paste-board, seized the ootheca by its fluted edge with her mandibles, straddled it with her front legs and thus carrying it, returned to the groove'. She went through the same procedure a second and third time because the groove was unsuitable and 'by this time she seemed to have decided that it was futile to attempt to place the ootheca in the originally selected location. She cleaned it with her mandibles, coated its exposed side and ends with a secretion from her mouth and from the bottom of the cage picked up loose bits of trash, attempting to conceal the ootheca by covering it over with them'.

In the majority of instances, the female American Cockroach deposits her ootheca on the day following its first appearance, but this period may be extended to six days. Both the American and Oriental Cockroaches attempt to use existing crevices in which to secure and conceal their oothecae; they are usually covered with debris torn up by the female, or sometimes by faecal pellets. In captivity, oothecae which are not well hidden are often eaten by other cockroaches or even by the parent. Rau[65] records a female *B. orientalis* carrying earth and debris, sometimes for considerable distances, and with this and saliva, daubing the ootheca until it was hidden. When no covering is available, the ootheca is dropped randomly or simply pasted onto surfaces and not covered.[77]

Rau[294] claims from his night vigils with *P. americana* and *B. orientalis* that these species rarely drop their egg cases indiscriminately. His observations 'show conclusively' that they usually make vigorous attempts to hide them with great care in crevices, or bury them in soft wood or workable material and 'cover them precisely'. He observed a female American Cockroach which spent half an hour chewing away to hollow out a cavity in rotten wood. The mouth secretion was introduced drop by drop over a period of 12 minutes before the ootheca was placed into the mass of adhesive material. The jaws were used to arrange the ootheca with the keel uppermost, presumably, he suggests, to allow free emergence of the nymphs.

This same author has detailed his observations on the egg-laying habit of *Blatta orientalis*. On a sandy surface, the female brushed away the sand with her front legs, using those on each side alternately, taking about 20 minutes to reach a stable surface. She then deposited the egg case in the cleared spot and after an interval of several minutes spread a thin layer of glutinous secretion from her mouth all over it, this taking a further three minutes. She then picked up the egg case in her mandibles and placed it with the keel uppermost; 45 minutes were spent covering the secretion with grains of sand until the ootheca was completely covered, and finally she brushed loose sand over the ootheca with her front legs until it was completely covered.

Structural features of the ootheca

Until Lawson[295] investigated the structure of the keel of the ootheca it was thought to be a sealed structure and the diffusion of gases into it seemed unlikely. At the same time it seemed equally unlikely that sufficient air could be sealed into the capsule to support respiration over a number of weeks. Lawson solved this anomaly by demonstrating the existence of tiny sutural openings in the keel which allow the embryos to respire.

The keel of the ootheca consists of two tightly opposed flanges but varies in structure in different species (Fig. 94). In *B. germanica* and *Parcoblatta pennsylvanica* it is composed of an upper and lower lamina enclosing a cavity with a sponge-like body above each egg. The lower lamina is thickened to form a floor to the cavity above the eggs, and the upper lamina forms a 'seam roof'. In these species, the sutural opening connects to the sponge body, *via* the keel cavity and a connecting duct. In *Supella*, *B. orientalis* and species of *Periplaneta* the sponge-like body is absent and the sutural opening connects with a duct opening directly above the eggs.

The remainder of the ootheca forms a sac-like structure with various ornamentations. In some species, for example the American and Oriental Cockroaches, the tops of the eggs within the ootheca are indicated by small rounded swellings either side of the keel. In others, e.g. *Blattella* and *Supella*, each egg is demarked by a groove in the oothecal wall running from the keel to the ventral surface (See Fig. 37, p. 100).

A few days before nymphs of the German Cockroach hatch, a dark band appears along the mid-line of the ootheca resulting from the accumulation of waste products within the alimentary canal of each developing embryo.[296] The oothecae of other species are often too dark for this to be visible.

These last two chapters have given an insight into the complexity of mating and ootheca production in cockroaches. Behavioural responses in getting the sexes together, the physiological processes regulating egg production, and the carrying of the ootheca externally by some species and

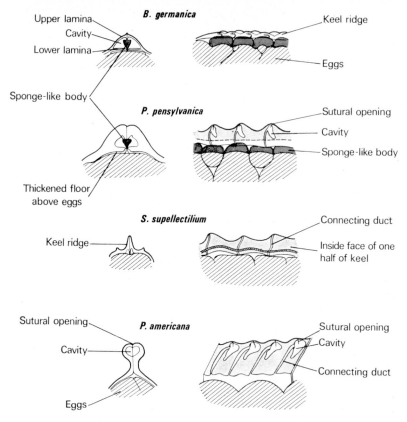

Fig. 94. Structural details of the keel of four species of cockroach (diagrammatic). The keel of *P. americana* is drawn to half the scale of the other species (after Lawson[295]).

internally by others are features which have obviously contributed towards the survival of these insects. There is no doubt that a great deal remains to be learnt about the mechanisms involved in insect reproduction, but there is clearly no better group than cockroaches for such investigations.

The reader who has patiently followed this description of cockroach reproduction must be convinced of two things. One, that although cockroaches are considered to be primitive insects the physiological processes concerned in reproduction—the perpetuation of these primitive external features—are very complex indeed. Secondly that from the information now available, it is not surprising that cockroaches have emerged as one of the most successful groups of insects, and often one of the most difficult for man to eradicate.

10

GROWTH, DEVELOPMENT AND
NATURAL ENEMIES

Embryological development: fate of the bacteroids; incubation period of the ootheca; hatching from the ootheca
Post-embryological development: characteristics of nymphal growth; growth of the antennae; growth of the cerci; growth of the terminal abdominal sternites of the female; growth of the wings
Growth and moulting: increase in weight; increase in size; number of moults and loss of appendages; regeneration of appendages; effects of individual and communal rearing—Effects of diet: protein requirements; vitamins—Seasonal variation in development
Inquiline cockroaches—Natural enemies of cockroaches: hymenoptera; other predators and parasites—Defence mechanisms against predators.

Growth and development in insects is divided into two phases: embryological development, which follows fertilisation of the egg and occurs within the egg membranes, and post-embryological development which occurs after the egg membranes have been shed.

Embryological development involves division of the zygote nucleus and the laying down of the primary layers, ectoderm, mesoderm and endoderm, and the differentiation of these layers into tissues and organs. The speed of embryological development is influenced principally by temperature and water availability.

After the egg has hatched (eclosion), post-embryonic development continues with periods of active growth punctuated by moults, or ecdyses. The increase in size of the insect is discontinuous because of the limitations of the cuticle, and the rate of growth following hatching is influenced primarily by temperature, humidity, diet and space.

Cockroaches belong to that group of insects referred to as the Hemimetabola (=Exopterygota) in which metamorphosis is direct or incomplete. The young are referred to as nymphs and resemble the adult in appearance and habit except for the absence of fully developed wings, external genitalia and adult colouring. There is no striking morphological change during development as in the Holometabola (=Endopterygota), in which a pupal stage is interposed between the immature (larval) and the mature (adult) stages.

In this chapter we shall examine the effects of environmental factors on the growth and development of cockroaches. Most of the information available has been obtained from studies of pest species held under controlled conditions in the laboratory. Some, however, has been obtained under varying conditions in buildings and demonstrates the marked effects of seasons.

Embryological development

The fertilised eggs, within the newly formed cockroach ootheca, are slightly curved, concave on one side, on which the future embryo will develop, and convex on the other. Each egg is composed of a zygote nucleus and yolk, contained in the cytoplasm, together with bacteroids which enter the oocyte in the ovary (see p. 201). The cytoplasm is enclosed by two layers, an inner vitelline membrane and an outer chorion, which allow free exchange of air and water.

As far as can be judged from accounts of the embryological development of cockroaches, the sequence of events is not unlike that of other orthopteroid insects. Briefly, development first follows the usual pattern for a heavily yolked egg: cleavage of the zygote nucleus is followed by the formation of a blastula, and subsequent gastrulation movements result in the formation of an embryo separated from the blastoderm by an amniotic cavity. A ventral plate gives rise to the three primary layers, ectoderm, mesoderm and endoderm, from which the various parts of the body are developed. The yolk is enclosed by the upward growth of the sides of the ventral plate which eventually meet along the mid-dorsal line. The nerve cord is formed by an infolding of ectoderm along the mid-ventral line, and the tracheal system arises from invaginations of ectoderm at regular intervals along the sides of the embryo. Rudimentary appendages form on the abdomen, but these are subsequently lost with the exception of those on the ninth segment which remain to form the cerci.

Throughout the whole of embryological development the yolk provides nourishment so that the space which it initially occupies in the egg comes to be taken up by the developing embryo. Water is absorbed by the eggs of all species of cockroach during development, but the amount varies in relation to that present in the ootheca at its formation.[297] The initial water content is high in species which deposit the ootheca (*Periplaneta* spp. 60–65 per cent; *Blatta orientalis*, 64 per cent), and those which carry the ootheca attached to the abdomen (*Blattella germanica*, 62 per cent; *B. vaga*, 60 per cent); it is low in those which incubate their oothecae internally (34–40 per cent). Among the latter species there is one exception, *viz. Diploptera punctata*, a false viviparous cockroach (p. 216) in which the eggs contain 65 per cent water at ootheca formation. It is the only cockroach known in which the eggs increase in both dry matter and water content during embryogenesis. The embryological development of *Diploptera* and *Blattella* have been described in detail by Hagan[292] and Wheeler,[298] respectively.

Fate of the bacteroids

During early embryogenesis, the bacteroids retain their position against the vitelline membrane, which they occupied at ovulation (p. 202). In the

American Cockroach, many of the first nuclei to reach the edge of the yolk do so after two days of incubation; some then sink back into the yolk accompanied by bacteroids. At the end of the second day some of the nuclei which are to form the blastodern pass into the masses of bacteroids at the poles of the egg, and between the third and fifth days the two polar masses of bacteroids move towards the centre of the yolk and form the primary mycetocyte. By the eleventh day of development the bacteroids begin to appear against the gut epithelium and eventually infect the cells of the fat body. Gier[272] suggests that at this time a few bacteroids also find their way into the developing ovary and become incorporated into the compact primitive cord of germ cells.

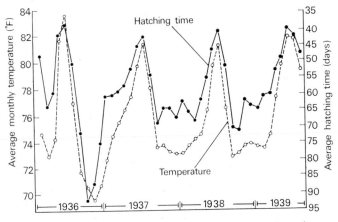

Fig. 95. Variation in hatching time of oothecae of *P. americana* (range 37–92 days) in a fluctuating environment (temperature range 70–80°F) (after Gould & Deay[21]).

Incubation period of the ootheca

The time required for completion of embryological development is greatly affected by temperature. In a fluctuating environment of 30–40 per cent relative humidity (Fig. 95), oothecae of the American Cockroach hatch in five weeks with periods averaging 84°F (29°C), but take up to 13 weeks to hatch at 70°F (21°C).[21] For each degree Farenheit rise in the average monthly temperature the hatching time is reduced by about three days. This compares with a reduction of 1·6 days for the ootheca of the German Cockroach, 2·6 days for the Oriental Cockroach and 5·1 for the Brown-banded Cockroach. Oothecae of *P. americana* held below about 10 per cent relative humidity fail to hatch. Under more closely controlled conditions, and at the higher relative humidity of 70 per cent, the incubation time of *P. americana* is shortened to 29–31 days at 29–32°C and the percentage hatch then exceeds 80 per cent (Fig. 96).

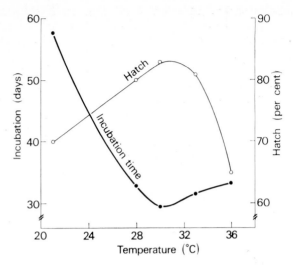

Fig. 96. The effect of temperature on the incubation time and hatching of oothecae of *P. americana*.

Hatching from the ootheca

When hatching occurs, the dorsal keel of the ootheca suddenly splits along its length, and the nymphs emerge abruptly. In *Supella*,[101] and probably in other species too, emergence from the ootheca is accomplished by the nymphs swallowing minute air bubbles which accumulate in the crop, so enlarging the abdomen that the resulting pressure helps to force the young out. The nymphs then wriggle from the ootheca, those near the middle, where the gap along the keel is usually widest, are first, those at the ends free themselves later. Nymphs which delay their escape too long may become trapped within the ootheca which tends to snap shut after the majority of nymphs have emerged. The process of emergence is complete within a few minutes (Fig. 97). The eyes of the emerging nymphs are darkly pigmented, but the remainder of the cuticle is white. Nymphs may hatch from the ootheca of the German Cockroach whilst the egg case is still held by the female (Fig. 98).

There is no evidence to support the suggestion that young secrete a fluid which dissolves the keel so enabling hatching. Neither is there any evidence that the female of any species of cockroach assists the young to escape. Immediately after hatching the young of some species undergo an embryonic moult (probably the shedding of the serosa, one of the embryonic membranes) leading to the formation of the first instar.

The nymphs are actively mobile from the moment they leave the ootheca. The abdomen is long and slim at eclosion but broadens somewhat after an hour or so and the cuticle soon tans. The nymphs often tend to

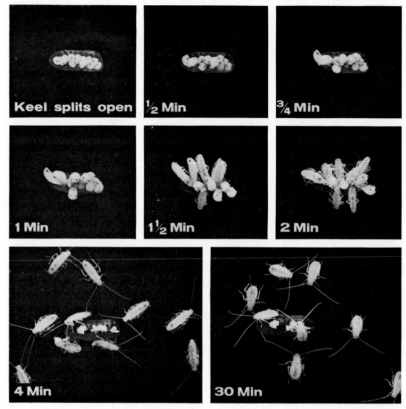

Fig. 97. Hatching of an ootheca of *Periplaneta*. Note the embryonic membranes left behind in the ootheca after the nymphs have emerged. (Courtesy: Drs. Roth & Willis, U.S. Army Natick Laboratories.)

remain together for a few hours after emergence having sought the nearest possible favourable environment. Nymphs of *Blaberus craniifer* consume the extruded ootheca, and have been observed to remain around and under the body of the female for a period after parturition.[261]

Post-embryological development
Post-embryonic growth consists of a series of nymphal stages separated by moults. The number of nymphal stages in each species remains reasonably constant, but may increase if environmental conditions are unfavourable. One sex may occasionally pass through more moults than the other and the duration of nymphal stages also varies between species, the sexes of the same species, and with season. It is possible for some individuals to reach maturity in half the time taken by others (Fig. 99).

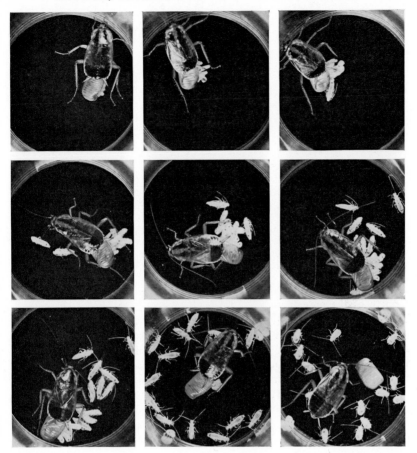

Fig. 98. Hatching of an ootheca of *B. germanica* while still attached to the female. The wings have been cut for clarity. (Courtesy: Drs. Roth & Willis, U.S. Army Natick Laboratories.)

Characteristics of nymphal growth

Nymphs of all species of cockroach are similar in general appearance to the adult except for the absence of wings, incompletely developed genitalia and adult colouring. Detailed examination also shows that certain of the appendages, such as the antennae and cerci, increase in their number of segments as nymphal development proceeds. Qadri[64] has studied the growth characteristics of the antennae, cerci, terminal abdominal sclerites and wings of the Oriental Cockroach in successive developmental stages. This species increases in body size (from the occiput to the end of the abdomen) from about 5 mm in the first stage nymph to 22 mm in the adult.

P

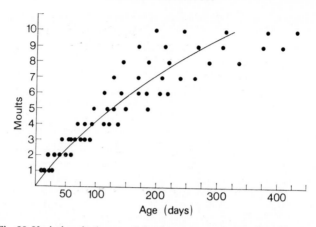

Fig. 99. Variations in the rate of development of nymphs of *P. americana* from hatching to maturity. Each point represents five individuals which moulted at about the same age. The curve gives the mean time for each moult (after Gier[75]).

Growth of the antennae

The antenna of the first instar nymph consists of 42 segments and is divisible into four regions (Fig. 100); the basal segment or scape, the second segment, which acts as a pivot for antennal movement, the third segment which constitutes the zone of growth or multiplication, and the fourth region, or flagellum, consisting of 39 segments in the first instar and of additional segments, divided off from the third segment in subsequent instars. The third segment of a newly moulted nymph is undivided but it becomes divided some hours after ecdysis. Thus according to Qadri the formation and subsequent separation of the new segments, from the third, appears to take place between moults. This process continues until the fourth instar but no further divisions occur in fifth or sixth stage nymphs. Fuller[299] has observed a similar process of growth which does not occur beyond the fourth instar in nymphs of termites. The growth pattern of the antennae of *B. orientalis* described here is not, however, in accord with the views of Gier[75] who states that the antennae of *P. americana* definitely increase in length *at* the moult and continue slight elongation by stretching of intersegmental membranes, *between* moults.

Growth of the cerci

The cercus of the first stage nymph of *B. orientalis* consists of three segments only (Fig. 101). All three divide to form eight in the second instar, and from then on only the terminal segment divides. The cercus has nine segments in the third instar, 10–11 in the fourth, 12 in the fifth, 14 in the sixth and 16 in the adult (Fig. 44, p. 115). The Brown-banded Cockroach

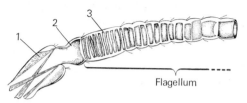

Fig. 100. Basal part of an antenna of a 2nd stage nymph of *B. orientalis* showing the zone of growth at the 3rd antennal joint (after Qadri[64]).

also starts life with a three-segmented cercus but acquires the full number of 15, by the fourth nymphal stage.[101]

Growth of the terminal abdominal sternites of the female
The last segments of the abdomen of the female nymph become considerably modified during development in relation to the formation of the genital pouch (p. 186). The most noticeable changes occur in the ventral sternites; in their relative size and shape, and in the extent to which they are visible externally. These changes are not identical in all species, but the end result is the same: the extensive development of the seventh sternite and the invagination of the posterior ones into the end of the abdomen (Fig. 101). The sequence of events in *Blatta* has been studied by Qadri[64] and in *Supella* by Hafez & Afifi.[101]

Growth of the wings
The first and second stage nymphs of the Oriental Cockroach are without traces of wings, but in the third stage, the hind margins of the meso- and metanota become concave posteriorly (especially in the male) and traces of wing rudiments are visible at the posterolateral angles. These rudiments in the fourth stage become distinct, notably in the male, with the growth backwards of these angles. In the next two stages, the developing wings are quite prominent: in the fifth stage the posterolateral margins of the mesonotum overlap the metanotum and those of the latter extend as far as the middle of the second abdominal segment. In the sixth and final nymph, the wing rudiments become thicker and more clearly defined from the thoracic sclerites. The tegmina and hind wings of the adult male cover about two-thirds of the abdomen whilst in the female they remain vestigial.

Growth and moulting
Moulting in insects is under the control of the 'juvenile hormone', ecdyson, which maintains the immature characteristics of nymphal stages. At the last nymphal stage the corpora allata are inhibited by the brain from producing the juvenile hormone. Severance of the corpora allata from the

brain in the last stage nymph of *Leucophaea* results in continued activity of the corpora allata with the production of supernumary moults.[300]

At moulting, air is taken into the crop causing the cuticle to split along the mid-dorsal line from the head backwards. By a series of rhythmical expansions and contractions of the body, the cockroach in its newly formed white cuticle emerges over a period of 15 minutes to one hour.

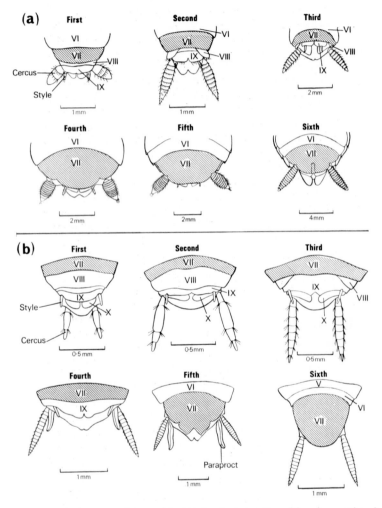

Fig. 101. Development of the terminal abdominal sternites of female nymphs of (a) *B. orientalis* (after Qadri[64]) and (b) *S. supellectilium* (after Hafez & Afifi[101]). The VIIth sternite has been shaded to show its enlargement to form the subgenital plate.

Fig. 102. Final moult of a last stage nymph of male *Blatta orientalis*. Escape from the old cuticle usually occurs with the head pointing downwards, gravity helping the newly-formed adult to emerge. Note the gradual expansion of the wings after emergence and the dorsal blood vessel clearly visible through the new soft white cuticle. (Courtesy: Drs. Roth & Willis, U.S. Army Natick Laboratories).

Moulting usually occurs with the head pointing downwards, gravity helping the insect to withdraw from the old cuticle. The new cuticle is at first white, without any signs of pigmentation except in the eyes. At this time the insect is highly susceptible to desiccation and to cannibalism by other cockroaches. At the final moult the wings of the emerging adult are small and crumpled, gradually expanding to their full size (Fig. 102).

Hardening and darkening of the cuticle which follow moulting have been studied by Pryor;[288] these changes are brought about by the formation of a protein similar to that found in the cockroach ootheca. A water-soluble protein and a dihydroxyphenol (probably dihydroxyphenyl acetic acid) are secreted into the outer layers of the cuticle where the protein is oxidised to form sclerotin. It is this which is responsible for giving the cuticle its rigidity and tanned appearance, the process being under the control of the hormone, bursicon (p. 146).

The sclerotised parts of an insect's body increase in size only at ecdysis

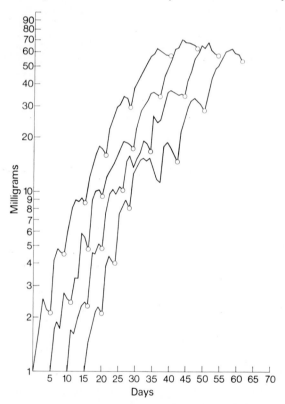

Fig. 103. Typical growth curves of four female nymphs of *B. germanica*. Each curve is displaced five days to the right. Moults are indicated by circles (after Woodruff[296]).

so that linear growth is discontinuous. The elasticity provided by the intersegmental membranes of the body does, however, allow an increase in weight between moults. Many generalisations have been put forward for the growth of insects as a result of studies on particular species. One of these (Przibram's Rule), based on studies with the Egyptian praying mantis, is that moults occur when the weight of the insect has doubled, and linear measurements of each stage increase by $\sqrt[3]{2}$ or 1·26. Dyar's Law, based on the measurements of head capsules of lepidopterous larvae, shows that linear growth between moults increases geometrically by a factor of 1·4 ($\sqrt{2}$). Wigglesworth[165] has pointed out the limitations of these rules as applied to insects in general; rarely do all the separate parts of an insect increase at the same rate, and rarely is the velocity of growth constant throughout the period of development of an insect.

Increase in weight

One of the most detailed studies on the increase in weight of a cockroach during development has been made on *B. germanica*;[296] isolated insects of an inbred laboratory strain were fed a constant diet and weighed daily. The usual number of moults in the German Cockroach is six but some individuals may have seven moults or occasionally more. These additional instars usually occur earlier in development rather than later.

Because active growth is punctuated by moults, increase in weight is irregular; weight is actually lost before and during a moult, since the insect

TABLE XX

MAXIMUM WEIGHT (Mg) OF THE NYMPHAL INSTARS OF *B. GERMANICA* AND MINIMUM WEIGHT AFTER MOULTING. TIME (DAYS) IN PARENTHESES. NYMPHS REARED IN ISOLATION AT 27–30°C
(After Woodruff[296])

Nymphal stage	Males		Females	
	Minimum after moulting	*Maximum*	*Minimum after moulting*	*Maximum*
I	(hatching)	2·5 (3·7)	(hatching)	2·6 (3·9)
II	2·2 (5·8)	5·1 (10·0)	2·2 (5·8)	5·1 (9·2)
III	4·5 (12·1)	9·1 (17·0)	4·6 (11·0)	9·9 (15·7)
IV	7·9 (19·4)	16·7 (26·8)	9·0 (17·5)	18·4 (24·7)
V	14·6 (29·0)	30·3 (36·6)	16·3 (27·1)	35·5 (34·1)
VI	27·6 (39·4)	55·3 (48·5)	32·1 (37·0)	68·2 (45·4)
Adult	45·0 (53·7)	—	57·4 (49·4)	—

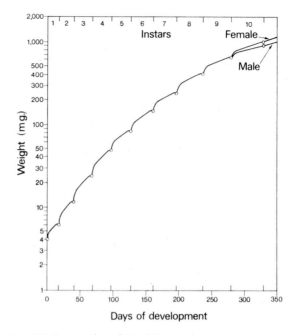

Fig. 104. Increase in weight of *P. americana* during nymphal
development. Differences between males and females occur
only in the last stage nymph and the adult (after Gier[75]).

eats sparingly for a few days before ecdysis, and there is also a loss of water
while the cuticle is soft. As a result, the minimum weight of the insect at
the beginning of each stage is noticeably lower than the maximum of the
preceding stage (Table XX). In addition to changes in weight at the moult,
there may also be periods between moults when growth is retarded, but
there is little correlation in the occurrence of this retarded growth, or its
extent, in different individuals (Fig. 103).

Both sexes of the German Cockroach increase in weight by the same
amount during early life, but differences occur towards the end of the third
nymphal stage and become more pronounced thereafter, with the result
that adult females weigh some 20 per cent heavier than males. This, however, is not so in the American Cockroach[75] which normally has 10
nymphal stages and in which differences in weight of the sexes are not
detectable until the last nymphal instar (Fig. 104).

Increase in size
Following a moult, feeding is resumed and there is then a sudden increase
in the length of the body caused principally by enlargement of the abdomen.

Sclerotised structures, however, such as the legs, can increase in size only at the moult. Woodruff[301] has made observations on four sclerotised structures of the German Cockroach to see if all increase in size by the same amount, and if the rate of increase of each is constant throughout development. The structures measured were the greatest width of the head, including the compound eyes, the greatest width of the pronotum and the length of the tibiae of the meso- and metathoracic legs. The ratio of increase was obtained by dividing the size of the structure in one stage by its size in the preceding stage. Each structure appeared to have its own rate of development and the average growth ratios obtained were 1·34 for the metathoracic tibia, 1·32 for the mesothoracic tibia, 1·24 for the pronotum and 1·18 for the head.

Woodruff has shown that the rate of development varies from one instar to the next; the growth curves for the four structures (Fig. 105) show a diminishing rate of increase in size with successive instars. The pronotum, for example, increases in size more rapidly than the other structures, but its development is complete by the fifth nymphal instar. Each part of the insect therefore has its own characteristic rate of growth, with differential rates for some and more regular rates for others. This same conclusion has been reached by Gier[75] from measurements on developmental stages of *P. americana*.

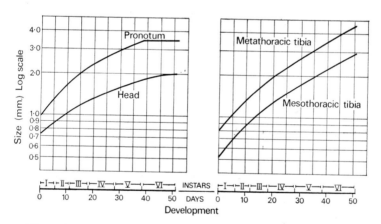

Fig. 105. Growth curves for sclerotised parts of the German cockroach (after Woodruff[301]).

Number of moults and loss of appendages

The number of moults in different species of cockroach varies considerably, but each has a reasonably constant number with the exception of a few individuals which appear to require an additional one, or occasionally two, before reaching maturity. In general, additional ecdyses appear to arise under adverse environmental conditions and can frequently be induced by maintaining cockroaches on a deficient diet. During investigations by Seamans & Woodruff[302] evidence was obtained that loss of legs can also induce an extra moult. To test this, one or two legs of newly emerged nymphs of the German Cockroach were deliberately amputated between the trochanter and femur. A single amputation involved the metathoracic leg and a double amputation included the mesothoracic leg of the other side. All amputations were made within 24 hours of hatching from the ootheca.

All uninjured cockroaches passed through six nymphal stages to reach maturity, but seven moults were required by nine out of 41 insects (22 per cent) with one amputation, and by 26 out of 73 cockroaches (36 per cent) with two legs removed. In no instances were more than seven moults observed.

Injury therefore appears to influence the need for an additional growth period and the greater the injury the more desirable an extension of nymphal development appears to be. Seamans & Woodruff comment on two striking features in connection with extra moults; first, the ultimate size attained by sclerotised parts is slightly greater in insects with a supernumary moult, and second, the additional instar is not merely appended to the sixth, but compensating growth, towards an increased size, becomes obvious early in nymphal development and is evident for the greater part of the developmental period. The overall growth rate of sclerotised structures is therefore reduced to allow time for the amputated leg to be regenerated. Thus measurements on different structures of amputated insects (Fig. 106) show a reduced rate of growth of the tibia, first apparent after the third moult. Slower growth of the head capsule can be detected at least at the second, or perhaps even the first ecdysis.

Regeneration of appendages

In contrast to higher animals, insects have an exceptionally high ability to regenerate a lost or injured appendage. A study made with *B. germanica*[303] indicates that cockroaches have at least 14 well-defined breaking points, or points of weakness: one on each of the antennae between the first segment (the scape) and the second (the pedicel) and two on each leg, at the immovable junction of the trochanter and femur and at the ball joint of the tibia and tarsus (Fig. 114). There are apparently no such weaknesses at the joints of the mouthparts or along the cerci although these may be separated if sufficient stress is applied. The flagellum of the antenna can also be broken at any of its segments but there is no indication of any specific breaking point along its length. The entire tarsus readily disengages from the tibia when pulled from the distal end but again there is no evidence of a fracture point between the tarsal segments. Clearly 'insects derive material advantage from the possession of predetermined loci of weakness in as

much as a leg or antennal segment may be easily severed at one of these
points when subject to external pull as might be exerted in the grasp
of an enemy'.[303]

In all insects and other Arthropods regeneration of lost appendages can
occur only at ecdysis. If injury is inflicted on a cockroach just before a
moult, regeneration of the lost part may be delayed until the moult following the next instar; the regenerated parts are usually smaller than the
normal structure, but with each subsequent moult the new structure grows
larger and given time may reach the size of a normal appendage.

Breaks along the flagellum of an antenna are readily regenerated and if
the break occurs near the tip, the pair are usually equal in length after the
following moult, or by the second moult. Should the break, however, occur
at the point of weakness, between the scape and the pedicel, regeneration
occurs more slowly and the resulting flagellum is considerably smaller in
diameter and length. Woodruff has shown that the cerci of the cockroach
may be regenerated in much the same way.

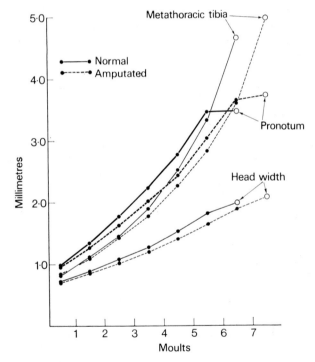

Fig. 106. Size of sclerotised parts of *B. germanica* undergoing six
moults (normal) and seven moults (following, e.g. amputation at
eclosion). The size of the parts in the adult are shown by open circles
(after Seamans & Woodruff[302]).

When breaks occur in the legs, the formation of a new tarsus takes place with much greater facility than when more leg segments are involved, and the regenerated tarsus almost invariably occurs with the next moult; it is frequently normal in length, but without exception consists of four sub-segments instead of the normal five. Should a break occur between the trochanter and femur, the lost parts are also regenerated at the next moult, but according to Woodruff the leg always has the reduced number of tarsal segments; the leg is smaller in size, but otherwise normal. Mutilation of one leg apparently has little effect upon the regeneration of another except that the normal movements of the insect are impaired. Multiple injuries to the legs or to the legs and antennae have no effect on rate of regeneration.

Effects of individual and communal rearing

There are many examples, particularly from studies on pests of stored food, that the density of insects in an environment influences their develop-mental period, fecundity and mortality. Under laboratory conditions these effects can be attributed to metabolic heat generated by the insects within the culture medium, cannibalism, mutual disturbance, and food availability.

The effects of population size on the development of cockroaches has

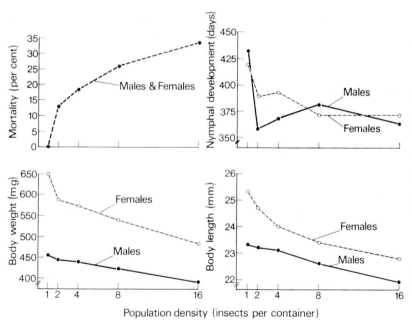

Fig. 107. The effects of density on the mortality, developmental period, body weight and length (anterior edge of prothorax to anus) of *B. orientalis* reared in standard size containers at 24–28°C and 95–100% RH (from Landowski[304]).

been examined by Landowski[304] for newly emerged nymphs of *B. orientalis* reared singly and in groups of 2, 4, 6 and 16 in standard sized containers. Mortality increases with density (Fig. 107), but the number of moults remains constant. All insects require the same developmental period for the first eight stages, but from the ninth moult onwards, the development of solitary nymphs lags noticeably behind. Heavier and larger adults are obtained when nymphs are reared in isolation, and both body weight and length decrease substantially with increasing population. Landowski attributes these results to an 'interference factor' (increased collisions during movement) rather than to shortage of food or oxygen, or to the accumulation of faeces. An increase in the period of development of cockroaches reared in isolation has also been noted by Pettit[305] for *B. germanica* at temperatures up to 23–25°C and by Willis *et al.*[44] for a number of species (Tables VII–X). Griffiths & Tauber[73] have recorded poorer reproductive performance of mating pairs of *P. americana* reared in small, compared with large, containers. Unfortunately, no detailed information is available on the rate of growth of pest species of cockroach at different densities in their natural surroundings.

Effects of Diet

The range of foods available to pest cockroaches in infested premises is usually very wide. To obtain information on the precise dietary needs of cockroaches it is necessary to make tests under sterile conditions in which the insects are fed a diet of known chemical composition. Cockroaches normally accept a variety of foods, but a high proportion of their intake consists of carbohydrates, which they are well equipped to digest with the abundance of carbohydrate-splitting enzymes in the gut (p. 128).

Many materials have been used as diets for maintaining stock colonies of cockroaches, including ground cereals, baby food, dog biscuits, dried skimmed milk powder, baker's yeast, bread, banana, raw potatoes and raw meat. In tests undertaken by Melampy & Maynard[306] in which natural foods were fed to seven-day-old nymphs (2·5–3 mg) of *B. germanica*, the average weights obtained after 42 days were 4·1 mg on wheat flour, 4·4 on commercial baby food, 6·3 on dried whole milk, 10·9 on dried skimmed milk, 19·1 on ground whole meat, 22·3 on a 1:1 mixture of whole wheat and dried blood, 22·8 on a mixture of whole wheat and dried skimmed milk and the highest, 23·5 mg, on dried beef steak. The poor results obtained with dried whole milk and commercial baby food demonstrate that the requirements for development of cockroaches are quite unlike those of the young mammal.

Protein requirements

Various attempts have been made to establish the protein requirements of cockroaches: Noland *et al.*[307] found that the growth of *B. germanica* was fastest on a diet of 30 per cent casein. Noland & Baumann[308] later suggested that 40 per cent was required for optimal growth, and for *P. americana* Sieburth et *al.*[309] found that 25 per cent casein best fulfilled the insect's protein demands.

Subsequently, Haydak[218] fed German, Oriental and American Cockroaches on diets containing various amounts of protein: the most rapid development and lowest nymphal mortality (Table XXI) occurred on 22–24 per cent protein for both the German and Oriental species, whilst for

TABLE XXI

INFLUENCE OF PROTEIN LEVEL ON THE MORTALITY OF NYMPHS
AND THEIR RATE OF DEVELOPMENT TO ADULT
(Data from Haydak[218])

Protein level (%)	Mortality (as nymphs %)	Nymphal development (days)	Total nymphal and adult life span (days)
		Blattella germanica	
11	38	162	444
22–24	12	115	338
49	12	150	236
74	38	136	213
86–91	100	–	–
		Blatta orientalis	
11	69	382	668
22–24	14	270	492
49	36	265	419
74–79	51	316	407
86–91	85	325	358
		Periplaneta americana	
11	75	787	1,391
22–24	32	431	1,172
49–79	20	366	1,058
86–91	28	378	844

the American Cockroach it was 49–79 per cent. Protein level greatly affects the longevity of all three species (Table XXII); the optimal level is 11–24 per cent for *B. germanica*, 22–24 per cent for *B. orientalis*, whereas for *P. americana* it is very variable at 2·5–49 per cent.

Precise information on the requirements of insects for different dietary constituents has been handicapped by the difficulty of formulating a completely 'synthetic' diet of known chemical composition on which insects will grow.[310] Noland et *al.*[307] studied the growth rate of nymphs of *B. germanica* on four diets at 29°C: those fed on crude diets matured in 40 days compared with 49–55 days on synthetic media. The insects were also noticeably larger (42–45 mg) after 30 days development on the crude diets compared with only 25 mg on the synthetic.

A deficiency of one or other amino acid in the diet of some insects has a drastic effect on body weight, but in *Blattella* deficiency symptoms are much less obvious. The omission of any one of the ten 'essential' amino acids from the food of the German cockroach (i.e. amino acids apparently

TABLE XXII

INFLUENCE OF PROTEIN LEVEL IN DIET ON THE LONGEVITY OF ADULT COCKROACHES
(Data from Haydak[218])

Protein level (%)	Protein intake (mg/day) Males	Females	Longevity (days) Males	Females
	Blattella germanica			
11–24	0·2	0·3	207	270
49	0·7	–	123	–
49–74	–	1·3	–	114
74–79	0·9	–	86	–
79–91	–	1·2	–	74
86–91	1·2	–	68	–
	Blatta orientalis			
0–11	0·2	–	204	–
22–24	1·1	2·4	233	185
49	2·4	5·2	148	151
74–70	3·5	–	109	–
74–79	–	6·4	–	90
86–91	3·7	7.2	56	63
	Periplaneta americana			
0–5	–	0·3	–	618
2·5–11	0·5	–	791	–
11–49	–	1·7	–	726
22–24	1·3	–	825	–
49	2·6	–	790	–
74–79	5·2	5·9	560	613
86–91	5·4	5·8	516	474

required by most insects for full development and adult survival) causes only a slowing of growth rate and a reduction in longevity. Only by the omission of alanine and leucine from the diet of *B. germanica* have marked deficiency effects been observed. A diet deficient in alanine causes a pronounced reduction in growth, but the presence of this amino acid in the tissues of cockroaches fed an alanine-free diet indicates that some is synthesised by the insect itself. Tests with cockroaches on a range of amino acids, normally required by insects for healthy development, point to the conclusion that *Blattella*, at least, is capable of synthesising many, if not all those that it requires, by means of its symbionts. The following amino acids appear unnecessary in the diet of the German Cockroach or can be synthesised by the insect: threonine, cystine (provided methionine is present), glutamic acid, aspartic acid, phenylalanine and tyrosine.

Vitamins
The vitamin requirements of insects are in general very similar to those of mammals, but the needs of the German Cockroach appear strikingly different. Two possibilities arise; either the German Cockroach can synthesise vitamins in its tissues or symbiotic microflora are responsible. Brooks & Richards[311] attempted to deprive cockroaches of their symbionts by feeding them aureomycin. Nymphs so treated were unable to grow on a diet which was adequate for normal nymphs, but it was believed that the aureomycin adversely affected the metabolism of the insects as well as the microflora.

Vitamin A is necessary to support the growth of rats, but the cockroach can develop normally in its total absence.[312] This was proved by exposing a mixture of equal parts of whole wheat flour and dried skimmed milk to hot air at 115°C for six hours to destroy any vitamin A or carotene, its precursor. The insects grew better on the heat-treated diet than on the original. Extracts of fat from the insects reared on the vitamin A-free diet showed that this vitamin had not been synthesised.

Studies on the importance of vitamin B to the German Cockroach[306] show that the weight of nymphs increases when fed vitamin B in increasing amount. Linear increases occur when the vitamin is supplied as dried baker's yeast at all concentrations up to 20 per cent. When given as vitamin B concentrate, however, the linear increase ceases at three per cent, and further amounts of vitamin in the diet have no effect on body weight (Fig. 108). In tests on vitamin C (ascorbic acid) Wollman et al.[313] were able to rear German Cockroaches for 46 generations under sterile conditions in a culture medium free of this vitamin. At the end of that time the insects contained as much vitamin C in their tissues as did normal cockroaches and in this instance it is believed that the symbionts were responsible.

Most insects have a requirement for choline and in *Blattella* the need for this vitamin is high, up to 4 mg/g of diet.[307] Insects make heavy demands on sterols and unlike higher animals are not capable of synthesising them. This demand can be satisfied by the addition of cholesterol to the diet but in *Blattella* this can again be synthesised, probably by the symbionts.[314]

Seasonal variation in development
In the greater part of the world, cockroaches can exist as pests in unheated buildings where their rate of development is influenced principally by ambient temperature, assuming that food, water and harbourage are adequate. In a temperature controlled environment of 82°F (27·8°C), the

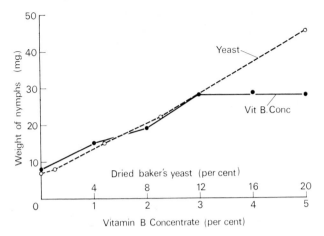

Fig. 108. Weight of young nymphs of *B. germanica* after feeding for 42 days at 27–28°C on diets containing increasing amounts of vitamin B as a concentrate or as yeast (from Melampy & Maynard[306]).

American Cockroach can reach maturity in 145 to 265 days, but under normal room conditions in Indiana development to maturity was found to require as long as 971 days.[21] Among six species for which the development time was recorded, maturity of the Brown-banded Cockroach was more influenced by temperature than any other: for each degree Farenheit rise in temperature between 76–86°F the nymphal development period of *Supella* is reduced by about 11 days (Fig. 109). This species is found in

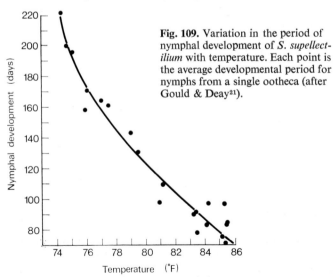

Fig. 109. Variation in the period of nymphal development of *S. supellectilium* with temperature. Each point is the average developmental period for nymphs from a single ootheca (after Gould & Deay[21]).

Q

houses all the year round in Egypt,[101] but is more abundant in spring and
summer (79–97°F and 50–75 per cent relative humidity). At that time of
the year female nymphs require 109 to 130 days to reach maturity compared with 215–245 days in winter (59–77°F and 45–65 per cent relative
humidity).

The climate of vast areas of the United States is highly favourable to
reproduction and development of pest cockroaches. In the south, the
American Cockroach is capable of breeding and developing in sewers
throughout the year. In Indiana, the Oriental Cockroach gives rise to a
preponderance of adults in spring, but nymphs may pass through two
winters before maturing. The Wood Cockroach, *Parcoblatta*, an essentially
outdoor species, also has a definite seasonal cycle, most individuals of this
species also maturing in the spring.

To some extent, the German Cockroach is less susceptible to seasonal
variations in climate, since the ootheca is carried by the female into
preferred environments, minimising hatching time and liberating the
nymphs where temperature, humidity and food are likely to be
optimal.

One of the best examples of seasonal variations in the abundance of a
pest species is that given by Rau[65] in his description of the occurrence of
the Oriental Cockroach in St. Louis. He says that adults in their natural
environment disappear during July and very soon young nymphs appear,
reaching some size in autumn and becoming adult in the following May or
June, the males emerging slightly in advance of females. The following
quote from Rau[65] emphasises what he believes to be a normal seasonal
occurrence in that part of the United States: 'The housewife has a justi-
fiable abhorrence of these creatures when they are adult; when thousands
of nymphs infest her home, either she sees them not, or she bothers not
about them, but the adults are conspicuous and at once arouse her wrath.
Forthwith she hies her to the nearest chemist and gets some good exter-
minator; two weeks later she will in good faith gladly tell the merits of
"XYZ" paste, and one cannot convince her that she spread her poison
just at the time when the roaches were dying a natural death, and that they
would have disappeared at that time of the year regardless of whether or
not she spread her paste'.

Inquiline cockroaches

Some cockroaches live as guests in the nests of Hymenoptera. A notable
example is the myrmecophilous cockroach, *Attaphila fungicola* (p. 94),
which lives with leaf-cutting ants of the genus *Atta*. Superficially resembling *Attaphila* is the cockroach *Sphecophila polybiarum* which has been
taken from the nest of the vespid wasp *Polybia pygmaea* in French Guiana.[322]
This wasp constructs a small paper nest which hangs from the undersides
of leaves or twigs; it is composed of a number of cells enclosed in a common covering of 'paper' and the entrance is by one orifice in the floor of

the nest. The female wasp feeds the larvae with insects or spiders that she brings to them and it is probable that the inquiline cockroaches living on the floor of the nest feed on any small fragments of food that may drop from the wasp larvae in the cells above.

Natural enemies of cockroaches

Cockroaches have many and varied associations with a wide range of organisms including bacteria, helminths, arthropods (mites, spiders, scorpions, centipedes and other insects) and various vertebrates (amphibia, reptiles, mammals and birds). For a detailed account of these associations reference should be made to the review by Roth & Willis,[4] who have emphasised the difficulty in distinguishing between those associations which are harmful to cockroaches and those which appear neither to harm or benefit the partners of the association. There are, however, a number of clearly defined instances of predation and parasitism on cockroaches, notably on their eggs and immature stages.

Hymenoptera

Representatives of six families of Hymenoptera are known to be capable of developing on cockroach eggs. Examples of these are species of *Evania* and *Hyptia* (Evaniidae) and *Tetrastichus* (Eulophidae). A number of wasps prey on cockroaches and carry them into crevices, or back to their nests, as a source of food on which to lay their eggs. Examples of cockroach-hunting wasps are species of *Ampulex*, *Podium* and *Tachysphex*.

Evania appendigaster

This parasitic wasp (Fig. 110) is distributed throughout the tropics and subtropics and parasitizes the oothecae of *P. americana* and *P. australasiae*. It has also been recorded from *B. orientalis* in Hungary and Egypt, and has been introduced and established in Britain. Its biology has been studied by Cameron:[315] the female lays one egg in each ootheca, puncturing the egg case with her ovipositor, and taking up to half an hour to deposit the egg. The resulting larva consumes the entire contents of the ootheca and pupates within. This parasite may have three or four generations per year and is not uncommon in cockroach-infested premises, where it may exercise some control over its host. Attempts have been made to introduce this parasite into certain areas for control purposes; it has established itself satisfactorily, but there is no supporting evidence to indicate its effectiveness in biological control.

Hyptia spp.

From 459 oothecae of *Parcoblatta* (mainly *P. pensylvanica*) collected from under loose bark of dead trees, Edmunds[316] obtained a total of 1,213 specimens of four species of parasitic Hymenoptera. These were *Hyptia harpyoides* (Fig. 111a) and *Hyptia thoracica*, which were present in almost

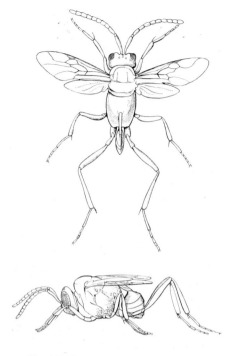

Fig. 110. *Evania appendigaster* (female).

seven per cent of the egg cases, there being one parasite per ootheca. They over-winter in the last larval stage, eventually emerging by chewing a hole 2 mm in diameter in the wall of the cockroach ootheca. The other parasites obtained were *Systellogaster ovivora* (Pteromalidae) with 262 adults in 11 oothecae, and *Syntomosphyrum blattae* (Eulophidae) which yielded an average of 92 wasps from each of ten oothecae. These species make minute exit holes in the egg case and may make two or three in the same capsule.[317]

Tetrastichus hagenowi
This is a small eulophid wasp (Fig. 111b), also widely distributed and a natural parasite of the oothecae of *P. americana*, *P. australasiae*, *P. fulginosa*, *B. orientalis* and species of *Parcoblatta*. It has not been found in Britain. The biology of this parasite has been described by Roth & Willis,[318] and by Cameron:[319] several eggs are laid in one ootheca and development is complete in 30–60 days depending on temperature and the number of wasp eggs laid. In oothecae containing few wasp larvae some cockroach eggs may complete their development and hatch. *Tetrastichus*

can have as many as six generations per year and oothecae of Wood Cockroaches may each give rise to as many as 100 adult parasites.[317]

Fig. 111. (a) Adult of *Hyptia harpyoides* with an ootheca of *Parcoblatta* sp. from which it has emerged. (b) *Tetrastichus hagenowi* ovipositing in an ootheca of *P. americana*. (Courtesy: Drs. Roth & Willis, U.S. Army Natick Laboratories.)

Ampulex compressa

This cockroach-hunting wasp is 15–25 mm long with a shining blue-green body and red femora. It is endemic throughout India, Burma and Ceylon, and its distribution extends into Africa, China, St. Helena and into some of the islands of the Indian Ocean. Williams[320] has described the biology and parasitic habit of this insect.

From observations in captivity, *Ampulex compressa* attacks the cockroach (*P. americana* and *P. australasiae*) from the side, in the region of the prothorax, and in a short lightning leap seizes the edge of the pronotum, immediately plunging her sting into the thorax. The wasp then cuts off the cockroach antennae about half way along their length and drags the insect into her nest. There, an egg (2 mm long) is glued to one of the mid-coxal plates and the nest is packed with debris to imprison the still active victim.

If the egg fails to hatch, or the larva dies when it is young, the cockroach may survive for many weeks.

The egg of *Ampulex* hatches in about three days and the larva feeds at, or near, the spot where it hatches, living externally on the coxal plate of its victim for four to five days. Entry into the cockroach occurs at the junction of the mid-coxa and the body; the larva feeds extensively within its weakening host, hollowing out its body even to the base of the legs. A cocoon of silk is then formed within the dead host. Development from egg to pupa varies from 34 to 140 days and there is often a resting larval stage within the cocoon before pupation occurs. At emergence, the wasp bites its way out of the dried cockroach. A female wasp once mated appears capable of parasitising dozens of cockroaches.

Podium spp.

These wasps occur in the southern United States[321] and have the habit of taking over the nests of the mud-daubing wasp *Sceliphron caementarium*. *Podium cardina* captures nymphs of *Parcoblatta pensylvanica* about one-third grown, on which she lays an egg, the host then being stored between mud partitions. The habit of using cockroaches as prey, is also character-istic of other species of this genus: *P. rufipes*, a solitary mason-wasp, collects Wood Cockroaches and places them in columns of clay. *P. flavipenne* digs a burrow in the ground about two inches deep: she stings the cockroach and carries the paralysed insect back to the nest where an egg is deposited behind the front coxa. This wasp carries water in her mouth to soften the clay as she makes her excavations and seals the nest containing the cockroach hosts with mud.

Tachysphex lativalvis

The only British insect recorded as preying on cockroaches is the sand wasp, *Tachysphex lativalvis*, which stocks its underground burrows with cockroach nymphs.

Other predators and parasites

A number of predators have been observed using cockroaches and their oothecae as food. Oothecae often become infested with larvae of dermestid beetles and nymphal stages are taken by the edible frog.[65] There are also numerous references in the literature to cockroaches found among the stomach contents of many species of frog and lizard. Rau quotes Wood ('Insects at Home') as saying that the cockroach is a favourite food of many animals and 'the hedgehog is so partial to it that one of these animals is sometimes kept in the kitchen for the express purpose of destroying these pests'. The same author also records cockroaches being eaten by garter snakes. In Puerto Rico, Pimental[323] found the insects in about 30 per cent of mongoose stomachs he examined, and mice, shrews and other small mammals were also predacious on cockroaches.

Overcrowded cultures in the laboratory often become infested by mites. Rau[65] found that the food used to rear Oriental Cockroaches often became infested with the 'mushroom mite' *Tyrophagus lintneri*, but the mites did not affect the health or mortality of his insects. The same author[5] believed that damp rearing conditions were responsible for the appearance of enormous populations of the mite *Rhizoglyphus tarsalis* in cultures of *P. americana*. These developed first on the mouldy food and then attacked living as well as dead cockroaches. The cockroach mite *Pimeliaphilus cunliffei* (previously *P. podapolopophagus*) (Fig. 112) lays its eggs indiscriminately in rearing cages and the nymphs feed on living and

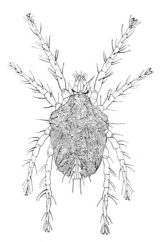

Fig. 112. The cockroach mite
Pimeliaphilus cunliffei (after
Baker *et al.*[324]).

dead cockroaches, sometimes completely destroying laboratory cultures.[318] The life history of this species has been described by Baker *et al.*[324] who indicate that one gravid female can give rise to several hundred mites under favourable conditions. Field *et al.*[325] quote instances of cultures of Oriental Cockroaches destroyed by this mite and of American Cockroaches which became heavily infested, with more than 180 mites in various stages of development observed on a single insect. Egg cases removed from infested colonies of *P. americana* and *B. germanica* failed to produce young. The same destruction can apparently occur in cultures of *Nauphoeta cinerea* attacked by the ant *Pheidole megacephala*.[109]

Defence mechanisms against predators
The principal defence mechanisms of cockroaches against natural enemies are their agility and concealment during the day. The effectiveness of 'cockroach odour' secreted by the cuticular glands in warding off predators is unknown. At least three species, however, secrete defence sprays.[326] *Eurycotis floridana* and *Neostylopyga rhombifolia* have a single gland

on the underside of the abdomen and the spray is ejected posteriorly; by turning the abdomen towards the stimulus these species can direct the spray with some degree of accuracy.

Diploptera punctata has two glands on opposite sides of the abdomen just behind the thorax; only that gland on the side of the body stimulated discharges at any one time and the spray is more broadly dispersed than that of the other species. Each gland has a sac-like reservoir in which the secretion is stored and this reservoir is associated with tracheoles which are thought to be responsible for expelling the secretion. The glands of *Eurycotis* and *Neostylopyga* are blind and in these species it is believed that ejection occurs by contraction of the muscles around the walls of the reservoir.

Tests of these defence mechanisms have shown that the spray of *Diploptera* repels most ants, carabid beetles, spiders and frogs. It produces un-co-ordinated movements of ants and beetles but recovery occurs within a few minutes. *Eurycotis* and *Neostylopyga* are not so adept at repelling other insects, but the fluid ejected by them is effective in repelling birds, lizards and frogs, especially if the spray contaminates the eyes.[326]

In addition to odours and defensive sprays, Roth & Hartman[327] are of the opinion that courtship stridulation in *Nauphoeta cinerea* (see p. 114) may have evolved as a 'disturbance sound' used for defence against enemies.

11

MOVEMENT

Voluntary movement: behaviour at rest; flight and running; articulation of the legs—
Mass migration; distance of movement; effects of population pressure; influence of
season—Night activity; night inspection—Measurement of the circadian rhythm; influence of temperature and food; changes in light and darkness; control mechanism of
diurnal rhythm; changes in the neurosecretory cycle; reset mechanism of the neurosecretory cycle
Involuntary movement: international dissemination; quarantine—Insects carried in
aircraft; cockroaches in aircraft before World War II; cockroaches taken from aircraft
in New Zealand; P. *brunnea* introduced into Britain—Cockroaches carried by ships;
incidence in food storage and food handling areas of ships; incidence in ships' holds—
Establishment of new infestations.

Movement of cockroaches may occur in two ways: (1) voluntary movement
over relatively short distances by running and flight, and (2) involuntary,
or man-assisted movement over longer distances, the insect being carried in
merchandise, by road and rail, and internationally by aeroplanes and ships.

For convenience we shall consider these two types of movement separately: under the heading of voluntary movement mention will be made of
the reports of mass migrations of cockroaches and the studies undertaken
with insects marked with paint and radioactive substances to provide
information on the distance of movement. Information of this type is of
considerable importance where it is suspected that cockroaches may have
access to disease organisms and be capable of spreading them, for example,
from sewers into nearby houses. Also under the heading of voluntary
movement we shall examine some of the laboratory studies undertaken to
explain the characteristic activity of cockroaches at night and their relative
immobility within harbourages during the day. This is a feature not only
of cockroaches, but of the behaviour of many insects of economic importance, notably of biting flies, midges, mosquitoes and many species of moths.

Under the heading of involuntary movement we shall discuss the importance of preventing the spread of unwanted insects around the world,
the functions of quarantine, and the records of cockroaches found in
aeroplanes and ships, both in the accommodation and among cargoes in
holds.

VOLUNTARY MOVEMENT

Local movements of cockroaches are known to be influenced by a large
number of factors, which together cause the insect to secure the optimum

environment; principally the optimum temperature, freedom from desiccation, and access to food and water. The preferred environment is sought by a series of discrete random movements resulting in the insect harbouring behind ovens for warmth, perhaps near tea urns for the required humidity, behind skirtings for minimum light and still air, or close to cold water pipes on which drops of condensation provide an adequate source of drinking water. In most premises, food in one form or another is likely to be readily available for consumption at night; in kitchens the small amounts of food required by cockroaches exist as residues beneath food preparation surfaces, crevices in the floor, or in the waste traps of sinks and gulleys.

The insect is made aware of its environment and of any disturbance by the many different types of sense organ discussed in Chapter 3. When alarmed, the reaction of the pest species is typified by rapid running or scurrying rather than by flight.

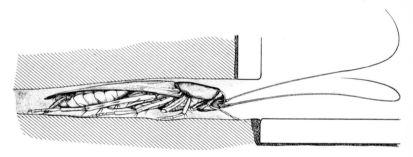

Fig. 113. Section of a narrow crevice showing the characteristic rest position of a cockroach within a harbourage.

Behaviour at rest

Cockroaches spend at least 75 per cent of their time at rest during which the pest species adopt a characteristic posture: the antennae point forwards and obliquely upwards angled at about 60° to each other. The legs hold the body a little above the surface, the terminal segment of the abdomen, or the ootheca if carried, rests on the supporting surface. The cerci extend in a slightly raised position, more vertical in nymphs than in adults. There appears to be no preferred orientation, that is to say with the body horizontal or vertical, with the head downwards or upwards, supported by, or hanging from a surface.

Within a harbourage the rest position is characterised by the antennae often being extended outside the harbourage so that these are the only structures visible (Fig. 113). The legs are held much closer to the body and the cerci are extended either horizontally or in contact with the supporting surface. In all species, the insect is able to compress the body considerably so that even minute crevices provide potential harbourages. Wille[328] has measured the minimum gaps within which the various stages of the German Cockroach are able to run. Whether or not the insect has fed does not influence the size of the crevice, but gravid females and those carrying oothecae require larger harbourages than males (Table XXIII).

If adult German Cockroaches are given a choice of spacings in which to harbour, ranging from $\frac{1}{16}$ to half an inch, 85 per cent of the insects congregate in spaces $\frac{3}{16}$ inch wide (4.8 mm).[329] The odour left in harbourages by cockroaches has a strong influence on their selection of resting sites, 83 per cent of insects occupying previously used harbourages when given the choice.

TABLE XXIII

MINIMUM VERTICAL DIMENSIONS OF HARBOURAGES IN WHICH THE DEVELOPMENTAL STAGES OF *B. GERMANICA* ARE ABLE TO MOVE
(From Wille[328])

Nymphs	mm	Adults		mm
First	0·5	MALE:	having eaten	1·6
Second	0·5		without having eaten	1·5
		FEMALE:	having eaten	1·6
Third	0·8		without having eaten	1·6
Fourth	1·0		with ootheca rotated horizontally	2·9
Fifth	1·4		before ootheca rotated	3·3
Sixth (male & female)	1·6		gravid, one day before ootheca formation	4·5

Flight and running

The German Cockroach and species of *Periplaneta* are capable of gliding flight, but this is not usually displayed except at very high temperatures. In the United States, the Brown-banded Cockroach is often attracted to lights in houses and has been observed flying indoors and out; this species does tend to fly when disturbed. Some of the outdoor woodland species (*Parcoblatta*) are capable of flight over long distances. A number of cockroaches have lost the ability to fly, and the protection to the abdomen offered by the tegmina and wings, because these have been reduced either in one sex (*B. orientalis*) or in both sexes (*E. floridana*).

The legs of cockroaches are well-developed for rapid movement. Their length enables the body to be raised well off the ground and with one exception, all the pest species are capable of climbing relatively smooth surfaces (glazed tiles and metal) immediately upon hatching from the ootheca. The Oriental Cockroach is not very adept at climbing because it is without an adhesive organ (arolium) between the claws.

Articulation of the legs

The agility of cockroaches can be attributed in some measure to the very efficient articulation of the joints of the legs. There are three types (Fig. 114): a ball and socket joint between the tibia and tarsus which allows multidirectional movement of the tarsal segments; condyles (or knuckle joints) at the junctions of the tibia and femur, and of the trochanter with

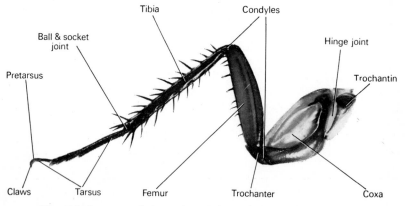

Fig. 114. Structure of the cockroach leg and the articulation of the various parts with each other and with the thorax. (Ventral view, *P. americana.*)

the coxa, allowing movements in one plane only; finally a hinge joint between the coxa along most of its length with the trochantin (the pleurite of the thorax to which the legs are attached). The three pairs of legs are all involved in walking; the forelegs, principally in gripping, the mid pair raising the thorax and abdomen off the surface on which the insect is moving and the hind pair providing thrust.

Mass migration

In early accounts of cockroaches and their behaviour, reference is made to their swarming in large numbers at certain times of the year; that *B. germanica* may develop a 'migratory instinct' has been witnessed by Marlatt[2] in Washington—'an army of thousands of roaches by one common impulse abandoned their old quarters and started on a search for a more favourable location'. The Shad roach of Philadelphia (*B. orientalis*) obtained its local name by swarming during May, coinciding with the arrival of the fish of this same name in the Delaware River.[43] Gould[59] quotes an instance of 'migration' of Oriental Cockroaches from a city dump to nearby houses and Roth & Willis[6] use a photograph, as a frontispiece to their paper on the 'Medical and Veterinary Importance of Cockroaches', showing *P. americana* issuing in enormous numbers from a sewage filter bed in Florida during flooding (Fig. 115). Gould & Deay[21] say that

B. orientalis frequently 'migrates' into homes through sewage drain pipes and Roth & Willis, referring to the domestic species write: 'they live and breed in close association with their food, or they may move out of sheltered areas under cover of darkness and migrate to obtain food and water. Natural migrations of cockroaches have been observed only a few times. Probably migrations are common, but as they undoubtedly occur at night, or other periods of low illumination, they have seldom been observed.' Nevertheless, these authors give a number of examples of mass movements of cockroaches of different species and under a variety of conditions: in one case, the march of cockroaches across a muddy street to the building

Fig. 115. Cockroaches migrating from a trickling filter at the University of Florida sewage treatment plant during the process of flooding. (Courtesy: Div. Pub. Relations, Univ. Florida, Gainesville).

opposite could not be stopped by several men with brooms who attempted to stem the advance!

Whilst swarm behaviour is characteristic of locusts and termites (to which cockroaches are closely related, see Chapter 2), it would seem that mass movements of cockroaches are not migrations in the sense of the well-defined directional movement characteristic of many butterflies. More probably the 'migrations' of cockroaches represent random foraging stimulated by high temperature, or adverse environmental conditions (as are some tropical species of ants during early rains), including depletion of food brought about by rapid increase in numbers. This type of movement has not been recorded among cockroaches in the United Kingdom despite the massive populations which are occasionally seen; nymphs and adults of *B. orientalis* have been observed actively moving on warm summer nights on the outside walls of infested properties and emerging from under paving stones, but not in the numbers implied in some of the descriptions given in the American literature.

Distance of movement

Where cockroaches are suspected of having access to organisms pathogenic to man, information on the distance and speed of movement is important for a proper understanding of the insect as a potential carrier of disease. With the concern that infections may be spread by cockroaches from sewers, a special investigation was undertaken in Tyler, Texas, in 1952 to study the bionomics of sewer cockroaches; this study was initiated jointly by the Communicable Disease Centre of the Public Health Service, Atlanta, Georgia and the Texas State Department of Health, and subsequently became known as the 'Tyler Project'. A great deal of information was obtained on the numbers of cockroaches infesting sewers, the relative abundance of the different species and the organisms associated with them (Chapter 13), but here we are concerned only with the information obtained on the extent and distance of movement of the principal species, *P. americana*.

As part of the Tyler Project cockroaches were marked and introduced into manholes; many specimens were recaught in adjacent homes and one in a grocery store a block away from the release point. One cockroach travelled 385 yards down the street to another manhole.[330] Observations at night showed that as many as 11 cockroaches left one manhole within an hour and because of their ability to disperse readily within a sewer system and into the discharge lines from property, investigations were carried out to determine whether cockroaches could enter houses through the common types of plumbing trap, having the usual water baffle.[331] In two experiments, 8 per cent and 18 per cent of test American Cockroaches negotiated the water barrier within a few days.

The results of the Tyler Project stimulated a number of investigations into cockroach movement. Examination of 22 selected manholes in Phoenix, Arizona,[332] during 1952 showed an average of about 100 *P. americana* per manhole (Fig. 116); 6,500 were trapped, marked with radioactive phosphorus and released back into the sewers at dusk through four selected manholes. The marked insects were allowed to distribute themselves over a period of 24 hours from a large dust-bin lowered into the sewer. To recover the cockroaches, 34 traps were distributed in the sewer within a radius of half a mile and ten additional traps were placed in premises very close to the release points.

During the next two months, over 1,700 cockroaches were caught, of which 900 were radioactive, all but one being trapped at the release points. The one caught elsewhere had travelled 60 feet above ground to the environs of a nearby building.

This result was contrary to the earlier reports of Gould & Deay,[21] of the migration of *P. americana* from restaurants and dumps, and it was also contrary to the results obtained the previous year in Tyler[330] demonstrating widespread dispersal of cockroaches from manholes into adjacent homes. The result could not go unchallenged. So the following year Jackson & Maier[333] repeated the experiment in the Phoenix sewers.

Fig. 116. Cockroaches (*Periplaneta* sp.) in a sewer manhole in Houma, Louisiana. (Courtesy: Public Works Journal Corp.)

In their first test they caught some 300 American Cockroaches living around a sewer manhole in an alley of a middle-class residential block. The nearest manholes on the same sewer lateral were 600 feet upstream and 460 feet downstream. They marked the 300 cockroaches with yellow paint and returned them into the manhole; 45 traps were sited in the immediate neighbourhood, next to refuse bins and in kitchens, which were examined for the following five days. The neighbouring manholes were also checked for yellow painted cockroaches, but again, disappointment; despite some traps being placed immediately above the 'release' manhole, none of the cockroaches caught had yellow marks, although marked adults held in the laboratory retained their yellow paint well for at least a week. The ratio of marked to unmarked cockroaches in the manhole used for release fell from 3:1 at the time of release to 1:4 a week later suggesting dispersal into the sewer lines. Two months later only one marked female was captured in a house about 125 feet from the release point.

Effects of population pressure

Undeterred, these same workers carried out two further tests using cockroaches marked with radioactive phosphorus as had Schoof & Siverly earlier. Jackson & Maier[334] were intent on finding out why extensive movement from the sewers could be obtained under one set of conditions, as in the Tyler Project, but not in another. These two tests were made in a low-rent housing area arranged in quadrangles each containing 20–24 apartments with a single manhole and its laterals servicing each quadrangle.

About 1,200 and 500 marked cockroaches were released in the two tests, which differed in one important regard; the 1,200 cockroaches were trapped from manholes outside the housing estate ('foreign' to the release site) and were superimposed on the population already living in the release manhole, whereas the 500 constituted almost all the visible population of the manhole from which they were caught and into which they were again released. During the next two weeks, 7,000 and 1,600 cockroaches, respectively, were caught in the two tests. Seventy-one of the 7,000 captives were marked, but only four marked ones were among the 1,600. In the first test, one of the marked cockroaches was taken in a kitchen 80 feet from the release point and 22 in a small hollow in the ground adjacent to the wall of an apartment 50 feet away. Excavation of the soil showed that the trap placed in this hole was adjacent to a disused sewer, connected through the system to the release manhole 65 feet down the sewer line. A further five marked cockroaches were caught above ground at a distance of up to 95 feet and an additional 43 tagged cockroaches were caught in manholes, some of the insects having travelled 350 feet. This result was in distinct contrast with the results of the second test in which only four marked cockroaches were recaptured and among these, the greatest distance of dispersal through the sewer was 170 feet.

Why then was there such a difference in the results; in the first test, nearly six per cent of released cockroaches were recaught outside the release manhole but less than one per cent in the second. The distance of movement was also small in the second test, and in all other experiments, where cockroaches were returned in comparatively small numbers into their own environment. But where strong population pressures were created by superimposing additional 'foreign' individuals onto an already existing sewer population, the catches above ground and along both directions of the sewer were high.

Jackson & Maier[334] compare this latter situation with the condition likely to be encountered with the partial flooding of a sewer system. They also suggest that high population pressure, the release of 1,000 insects superimposed on natural sewer populations, is the likely explanation for the emigration obtained in the Tyler Project. About the same numbers of released insects were also used by Schoof & Siverly[332] in each manhole in the Phoenix experiment, but these manholes were as much as 720 feet apart,

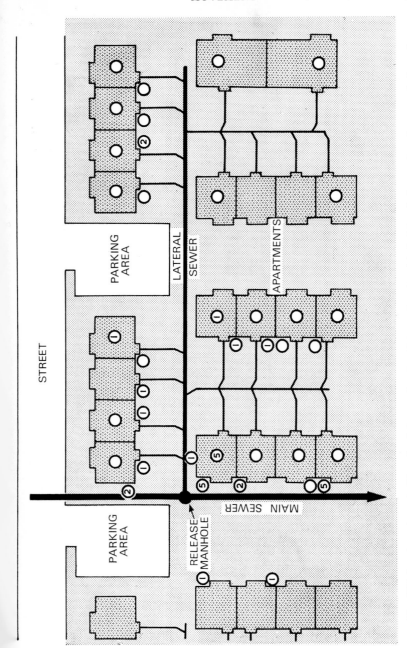

Fig. 117. Apartment area in Phoenix, Arizona, showing the trapping sites (circles) in relation to the release manhole, and the numbers of marked cockroaches caught. In this experiment, undertaken in June, the natural population of the sewer manhole (400 cockroaches) was increased by the release of 2,000 additional marked *P. americana* (after Jackson & Maier[334]).

considerably greater than the relatively short distances over which cock-roaches normally move.

Influence of season

The final experiment carried out by Jackson & Maier in Phoenix[334] was to compare the effects on cockroach movement of 'undisturbed' and 'stressed' populations during January 1954 (with an average maximum temperature in the sewer of 22°C and average minimum of 13°C) and during June 1954 (with a mean sewer temperature of 35°C±3°C).

When large numbers of extraneous cockroaches were superimposed on normal manhole populations extensive emigration occurred during warm weather (Fig. 117) but not during the winter. When the numbers of released cockroaches did not increase the manhole population, only limited move-ment was experienced in both seasons. Jackson & Maier are therefore of the opinion that while an occasional cockroach moving out from a contami-nated sewer is of little epidemiological importance, extensive emigrations which may result from sudden increases in population in warm weather could convert cockroaches into important vectors of disease. Certainly these studies with released cockroaches in sewers throws some light on the probable cause of the 'mass migrations' referred to earlier in this Chapter.

Night activity

There are now many recorded observations to indicate that biological organisms are able, endogenously, to measure the course of the time of day. They have a sense of time, or a time memory. This physiological clock operates on 24-hour cycles; the endogenous rhythm becomes established by heredity and is not induced in the early stages of the individual's de-velopment.[335] This pattern of behaviour occurs in many species of insects: they show a peak of activity at a certain time of the day and maintain that same rhythm even though environmental conditions may change. Mosqui-toes bite particularly at dusk, and the flour mill moth, *Anagasta kühniella* also flies actively at dusk at a time when the machines of a flour mill are normally turned off, and again at dawn some hours before the machines are turned on.

There is still considerable controversy as to whether some of the daily rhythms or 'biological clocks' of insects are governed by influences within the organism or externally. Halberg[336] has proposed the term 'Circadian' rhythm to describe cycles of activity which have a periodicity of about 24 hours (Circa = about, diem = day).

Under the normal sequence of light and dark, *P. americana* and many other pest species of cockroach show a marked increase in activity just as it begins to get dark, but activity ceases after five or six hours and they remain quiescent throughout the following day. After the period during which they remain immobile, slight movement is resumed which then builds up to a peak again at dusk (Fig. 118a).

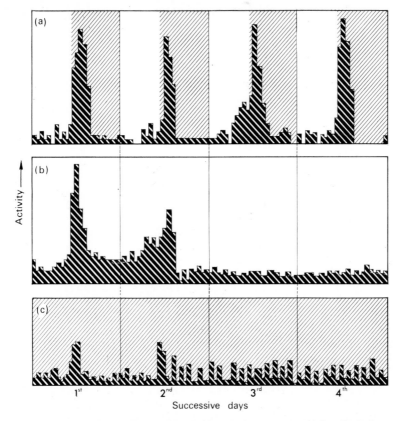

Fig. 118. The activity of *P. americana* at room temperature (a) in alternating light and darkness, (b) in continuous light, (c) in continuous darkness. Hatched areas represent dark periods (after Harker[338]).

Harker[337] has analysed the locomotor activity of *Periplaneta* during alternating 12-hour periods of light and dark (Fig. 119). Six stages may be recognised:

Stage A   some time before the onset of darkness the level of activity may rise.

      B   after the onset of darkness the increase in activity is sudden and marked.

      C   a period of two to three hours is reached, in which activity is high.

      D   the level of activity decreases sharply over a period of about two hours.

      E   activity remains at a fairly low level during the latter half of the dark period.

F   about five hours after the onset of light, activity is at a minimum or may cease completely for an hour or two.
This same sequence of activity is also maintained when artificial light is used in place of daylight.

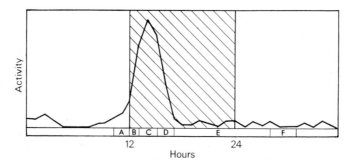

Fig. 119. The six stages of the locomotor activity rhythm of *Periplaneta americana* in alternating light and darkness. Hatched area represents dark period (from Harker[337]). For explanation of lettering, see text above.

Night inspection

Those concerned with cockroach control are well aware of the apparent absence of cockroaches in an infested building when visited during the day. Pyrethrum sprays to 'flush out', or stimulate cockroaches to move from their harbourages are required if all locations of the infestation are to be discovered. The same premises visited at night can give a totally different impression of the size and distribution of the infestation, and a 'night inspection' has long been recognised among pest control operators as the ideal method for assessing the extent of residual infestations following insecticide application.

At night when cockroaches are foraging for food they will readily disperse if disturbed by excessive noise. The turning on of an electric light, however, will not drive German Cockroaches from their food, providing the switch is operated quietly. The relative insensitivity of cockroaches to disturbance at night is well described by Wille[328] from observations made at the turn of the century: 'during the 1905–6 winter in a kitchen of a large restaurant in Halle, which was brightly lit at night where cooking went on all night long, German Cockroaches ran around on the walls, ceiling and floor in vast numbers and were not in the slightest affected by the light. The creatures dropped into the cooking pots and were constantly being fished out. Similarly in a large Berlin hospital, in the sick rooms in which lights burned, German Cockroaches ran around quite unaffected by the light and even crawled into the beds of the patients'.

The lack of evasive movement caused by turning on a light at night is emphasised because of the two commonly held views that a 'night inspection' should be carried out by torchlight, without turning on the lights of the room, and that if an inspection is to be carried out late at night, the lights should be left on when the working staff leave the premises rather than put on when the inspection begins. Neither of these 'precautions' is necessary. More important, pest control operators should recognise that the peak of maximum activity (period C of Fig. 119) occurs at different times of the year with the alteration in day length; in Britain, this period is between about 6 p.m. and 9 p.m. in winter and between midnight and 3 a.m. in summer.

Measurement of the circadian rhythm

Many research workers have devised equipment capable of measuring the phases of activity of cockroaches so that the insects can be studied undisturbed. Harker[338] recorded activity by attaching one end of a fine thread to the pronotum of an American Cockroach, and the other end to a marker on a revolving drum. Roberts[339] used an actograph in which cockroaches were contained in a wheel cage mounted on a delicate bearing, so well balanced, that they rotated the whole assembly with ease and the movements were recorded electrically. A similar but more primitive device was used 40 years earlier by Wille[328] whereby movement of *B. germanica* caused a lever to record directly onto a chart. By dividing the period of movement by the period of rest he obtained a 'mobility quotient' which for different insects (at 18·5–22°C) ranged from 0·07 to 0·26.

To explore the use of cockroaches in space, Sullivan & colleagues[340] devised a simple electronic apparatus to monitor the electrophysiological activity of the Madeira Cockroach. Their 'biopack', developed with the requirements for space studies of light weight, reliability and simplicity, involved the insertion of fine electrodes into the rear legs of the immobilised insect, but as Dr. Dutky accepts[341] 'however simple or sophisticated the equipment might be to record this information, the need to immobilise the insect on a glass slide by securing it by its wings with adhesive tape is a very serious physiological insult to any kind of animal'! Subsequently Dutky and his colleagues devised a method which allowed the cockroach limited freedom of movement and access to food and water but still on a leash of flexible connecting wires. Their studies showed that the peak levels of electrophysical activity in the insect, at about sunset (1900–2100 hours), coincided with the onset of circadian activity in *Leucophaea maderae*.

The most sophisticated equipment for monitoring cockroach activity has been devised by Schechter *et al.*[342] which does not involve any attachments to the insects. This equipment was used to record the locomotor activity of the Madeira Cockroach over many months and consisted of a capacity-sensing device in which movements of the cockroach within a cylinder produced electrical signals. This equipment gave the type of 'trace' recorded in Fig. 120.

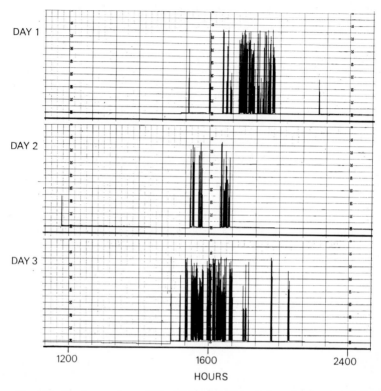

1200   1600   2400

HOURS

Fig. 120. The locomotor activity of the Madeira cockroach over a period of three consecutive days, recorded with a capacity-sensing device (photograph by Schechter, Dutky & Sullivan[342])

Influence of temperature and food

When *Periplaneta* is held at a constant temperature and then subjected to a sudden increase or decrease, there is an immediate increase or decrease in the length of the normal 24-hour cycle, which then rapidly adjusts itself. Thus Bünning[343] found that the period of the rhythm of *P. americana* at 22°C was 24·5 hours, but after chilling for 12 hours at 5°C the first period dropped to 21·5 hours and then increased in successive cycles to 23·0, 23·5 and 24·5 hours. The 'speed of the clock' was not, however, affected when *Periplaneta* was given short, four-hour periods of high temperature (32°C).

According to Bünning the well defined activity rhythms of *P.*

americana are lost below 18°C and this has been confirmed at 17°C by Roberts.[339] Within the normal temperature ranges of the American Cockroach the activity periods in total darkness are 25·1 hours at 20°C, reducing to 24·4 hours at 25°C and 24·3 hours at 30°C. Roberts concludes that the rhythm of *P. americana* is temperature compensated at least within the range 20°–30°C.

In their normal environment cockroaches eat during the period of activity at night. If, however, food and water are not made available at that time, but only during the day (Fig. 121) hunger does not appear to modify the activity cycle.[338]

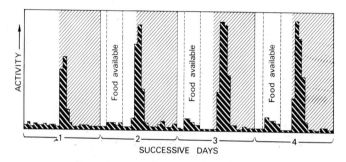

Fig. 121. The activity of *P. americana* in alternating light and darkness (hatched areas), when food is available only in the light period (between the dotted lines). The cockroaches have been starved for 4 days previous to the experiment (after Harker[338]).

Changes in light and darkness

In some industrial and catering establishments infestations of cockroaches are subject to artificial light for long periods of the day and night. Occasionally too, in cellars and ducts, cockroaches may experience total darkness throughout 24 hours.

Using the Madeira Cockroach, Schechter *et al.*[342] were able to show that this insect begins its cycle of activity near sunset (5–6 p.m.) under all three conditions of (1) alternating daylight and darkness, (2) continuous darkness and (3) continuous light. However, if darkness and light were continuous and not alternated, the average circadian rhythm became gradually shorter than 24 hours, and a pronounced secondary period of activity occurred at dawn which was more noticeable in continuous light than under the other conditions.

Harker[338] did similar experiments with *P. americana* to find out the effects of reversing the periods of light and darkness. Under these new conditions the normal activity rhythm continued for up to four days, but was then gradually replaced by a new rhythm with the peak of activity starting at the beginning of the new dark period. She found that in both continuous light and continuous darkness, the original rhythm of *P. americana* was maintained for up to five days but was soon lost to 'a sequence of random or spasmodic movements' (Fig. 118b and c).

Roberts[339] also examined the effects of total darkness and of constant light of several intensities. He used three species of cockroach: the Madeira Cockroach, the American Cockroach and *Byrsotria fumigata*. Because his experiments showed that the activity patterns of females were generally more erratic than males, he confined his tests to males only. In constant darkness the rhythm of *L. maderae* and *B. fumigata* persisted for at least three months without any indication of a gradual loss in periodicity. The cycle ranged for different individuals from 23·5 to 24·5 hours. Similarly, Roberts was unable to find any loss of rhythm in any of the three species after a few days in continuous light as had been reported for *Blatta*[344] and for *Periplaneta*.[338] What he did find, however, was that in continuous light the periodicity of the cycle was lengthened by an increment of 20–60 minutes when the insects were placed in light intensities of up to 25 foot candles. Exposure to constant light also introduced a secondary peak of locomotor activity about ten hours after the onset of the primary peak, an observation which was later supported by Schechter *et al*.[342]

Roberts suggests that the secondary peak which occurs in continuous light, and sometimes among cockroaches in alternating darkness and light, closely coincides with dawn in the insect's natural environment 'stirring it to activity until it reaches an optimally dark refuge where its movements will cease'.

Control mechanism of diurnal rhythm

Janet Harker, in a series of papers, has done much to explain the physiology of circadian rhythm in cockroaches. In a previous chapter of this book mention is made of the many physiological processes of the cockroach which are controlled by hormones, or neurosecretions, produced by tissues associated with the brain and ganglia. Scharrer[345] was the first to show that the suboesophageal ganglion of the cockroach contains neurosecretory cells which form an integral part of the endocrine system, and it is these cells which are now known to play an important part in the control of cockroach activity.

In early experiments, Harker[346] removed the heads from American Cockroaches and found that the decapitated insects could continue to move quite actively for about ten days, but showed no rhythm. This suggested that the internal mechanism controlling the activity cycle was located in the head and since changes in light and dark are likely to be perceived by the compound eyes or ocelli, experiments were carried out to discover the effects on activity when these were covered.

Occlusion of the compound eyes or cutting of the nerve from the eye to the brain failed to prevent cockroaches from displaying their normal rhythm, but when the ocelli alone were destroyed or painted over, cockroaches in alternating light and darkness gradually lost their activity rhythm (Fig. 122). By contrast, the cockroaches became active during the day, but this too could be eliminated if the compound eyes were blackened. This suggested to Harker that the ocelli acted as 'time keepers' but the manner in which the ocelli performed this function remained to be discovered.

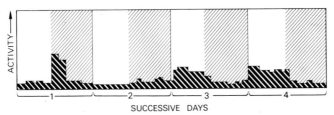

Fig. 122. The activity of *P. americana* in alternating light and darkness (hatched areas) after the ocelli have been blackened (after Harker[338]).

At about the same time, Hoyle[347] showed that in darkness, or when the ocelli are occluded, there is a continuous discharge of nerve impulses in the commissures which link the brain to the suboesophageal ganglion. Harker postulated that these impulses could be the means by which the suboesphageal ganglion is stimulated to produce an activity promoting secretion. She proved this to be so by removing the suboesophageal ganglia from normal cockroaches and implanting them into the abdomens of headless cockroaches held in continuous light. These insects showed the normal activity cycle demonstrating that the stimulus for activity could be relayed from one insect to another (Fig, 123).

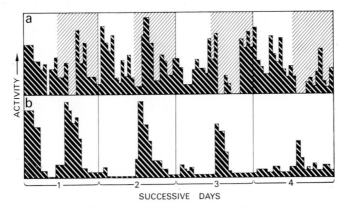

Fig. 123. The activity of a headless *P. americana*, (a) in alternating light and darkness (hatched areas), (b) in continuous light after implantation with a sub-oesophageal ganglion from a normally rhythmic cockroach (after Harker[338]).

From these experiments Harker[338] was able to conclude that 'at least part of the mechanism of the internal clock is an endocrine secretion released by the suboesophageal ganglia and that this is governed by the extrinsic factors of light and darkness through the medium of the ocelli. The suboesophageal ganglia themselves appear to be the "retainers" of the rhythm in that they can be completely isolated (as in implantation experiments) and yet continue to secrete at definite times'.

Changes in the neurosecretory cycle

In her more recent studies, Harker[337] set out to discover the extent to which the neurosecretory mechanism of the American Cockroach could be modified by changing the onset of light and darkness. In the normal condition, secretion is produced at the beginning of cockroach activity which in turn corresponds with the onset of darkness. But what would happen if darkness occurred when secretion was not normally taking place?

Implantation experiments in which suboesophageal ganglia from cockroaches placed in darkness at different times of the day, were transferred to cockroaches not showing the normal rhythm, provided a picture of the periodicity of neurosecretion. When a rhythmically secreting ganglion is implanted in this way the recipient cockroach follows an activity rhythm in phase with the implanted ganglion.

These experiments showed that there are three stages in the neurosecretory cycle, (1) when secretion will take place whatever the external conditions, (2) another when secretion will take place if there is a change from light to darkness (Harker calls this the period of 'possible' secretion) and (3) a stage when no secretion can be evoked (the period of 'impossible' secretion) (Fig. 124). She sums this up by saying that 'if a change from light to darkness occurs at a time when secretion is already taking place, the phases of the cycle appear not to be reset in any way and the next secretory period occurs at the normal time. If the onset of darkness occurs at a time when secretion would not normally be taking place, but when the cells are able to respond to the stimulus, then the cycle is reset so that secretion next occurs 24 hours after the stimulus. If secretion cannot take place at the time of the stimulus (a change from light to dark) then the neurosecretory cycle appears to be unaffected and secretion continues to take place at the normal time'.[337]

Reset mechanism of the neurosecretory cycle

Without wishing to over-complicate this account of the factors involved in the control of cockroach activity, it must be emphasised that the suboesophageal ganglion is not alone in its control of circadian rhythm. In a further study, Harker[348] was able to chill the neurosecretory cells of the suboesophageal ganglion of intact insects to very low temperatures, without lowering the temperature of the rest of the insect's body. When the ganglion was chilled for four hours, the rhythm of the test cockroach

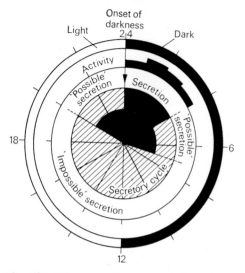

Fig. 124. Diagrammatic representation of the neurosecretory cycle in relation to time of darkness and locomotor activity (from Harker[337]).

remained unchanged. When, however, the ganglion was chilled for this same period, but dissected out and immediately implanted into a cockroach not showing a normal activity pattern, a rhythm was induced, which was four hours late. By contrast, ganglia chilled for four hours but not dissected out or implanted into other cockroaches until 24 hours after chilling, caused no delay in the onset of the rhythm. This has prompted Harker to suggest that there is some factor in the insect other than the ocelli or sub-oesophageal ganglion which can reset the neurosecretory cycle but which requires time to take effect.

INVOLUNTARY MOVEMENT

During the course of servicing work by pest control operators, many examples come to light of cockroaches carried by transport in local trade. Oothecae of *B. orientalis* carried in beer crates between the bottling plants of breweries and hotels is not uncommon. In some instances it is possible to trace these involuntary movements back to infestations in manufacturing premises. Mallis *et al.*[349] give an excellent example of a problem where a large modern brewery was receiving German Cockroaches in returnable cartons which were then being shipped out to its customers in the refilled cartons. Modification in the design of the carton to remove as many crevices as possible and treatment with a cockroach repellent (see Vol. II) were successful in preventing cockroaches from being carried in this way. Because certain species of cockroach, such as *P. americana* and *P. australasiae*, are relatively rare in Britain the task of tracing the means by which these come to be introduced into premises of manufacturing industries— *via* the road transport and the ship from which the infested consignment was unloaded—is relatively easy.

Two myths which it is felt necessary to dispel in connection with cockroach movement are first, the widespread belief that cockroaches (*B. orientalis*) are introduced into premises in coke, and secondly that laundry baskets are a common means by which cockroaches are introduced into hotels and hospitals. Why should the gas works be a source of infestation of cockroaches? It seems far more plausible that cockroaches infesting a boiler house are seen at some time to crawl over coke, which provides them with excellent harbourage and moisture, for which cockroaches in such an environment would show considerable interest, rather than the coke itself being the means by which the insects are introduced. Similarly there are many instances in hospitals where the warmth of linen cupboards provides an ideal environment for cockroach infestation; the fact that these areas, and laundries too, become foci for infestations has led to the belief that laundry baskets are the common link. The occasional presence of cockroaches or their oothecae in laundry baskets is probably no more than a fortuitous association.

International dissemination

Most of the common domiciliary species of cockroach have become distributed widely. Yet not so long ago, probably not before the slave trade between West Africa and the United States, many of these cockroaches, the American, Australian, the Brown-banded and Madeira Cockroaches, did not exist in the New World. The evidence strongly suggests that these insects crossed the Atlantic in slave ships and became established in the southern states of America, in some instances possibly by way of the West Indies.[1] The Lobster or Cinerous Cockroach also reached the United States from Africa but by a more circuitous route (Fig. 27).

Once an exotic species of cockroach gains a foothold in a new territory there can be no better example of its potential rate of spread than that demonstrated by the Brown-banded Cockroach in the United States; this species was first recorded on the southern tip of Florida in 1903 and is now reported from every State but one throughout North America (p. 68).

The two species of cockroach common in Britain, viz. *B. orientalis* and *B. germanica*, came, it is believed, from north and north-east Africa, entering Europe by way of early trade in the eastern Mediterranean. There seems little doubt that the trading vessels of the Greeks and Phoenicians and later, of the Spanish and Portuguese, did a great deal to colonise the world with cockroaches.

Even today, in the late twentieth century, ships continue to arrive at our ports carrying cockroaches. *B. germanica* is the principal species in the galleys and accommodation of ships; cargoes in the holds are also associated with cockroaches, both of non-pest species (notably *Panchlora* and *Henschoutedenia* which often arrive on imports of bananas) and of the already long-established domiciliary cockroaches, *B. germanica* and *P. americana*. As Laird[350] rightly comments in connection with species found in aircraft, 'some of the insects are so intimately associated with man and his foodstuffs that their non-discovery in association with international transport would be more surprising than their discovery'.

Quarantine

The inadvertent introduction of undesirable insects into countries throughout the world is now much reduced by quarantine. Early in the fourteenth century, the city of Venice required that all ships which wished to trade there had to remain at anchor for 40 days prior to docking. The word quarantine (derived from the Italian *quarantina*, meaning 'forty') has now come to mean, not 40 days of isolation to ensure freedom from disease, but a system of scientifically established restrictions, involving in some instances embargoes on the import of certain commodities, and in others, inspection and treatment of people, animals, cargoes and the fabric of the vessels in which goods are introduced.[351]

California was the first North American State to take action in 1886 to prevent the introduction of agricultural pests and plant diseases from foreign countries and from other States. In 1912 the Federal Plant Quarantine Act established regulations covering the whole of international commerce with the result that today regulations are in force covering goods handled in trade, as well as the possible accidental introduction of insects in passenger baggage.

International quarantine involves an extensive knowledge of pests and their status throughout the world. Reagan,[352] estimates that there are 20,000 pests of economic importance not so far introduced into the United States, many of which could readily become established, given the opportunity. Many of the land masses over which plants, plant products and livestock are transported, are so large that quarantine must also be imposed to prevent internal spread within a country. Thus the inspection and treatment of goods at inter-state boundaries (e.g. in Australia) makes as significant a contribution to pest confinement as quarantine applied at ports.

More difficult to control than the spread of unwanted insects by national and international trade, however, is the unwitting spread of insects by the internationally travelling public, notably by air. Since World War II, the great increase in air travel has magnified the problem of quarantine very many times. One hundred and eighty-six million people passed through the borders of the United States in 1965, nearly equal to the population of that country. Of 446,000 consignments inspected by United

States quarantine personnel, 32,000 (seven per cent), were infested. How many infested lots escaped detection is not known. This vast increase in international travel, exchange of goods in trade, and the speed of movement from one part of the world to another, requires the strictest measures to prevent world-wide dissemination of unwanted insects.

The setting-up of import permits, quarantine regulations and the subsequent policing of such regulations by inspection and treatment cannot, by virtue of the size of the problem, be 100 per cent effective, but they can act as a useful deterrent to the spread of undesirable insects of economic importance. Where infested goods escape the net of port inspection, and insects establish themselves in an importing country, there is every justification for using the full range of pest control procedures to eliminate the unwanted species.

The philosophy of quarantine, as summarised by Reagan[352] of the United States Department of Agriculture, 'is to:

1. Keep foreign pests out rather than have to control them;
2. Eradicate, rather than live with them;
3. Contain and suppress their spread wherever possible if eradication is not feasible;
4. Use the best methods available;
5. Deny entry of a commodity if an effective means of treatment is not possible.'

Insects carried in aircraft

One area of the world in which the author has had personal experience of extremely strict quarantine control is the mid-Pacific. The Hawaiian islands support agricultural pests, notably of fruits and vegetables, not so far established on the American mainland. Hawaii is an international 'all change' and the holiday resort of at least a quarter of a million Americans each year. The possibility of exotic insects of considerable economic importance becoming disseminated around the world *via* Honolulu airport in the absence of quarantine control would indeed be great.

On the chance of discovering as soon as possible after arrival any new insects which might arrive alive in Hawaii, particularly mosquito vectors of malaria, the U.S. Navy and Public Health Service operated, towards the end of World War II, light traps primarily at or near the large airports.[353] Over 150,000 insects were collected between 1944 and 1946. In 1945 alone, between 1,200 and 1,500 planes were estimated to have arrived each month from outside the territory. During the last 18 months of the war 15 insect species new to the Hawaiian islands, and apparently recently arrived, were caught, the majority of them firmly established.[354]

It was not possible to prove that any one of these new species became established as a result of introduction by airplane, but one of them was a beetle (*Rhipidius* spp.) whose larvae parasitise *B. germanica*. Eight of these beetles were taken in light traps on the island of Oahu during 1945 and a

German Cockroach parasitised by this beetle was taken from a plane arriving at Honolulu from the South Pacific. Thus, not only may new pest species be introduced by air transport but parasites of already established species may be introduced by the same route.

Cockroaches in aircraft before World War II

Over the last two decades the type and number of aircraft travelling international routes has changed out of all recognition. Nevertheless, the records listed by Whitfield[355] for cockroaches collected from aircraft principally at Khartoum and Miami before World War II are of interest. His main purpose was to appraise the inter-relation between air transport and the possible spread of Malaria and Yellow Fever. He lists 227 different species of insects taken in commercial aircraft: they include 24 identified cockroaches belonging to three species (Table XXIV), and almost as many unidentified cockroaches. In some instances cockroaches were recorded

TABLE XXIV

COCKROACHES RECORDED IN COMMERCIAL AIRCRAFT BEFORE
WORLD WAR II
(From Whitfield[355])

Species	No. of insects	Date	Where collected	Plane from
Identified:				
S. *supellectilium* (nymph)	1	July 1935	Khartoum	Capetown
,, ,,	1	Dec. 1935	,,	,,
,, ,,	1	Dec. 1935	,,	,,
,, ,,	5	Dec. 1935	,,	Cairo
,, (adult)	3	Mar. 1938	,,	Asmara
,, ,,	1	July 1938	,,	Durban
B. *germanica* (nymph)	1	June 1936	,,	Capetown
,, (adult)	7	May 1936	,,	,,
,, ,,	1	June 1936	,,	,,
,, ,,	2	Jan. 1937	,,	Cairo
P. *australasiae*	1	1938	Miami	Maracaibo
Unidentified:				
Supella sp.	1	1938	Miami	Rio de Janeiro
Blattella sp.	1	July 1938	Khartoum	Durban
Other cockroaches	1	1934	Kisumi	(not known)
,,	1	1934	,,	,,
,,	1	Sep. 1935	Khartoum	Capetown
,,	11	1938	Miami	Barranquilla
,,	6	1938	,,	Cristobal
,,	1	1938	,,	Port of Spain

living in the wings of airplanes where they were apparently feeding on glue and 'dope'.

Cockroaches taken from aircraft in New Zealand

At present New Zealand and its neighbouring islands are free from *Anopheles* mosquitoes, and their continued exclusion is one of the reasons for examining aircraft arriving from the South Pacific area.[356] Laird found that the basal rims of astrodomes function as light traps for some species and 76 insects were collected from the astrodomes of two aircraft alone.

During 1943–44, insects belonging to 100 species were collected from 16 aircraft which had arrived from the Pacific Islands. Among these were 26 of medical and economic importance. Four cockroaches were included, two being identified as *B. germanica* and *Leucophaea* (*Pycnoscelus*) *surinamensis*.[350] The aircraft carrying these cockroaches had flown to New Zealand direct from the New Hebrides or *via* New Caledonia.

In 1951, 540 insects were found in aircraft arriving in New Zealand, including 32 cockroaches taken from 27 planes; these comprised 17 *B. germanica*, 10 *P. australasiae* and 5 *P. americana*, chiefly from the baggage compartments of the aircraft from Australia, Norfolk Island and Fiji.[356] To relate these introductions to the species already present in New Zealand, Laird[357] states that '*B. germanica* is already an abundant pest, but *P. americana* although very common throughout most of the Pacific and sometimes found in New Zealand wharf sheds, does not seem to have gained a firm foothold'. Laird gives an analysis of the distribution within the aircraft of the 540 insects (Table XXV); in addition to the baggage

TABLE XXV

THE NUMBER OF COLLECTIONS OF VARIOUS INSECTS MADE FROM DIFFERENT SECTIONS OF 111 AIRCRAFT AND THE NUMBER OF SPECIMENS FOUND: 343 AIRCRAFT WERE INSPECTED
(From Laird[356])

Section	Number of collections	Number of specimens
Baggage and cargo	12	217
Main accommodation compartment	48	144
Astrodome	12	123
Pantry, servery	13	22
Baggage compartments	12	22
Pilot's compartment	6	9
Toilet compartment	3	3
Exterior of fuselage	32	Many egg masses
Totals	138	540

compartment, cockroaches were taken from the servery, luggage racks and main compartment.

P. brunnea introduced into Britain

One of the best documented and most recent examples of a cockroach introduced into Britain, which succeeded in producing infestations in nearby buildings, is that of *Periplaneta brunnea* at London Airport. This cockroach has been introduced into Britain in the holds of ships carrying Dominican bananas[89],[90] but no established infestations had been recorded prior to 1965. London Airport currently handles, annually, more than 13 million international travellers and is involved in a quarter of a million air movements.

The first infestation was found in one of the airport buildings which contained four calorifiers (heat exchange units) supplying domestic hot water. This room averaged 21–23°C, and its door opened into a service corridor from which short passages ran directly to the airfield. Here trolleys loaded with baggage constantly passed to and from the planes. It is possible that *P. brunnea* may have been introduced in this way, but more probably, it gained entry from the baggage conveyors directly above the ceiling of the calorifier room. Bills[91] suggests that baggage coming in from the southern states of the U.S.A. and destined for Europe or elsewhere, could have carried *P. brunnea* which subsequently gained access to this section of the building.

A year later, Bills[92] discovered a second infestation of *P. brunnea* at the same airport in buildings about one and a quarter miles from the first, this time in an animal transit centre. The number of animals passing through was reported as 50,000 a month. This time the infestation occurred in a stable heated to 21–24°C, which had no connection by underground duct, or by traffic, with the previous infestation. The introduction of cockroaches in this instance was possibly by way of food containers which frequently accompany the animals.

Cockroaches carried by ships

Many of the early records of cockroaches on ships leave little doubt that the principal species carried in the accommodation was the American Cockroach. This may have been true of the early sailing vessels and even as recently as 1912, a paper in *The Entomologist's Record* by Shelford[358] refers to *P. americana* as 'the well known ship's cockroach'. But this is certainly not true of modern cargo vessels and passenger liners, in which *P. americana* is now rare, having been displaced by *B. germanica*. What feature of ship construction has caused this change in species dominance is not known. Could it be that the German Cockroach has risen to this position by virtue of its greater tolerance of modern insecticides compared with *P. americana*, and by its more recent development of resistance to compounds such as chlordane and dieldrin. This is certainly one possible

S

explanation, since the environment provided for cockroaches on ships would appear to suit both species equally well (see Chapter 12).

Roth & Willis[4] give an interesting resume of the early records of cockroaches found on ships: 'The earliest recognisable record of cockroaches on shipboard is Moffett's (1634) statement that when Drake captured the ship *Philip*, he found it overrun with cockroaches (*Blattarum alatarum*). Bligh (1792) described disinfesting H.M.S. *Bounty* with boiling water to kill cockroaches. Chamisso (1829) reported that he had seen ships' casks, in which rice or grain had been stored, that were found to be filled with *Blattella germanica* when opened. During a voyage from England to Van Diemen's Land, Lewis (1836) was greatly annoyed by hundreds of cockroaches flying about his cabin at night; the most numerous resembled *Periplaneta americana* and another was similar to *Ectobius lapponicus*.[359–362] Lewis describing the infestation of *P. americana* says that the cockroaches occurred 'in immense profusion, and had communication with every part of the ship, between the timbers or skin. The ravages they committed on everything edible were very extensive; not a biscuit but was more or less polluted by them, and amongst the cargo 300 cases of cheeses, which had holes in them to prevent their sweating, were considerably damaged, some of them being half devoured and not one without some marks of their residence'.

Incidence in food storage and food-handling areas of ships

Evans & Porter[363] recorded the incidence of insects in the food storage and handling areas of 1,193 ships inspected at New Orleans during 1960–63, and 235 ships at Miami from 1957 to 1961. These records were acquired by the Inspectors of the Division of Foreign Quarantine, U.S. Public Health Service, who promote efforts to achieve good sanitation on ships entering the United States from foreign ports. Among cockroaches found in the galleys and mess rooms, the German Cockroach was encountered by far the most frequently, followed by the American Cockroach as a very poor second (Table XXVI). Populations of *B. germanica* were reported as very large on some vessels, occurring on 205 (i.e. 14 per cent) of the 1,428 vessels inspected. The next most common insects were various species of ants, notably at Miami (107 occurrences), followed by species of *Tribolium* (100) and saw-toothed grain beetle, *Oryzaephilus surinamensis* (43 occurrences).

Incidence in ships' holds

As part of the responsibility of the Ministry of Agriculture, Fisheries and Food, a similar inspectorate operates at British ports concerned with infestation in cargoes in ships' holds. Among 3,632 cargoes inspected in Britain on arrival from West Africa during the eight years 1945–52, *B. germanica* occurred most often.[364] Other species found in the holds were

TABLE XXVI

FREQUENCY OF OCCURRENCE OF COCKROACHES COLLECTED
FROM FOOD STORAGE AND HANDLING AREAS ON 1,193 SHIPS
ENTERING NEW ORLEANS (1960–63) AND 235 VESSELS ENTERING
MIAMI (1957–61)
(From Evans & Porter[363])

Species	Number of vessels from which each species was collected	
	New Orleans	Miami
Blattella germanica	188	17
Periplaneta americana	9	—
Periplaneta fuliginosa	2	—
Periplaneta spp.	2	1
Nahublattella ecuadorana	2	—
Blatta orientalis	1	—
Panchlora irrorata	1	—
Parcoblatta sp.	1	—
Litopeltis sp.	1	—
Nyctibora sp.	—	1
Anaplecta sp.	—	1
Unidentified cockroaches	—	15

P. americana, P. australasiae and *Neostylopyga rhombifolia* (formerly *Dorylaea rhombifolia*).

Cargoes arrive at British ports from all over the world and inspections are carried out on about 4,000 vessels each year. Over the nine years, 1958–66, 151 instances were recorded of the more common species of cockroach in holds involving cargoes from 22 different countries (Fig. 125); *Blattella germanica* and *Periplaneta americana* occur most often, but *Blatta orientalis* and other species of *Periplaneta* relatively infrequently (Table XXVII). It must be appreciated that these records do not include the 'rare' tropical species which may be carried in small numbers.

The number of commodities associated with pest species of cockroach in the holds of ships is considerable; it is not possible to relate the species found to type of commodity, because many shipments involve mixed cargoes. Moreover, with the exception possibly of bones imported from Nigeria, where cockroaches are not uncommon on the stacks awaiting shipment, it is the view of Dr. J. A. Freeman, Head of the Entomology Department of the Infestation Control Laboratory, that the association of cockroaches with commodities is in general fortuitous. In addition, it should be recognised that cockroaches in ships' holds are not always associated with foodstuffs; as an example a ship loaded with wood pulp

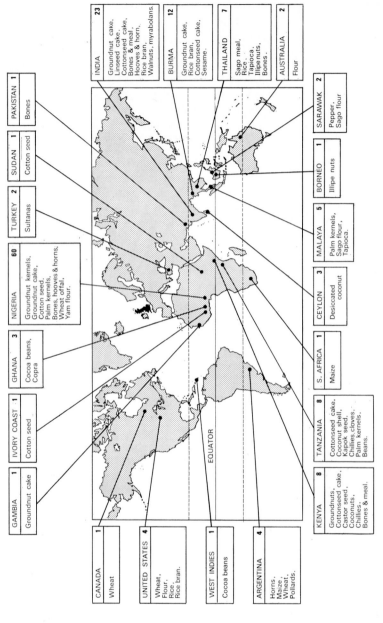

Fig. 125. The number of cargoes infested with cockroaches which arrived in Britain between 1958 and 1966 from 22 overseas countries.

| CANADA | 1 |
| Wheat |

| UNITED STATES | 4 |
| Wheat, Flour, Rice, Rice bran. |

| WEST INDIES | 1 |
| Cocoa beans |

| ARGENTINA | 4 |
| Horns, Maize, Wheat, Pollards. |

| GAMBIA | 1 |
| Groundnut cake |

| IVORY COAST | 1 |
| Cotton seed |

| GHANA | 3 |
| Cocoa beans, Copra |

| NIGERIA | 60 |
| Groundnut kernels, Groundnut cake, Cotton seed, Palm kernels, Bones, hooves & horns, Wheat offal, Yam flour. |

| TURKEY | 2 |
| Sultanas |

| SUDAN | 1 |
| Cotton seed |

| PAKISTAN | 1 |
| Bones |

| INDIA | 23 |
| Groundnut cake, Linseed cake, Cottonseed cake, Bones & meal, Hooves & horn, Rice bran, Walnuts, myrabolans. |

| BURMA | 12 |
| Groundnut cake, Rice bran, Cottonseed cake, Sesame. |

| THAILAND | 7 |
| Sago meal, Rice, Tapioca, Illipe nuts, Bones. |

| AUSTRALIA | 2 |
| Flour |

| KENYA | 8 |
| Groundnuts, Cottonseed cake, Castor seed, Coconuts, Chillies, Bones & meal. |

| TANZANIA | 8 |
| Cottonseed cake, Coconut shell, Kapok seed, Chillies, cloves, Palm kernels, Beans. |

| S. AFRICA | 1 |
| Maize |

| CEYLON | 3 |
| Desiccated coconut |

| MALAYA | 5 |
| Palm kernels, Sago flour, Tapioca. |

| BORNEO | 1 |
| Illipe nuts |

| SARAWAK | 2 |
| Pepper, Sago flour |

EQUATOR

and plywood in western Canada, discharged large numbers of German cockroaches with the plywood at the port of Hull in 1964.

TABLE XXVII

INCIDENCE OF THE MOST COMMON COCKROACHES IN THE HOLDS OF SHIPS INSPECTED AT BRITISH PORTS DURING 1958–66

Year	Number of shipments			
	B. germanica	B. orientalis	P. americana	Other Periplaneta spp.
1958	—	—	3	—
1959	6	1	3	1 (P. australasiae)
1960	4	1	4	1 (P. australasiae)
1961	1	2	—	—
1962	6	—	5	1 (P. australasiae)
1963	6	1	9	—
1964	19	1	9	2 (Unidentified)
1965	24	1	14	1 (P. brunnea)
1966	13	—	12	—
Totals	79	7	59	6

(Information provided by the Infestation Control Laboratory, Ministry of Agriculture. Fisheries & Food, based on reports from the Insect Inspectors of that Ministry and of the Department of Agriculture and Fisheries for Scotland.)

Establishment of new infestations

In modern food storage practice, and in the transport and marketing of perishable foodstuffs, chilling and refrigeration are playing an increasingly important part. How does the cockroach react to sudden changes of temperature when carried perhaps in refrigerated vehicles, and once unloaded with goods finds itself in chilled areas or normal ambient temperatures? Does the insect's previous temperature experience influence its activity or chance of survival? Whether or not a German Cockroach carrying an ootheca is capable of surviving and producing an infestation in a new environment depends in large measure on whether the temperature which it encounters lies between the insect's low and high thermal death points. Very often this will be so; then other factors, the level of humidity and availability of food and water will determine the period of survival and the chances of the ootheca hatching and the nymphs surviving to establish an infestation. These are some of the questions examined in the next chapter on the influence of the environment.

12

INFLUENCE OF THE ENVIRONMENT

Effects of temperature: immobilisation at low temperatures; acclimatisation; recovery from chill-coma; the cold death point; survival outdoors; the upper lethal temperature; long and short exposures to high temperatures; the temperature preferendum; preferred temperatures of different species—Response to humidity alone; desiccation in different species—Effects of air movement—Environmental factors in relation to cockroach habits

The environment of air travel: effects of low pressures; tests in jet aircraft; cockroaches in space; gaseous environments—Absence of food and water

The hatching of oothecae; water content of oothecae; loss of water from oothecae

Pest cockroaches establish themselves within buildings in harbourages which provide micro-climates similar to the climate of the out-door tropics, from which they originated. Examples of such harbourages are behind plaster, pipe runs, skirting and architraves, beneath kitchen equipment and within floor and wall cavities. Cockroaches require relatively high temperatures and humidities and preferably situations where water is freely available. They are confined to their harbourages during the day, where there is relatively little air movement, and become active at night at a time coinciding, except in centrally heated buildings, with a drop in temperature and an increase in the water holding capacity of the air.

The pest species can survive in full sunlight, but their negative response to light guides them to micro-climates offering the maximum chance of survival. Harbourages of the German and American Cockroaches are often close to water pipes, sinks, baths, toilets and washbasins where humidity is further increased by moisture lost from the many insects crowded together which Pimental suggests is a further aid to their survival.[323]

In this chapter we are concerned with the effects of different physical components of the environment on the behaviour of cockroaches; we are concerned with the 'preferred environment' and the range, the upper and lower limits, which cockroaches can tolerate. Towards the end of this chapter we shall consider the factors which influence the hatching of oothecae. If we are to appreciate the conditions under which pest species are able to give rise to infestations we are concerned also with chemical components of the environment, the presence or absence of food and water. The effects of environmental factors on the rate of development and growth of cockroaches are considered in Chapter 10.

278

The three physical factors of the environment which most influence cockroaches are:

1. Temperature,
2. Humidity, or water-vapour content of the air, and
3. Air movement.

These three factors are inter-related. To avoid confusion it is perhaps necessary to point out that when a given sample of air is warmed, its relative humidity drops and its drying power, or saturation deficit, increases.

Relative humidity is defined as the ratio (usually expressed as a percentage) of the actual vapour pressure of the air (measured in mm of mercury) to the full amount of water that the air can hold at that same temperature (the saturation vapour pressure). When air is warmed its water holding capacity increases. As an example, the saturation vapour pressure of air at 20°C is 17·6 mm Hg and increases to 31·8 mm at 30°C. When the air is only half saturated (i.e. it has a relative humidity of 50 per cent) the vapour pressure at the same two temperatures is 8·8 and 15·9 mm. The drying power of the air, or saturation deficit is obtained by subtracting the actual vapour pressure from the saturation vapour pressure.

Air movement interacts with temperature and humidity in that it may displace moist air with drier air causing loss of moisture from surfaces by evaporation. This has the effect of cooling the surface, which in turn may cool the air in the immediate vicinity of that surface.

Additional factors which cockroaches may experience, notably in transport, are:

4. Reduced pressures in aircraft, and
5. Starvation and lack of water.

Many insects, especially those of stored foodstuffs, are capable of obtaining their water requirements from relatively dry food. This, however, is not the case for the cockroach for which freely available water is vitally important.

Effects of temperature
Like other insects, the body temperature of the cockroach is entirely dependent on that of its surroundings; low temperatures inhibit cockroach activity and high temperatures usually stimulate activity. The one environmental factor, more than any other, which limits the spread of insects, is the temperature below which activity cannot normally occur.

Immobilisation at low temperatures
At a certain low temperature, varying with the species, insects become immobilised. Mellanby[365] calls this the 'chill-coma temperature'. Using the Oriental Cockroach, experiments were undertaken to find out whether previous exposure to different temperatures could modify the response of the cockroach, so enabling it to exist more easily at low temperature.

To eliminate the effects of humidity, the air in which the cockroaches were contained was always fully water saturated.

These experiments showed that the cooler the conditions in which Oriental Cockroaches are held before being moved towards the chill-coma temperature, the lower the temperature at which activity is possible. Thus, the lowest temperature at which nymphs and adults of *B. orientalis* are active is 2°C when previously exposed to 14–17°C, increasing to 7·5°C for previous experience at 30°C and 9·5°C if held previously at 36°C.

Acclimatisation

To discover how long cockroaches must be subjected to different temperatures in order to modify the chill-coma temperature they were transferred from 30°C to 15°C for different periods and the acclimatisation period was measured—in this case the time required for the chill-coma temperature to drop from 7·5 to 2°C. It was found that although cockroaches kept at 15°C became acclimatised to 30°C within 20 hours, others kept at 30°C and moved to 15°C do not become fully acclimatised to the lower temperature for two to three days.

Even more interesting, acclimatisation is possible only if the cockroach is capable of movement. It cannot take place in cockroaches actually in chill-coma. Thus when cockroaches from 30°C are held for five days at 2–3°C they remain completely immobile. When warmed to 15°C they recover after some time, but an immediate determination of their chill-coma temperature shows that it is still the same (7·5°C) as when they left 30°C and is not modified by the period at 2–3°C.

Recovery from chill-coma

If Oriental Cockroaches are cooled to, but not below, the chill-coma temperature and then warmed again they recover very quickly. Even when held at the temperature of immobilisation for as long as three days the recovery time is less than one minute (Table XXVIII). If, however, they

TABLE XXVIII

TIME TAKEN FOR *B. ORIENTALIS* ACCLIMATISED TO 15°C AND 30°C TO RECOVER FROM EXPOSURE TO LOW TEMPERATURE
(From Mellanby[365])

Temperature of exposure (°C)	Period of exposure (hr.)	Time taken to recover at 15°C after transfer from low temperature exposure	
		Acclimatised to 15°C	Acclimatised to 30°C
1	24	Under 1 min.	$1\frac{1}{2}$–$2\frac{1}{2}$ hrs.
1	72	Under 1 min.	$1\frac{1}{2}$–$2\frac{1}{2}$ hrs.
−3	1	12 min.	2–$2\frac{1}{2}$ hrs.

are cooled some degrees below the chill-coma temperature, the period of recovery is appreciably longer. The higher the temperature to which cockroaches are transferred from chill-coma, the sooner they become mobile,[365] e.g. in 90 minutes when transferred to 15°C compared with only 15 minutes at 35°C.

The cold death point

In reviewing resistance to cold, Wigglesworth[165] divides insects into three groups: (1) those accustomed to warm environments, such as insects of stored foodstuffs, which die at temperatures well above freezing point, death being attributed to the accumulation of toxic products which cannot be eliminated; (2) those which are killed as soon as their tissues freeze, death being attributed to dehydration of the tissues and perhaps to mechanical injury by ice crystals, and finally, (3) those which can withstand freezing, but which die at still lower temperatures, the cause of death being unknown. Cockroaches fit most conveniently into the third group; when nymphs and adults reared at 27°C are held at low temperatures for one hour, mortality increases from two per cent at freezing point, to 71 per cent at −5°C and 98 per cent at −10°C. All are killed in one hour at −15°C.[366]

Survival of cockroaches at low temperatures is also influenced by previous temperature experience. Thus, Mellanby found that all Oriental Cockroaches which had been living at 15°C, survived for three weeks when moved to 2–5°C and were able to crawl for the whole of this period. Others moved from 30°C to this low temperature began to die within five days.

Once cockroaches have become acclimatised to their environment, the temperature at which they die from freezing is well-defined and mortality is not greatly modified by the period of exposure. Thus, all *B. orientalis* acclimatised to 15°C survive at −5·5°C, whether they are exposed to this low temperature for one or nine hours. Most, however, die within one hour at −8°C (Table XXIX).

TABLE XXIX

DEATH (D) AND SURVIVAL (S) OF *B. ORIENTALIS* ACCLIMATISED
TO 15° AND 30°C WHEN EXPOSED TO BELOW ZERO TEMPERATURES
(Six insects per test; from Mellanby[365])

Temperature of exposure (°C)	Period of exposure (hr.)	Cockroaches previously kept at	
		15°C	30°C
−3·0	1½	S	S
−5·5	1	S	D
−5·5	9	S	D
−6·8	1¼	S	D
−8·0	1	5D, 1S	D
Between −4·0 & −8·0	15	D	D

It is clear from these studies that cockroaches which live in buildings without heating are considerably more cold hardy when exposed to winter conditions than those from centrally heated premises. The experiments would also indicate that cockroaches carried accidentally but quickly in the heated parts of jet aircraft, say from the warmer parts of the United States to Britain, have less chance of surviving here in the absence of a favourable environment on arrival, than insects carried in the opposite direction. The influence of the environment in jet aircraft on the survival of cockroaches is dealt with in greater detail on page 292.

Survival outdoors

In warm climates most of the domiciliary species of cockroach live out-doors. It is now widely recognised that the Oriental Cockroach is capable of doing so in Britain although records of such occurrences are few. As examples, Gardner[367] found an immature male at the roots of plants about a mile away from the nearest house at Stanford-le-Hope, in Essex, and Lucas[48,368] has found the Oriental Cockroach outdoors in rubbish heaps. Considerable numbers were found on open ground around refuse filling a disused gravel pit near Sevenoaks, Kent, during September 1964 (Edwards, personal communication).

In an attempt to establish the cold-hardiness of *B. orientalis* in Britain, small numbers of nymphs were subjected to various climatic conditions during the winters of 1949–50 and 1951–52. With an average minimum of 2·9–3·2°C, during the three coldest months, the insects failed to survive beyond the following early spring. At temperatures a little higher, with an average minimum for the three months of 4·6–5·1°C, some nymphs survived into May and June. The Oriental Cockroach is thus capable of surviving outdoors through the winter, but Solomon & Adamson[369] suggest that in these tests lack of moisture as well as cold probably contributed towards mortality.

The upper lethal temperature

The death of cockroaches exposed to high temperatures for long periods is brought about by lack of moisture. High temperatures increase the metabolic activities of insects causing an increased demand for oxygen. At low temperatures, respiration occurs by a process of diffusion but at high temperatures it is replaced by forced ventilation, involving pumping movements of the abdomen which ventilate the tracheae. Gunn[207] was unable experimentally to discover at what temperature *B. orientalis* abandons one type of respiration for the other, since below 30°C pumping movements occur during and after great activity, but at 32°C they never cease, becoming more frequent as the temperature rises.

Gunn postulated that at high temperatures forced ventilation of the tracheae causes cockroaches to lose water rapidly and at about 30°C the loss increases out of all proportion to the gain of oxygen, with the result that the water conservation mechanism of the respiratory system fails (Fig. 126). He says that, 'if the air is dry and supplies of water for drinking are not available, cockroaches kept at temperatures above 30°C must speedily die. Here then is an upper limit to the temperature range of *B. orientalis*, fixed by the speed of desiccation. At 40°C the animal dies in about four hours whatever the humidity, so that in saturated air, heat stroke fixes the upper limit of temperature at 36–40°C, while for dry air desiccation fixes it at a little above 30°C'.

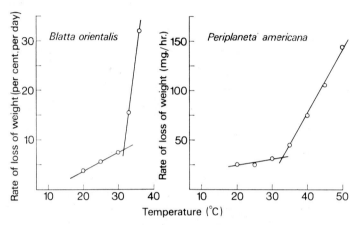

Fig. 126. Rate of loss of weight (water) in relation to temperature from live adult *B. orientalis* and dead *P. americana*. Both species show the sudden increase in rate of evaporation just above 30°C (after Gunn[207] and Ramsey[135]).

Ramsey[135] working with *Periplaneta* could not support Gunn's contention that death at high temperatures occurs because of excessive loss of water through the spiracles. In *P. americana* evaporation also increases rapidly at temperatures above 30°C (Fig. 126), but equally whether the insects are dead or alive and whether the spiracles are open or blocked with paraffin wax.

Ramsey's experiments suggest that at high temperatures some modification occurs to the body surface. Observations on the nature of the film covering the cuticle of the American Cockroach show that it undergoes a change of phase at 30°C which greatly increases permeability of the cuticle to water molecules. His experiments, and those of more recent workers, show conclusively that a considerable fraction of the total amount of water lost from the cockroach at high temperatures does indeed take place through the body surface.

Long and short exposures to high temperatures

The three pest species, *B. orientalis*, *B. germanica* and *P. americana*, differ in their susceptibility to high temperatures in moist and dry air.[370] With long exposures of 24 hours in *moist* air practically no deaths occur below 37°C and few survive more than 39°C, irrespective of the species (Fig. 127). In *dry* air, however, there is considerable variation; the largest cockroach, *P. americana*, desiccates more slowly, and the smallest, *B. germanica*, loses water at about the same rate as *B. orientalis* (see also Fig. 131). This results in these two species dying more readily at low temperatures (35–37°C) than *P. americana*.

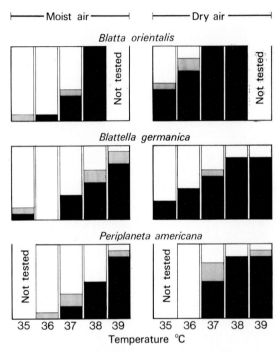

Fig. 127. Proportions of dead (black), moribund (shaded) and live (open) cockroaches of the three pest species after exposure to various temperatures (35–39°C) in moist air (90% R.H.) and in relatively dry air for 24 hours (after Gunn & Notley[370]).

With short exposures of one hour all three species survive temperatures above 41°C, and contrary to the effects of a 24-hour exposure, cockroaches survive in dry air more readily than in moist. This points to confirmation of Mellanby's earlier suggestion that evaporation of water from the body can cool the insect in dry air allowing it to remain alive at temperatures some degrees higher than when the air is moist.[371]

The temperature preferendum

Within their normal habitat all insects have a preferred temperature range; they avoid unfavourable temperatures by responding to temperature gradients which induce movement back to the thermo-preferendum.[165]

In the early part of this chapter we have seen that two of the environmental parameters which affect the Oriental Cockroach—the chill-coma temperature and the cold death point—are influenced by the insects' previous temperature experience. Gunn[188] has shown that the preferred temperature of the Oriental Cockroach—the temperature at which it congregates—is also influenced by previous experience, but is, in this case, related to the amount of water vapour in the air.

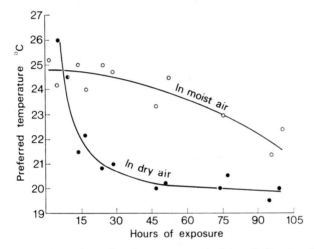

Fig. 128. Change in preferred temperature of adult male *B. orientalis* in a temperature gradient containing moist and dry air. As the water content of the insect drops it moves to a lower temperature, into air with a lower saturation deficit thereby reducing further water loss (after Gunn[188]).

This information came from two experiments lasting over a period of four days with adult Oriental Cockroaches in a temperature gradient, one experiment in dry air and the other in moist. The preferred temperature, at which the cockroaches settled, changed with time, more so in dry air than in moist (Fig. 128). At any particular temperature, Oriental Cockroaches lose water by evaporation at a rate proportional to the drying capacity of the air. When the amount of water in the cockroach falls below a certain level, the insect moves to a lower temperature, with the result that it experiences air with a smaller saturation deficit and hence further loss of water is reduced.

Preferred temperatures of different species

The preferred temperature, or 'indifference zone', as it is called by Gunn,[372] is similar for adult male *B. germanica* and *P. americana*. When these species have had access to food and water the temperature preferendum ranges from about 24° to 33°C. For similarly fed *B. orientalis*, the range is a little lower, 20–29°C. All species actively avoid temperatures at the higher end of the indifference zone more so than at the lower end (Fig. 129).

Under conditions of changing humidity the Oriental Cockroach shows very little inclination to move from an acceptable temperature providing the insect has had food and water; humidity may cause a very slight change in temperature preference but this varies with individuals.[373] If the

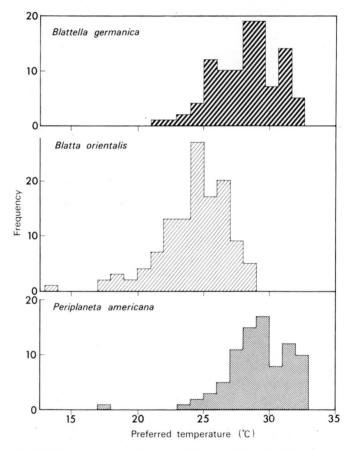

Fig. 129. Temperature preferences of German, Oriental and American cockroaches as shown by the number of 20-minute periods during which individuals remained at each temperature (excluding aberrant individuals; after Gunn[374]).

cockroach has been given water, but no food, its reaction is still unchanged. Only when deprived of water, to the extent that the insect has become desiccated, does it prefer a lower temperature, since the cockroach then loses water more slowly because the air has a lower saturation deficiency. When water is given to the insect it returns to its normal temperature preference zone (Fig. 130). Gunn[372] refers to this as a 'compensating reaction' to conserve low levels of body moisture, which conflicts with the normal temperature preference of the insect. The Oriental Cockroach can lose and regain about 30 per cent of its weight by adjusting itself to air of varying water vapour content.

Response to humidity alone

When cockroaches move from one temperature to another it is difficult to demonstrate whether they are responding to the temperature alone, or to the joint action of temperature and humidity. This comes about because, as

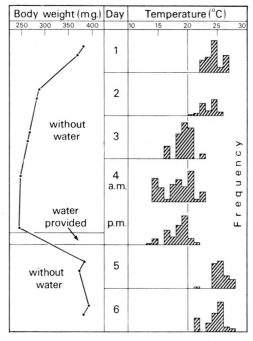

Fig. 130. The loss in body weight of adult *B. orientalis* caused by desiccation over a period of four days without water and the recovery in weight following the provision of water during the afternoon of the fourth day. The histograms show the fall in preferred temperature with desiccation and the rise again following drinking. The histograms were obtained by summing the periods longer than 2 minutes during which cockroaches remained at a given temperature (after Gunn[372]).

already mentioned, air at a low temperature has a higher relative humidity, and a lower drying power, than the same air at a high temperature. This problem was resolved by devising a humidity gradient ranging from 20 to 90 per cent, divided into three zones, 'dry', 'medium' and 'wet' with a uniform temperature throughout.[373] The time spent by Oriental Cockroaches in the dry and wet zones was recorded over a period of an hour.

Normal, undesiccated cockroaches spent half their time on the dry side and over a quarter on the wet, showing that humidity *per se* appears to be a weak stimulus to movement (Table XXX). Nevertheless, after these same insects had been desiccated to varying extents, their preference for the wet side increased considerably, demonstrating conclusively that cockroaches on desiccation do respond to atmospheric humidity.

TABLE XXX

TIME SPENT BY NORMAL AND DESICCATED *B. ORIENTALIS* IN DRY AND WET AREAS OF A CHOICE CHAMBER
(From Gunn & Cosway[373])

Temp. (°C)	Condition of insect	Time spent in each zone (%)		Ratio Dry/Wet
		Dry	Wet	
16–23 25	Normal	49	29	1·7
25	Normal	50	38	1·3
	Slightly desiccated	41	42	1·0
	Desiccated to more than 20% of body weight	34	51	0·7

Desiccation in different species

The experiments reported by Gunn in his various papers, show quite clearly the existence of an interaction between environmental temperature, water deficit in the air, and body moisture content; these jointly influence the environment favoured by the Oriental Cockroach. But not all species are equally susceptible to desiccation: in dry air (with a high saturation deficit), adults of the small species, B. *germanica*, lose water at about the same rate as *B. orientalis*, but more rapidly than the larger *P. americana* (Fig. 131); at temperatures below 30°C and a saturation deficit below 32 mm of mercury, the water loss from *B. germanica* (as percentage of initial weight) is nearly twice that of *B. orientalis* and *P. americana*.[374] From calculations which take into account body weight, surface area and respiration rate of these three species, it would appear that the differences which they show in the threat of desiccation are unrelated to rates of

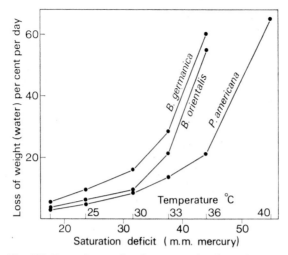

Fig. 131. Rate of water loss by evaporation from German, Oriental and American cockroaches in air of increasing dryness at the temperatures specified. The loss of weight per day is expressed as a percentage of original weight (after Gunn[374]).

water loss through the spiracles or through the integument (Table XXXI). These calculations do not, however, take into account differences in the composition of the wax on the surface of the cuticle which is most likely to be the controlling factor.

TABLE XXXI

WATER LOSS FROM THREE SPECIES OF COCKROACH IN RELATION TO WEIGHT, SURFACE AREA AND RESPIRATION RATE
(From Gunn[374])

Factor	B. germanica	B. orientalis	P. americana
Average weight (mg)	47·0	380·0	912·0
Oxygen consumption at 30°C (mg/g/day)	24·1	16·0	13·0
Water loss in dry air at 30°C (mg/g/day)	159·0	95·0	86·0
Ratio of cuticle area: weight (cm²/g)	21·9	11·0	8·2
Water loss/cuticle area: weight ratio (mg/cm²/g/day)	7·3	8·6	10·5
Oxygen consumption/cuticle area: weight ratio (mg/cm²/g/day)	1·1	1·5	1·6
Water loss/mg of oxygen consumed (mg)	6·6	5·9	6·6

T

Effects of air movement

Cockroaches within harbourages are protected from air movement, but when they forage for food they encounter air displacements, which although usually of low velocity, affect the conservation of body moisture.

Ramsey,[135] using a wind tunnel in which he could control the temperature and humidity of the air, found that for *P. americana* the effect of air movement is much less in causing evaporation from the body surface than in causing water loss from the tracheae. With the spiracles blocked by paraffin wax, so that water could be lost only *via* the cuticle, an increase in air movement from 5 to 20 metres per second increases the rate of evaporation by about one-third. However, with the spiracles open, this same range of air movement increases evaporation four times from 3 to 12 mg/hr. Moreover, if the insect is placed across the stream of air rather than head on, evaporation, at 20 metres per second, increases by about three times.

Environmental factors in relation to cockroach habits

This brief review of the effects of temperature and humidity on cockroaches has shown that they are strongly influenced by environmental factors. It ought, therefore, to be possible to relate what we know from these experiments to the behaviour and habits of the pest species.

Haber[206] made some 30 observations on the micro-climates within five separate habitats infested by *B. germanica*. The average was 20·6°C, close to the low end of the preferred temperature range (Fig. 128), and 72 per cent relative humidity. In kitchens with poor ventilation, layering of the air causes quite marked temperature differences between floor and ceiling, in some instances as much as 7–10°C. These higher temperatures near the junction of wall and ceiling are often responsible for the activity of domiciliary species high up in rooms.

On the supposition that the night activity of cockroaches is due to the absence of daylight, and that ultra-violet light might be the cause of their hiding and inactivity by day, Necheles[375] undertook experiments which showed that neither full sunlight nor light of different wavelengths exert any direct influence on the activity of *P. americana* or *B. orientalis*. He concluded that cockroaches do react to light, but very slowly: 'their usual flight when light is suddenly switched on in a room has led to the belief that they flee from light. If the light is turned on from outside the room, one may observe from outside, that no sudden flight takes place and that it is some time before all the cockroaches have retired'. As we have seen in Chapter 4 cockroaches are well equipped with sense organs (the cerci) for detecting vibrations, low levels of noise and air movements and it is probably these factors, rather than light, which stimulate the avoidance reaction. This subject is dealt with in greater detail in Chapter 11, in connection with the value of 'night inspection' for cockroach control, and where the night activity of cockroaches is discussed in relation to circadian rhythm, believed to be mediated by stimulation of the ocelli.

Water is probably the most important limiting factor to the establishment of cockroaches in buildings. The hiding of cockroaches during the day is attributed by Necheles 'to the necessity of seeking refuge from the excessive evaporating power of day air and their activity at night to the reversal of air conditions, the night air being cooler and more humid'. Gunn & Cosway,[373] however, are of the opinion that the humidity in harbourages at night is likely to be little different from that of the freely moving air. In any event, we have seen (p. 287) that the reaction of the cockroach to humidity, providing it has had water to drink, is not all that intense.

Gunn[374] discusses the temperature preferences of the three most common domiciliary cockroaches to account for their difference in ecological habit. All three can safely stand a loss in body weight of 30 per cent through desiccation and recover their loss on drinking. Among the three species, however, the temperature preference of the German Cockroach may take it into conditions where it could desiccate to death in two days. Infestations of the German Cockroach, or steam fly, are closely associated with conditions where water is freely available; the rapid loss of water from this species almost certainly accounts for its preferred industrial environment of warm, steamy kitchens.

By comparison, the Oriental Cockroach has a lower temperature preference extending well below 20°C (Fig. 129), and at these low temperatures loss of water is small. In the event of water not being available this species prefers the range 12–23°C and this understandably explains why *B. orientalis* usually infests drier and cooler conditions than *B. germanica*.

Gunn has made a similar practical appraisal of the requirements of *P. americana*. This species thrives well, almost to the exclusion of others, in the stable environments of sewers in the United States (Chapter 11), but rarely establishes itself in the United Kingdom. When this does happen it is often to be found in the constant, artificial and warm environments of greenhouses and tropical houses of Zoos and Botanic gardens, or more usually in the nearest favourable environment to where imported goods, carrying this species, have been temporarily placed or stored (see p. 54). The American Cockroach rarely remains at temperatures above 33°C where its rate of desiccation would be high, and its long life cycle, requiring favourable conditions for development for at least a year, probably accounts for its failure to become an industrial pest in the United Kingdom. Nevertheless, there is reason to believe that with the wider acceptance over the next decade of central heating and temperature control in buildings in the United Kingdom, incipient infestations of *P. americana* could become more widely established here in certain types of property.

The environment of air travel

The development of resistance to modern insecticides by a great many insects of economic importance has drawn attention to the ease of spread of this problem through air travel. The growth of international traffic with the possibility of insects being introduced very quickly from one country to another, places an increasing responsibility on quarantine authorities.

In one respect, however, Knipling & Sullivan[366] suggest that perhaps the coming of jet travel has brought an answer to some of the problems of preventing the introduction of undesirable insects and resistant strains: these authors have pointed out that for jet transport to operate efficiently, aircraft must fly at near 40,000 ft. where outside temperatures range from $-42°C$ to $-65°C$ and cooling of the unheated parts of airplanes is likely to provide an environment, although of short duration, unfavourable to insect survival.

Effects of low pressures

The air pressure on the surface of the earth fluctuates around 760 mm of mercury. It falls to about 520 mm at an altitude of 10,000 ft, to 430 mm at 15,000 ft and to 225 mm at 30,000 ft. At 200,000 ft (about 40 miles up) pressures drop to less than 0·05 mm of mercury.

Packchanian[376] devised an apparatus for studying the effects on insects of the low temperatures and reduced pressures that exist at various altitudes. He showed that the positive and negative pressures in the range in which insects may occasionally find themselves are not detrimental to survival. In studies using eight species of insect, death increased directly with the period of exposure at a given altitude. The factor chiefly responsible for death is low temperature, reduced pressures alone being without ill effect.[377]

Tests in jet aircraft

To test these experimental conclusions, Sullivan et al.[378] subjected German Cockroaches to the low temperatures, reduced pressures, and low humidities in the unpressurised and unheated sections of jet aircraft. In two flights in jet fighters, lasting 50 and 95 minutes, and ranging in altitude from 20,000 to 40,000 ft, all the cockroaches were killed. The outside air temperature during these flights ranged from $-30°C$ to $-60°C$. All American Cockroaches in a similar flight lasting 90 minutes were also killed. Complete mortality of German Cockroaches was obtained in a three-hour flight in a jet bomber at 40,000 ft, when the outside air temperature fell to $-51°C$; nevertheless, in a bomb bay of a similar aircraft where heat was being generated, all the cockroaches survived. These trials showed that with flights in the stratosphere of 40 minutes or less, or with long flights at low altitudes, a proportion of cockroaches which become passengers on jet aircraft may be alive on landing.

Cockroaches in space

To increase our knowledge of the effects of the environment of outer space a number of animals, including various insects, have been used as 'guinea pigs' in place of man. Among five species exposed by Thornton & Sullivan[379] for different periods to the very low pressures of 2C0,0C0 ft (less than 0·05 mm of mercury) the cockroach *Leucophaea maderae* survived best; 60 per cent lived for one day following a one-hour exposure, and 20 per cent were still alive after four days. The cockroach also suffered the smallest loss in weight (14 per cent) compared with the maximum (47 per cent) by the house fly (*Musca domestica*). In these tests, the temperature within the abdomens of the cockroaches exposed to very low pressures failed to drop below 10°C indicating that mortality may have resulted from desiccation and internal damage rather than cold. Unlike the other insects exposed, Madeira Cockroaches were not entirely quiescent at low pressures; they twitched their legs in muscle spasms lasting more than a minute, but all the insects showed marked abdominal swelling.

To enable insects to be used effectively in studies in satellites, Starkweather & Sullivan[380] considered all the possible environmental factors: insects are much more resistant than mammals to high speed acceleration[381] and many studies have shown the relative resistance of insects to ionising radiations compared with mammals (see Vol. II).

Starkweather & Sullivan investigated the effects of increased atmospheric pressures: Madeira Cockroaches and houseflies were given a pad of cotton wool saturated with a solution of ten per cent sugar while being

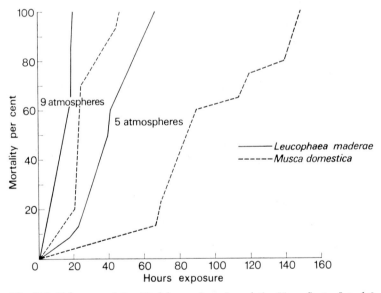

Fig. 132. Tolerance of the Madeira cockroach and the Housefly to 5 and 9 atmospheres pressure with constant exchange of air (after Starkweather & Sullivan[380]).

subjected to one, five and nine atmospheres. At five atmospheres all the cockroaches died in three days, compared with some of the flies which survived for six days. At nine atmospheres pressure all the cockroaches died in one day and the houseflies in two days (Fig. 132).

Gaseous environments

The response of cockroaches to different gases is of interest to the use of insects in satellites as well as to the more utilitarian purpose of immobilising insects to facilitate laboratory handling (see Vol. II).

Using one-month old adult males of the Madeira Cockroach, experiments undertaken by Sullivan et al.[382] showed that at room temperatures and atmospheric pressure insects starved and without water survived for two days or less, in both very high and very low concentrations of oxygen. But they lived for at least 20 days in 40–80 per cent oxygen provided that the carbon dioxide was removed. The optimum atmosphere was 55–58 per cent oxygen and 42–45 per cent nitrogen, which, with the carbon dioxide removed was sufficient to oxidise the food reserves of the starving cockroaches, keeping them alive for the maximum period.

Absence of food and water

Cockroaches are essentially scavengers on dead plant material, preferring carbohydrates to protein and fat. Although they are omnivorous, cockroaches do discriminate when given a choice: P. americana will eat dead and maimed individuals and egg cases of its own species, cardboard and paper. In captivity, they take bread, pastry, cheese and various vegetables and fruits; potatoes, carrots, sweetcorn, lettuce and cabbage, as well as banana and cantaloup. In greenhouses they eat the open flower petals of Cattleya orchids as well as the aerial roots and flower spikes of the Vanda orchid.[5]

Within their normal habitats, indoors and out, there is sufficient food and water for cockroaches to survive and reproduce, but in transport they may find themselves without. Under these circumstances low humidities may enhance the adverse effects of food and water shortage.

In India, Nigam[66] observed that second instar nymphs of P. americana can survive almost without food for a week. Willis & Lewis[383] subjected two-week old adults of both sexes of ten species of cockroach to partial and complete starvation: they were given (1) dry dog biscuits without water, (2) water alone, and (3) no food or water, at 27°C and 36–40 per cent relative humidity.

Cockroaches completely starved (Fig. 133) live for as short a time as five days (male B. vaga) and as long as 42 days (female P. americana). Generally, the larger the insect the longer it survives. Cockroaches with access to dry food but no water remain alive for about the same time as completely starved insects, but drinking water enables most, with the notable exceptions of male B. germanica and S. supellectilium, to live significantly longer. Females survive longer than males probably because of their greater body reserves. Water alone is sufficient to sustain some species, notably *P. americana*, *N. cinerea* and *P. surinamensis*, for two to three months.

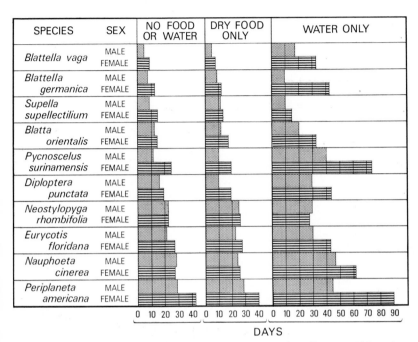

SPECIES	SEX	NO FOOD OR WATER	DRY FOOD ONLY	WATER ONLY
Blattella vaga	MALE / FEMALE			
Blattella germanica	MALE / FEMALE			
Supella supellectilium	MALE / FEMALE			
Blatta orientalis	MALE / FEMALE			
Pycnoscelus surinamensis	MALE / FEMALE			
Diploptera punctata	MALE / FEMALE			
Neostylopyga rhombifolia	MALE / FEMALE			
Eurycotis floridana	MALE / FEMALE			
Nauphoeta cinerea	MALE / FEMALE			
Periplaneta americana	MALE / FEMALE			

0 10 20 30 40   0 10 20 30 40   0 10 20 30 40 50 60 70 80 90

DAYS

Fig. 133. Longevity (days) of cockroaches on starvation diets at 27°C and 36–40% R.H. (after Willis & Lewis[383]).

Willis & Lewis also present some previously unpublished data of Dr. Jean Leclercq (Université de Liège), which shows that the survival of completely starved adults and nymphs of *B. orientalis* is correlated with relative humidity; values below 40 per cent would not appear to affect survival but longevity is increased by humidities above 40 per cent.

These studies on food and water requirements show that it is possible for cockroaches to live for relatively long periods in shipments of material not ordinarily considered food: starvation is not a limiting factor for cockroaches travelling in the heated parts of aircraft. In most other forms or transport, too, limited access to water does enable most species to complete the journey alive.

The hatching of oothecae
In the earlier part of this chapter we considered the many environ-

mental factors which affect the mobility and survival of cockroaches as nymphs and adults in buildings and during dissemination in transport. One of the ways by which pest cockroaches become readily introduced into properties is by means of oothecae in crates of foodstuffs and beverages and in a variety of packing materials. The remainder of this chapter is concerned with the effects of the environment on embryological development and hatching of oothecae.

In Chapter 9 three types of ovipositional behaviour among cockroaches are distinguished. To understand the factors which influence oothecal development of the pest species, we are concerned here with only: (1) oothecae which are deposited soon after formation, e.g. by *Blatta orientalis*, *Supella supellectilium* and all species of *Periplaneta*, and (2) oothecae which are carried by the female until or shortly before the eggs hatch, e.g. by *Blattella germanica*.

Water content of oothecae

Water content is the principal factor which determines whether oothecae hatch after being deposited. Roth & Willis[41] have shown that the amount of water within newly formed oothecae and enclosed eggs of the pest species of cockroaches, averages about 60–65 per cent. Oothecae of cockroaches which deposit their egg cases almost immediately after formation are hard and impermeable, and the water content remains constant during embryological development.

In contrast, the end of the ootheca which remains attached to female *Blattella germanica* during egg development is soft and permeable to water, and when first formed this ootheca contains about 62 per cent water but increases steadily to 76 per cent at time of hatching (Fig. 134). This increase derives from both loss of dry matter and uptake of water from the female.

Loss of water from oothecae

Water is essential to the development of eggs: the hardened wall of the ootheca of some species (see Chapter 9) and its retention by others in the genital pouch until the eggs hatch are means by which desiccation is prevented.

The egg case of *B. orientalis* is the most resistant to water loss; it is covered with a water-proofing material, which although differing from that on the cuticle of the cockroach, is sufficiently impermeable to allow eggs to hatch from oothecae retained continuously in completely dry air. During early development, the inside of the ootheca is very moist, but as development proceeds the inner surface becomes progressively drier until at about four weeks the chorion surrounding each egg becomes very brittle. The inside of the chorion and the embryo itself, however, remain moist. Roth & Willis[41] believe that water is absorbed by the developing eggs from the spongy inner surface of the ootheca, which results in a

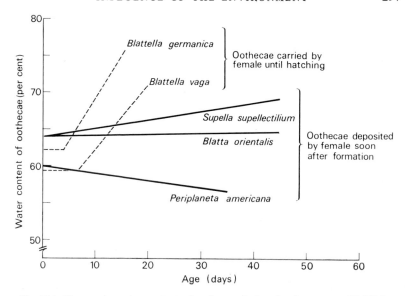

Fig. 134. Changes in water content of oothecae during development at 27–29°C. Females of *Blattella* sp. had access to drinking water. Oothecae of species which deposit them were kept at 30% relative humidity (after Roth & Willis[41]).

progressive increase during development in the water content of the eggs from 63 per cent when 12 days old to 71 per cent when 33 days old. The little water that is lost from the ootheca occurs through the respiratory ducts in the keel, rather than through the oothecal wall; there is very little increase in water loss with temperature over the range 30–40°C, indicating that the waterproofing material on the ootheca is not the same as the mobile wax on the cuticle of the cockroach (see page 105).

It is apparent from these studies that the ootheca of the Oriental Cockroach can develop and hatch under the most adverse environmental conditions. Nevertheless, experiments suggest that if the eggs of this cockroach are to hatch satisfactorily, it is important for the ootheca to remain dry since contact with water or abrasive agents considerably increases permeability.[384]

The ootheca of *P. americana* is not quite so impermeable to evaporation. In laboratory cultures of the American Cockroach it is common for adults to damage their oothecae by attacking the keel: this causes rapid loss of water, preventing embryological development, particularly at low relative humidities (Table XXXII). The membranes which surround the newly laid eggs are so freely permeable to water that the oothecal case itself protects the eggs from desiccation. Whether or not eggs of *P. americana* and *S. supellectilium* are able to complete their development in infested premises

TABLE XXXII

EFFECTS OF HUMIDITY AND THE REMOVAL OF KEELS FROM
OOTHECAE OF *PERIPLANETA AMERICANA* ON THE HATCHING
OF OOTHECAE AND EGGS
(From Roth & Willis[384])

Relative humidity	Age (days) at treatment	Condition of oothecae	Percentage oothecae from which some eggs hatched	Percentage egg hatch from viable oothecae
15%	Less than 1	Normal	87	92
		Keels removed	0	0
	14	Normal	65	93
		Keels removed	0	0
90%	3–5	Normal	92	97
		Keels removed	56	87
	16	Normal	100	99
		Keels removed	90	99

depends on the evaporating capacity of the air. In completely dry air at
27–28°C, they lose up to 60 per cent of water within 30 days and fail to
hatch (Fig. 135).

Oothecae of the German cockroach differ from those of *B. orientalis*
and *P. americana* by not being uniform in colour; the anterior part held
by the female is not as heavily sclerotised as the posterior part, and by
covering the anterior and posterior halves with beeswax, Roth & Willis[384]
showed that the two areas differ considerably in permeability. Of 30 per
cent water lost in 24 hours, 28 per cent could be attributed to evaporation
through the pale anterior end and only two per cent through the dark
posterior end.

Premature detachment of the ootheca from female *B. germanica* has a
marked effect on hatching. Early observations[60] suggested that if oothecae
were detached nine days after formation, the eggs would hatch if kept
moist, but would not do so under any conditions if removed earlier. The
more recent studies of Roth & Willis[385] show that the age of the ootheca
at time of separation from the female is not the sole factor which influ-

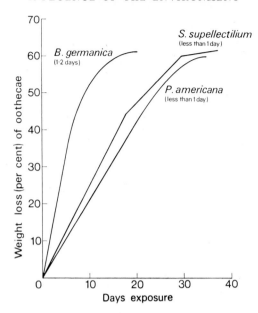

Fig. 135. Rate of loss in weight (%) of oothecae at 0% relative humidity and 27–28°C, which failed to provide young. Figures in parentheses give age of ootheca at removal (*B. germanica*) or deposition (other species) (after Roth & Willis[41]).

ences hatching; when detached oothecae are kept at a favourable temperature (27–29°C), but low humidity (30–50 per cent), eggs fail to hatch unless the oothecae are removed from females on the day prior to hatching when development is almost complete. If kept in moist air, however (90 per cent relative humidity), eggs hatch from oothecae detached when only one day old, or when more than seven days old (Fig. 136).

There is sufficient water in the newly formed ootheca of the German Cockroach (62 per cent), to allow development and hatching of eggs when kept at high humidities, without additional water being supplied by the female. If however the ootheca is detached or prematurely dropped by the female, as so often occurs with German Cockroaches poisoned by carbamate insecticides (see Vol. II), the permeability of the egg case allows water to be lost at ordinary room humidities and more rapidly in dry air. At zero per cent relative humidity and 27–28°C, 60 per cent of water is lost in 20 days (Fig. 135). But, irrespective of humidity, the amount of water lost varies considerably with the age of the ootheca: little is lost from eggs of oothecae detached when one day old, evaporation increases to a maximum between four and six days and falls to a constant amount between seven and 16 days (Fig. 137). Thus the hatching of oothecae dropped

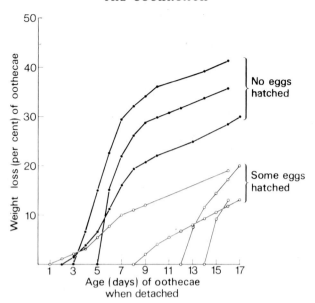

Fig. 136. Relationship between age of oothecae when detached from female *B. germanica* (at 1, 2, 3, 5, 8, 12 and 14 days) and loss in weight at 27–29°C and 90% relative humidity. Also relationship between age at removal and the ability of the eggs to hatch (after Roth & Willis[385]).

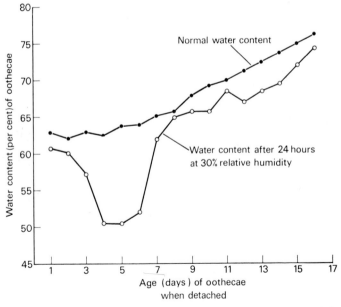

Fig. 137. The normal water content of oothecae when detached from female *B. germanica*. Also the water content of detached oothecae after exposure to 30% relative humidity for 24 hours (after Roth & Willis[385]).

prematurely by the German Cockroach depends on (1) the amount of water present in the ootheca, which increases with age, (2) the age of the ootheca which determines the rate of water loss, and (3) the saturation deficit of the air.

This examination of the influence of the environment on adults, nymphs and oothecae of the pest species of cockroach has drawn attention to their ability to withstand most of the adverse conditions likely to be encountered in buildings and during movement to and from properties. This ability, together with their cryptic habits, undoubtedly account for their success as pests and the relative ease with which new infestations become established as a result of dissemination in trade.

13

DISEASE

Cockroaches in sewers, latrines and cesspools—Bacteria isolated from cockroaches associated with disease outbreaks—Viruses, protozoa and parasitic worms—Experimental transmission of disease organisms—Gastroenteritis and food poisoning organisms—Vector capabilities of different species of cockroach—Typhoid—Persistence of bacteria in cockroach excrement and on utensils and food—Allergy to cockroaches—The role of cockroaches in disease transmission

---

'People living in civilised, highly sanitised areas are rarely aware of the truly tremendous cockroach infestations that may exist under poor hygienic conditions'.[6] It is regrettable, but nevertheless the case, that in many areas of the world people work, eat and sleep with the cockroach: even in certain parts of Europe it is still commonly believed that once cockroaches have taken up residence within a building they are there to stay; their presence is inevitable, and they are tolerated and accepted as part of normal living.

The extent to which pest species of cockroaches, under poor conditions of hygiene and sanitation, are accidental carriers of infections is largely unknown. Roth & Willis[6] have published an excellent and comprehensive review of the information available on the association of cockroaches with disease organisms and in the Foreword to that review, Lt. Col. Ley of the U.S. Army wrote: 'although the cockroach has long been the target of intensive control efforts in both civilian and military communities, my personal grudge against the insect has been based more on suspicion than on fact. . . . This review has replaced a complacent acceptance of the insect as an unpleasant nuisance in areas of poor sanitation, with a firm belief that greater attention must be placed on increased attempts to demonstrate, both in the laboratory and in the field, possible relationships between the prevalence of cockroaches and the incidence of certain diseases'.

This has been the precise aim of very many workers over the last 30–40 years. Whilst the information now available undoubtedly points to the conclusion that cockroaches may transmit disease organisms if given the chance, the inevitable question remains: how often are they involved as vectors of disease, and have they ever been responsible for a major disease outbreak?

A great deal of the stimulus for medical studies has come from the close association of cockroaches with food storage and food handling areas—kitchens, canteens, cafés and restaurants—as well as their presence in

302

latrines, toilets and privies, and in warm countries in sewers. In these locations, cockroaches become contaminated with urine and faeces and have access to a variety of pathogens. They have the opportunity of carrying infections on the outside of their bodies as well as internally. They consume indiscriminately both the food and faeces of man and domestic animals and in this way, parasites of the alimentary canal as well as viruses, bacteria and protozoa may be readily transferred from animal to animal and from animal to man.

The establishment of cockroaches in hospitals brings them again into close association with a variety of disease organisms. In wards and surgical units their presence foils all attempts at good hygiene as well as being psychologically disturbing to patients.

In the first part of this chapter we shall examine some of the information obtained on the numbers and species of cockroach found in locations where they may become closely associated with pathogenic organisms. Secondly we shall briefly review those instances where cockroaches have been found actually carrying disease organisms, and where the isolation of pathogens from the insects appeared in some instances to be related to the existence of disease outbreaks. Finally, we shall look at the potential of cockroaches as disease carriers as indicated by laboratory studies in which bacteria and other organisms have been fed to cockroaches in an effort to find out whether pathogens are able to remain viable in the alimentary canal and in the excreta of the insect.

Cockroaches in sewers, latrines and cesspools

There are reports from many countries of the association of cockroaches with excreta: Antonelli,[386] during an investigation into typhoid outbreaks in Italy found Oriental Cockroaches in sewers and open latrines where they were potentially capable of carrying infection into houses. The American Cockroach has been recorded in large numbers in latrines in Iran,[387] in Venezuela,[388] in septic tanks in Malaya[389] and in cesspools and sewer manholes in Hawaii.[390] In Queensland, Australia, P. americana is more prevalent in sewers and manholes than P. australasiae.[62]

Already in Chapter 11 reference has been made to Tyler, a town in Texas of about 40,000 people in which studies were made of cockroaches in sewers. Of the 670 manholes examined, 40 per cent contained cockroaches; 1–25 insects were found in 17 per cent, 26–100 in 10 per cent and more than 100 cockroaches in 13 per cent. P. americana was the dominant species and the heaviest infestations occurred in the oldest sections of the sewers.[391] Other species found in the Tyler sewers, but less frequently, included P. fuliginosa, B. orientalis and the Wood Cockroaches, Parcoblatta pensylvanica and Parcoblatta bolliana.

Studies in other Texas towns have given similar information. In Austin, 80 per cent of manholes examined by Eades et al.[331] contained P. americana, and in Galveston, Houston and Corpus Christi, the American Cockroach was found in over half the manholes inspected. It is of interest to mention here that references to Corpus Christi are often to be met with in cockroach literature since in this town resistance to chlordane was first detected among German Cockroaches.

The enormous size to which populations of cockroaches can develop in sewers is illustrated by the description of a campaign against *B. orientalis* in Bedford, Indiana;[392] 'not one house in the city of 18,000 was free of the pest. A heavy infestation was found in most manholes, and in one there was one cockroach for every three square inches of surface. Cockroaches invaded homes and apartments from outlets in bath tubs, sinks and lavatories. Basements were heavily infested with "water bugs" coming up through the drains'. In Phoenix, Arizona, Schoof & Siverly[332] surveyed 22 manholes over a seven-week period and obtained a weekly average of 92–143 *P. americana* per manhole. In the same city, Jackson & Maier[333] found 300–400 cockroaches in some of the manholes.

In two other towns in southern Texas, Pharr and Donna, cockroaches were trapped in the Latin-American sectors to discover whether poliomyelitis virus was being carried; 72 pairs of traps were operated simultaneously in houses and out-door privies over a period of several weeks.[393] German Cockroaches were encountered much more often in houses, 1,692 insects in 60 per cent of the traps, compared with only 51 in 15 per cent of the traps located in privies. The American Cockroach was more prevalent in privies, but *P. brunnea* outnumbered *P. americana* in houses.

Some of the most detailed information from the United States on the relative abundance of the pest species of cockroach in and around homes and privies comes from the study made in 12 towns in south-west Georgia.[93] Again using traps, 80 samples of cockroaches were taken each week during 1952 and 1953 (Table XXXIII); German Cockroaches were most prevalent inside homes and American Cockroaches were most prevalent in sewer manholes. The species which most consistently outnumbered all others outside homes and in and around privies was the Smoky-brown Cockroach, *Periplaneta fuliginosa*. In Georgia, the season has a marked effect on the relative abundance of species; *B. germanica* is less abundant in homes during the hottest months when *P. americana* and *P. brunnea* are at a maximum, and these two species are also more abundant in and around privies during the warmer months.

No records exist of cockroaches occurring in sewers in the United Kingdom. There is no doubt that cockroaches would have been seen if present, since many thousands of manhole covers are lifted each year in connection with rodent control. This absence of cockroaches is not however surprising since in those countries in which the sewers are infested, the American Cockroach, which is rare in Britain, appears to be best suited to this environment. Nevertheless, Oriental Cockroaches are not uncommon within premises around drains and gulleys where they have access to a variety of infectious bacteria. This is especially true in hospitals where

TABLE XXXIII

COMPARISON OF COCKROACH DISTRIBUTION IN FOUR ENVIRON-
MENTS IN S.W. GEORGIA (1952–53). AVERAGE NUMBER OF COCK-
ROACHES PER 100 TRAPS
(From Haines & Palmer[93])

Environment	Season	Species			
		P. fuliginosa	P. americana	P. brunnea	B. germanica
Inside	Spring	7	2	9	171
homes	Summer	15	9	154	47
(3,713	Autumn	45	1	7	657
traps)	Winter	4	1	1	203
Outside	Spring	10	1	1	5
homes	Summer	34	0	11	0
(1,027	Autumn	27	0	7	17
traps)	Winter	21	0	5	1
In or	Spring	11	2	0	7
around	Summer	121	83	25	4
privies	Autumn	77	0	50	2
(164 traps)	Winter	120	0	0	6
In sewer	Spring	7	720	0	0
manholes	Summer	1	51	3	1
(2,071	Autumn*	–	–	–	–
traps)	Winter	1	90	1	1

* No records available.

infestations of B. orientalis outnumber B. germanica by more than four to
one, and where the incidence of the Oriental Cockroach in and around
toilets is almost as high (33 per cent of hospitals) as in any other type of
premises containing this species (Table XLII). According to the survey
data for the United Kingdom (Chapter 14), Oriental Cockroaches occur
in and around toilets in 22 per cent of infested properties and in 16 per
cent of premises infested by B. germanica.

Bacteria isolated from cockroaches associated with disease outbreaks
Organisms which it is thought are most likely to be carried by cockroaches
and responsible for human infections are those belonging to the Salmonella
group, the causative bacteria of food poisoning. Salmonellae were recovered
from 12 of 360 batches of cockroaches taken from sewer manholes during
the Tyler Project (see page 254). Examples of pathogenic bacteria found
naturally infecting cockroaches taken from sewers, hospital wards and
other locations include seven species of Salmonella (Table XXXIV). The
list incriminates the three most common pest cockroaches, B. germanica,
B. orientalis and P. americana.

U

TABLE XXXIV

EXAMPLES OF PATHOGENIC BACTERIA FOUND NATURALLY INFECTING COCKROACHES FROM
SEWERS, HOSPITAL WARDS AND OTHER LOCATIONS
(Derived from information compiled by Roth & Willis[6])

Disease of man	Species of bacterium	Species of cockroach carrying infection	Part of cockroach from which extracted	Location in which cockroaches found	Country
Lesions and infections of urinary tract	Pseudomonas aeruginosa	Blaberus craniifer Blattella germanica	faeces faeces and alimentary canal	— —	U.S.A.[399] U.S.A.[400]
Boils, abscesses	Staphylococcus aureus	Blaberus craniifer Blatta orientalis Blattella germanica	faeces intestinal contents antennae	— — —	U.S.A.[399] Italy[401] U.S.A.[402]
Associated with pus	Staphylococcus spp.	Blattella germanica	outer surfaces of insects	From 19 cockroaches taken from hospital operating room	Germany[403]
Infections of genital urinary tract and intestine	Escherichia coli	Blatta orientalis Blattella germanica	gut contents and faeces gut contents	—	Italy[401,404] France[405] Poland[406] U.S.A.[394,407]
Enteric fever and gastroenteritis	Salmonella schottmuelleri, S. bredeney, and S. oranienburg	Periplaneta americana	intestinal tract	Sewer manholes	U.S.A.[394]

Disease of man	Species of bacterium	Species of cockroach carrying infection	Part of cockroach from which extracted	Location in which cockroaches found	Country
Gastroenteritis	Paracolobactrum aerogenoides and P. coliforme	Blattella germanica	faeces and alimentary canal intestinal tract	—	U.S.A.[400]
		Periplaneta americana			U.S.A.[394]
	Salmonella morbificans	Periplaneta americana	gut contents	From 16 cockroaches taken from hospital ward containing cases of gastroenteritis	Australia[112,397]
Intestinal infections	Salmonella anatis	Periplaneta americana	—	Sewer manholes	U.S.A.[331]
Food poisoning	Salmonella typhimurium	Blattella germanica	—	A cockroach captured in a hospital ward during an epidemic of gastroenteritis	Belgium[408]
		Nauphoeta cinerea	gut	A cockroach captured in a hospital ward where Salmonella infections were occurring	Australia[112,397]
Typhoid fever	Salmonella typhosa	Blatta orientalis	legs and faeces	Cockroaches captured within homes of people who had contracted typhoid	Italy[386,396]

Table XXXIV (Cont.)

Disease of man	Species of bacterium	Species of cockroach carrying infection	Part of cockroach from which extracted	Location in which cockroaches found	Country
Dysentry	Shigella alkalescens	Periplaneta americana	intestinal tract	—	U.S.A.[394]
Summer diarrhoea in children	Shigella para-dysenteriae	Blatta orientalis	mid gut	Cockroaches from food cupboard in hospital	U.S.S.R.[395]
Bubonic plague	Pasteurella pestis	Blatta orientalis	—	Cockroaches collected from plague-infected foci	Hong Kong[409]
Leprosy	Mycobacterium leprae	Blattella germanica	in cockroaches and faeces	55 of 230 cockroaches caught in native huts	S. Rhodesia & Kenya[410,412]
		Periplaneta americana & P. australasiae	alimentary canal	Among many cockroaches caught in wards of a leprosy sanatorium	Formosa[413,414]

In an attempt to correlate cockroaches with an outbreak of summer diarrhoea among children in San Antonio, Texas, Bitter & Williams,[394] looked for the causative bacteria (*Shigella sonnei* and *Shigella paradysenteriae*) in the gut contents of cockroaches collected from several manholes. Cultures of organisms from 94 insects gave no grounds to connect cockroaches with the epidemic. Nevertheless, organisms which were isolated from these cockroaches included *Salmonella schottmuelleri* which causes enteric fever in man, and *S. oranienburg* and *S. bredeney*, both of which cause gastroenteritis.* Eades *et al.*[331] have also isolated S. *oranienburg* and *S. panama*, another bacterium which causes food poisoning, from the intestinal tracts of *P. americana* taken from manholes in the United States.

Despite the failure of Bitter & Williams to detect among *P. americana* the causative organisms of summer diarrhoea, this did prove possible with *B. orientalis*.[395] This species was found naturally infected with *Shigella paradysenteriae* when caught in a food cupboard of a hospital in the Republic of Tadzhikistan (U.S.S.R.). In Italy this cockroach has also been found carrying *Salmonella typhosa* on its legs and in its faecal pellets in homes of people suffering from typhoid.[386,396] In Australia, Mackerras & Mackerras[112,397] have implicated *P. americana* as secondary foci of infection in a hospital outbreak of gastroenteritis among children. The insects were carrying *Salmonella morbificans*.

Viruses, Protozoa and Parasitic worms
Viruses and protozoa are also carried by cockroaches. Four strains of poliomyelitis virus have been isolated by Syverton *et al.*[415] from *B. germanica*, *P. americana* and *S. supellectilium*, taken on the premises of patients suffering from paralytic poliomyelitis. It was possible to transmit the virus from the naturally infected insects to susceptible hosts. Laboratory tests in which mice have been injected with suspensions of faeces and tissues from cockroaches (*P. americana*) artificially fed Lansing poliomyelitis virus indicate that the insect loses its infectivity within 24 hours.[416]

Among the many protozoa carried by cockroaches, the most important is *Entamoeba histolytica*, responsible for amoebic dysentery. Cysts resembling those of *E. histolytica* have been found among many species of cockroach from widely separated sources, including Egypt, Venezuela and Peru. In addition, cockroaches serve, naturally, as the intermediate hosts for 12 species of helminths including the eggs of various hookworms and the larvae of many round worms. The most well-known of these worms is

* *Salmonella schottmuelleri* is a natural pathogen of man, causing enteric fever, and is occasionally a pathogen of farm animals. *S. oranienburg* was first isolated from the faeces of a child in a children's home near Oranienburg, just north of Berlin. It was later isolated from cases of gastroenteritis in man and has also been taken from chickens and powdered egg. *S. bredeney* was first found by Hohn and Herrman in Bredeney, Germany, from cases of human gastroenteritis and an abscess of the lower jaw. It is also found in pigs and chickens.[398]

Oxyspirura mansoni, the eye worm of poultry, for which *Pycnoscelus surinamensis* is one of the natural intermediate hosts.

Experimental transmission of disease organisms

To explore further the potential of cockroaches in their natural environments to carry disease organisms, many attempts have been made to examine the fate of organisms fed artificially to cockroaches. To determine the period that bacteria and other organisms may remain viable in the alimentary tract, faeces have been collected from test cockroaches over many weeks. In these experiments it has been necessary to immobilise the cockroaches in some way so that they have no opportunity to contaminate other parts of the body while receiving infective food, or to pass infection from the mouthparts to faeces other than through the gut. In addition, organisms have been inoculated onto the cuticle to explore the potential of cockroaches to spread disease by physical contact.

From early experiments of this type, it was concluded that cockroaches could, by contamination with their faeces, infect food and milk with intestinal bacteria, transmit the bacillus for human tuberculosis, disseminate various pathogenic staphylococci and carry destructive moulds.[417] Also cockroaches could carry *Escherichia coli* and other pathogenic bacteria on their legs, and these too could be found in faeces.[418]

In the Philippines, Barber[419] found that *P. americana* and *L. maderae* were able to carry *Pasteurella pestis* (the causative organism of plague) and that *Vibrio comma* (the cholera bacteria) multiply in the alimentary canal of cockroaches and are discharged in the faeces, without loss in virulence.

In Accra, Macfie[420] established that *P. americana* fed on sputum containing tuberculosis bacillus failed to pass bacteria in faeces on the first day after infective feeding but bacteria were present from the second to the fifth. Also, cockroaches given scrapings from the nose of a leper passed faeces containing *Mycobacterium leprae* one or two days later. In addition positive results were obtained with *Entamoeba histolytica* taken from stools of African patients suffering from acute dysentery. Cysts of this organism were found in cockroach excreta for one to three days after infective feeding and again appeared unharmed by passage through the insect gut.

Macfie also obtained positive results with various parasitic worms; eggs of *Ancylostoma duodenale* (human hookworm) and *A. ceylanicum* (dog hookworm) passed unharmed through the gut of *P. americana* and appeared in the faeces for one to three days after the infective meal. The same result was obtained with the beef tapeworm (*Taenia saginata*), intestinal round worm (*Ascaris lumbricoides*), and human whipworm (*Trichuris trichiura*).

Gastroenteritis and food poisoning organisms

Whilst sources of tropical disease organisms are unlikely to be readily available to cockroaches in cool climates, a number of bacteria are available under conditions of poor hygiene and sanitation in temperate countries. These include the *Salmonella* bacteria responsible for food poisoning and gastroenteritis.

In preliminary tests with food poisoning bacteria, Olson & Rueger[421] were able to show that *Salmonella enteritidis* fed to *B. germanica* could be recovered from the faeces within two days. Similarly, *Salmonella typhimurium* could be recovered from the digestive tract up to nine days after infective feeding. Studies also with the German Cockroach by Janssen & Wedberg[400] provided infected faecal pellets for seven days and viable *S. typhimurium* in the alimentary canal for up to nine days. In Australia, this bacterium was recovered from the gut and faeces of *P. australasiae* and *S. supellectilium*,[422] and it can also be carried on the exoskeleton of *B. germanica* for at least ten days.[408]

Jung & Shaffer[423] investigated the survival of ingested Salmonellae (*S. typhimurium* and *S. montevideo*) by allowing starved cockroaches to feed on faeces (from healthy humans) inoculated with varying doses of bacteria. The amounts ingested in a single meal varied from 0·02 to 0·1 gram. Survival of these Salmonellae in the gut of *P. americana* occurred fairly regularly and persisted for at least seven days when the insects ingested amounts of faeces containing 10,000 or more viable bacteria. Previously, Wedberg *et al.*[399] had shown that at least 5,0C0 *S. typhimurium* had to be consumed to obtain infection in *Blaberus craniifer*.

Vector capabilities of different species of cockroach
In more extensive tests with *S. oranienburg* isolated from a food poisoning incident in which 16 people became infected, attempts were made to examine the vector capabilities of the three common species of pest cockroaches. After feeding, *P. americana* produced infected faeces within 24 hours and for up to ten days; faecal pellets produced during the first few days were 100 per cent positive. Infected pellets were also obtained from *B. germanica* for up to 12 days, and for as long as 20 days from *B. orientalis*. A post-mortem on Oriental Cockroaches showed that the bacterium remained viable in the gut of this insect for as long as six weeks.[421]

Using four species of cockroach (*P. australasiae*, *P. ignota*, *S. supellectilium* and *N. cinerea*), and five species of *Salmonella*, Mackerras & Pope[422] obtained no indication that different species of cockroach were more efficient than others as carriers, or that different Salmonellae were more infective than others. The bacteria were isolated either from the faeces during life, or from the gut at post-mortem, and of the 44 cockroaches used, 15 remained infective for 8 to 42 days and seven (about 16 per cent) became 'chronic carriers', producing infected pellets intermittently for more than a fortnight.

Typhoid
The potential of cockroaches to transmit *Salmonella typhosa*, the causative

organism of typhoid, is open to question. In 1903, Englemann[424] described an outbreak of typhoid in Chicago and suggested, without any evidence, that cockroaches were acting as carriers.

Reference has already been made (see page 309) to the successful isolation of *S. typhosa* from the legs and faeces of *B. orientalis* associated with typhoid patients in Italy, yet attempts to pass this bacterium through a number of experimental vectors has given variable results.

For example, massive doses of the bacterium fed to *Blaberus craniifer*[399] failed to show its presence in the gut or faeces, and *B. germanica* fed billions of *S. typhosa*[400] produced only two positive faecal pellets among 45 passed within the first 18 hours of infective feeding, and none after 24 hours. Moreover, the contents of the alimentary canal of these insects gave only one positive culture between 12 and 15 hours after the massive doses were given.

Macfie[420] also failed to recover *Salmonella typhosa* from *P. americana*, although other workers with this cockroach[425] and with *P. australasiae*[426] were able to isolate the organism from excreta for up to three days. Using *Blatta orientalis*, Spinelli & Reitano[404] recovered *S. typhosa* from the insect's gut for up to nine days and from the faeces for up to three days. In contrast, McBurney & Davis[427] again using the Oriental Cockroach fed the typhoid bacterium for five days, obtained isolates which could only once be confirmed as *S. typhosa* by the recognised tests.

Accordingly, there is reason to believe that the typhoid bacterium may require more precise conditions for its passage in a viable state through the gut of cockroaches than is the case for the food poisoning organisms previously discussed. In this regard it seems probable that some species of cockroach may be more effective vectors of *S. typhosa* than others.

Persistence of bacteria in cockroach excrement and on utensils and food
One of the features of bacteria which plays an important role in the spread of infections is that many are able to remain infective on inert surfaces for long periods. *Salmonella oranienberg* can remain viable in the excrement of *P. americana* for 85 days at 52–56 per cent relative humidity and for over six months at 30 per cent relative humidity. On glass, which cockroaches may contaminate with faeces or vomit, *S. oranienburg* can survive at room temperature for 34 days, whilst on cornflakes this period is extended to at least 62 days and on dry biscuits to 88 days. It is also apparent that cockroaches with access to infected material can contaminate liquids by mouth contact or regurgitation, for at least four days, and that bacteria can remain viable on the relatively smooth pronotum of the insect for as long as 78 days.[421]

Allergy to cockroaches
The varying sensitivity of humans to the stings of bees and wasps is well known, but far less information is available on the reactions of humans to

contact with cockroaches. In a preliminary study on this subject, Bernton & Brown[428] found that 28 per cent of 114 patients suffering from various allergies gave positive skin tests with extracts of cockroaches as compared with only 7.5 per cent of 253 normal individuals. In subsequent work[429] these authors give evidence to suggest that the greater the exposure of humans to German Cockroaches the greater is the likelihood of development of skin sensitivity to cockroach allergen; the allergen can be detected in food partially consumed by cockroaches, and is not destroyed by a cooking temperature of 100°C. Among almost 600 allergic patients belonging to four ethnic groups, routinely visiting seven hospitals in New York City, over 70 per cent reacted positively to the cockroach allergen. Positive reactions were most marked among Puerto Ricans (59 per cent), less marked among Negroes (47 per cent) and Italians (17 per cent) and least among Jews (5 per cent); this is the same order as the severity of cockroach infestations (*B. germanica*) reported in the homes of these four groups in New York City (unpublished).

The role of cockroaches in disease transmission

Only a small proportion of the large amount of information on the incidence of cockroaches and their association with disease organisms, under natural or experimental conditions, has been cited in this chapter. For more detailed information the interested reader can do no better than consult 'The Medical and Veterinary Importance of Cockroaches' by Roth & Willis[6] which has proved of immense value in compiling this review.

We now have the task of drawing together the facts to provide a proper understanding of the practical importance of cockroaches in disease transmission. Almost every author who has faced this task has prefaced his remarks with cautions, which range from 'the cockroach, like many other household insects, can be regarded *only* with suspicion'[430] to 'cockroaches are decidedly one of our most serious public health problems'.[431] The truth probably lies somewhere in between!

The facts presented in this chapter incriminate the cockroach beyond it being just an insect with repulsive habits. In the context of disease, three points arise.

(1) Cockroaches favour the environments created by man for the discharge of effluent, waste disposal and human sanitation. That cockroaches also favour the environment of kitchens where food is prepared for public consumption is only too well known. The movement of cockroaches from one location to another provides a ready means for the contamination of food and food preparation surfaces with disease organisms.

(2) There is ample evidence that cockroaches carry pathogens in and on their bodies and that these organisms may remain viable on the cuticle, in the alimentary canal and in their excreta for several days or weeks. Disease transmission may occur readily by regurgitation from the mouth-

parts or it may be attenuated over long periods by cockroaches acting as 'chronic carriers' with the intermittent production of faecal pellets containing infective organisms.

(3) At present there is only circumstantial evidence to link diseases which it is known can be carried, or are carried by cockroaches, with disease outbreaks. The evidence, however, is sufficient to justify the immediate control of cockroach infestations as soon as they arise in all areas where they may create a possible hazard to public health.

Perhaps the most striking piece of evidence tending to incriminate the cockroach as a carrier of disease, is that given by Graffer & Mertens[408] involving an epidemic of food poisoning caused by *Salmonella typhimurium* among children in the nursery of a hospital in Brussels. This infection persisted for two months, despite isolation of the patients from possible healthy carriers. Cockroaches had not been considered as possible carriers because none had been seen by day. Attention was however drawn to an infestation of *B. germanica* by a night nurse when cockroaches were seen to run over the bed clothing and over the children at night. Among the cockroaches caught, one was found to be carrying numerous bacteria identified as *S. typhimurium*. When the cockroach infestation was controlled with DDT and no more living cockroaches were seen, there was also an immediate check on the epidemic of food poisoning.

14

THE INCIDENCE OF PEST COCKROACHES IN THE BRITISH ISLES

Changes in post-war Britain—The survey—The sample: geographical distribution; types of property; age of properties in relation to distribution and type; heating—Incidence of cockroach species: infestations in different types of property; infestations and the age of properties; infestation and central heating—Locations of infestations within buildings—Geographical variation in the incidence of species; infestations in cities and large towns—Other species—Conclusions from the survey

Apart from the occasional establishment of the American and Australian Cockroaches in Britain, and even more rarely of such species as *Periplaneta brunnea* (see p. 64) and *S. supellectilium* (p. 68), there are only two pest species which occur regularly, namely, the German Cockroach and the Oriental Cockroach.

This situation contrasts markedly with certain areas of the United States where at least four or more pest cockroaches may occur within a group of premises and two or three species within one building. As an example, a survey of the occurrence of cockroaches in apartments in North Carolina[432] has shown that the German Cockroach occurs about four times more often than the Brown-banded Cockroach, but together with the occasional occurrence of the American, Oriental and Smoky-brown Cockroach (*P. fulginosa*).

The occurrence of different cockroaches in buildings is influenced to a marked extent by the type of property: thus in three cities in North Carolina, in which 44 per cent of the buildings were found infested, *B. germanica* occurred about twice as often as *B. orientalis* in houses, where *P. americana* and *S. supellectilium* were found only infrequently, yet in shops, the German and Oriental species were found in about equal numbers. In restaurants, infestations of *B. germanica* were found three times more often than *B. orientalis* (Table XXXV). Disregarding the type of premises, infestations of *B. germanica*, *B. orientalis*, *P. americana* and *S. supellectilium*, occurred in the ratios 16 : 10 : 2 : 1.[433]

In a country as large as the United States with a wide range of climate the incidence of different cockroaches varies with geographical location. Those which live outdoors are frequently found indoors and the numbers of pest species increases as one travels south. In a temperate climate, like that of the British Isles, infestations of pest cockroaches are rarely encountered outdoors, and the three outdoor species of *Ectobius* (p. 90)

315

are not found indoors. Moreover infestations of *B. germanica* and *B. orientalis* within properties are buffered from the small outdoor variations in climate which exist in different parts of the country.

TABLE XXXV

FREQUENCY OF OCCURRENCE OF COCKROACHES IN BUILDINGS
IN N. CAROLINA

(Data from Wright[433])

Type of building	No. with cockroaches	Frequency			
		German	Oriental	American	Brown-banded
House	157	116	64	4	7
Shop	17	14	14	4	0
Restaurant	12	12	4	1	0
Apartment	5	5	3	2	2
Others	30	17	18	12	1
Total	221	164	103	23	10

Accurate statistics on the incidence of pest insects are difficult to obtain. Only in recent years have we begun to recognise the value of factual data on pest abundance, especially of agricultural pests, when we come to consider control by management of the environment as opposed to the use of chemicals. It has been wisely said that the density of cross-hatching on most insect distribution maps can be correlated with the density of entomologists. This would appear true for recent maps of the distribution of the German and Oriental Cockroaches in the British Isles (Fig. 138) where many blanks appear but where the species is by no means absent.[45]

Changes in post-war Britain

Early references to cockroaches in Britain indicate that the Oriental Cockroach is by far the most common, but with the change in eating habits, involving the growth of the hotel and catering industries and the gradual introduction of such amenities as central heating, there is reason to believe that the relative incidence of the species may have changed, at least in certain types of property. As an example of such a change, but for reasons not yet understood, reference has already been made to the replacement of the American Cockroach by the German Cockroach in the accommodation of modern ships. Because of the absence of factual data, one is tempted to ask whether the German Cockroach has recently assumed this position, or is it that the smaller German Cockroach has been mistaken for many years for nymphs of the American species?

Statistics on the numbers of different types of properties constructed in

(a)

(b)

Fig. 138. The recorded distribution of (a) the German cockroach, *B. germanica*, and (b) the Oriental cockroach, *B. orientalis* (after Ragge[45]).

Britain since the last World War are not accurately known, but it is estimated that about 20 per cent of existing properties were built during the last 25 years.

This extensive rebuilding has involved the use of new materials and constructional methods. Our appreciation of modern internal décor has changed; panelling is used extensively to give smooth lines to internal surfaces and new insulation materials are being employed. The boiler house of a modern office block offers far less favourable accommodation to cockroaches than its old fashioned predecessor. Oil-fired and gas central heating have partly replaced solid fuel. Much of present-day plumbing consists of small bore piping within well-insulated service ducts minimising the available water for insects by way of condensation. Air extraction and ventilation are relatively new features in modern kitchens, where equipment is fitted close to walls, floors and skirtings, but leaving the inevitable gaps which fail to exclude cockroaches. Nevertheless the kitchens of modern catering establishments are designed for better hygiene and ease of cleaning and show a tremendous improvement over kitchens of pre-war design. The importance of hygiene has grown with increasing competition between the food industries and the level of hygiene in homes has seen an enormous change within the present century. But there has been an increased spread of imports, and therefore of insects, from ports to inland production areas as well as greater trade between different parts of the country. More packaging materials are being used than ever before, increasing the opportunity for spread of cockroaches from one premises to another. Straw is a packaging material of the past, having been replaced by synthetic materials, and more and more crates are marked 'non-returnable'. How have all these factors influenced the environments and movement of the Oriental and German Cockroaches and affected the relative abundance of the two species?

The absence of statistical records precludes an answer to this question but Green[434] suggests that 'if an accurate assessment could be made it would probably be found that the position has been reversed and that the German Cockroach now outnumbers its Oriental cousin both in numbers of infestations and numbers of individuals'.

This chapter is concerned with the incidence of cockroaches in buildings in the British Isles *at the present time*. It is concerned with the results of a survey in which information on 4,004 premises was reported by the Service Staff of Rentokil Laboratories who were responsible for pest control in those premises. These staff had been trained, as part of their servicing work, to distinguish between cockroach species. Since only two are involved, with the very rare occurrence of others, the accuracy of identifications is considered high. Among the 4,004 premises investigated, only 15 contained species other than *B. germanica* and *B. orientalis*, and the validity of these identifications was checked.

The survey

Space is given here to the conduct of the survey because it may be useful as a model for obtaining information on other industrial pests. Each serviceman was asked to answer seven questions about infested premises where he personally had seen cockroaches alive or dead. One of the forms for reporting the information is reproduced opposite.

It is the practice of Servicing Companies to allocate a contract number to each premises treated for pest control. This is required simply for reference purposes but proved useful for checking some of the cockroach identifications. The type of premises or industry had to be selected from a list of 50, issued with the report forms, but to aid in analysis many similar types of property were grouped. The age of the property was often difficult to assess; properties built before the Second World War, but with post-war additions, were grouped with pre-war properties.

The species of cockroach in each of the premises was based on the visual observations of the serviceman. In most, the infestation had been controlled at the time of reporting so that this information and details of the locations of the infestation, relied to some extent on the memory of the man, supported by information on the treatment card which records the history of the infestation over the previous months. The type of heating in the premises was in many cases difficult to describe. Servicemen were instructed to answer 'no' if the building was not above average temperature, 'centrally' if a heating plant was installed, and 'otherwise' if portable, oil or other equipment was used. Premises with part central heating were included among those with full central heating.

FILL IN THIS REPORT ON THE PREMISES.

1. Contract No._____72510092_____

2. Type of premises or
   industry carried on ___Restaurant._____

3. Age of premises (state pre-
   or post-war) _____Pre-war._____

4. Address (town & county only) ____London, W.1.____

_____   _____

5. Have you personally seen, at any time (live or dead)?

	Steamflies B.germanica	Black beetle B.orientalis	Others P.americana
(tick box) Yes	✓	✓	☐
No	☐	☐	✓

6. Where in the premises? (tick locations for species seen)

	Steamflies B.germanica	Black beetle B.orientalis	Others P.americana
Cellar/basement		✓	
Boiler room		✓	
Ducts			
Kitchens	✓	✓	
Larder/stores		✓	
Eating areas	✓		
Lounges	✓		
Bars	✓		
Service pantries	✓		
Bedrooms			
Bathrooms		✓	
Toilets	✓		
Linen stores			
Laundry			
Offices		✓	
Other places (state)			

7. Are the premises heated (above average temperature)?

(tick box)   No ☐   Centrally ✓   Otherwise ☐

The sample
The 4,004 premises cannot be considered a random selection of properties, since (1) they all contained cockroaches at sometime, (2) the owner of the premises asked for the pest to be eradicated, and (3) a disproportionately high number of certain types of property were examined in one area compared with another.

Geographical distribution
Information was obtained from all but one county in England and one in Wales, and from all but three counties in Scotland and four in Ireland. These omissions are believed to have little significance in relation to the conclusions reached from the survey. To handle the data more easily, and to study geographical variations, the country was split into ten arbitrary units (Fig. 139). These were not equal in area, but the sample in each unit comprised not less than 200 infested properties.

A brief description of the geographical units will help to distinguish them. 'North Scotland' comprised the Highlands and some information was obtained from the Western Isles and Orkneys. A high proportion of the data for 'South Scotland' came from Glasgow. 'North England' contained the highly populated areas of Liverpool, Manchester and Tyneside as well as the large rural areas of Yorkshire and the Lake District. The 'East' was characterised by the agricultural counties of Lincoln, Norfolk and Suffolk together with the urbanised areas north of London. The 'Central' area comprised the industrial Midlands centred on Birmingham. In complete contrast, the 'West' consisted of Wales, with its sparsely populated sheep-country, together with the south Wales coalfield and the industrial port of Cardiff. This area also included Birkenhead in the north and Newport in the south.

The 'South West' was made up of five counties extending eastward to the borders of Hampshire and Berkshire, comprising that part of the country with the warmest winters and characterised by numerous holiday resorts. The 'South East' stretched from Bournemouth to Margate and from Oxford to Eastbourne. This area included the Isle of Wight, many south coast holiday towns as well as the dormitory areas of south London. The density of population in this area varies considerably with proximity to London and the coast.

'London', composed heterogeneously of the City, dockland, and the West End, embraced the London Boroughs. Relatively few observations were made in Ulster and Eire so these were grouped into one area, 'Ireland', where about one-third of the data came from the cities of Belfast and Dublin.

Types of property
The types of properties in the geographical units varied considerably (Table XXXVI). Thus, although 910 (23 per cent) were hotels, these

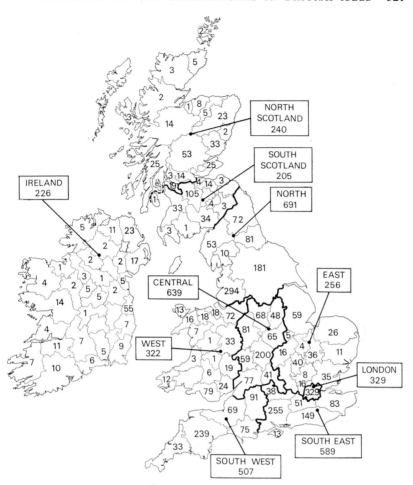

Fig. 139. The sampling areas and the numbers and distribution of infested premises.

accounted for only 3 per cent of the properties in London, compared with 36 per cent in the 'South West' and 37 per cent in Ireland. Half the textile factories were in the 'North', a quarter of the schools and colleges in the 'South East' and over a third of public houses in the 'Central' area. Other examples of heterogeneity can be found in the Table; relatively few schools were included in London and in North and South Scotland, and a disproportionately large number of chemical and engineering factories were among the properties of the 'Central' area. Many of these variations result, of course, from the differences in geographical distribution of popu-

X

lation and of industry in Britain, but not, it is believed, of educational requirements or drinking habits!

TABLE XXXVI

COCKROACH SURVEY: NUMBERS AND DISTRIBUTION OF DIF-
FERENT TYPES OF INFESTED PROPERTIES COMPRISING THE
SAMPLE

Type of property	Geographical unit										
	South West	South East	London	East	Central	West	North	S. Scotland	N. Scotland	Ireland	Total
Hotels	183	186	10	47	105	74	100	29	92	84	910
Restaurants & cafés	69	101	93	43	74	25	102	50	23	19	599
Food factories	66	54	46	61	73	54	98	33	33	40	558
Hospitals	29	54	21	14	61	37	53	30	39	34	372
Shops	40	34	29	11	41	27	58	21	11	8	280
Schools, colleges & convents	18	37	2	18	34	15	21	2	2	16	165
Houses, flats & conval. homes	36	39	12	6	18	10	24	2	7	5	159
Chemical & eng. factories	8	11	13	9	54	12	39	6	3	3	158
Cinemas & theatres	10	14	7	13	37	16	34	5	1	2	139
Laundries	11	22	18	6	12	6	31	4	7	4	121
Public houses	10	6	13	4	41	6	21	5	2	2	110
Textile factories	1	1	5	2	30	7	49	4	9	1	109
Clubs & public halls	3	10	25	2	18	8	18	4	2	3	93
Hostels & holiday camps	8	7	9	6	15	6	4	1	3	0	59
Breweries	4	5	5	4	11	6	12	1	2	1	51
Offices	5	1	11	2	5	2	13	4	2	0	45
Others	6	7	10	8	10	11	14	4	2	4	76
Total	507	589	329	256	639	322	691	205	240	226	4,004
Pre-war	467	542	303	229	575	274	609	183	211	193	3,586
Post-war	40	47	26	27	64	48	82	22	29	33	418

Age of properties in relation to distribution and type

About 90 per cent of the properties were built before World War II and 10 per cent after the war. This ratio, however, varied for different parts of the country (Table XXXVI) and with the type of premises (Table XXXVII). Thus in the south of England (S.W., S.E. and London), post-war properties comprised only 8 per cent of the sample whereas in the 'West', 'North' Northern Scotland and Ireland, the sample contained up to 15 per cent new buildings. Among different types of property, very few hotels (5 per cent) and few hospitals (6 per cent) were built after the war, whereas 14 per cent of food factories, 15 per cent of chemical and engineering

TABLE XXXVII

COCKROACH SURVEY: NUMBERS OF PRE- AND POST-WAR PROPERTIES COMPRISING THE SAMPLE

Type of property		Total	Pre-war	Post-war
Hotels		910	870	40
Restaurants & cafés		599	524	75
Food factories		558	483	75
Hospitals		372	349	23
Shops		280	236	44
Schools, colleges & convents		165	150	15
Houses, flats & convalescent homes		159	144	15
Chemical & engineering factories		158	134	24
Cinemas & theatres		139	129	10
Laundries		121	112	9
Public houses		110	96	14
Textile factories		109	99	10
Clubs & public halls		93	78	15
Hostels & holiday camps		59	48	11
Breweries		51	45	6
Offices		45	39	6
Others:				
Military establishments	13			
Warehouses	13			
Farms	12			
Laboratories	11			
Public baths	10			
Garages & transport	7	76	50	26
Electricity & gas works	4			
Mines	3			
Fire stations	1			
Markets	1			
Studios	1			
Total		4,004	3,586	418

factories and 16 per cent of shops were post-war. Proportionately fewer cinemas and theatres have been built since the war (7 per cent), whereas clubs and public halls (16 per cent) and hostels and holiday camps (18 per cent) have become more numerous.

Heating

Of the 4,004 infested premises, 2,973 (74 per cent) were centrally heated. The incidence of central heating varied little between pre- (74 per cent) and post-war properties (80 per cent). Accordingly, other types of heating, or none, occurred in 1,031 premises (26 per cent), this same percentage in pre-war properties and 20 per cent in those built after the war. For the purposes of analysis, 'other types' of heating and 'none' are considered as one group.

The presence or absence of central heating varied considerably with different types of property and with their age (Table XXXVIII). Thus 55 per cent of post-war food factories were heated centrally compared

TABLE XXXVIII

COCKROACH SURVEY: THE INCIDENCE OF CENTRAL HEATING IN PRE- AND POST-WAR PROPERTIES COMPRISING THE SAMPLE

Type of property	Pre-war properties		Post-war properties	
	Number with central heating	Percentage of total	Number with central heating	Percentage of total
Hospitals	343	98	22	96
Cinemas & theatres	124	96	10	100
Hotels	802	92	39	98
Hostels & holiday camps	44	92	10	91
Schools, colleges & convents	137	91	15	100
Chemical & eng. factories	118	88	21	88
Textile factories	86	87	10	100
Offices	34	87	6	100
Clubs & public halls	63	81	14	93
Houses, flats & conv. homes	99	69	12	80
Restaurants & cafés	338	65	59	79
Public houses	57	59	13	93
Laundries	63	56	6	67
Breweries	25	56	5	83
Shops	109	46	30	68
Food factories	159	33	41	55
Others	36	72	23	88
Average	(2,637)	74%	(336)	80%

with only 33 per cent pre-war; central heating was present in 68 per cent of post-war shops compared with 46 per cent pre-war, and in 79 per cent of post-war restaurants compared with 65 per cent pre-war. Among recently built hotels, 98 per cent were heated centrally, a figure only a little above the 92 per cent for hotels constructed before the war.

This analysis of the ten geographical areas has shown variation in the type of properties and in their age. These two factors combine to influence the distribution of central heating (Table XXXIX). Thus, the sample of pre-war properties in London contained 62 per cent with central heating, 66 per cent in the 'East' and 81 per cent in Northern Scotland. Among post-war properties, London contained 73 per cent with central heating, Ireland with even fewer, 70 per cent, yet Southern Scotland with the maximum of 91 per cent.

TABLE XXXIX

COCKROACH SURVEY: THE INCIDENCE OF CENTRAL HEATING IN PRE- AND POST-WAR PROPERTIES IN GEOGRAPHICAL AREAS

Geographical area	Pre-war properties		Post-war properties	
	Number with central heating	Percentage of total	Number with central heating	Percentage of total
North Scotland	171	81	26	90
Central	461	80	50	78
South Scotland	142	78	20	91
West	215	78	37	77
North	455	75	67	82
South West	341	73	33	82
Ireland	137	71	23	70
South East	378	70	41	87
East	150	66	20	74
London	187	62	19	73

Incidence of cockroach species

Taking the British Isles as a whole, B. germanica occurred in 859 of the infested properties (21 per cent) and B. orientalis in 3,552 (89 per cent), a ratio of infestations of 1 : 4·1. The two species occurred together in 415 properties (10 per cent). Periplaneta americana was found in 14 properties (0·35 per cent); these included seven properties in which B. germanica or B. orientalis, or both, also occurred. One property only contained Supella supellectilium and no other species. As infestations of the German and Oriental Cockroaches are by far the most common, these species will be considered first.

Infestations in different types of property
The incidence of German and Oriental Cockroaches in different types of property varies considerably (Fig. 140). Infested premises which most favour the German Cockroach are clubs and public halls (42 per cent), restaurants and cafés (39 per cent), and breweries (39 per cent). Those which most favour Oriental Cockroaches are cinemas and theatres (97 per cent), houses, flats and convalescent homes (96 per cent), and laundries (94 per cent). Accordingly the ratio of infestations of the two species, in different types of property, deviates considerably from the average of 1 : 4·1. Clubs and public halls are ten times more susceptible to infestation by *B. germanica* (ratio 1 : 1·7) than dwellings (ratio 1 : 17·0). In contrast, properties which deviate only slightly from the average are hospitals, offices, shops and hotels (ratios of 1 : 4·1 to 1 : 4·6).

Infestations and the age of properties
Pre-war properties comprised 90 per cent of the sample. In these, German Cockroaches were found in 714 (20 per cent) and Oriental Cockroaches in 3,241 (90 per cent). Infestations of both species occurred in ten per cent. The ratio of infestations by German to Oriental Cockroaches in pre-war properties is therefore 1 : 4·5.

Post-war properties contained 145 infestations of *B. germanica* (35 per cent) and 319 of *B. orientalis* (76 per cent). Both species occur in 11 per cent. Accordingly, the ratio of infestations for post-war buildings, 1 : 2·2, is much lower that that for pre-war buildings (Fig. 141).

The most striking feature about the greater incidence of German Cockroaches relative to *B. orientalis* in post-war buildings is that it occurs in almost every type of property (except schools, colleges and convents, cinemas and theatres). Infestations of Oriental Cockroaches relative to *B. germanica* were fewer in 11 types of premises and greater in only five. This change in the incidence of the two species with the age of properties lowers the ratio of infestations of *B. germanica* to *B. orientalis* in 14 of the 16 types of premises examined.

To study in more detail the greater incidence of *B. germanica* relative to *B. orientalis* in new compared with old properties, premises were considered as four groups. These contained roughly equal numbers and are arranged in order of decreasing incidence of *B. germanica* in Table XL. In those with a high incidence of German Cockroaches (Group I) infestations rise from 34 per cent in pre-war buildings to 62 per cent in post-war, with a corresponding drop in *B. orientalis* from 80 to 51 per cent. A much smaller change occurs in those premises least susceptible to infestation by *B. germanica* (namely, Group IV). In these, infestations of German Cockroaches rise from only 9 to 14 per cent and infestations of Oriental Cockroaches decrease only slightly from 94 to 92 per cent.

TABLE XL

INFESTED PREMISES GROUPED IN ORDER OF DECREASING INCIDENCE OF *B. GERMANICA* TO SHOW THE EFFECTS OF POST-WAR BUILDING ON THE GREATER INCIDENCE OF THIS SPECIES RELATIVE TO *B. ORIENTALIS*

Group	Type of property	Age of property	Number of infested properties	Percentage infested by *B. germanica*	Percentage infested by *B. orientalis*	Ratio of infestations *B. germanica* : *B. orientalis*
I	Clubs, restaurants, cafés, breweries & public houses	Pre-war	743	34	80	1 : 2·3
		Post-war	110	62	51	1 : 0·8
II	Chem. & eng. factories, hospitals, offices & shops	Pre-war	758	21	92	1 : 4·3
		Post-war	97	35	78	1 : 2·2
III	Hotels, hostels, holiday camps, schools, colleges convents & textile factories	Pre-war	1,167	18	93	1 : 5·2
		Post-war	76	25	87	1 : 3·5
IV	Food factories, cinemas, theatres, laundries, houses, flats & conv. homes	Pre-war	868	9	94	1 : 10·7
		Post-war	109	14	92	1 : 6·7

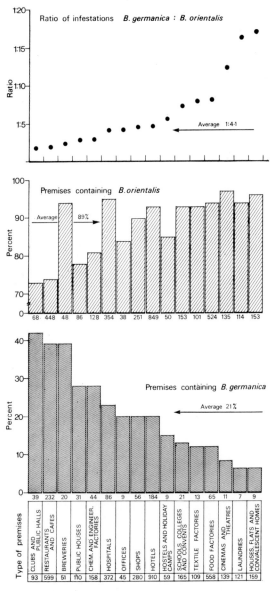

Fig. 140. The ratio and incidence (%) of *B. germanica* and *B. orientalis* in different types of infested premises arranged in order of decreasing incidence of *B. germanica*. The numbers of infested premises and those containing *B. germanica* and *B. orientalis* are given at the bottom of the histograms. Because about 10% of premises contain both species, the combined percentage incidence exceeds 100%.

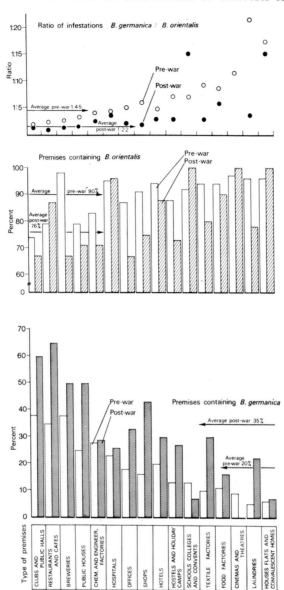

Fig. 141. The ratio and incidence (%) of *B. germanica* and *B. orientalis* in different types of infested premises built pre- and post-war. Premises arranged in order of decreasing incidence of *B. germanica* (cf. Fig. 140). The ratio of infestations of the two species could not be calculated for post-war cinemas and theatres since none contained *B. germanica*.

Infestation and central heating

The most plausible explanation for the apparent increase in German Cockroaches relative to *B. orientalis* in post-war buildings is a change in the environment. With the preference of the German Cockroach for higher temperatures the explanation may lie in the type of heating. On the other hand, most post-war offices and industrial buildings now incorporate a canteen and the presence of more kitchens, for which the German Cockroach has a predilection, could be an influencing factor.

Reference has already been made to the relatively small difference in the amount of central heating (74 per cent and 80 per cent) in pre- and post-war properties. It would appear unlikely therefore that changes in the method of heating are responsible for the greater incidence of *B. germanica*. This conclusion is supported by the very small difference between the occurrence of the two species in pre- and post-war buildings which have different types of heating (Table XLI). Nevertheless, analysis of these data by the method of chi-squared reveals an important fact, namely, a deficiency in the numbers of infestations of both species of cockroach in non-centrally heated, post-war buildings. (Chi-squared $= 11{\cdot}3$; Probability < 2 per cent.) As the staff who reported the information could not have specifically set out to avoid reporting on this type of building, one is led to the conclusion that relative to older properties, *modern* properties, without central heating, are less liable to infestation by cockroaches, of either species, than properties with heating.

TABLE XLI

INCIDENCE OF INFESTATIONS OF GERMAN AND ORIENTAL COCKROACHES IN PRE- AND POST-WAR PROPERTIES, WITH AND WITHOUT CENTRAL HEATING

Age of property	Type of heating	No. of infested properties	Number and percent of infestations B. germanica	B. orientalis	Ratio of infestations B.g. : B.o.
Pre-war	Central	2637	548 (21%)	2405 (91%)	1 : 4·4
	Other or none	949	166 (17%)	836 (88%)	1 : 5·0
Post-war	Central	336	119 (35%)	257 (76%)	1 : 2·2
	Other or none	82	26 (32%)	62 (76%)	1 : 2·4

If the German Cockroach has been dependent for its increase in post-war properties (cf. *B. orientalis*) on the growth of central heating, we would anticipate a correlation between the relative incidence of German Cockroaches and heating in pre-war properties. This quite clearly is not so. Inspection of Table XXXVIII shows that those premises in which *B. germanica* are most often found, namely clubs, restaurants, cafés, breweries and public houses, have the minimum of central heating (an average of 65 per cent) whereas those (Group III, Table XL) in which *B. germanica* is encountered far less often, namely, hotels, hostels, schools and textile factories have a much higher incidence of central heating (average 92 per cent). We must conclude therefore that even among pre-war properties, central heating is not the primary factor which influences the presence of one or other species.

Perhaps the strongest argument against the suggestion that the increase in German Cockroaches might be associated with the growth of post-war central heating comes from an analysis of different types of property. It so happens that the greatest increase in central heating, 65 to 83 per cent, has occurred in properties (Group I) which have both the highest incidence of German Cockroaches and the greatest increase of the species in post-war properties. Incongruously, though, properties (Group IV) in which the next highest increase in central heating has occurred (51 per cent in pre-war to 63 per cent post-war) have the lowest incidence of *B. germanica* and show the lowest increase with post-war development.

Locations of infestations within buildings

The environmental requirements for cockroach reproduction and survival are warmth, food and water. Different parts of premises in which cockroaches are found are analysed in Fig. 142. Because, for example, bedrooms and bathrooms occur only in certain types of property and bars and lounges in some, but not in others, each type of premises has been examined separately.

As expected, kitchens provide one of the most favoured locations for cockroach infestation; both species occur most often here in restaurants and cafés, hotels, houses, flats and convalescent homes, hostels and holiday camps, schools, colleges, convents and hospitals. The kitchen is also the most favoured location of *B. germanica* in clubs, cinemas and theatres, offices, shops, laundries and all types of factories. In public houses, most infestations of German Cockroaches occur in the bar, with the kitchen favoured secondarily. The basement or cellar is the most favoured location of *B. orientalis* in public houses, clubs, offices and shops.

Comparing the two species, the cellar, boiler room, and heating ducts almost invariably provide a more favourable environment for *B. orientalis* and the kitchen a more favoured micro-climate for *B. germanica*. Nevertheless, there are certain types of property, namely restaurants and cafés, hotels, hostels, teaching establishments and hospitals, where the warmth and food of kitchens provide an equally favourable environment for both species. In laundries, the most frequently encountered sites of infestation of *B. germanica* are the ducts and boiler room.

Assuming that the kitchen is infested, the next most favoured sites for cockroach harbourage in eating and drinking houses are larders and service pantries, eating areas and lounges. Toilets of most properties tend to

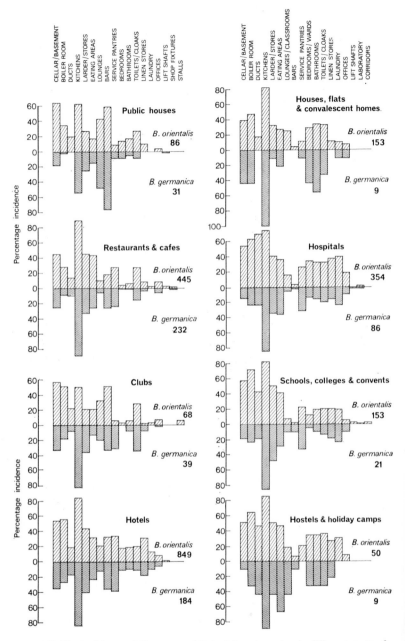

Fig. 142. The incidence of German and Oriental cockroaches in different parts of infested premises. The number of occasions cockroaches were reported in each

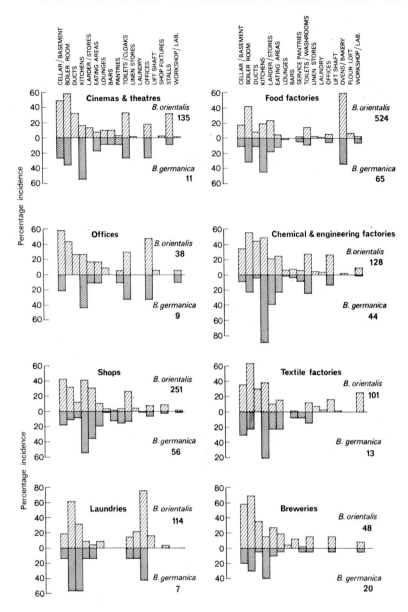

location is expressed as a percentage of the number of premises containing the species. The numbers of premises on which each histogram is based are given.

favour the Oriental Cockroach (Table XLII): the incidence of Oriental Cockroaches in toilets in 1 in 5 of properties infested by this species and of *B. germanica* in 1 in 6 of properties containing this insect, emphasises the health hazards associated with cockroach infestations in premises where food is sold or consumed.

TABLE XLII

THE INCIDENCE OF ORIENTAL AND GERMAN COCKROACHES IN TOILETS OF INFESTED PROPERTIES

Type of property	Properties infested with *B. orientalis*		Properties infested with *B. germanica*	
	Number	% with *B. orientalis* in toilets	Number	% with *B. germanica* in toilets
Hostels & holiday camps	50	34	9	33
Houses, flats & conv. homes	153	33	9	33
Hospitals	354	33	86	19
Cinemas & theatres	135	32	11	27
Clubs & public halls	68	28	39	31
Restaurants & cafés	445	27	232	16
Public houses	86	26	31	7
Offices	38	24	9	33
Chem. & eng. factories	128	22	44	25
Shops	251	21	56	14
Schools, colleges & convents	153	20	21	14
Hotels	849	20	184	11
Breweries	48	15	20	0
Laundries	114	14	7	14
Textile factories	101	12	13	15
Food factories	524	11	65	9
Average (all properties)	22%		16%	

The Oriental Cockroach is frequently found in the auditorium of cinemas and theatres, and in the offices of clerical staff. In these locations food for cockroaches is provided by the 'nibbling' public while being entertained, as well as by partially consumed office sandwiches. Areas around presses in laundries and around ovens in food factories present ideal environments with steam and heat, which are highly favoured sites for both *B. orientalis* and *B. germanica*.

Within the 4,004 premises, German Cockroaches were reported in 2,486 locations and Oriental Cockroaches in 13,451. If the number for each type of property is divided by the number of infested premises, an average is obtained which allows a comparison of the extent of infestation of the two species within each type of buildings (Fig. 143).

Without exception, infestations of *B. orientalis* are more widespread than *B. germanica*. Analysis of the means by the method of paired comparison shows a highly significant difference ($t = 5 \cdot 7$; Probability $< 0 \cdot 1$ per cent). This is a reflection of the greater tolerance of *B. orientalis* to lower temperatures and its lower susceptibility to desiccation (Chapter 12).

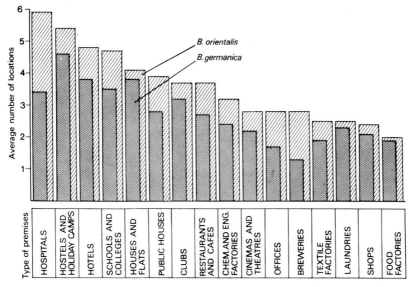

Fig. 143. The average number of locations infested by Oriental and German cockroaches within different types of premises. Properties arranged in order of decreasing distribution of *B. orientalis*. Infestations of *B. germanica* are significantly more restricted in distribution than *B. orientalis* (Probability $< 0 \cdot 1 \%$).

The Oriental Cockroach is most widespread in hospitals occurring on average in six different locations. It is least widely distributed in food factories, where it occurs most often in the boiler room and around ovens. The German Cockroach is most widely distributed in hostels and holiday camps with an average of 4·6 harbourage sites, and least widely distributed in breweries, 1·3 locations.

Using the same technique, but averaging over all types of premises, values can be obtained for pre- and post-war properties. Infestations of German Cockroaches occur in 2·9 locations in both old and new property, whereas the average for *B. orientalis* drops from 3·9 for pre-war buildings to 3·1 for post-war. This suggests that newer buildings, because of design or cleanliness, exercise greater restriction on the activities of *B. orientalis* than *B. germanica*, or perhaps, that it takes a number of years before the

Oriental Cockroach occupies all the favourable harbourages in a building during which the fabric of the building or level of hygiene may deteriorate.

Geographical variation in the incidence of species

The information contained in the previous paragraphs, on the places where cockroaches are usually found, emphasises that many factors influence the suitability of a building for infestation by one or other species, or both; principally the existence of kitchens, boiler room, basement, heating ducts and a bar, which jointly influence the available warmth, food and water. Because the properties examined in different parts of the country were of many different types, with heterogeneity in the sample for different areas, it would not be surprising to find considerable variation in the relative abundance of *B. germanica* and *B. orientalis* in different parts of the country.

If the areas are considered, irrespective of the properties they contain, German Cockroaches are most prevalent in London and least common in the north of Scotland (Table XLIII). This information, however, is biased: few hotels were examined in London but a large number were included for

TABLE XLIII

GEOGRAPHICAL AREAS ARRANGED IN ORDER OF DECREASING INCIDENCE OF INFESTATIONS OF *B. GERMANICA*. DATA NOT CORRECTED FOR THE DIFFERENCES IN TYPE OF PROPERTIES IN EACH AREA

Geographical area	No. of infested properties	Infestations of B. germanica		Infestations of B. orientalis		Ratio of infestations B.g. : B.o.
		No.	Percentage of infested properties	No.	Percentage of infested properties	
London	329	146	44	214	65	1 : 1·5
Ireland	226	72	32	190	84	1 : 2·6
South East	589	168	29	507	86	1 : 3·0
South Scotland	205	54	26	179	87	1 : 3·3
Central	639	148	23	581	91	1 : 3·9
East	256	56	22	225	88	1 : 4·0
West	322	54	17	302	94	1 : 5·6
South West	507	75	15	476	94	1 : 6·3
North	691	69	10	654	95	1 : 9·5
North Scotland	240	17	7	232	97	1 : 13·6
Total	4,004	859	21	3,560	89	1 : 4·1

Note: The percentage of infested properties containing *B. germanica* and *B. orientalis* added together do not make 100 per cent since both species occur together in about 10 per cent of properties.

Scotland; the ratio of infestations, of German to Oriental Cockroaches, cannot be reliable if one area contains an abundance of properties which provide a favourable environment for one species but not for the other.

To correct this bias, the premises for each area were grouped into four categories. This was done, as previously (Table XL), according to the relative incidence of species. Treatment of the data in this manner shows that the greater incidence of *B. germanica* (Fig. 144a) and the lowest incidence of *B. orientalis* (Fig. 144b) occurs in London, irrespective of the type of property, and that the reverse is true towards the west and north.

Division of the properties into four groups allows the calculation of four ratios of infestations of *B. germanica* : *B. orientalis* for each area (Fig. 145). Ratios for properties in Group I vary little between geographical areas, whereas those for Groups II and III show a more marked preponderance of infestations of Oriental Cockroaches in areas most distant from London, (with the exception of 'South Scotland'). Properties in Group IV, with the lowest incidence of *B. germanica* to *B. orientalis* provide the maximum geographical variation, a ratio of 1 : 5 in 'South Scotland' and 1 : 48 in 'North Scotland'.

We are now part way to showing the existence of a true geographical variation in the relative incidence of the two species. By combining the ratios for the four groups of premises it is possible to obtain an average value for each area, free of bias for different types of properties, since each group contributes equally to the mean (Fig. 146).

The greatest incidence (lowest ratio) of German to Oriental Cockroaches does indeed occur in London. A very similar figure is obtained for southern Scotland where much of the information is contributed from Glasgow. This suggests that densely populated areas offer an environment favourable to *B. germanica* which is not to be found in rural areas. In this regard the ratio for Ireland appears anomalous, but again, it must be remembered that a great deal of the information for Ireland came from Belfast and Dublin.

Blatta orientalis increases in dominance from the south-east (1 : 4·2) to the west (1 : 7·8) and north of England (1 : 11). This species outnumbers infestations of *B. germanica* in northern Scotland by 20 : 1. (Fig. 147). Here population density is lowest for the whole country and here too the German Cockroach occurs in only eight per cent of the premises sampled. Joint infestations by both species are lower in the north of Scotland than anywhere else.

The picture now obtained for the distribution of the German Cockroach agrees surprisingly well with the map (Fig. 138) based on previously reported evidence compiled by Ragge.[45] Not all of the geographical variation, however, can be correlated with population density. The ratios for the 'East' and 'South-East' are very similar, yet the two areas differ considerably in the extent of urban development. The 'Central' area is greatly industrialised, yet this and the two areas previously mentioned differ only slightly in the relative abundance of species.

Y

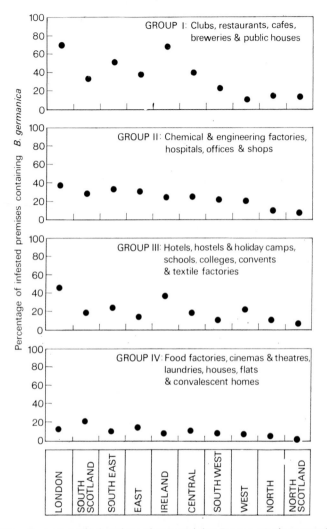

Fig. 144. a. Percentage of infested premises containing *B. germanica* in geographical areas. Premises grouped in order of decreasing incidence of the species. Areas ranked in order of decreasing incidence of *B. germanica* relative to *B. orientalis*.

Clearly, outdoor climate plays no contributory role. 'Southern Scotland' is not sufficiently different in climate from the 'North of England' to influence the ratio of species by a factor of three. The 'South-West' certainly has warmer winters than the 'East', yet the incidence of *B. germanica* is higher in the colder area.

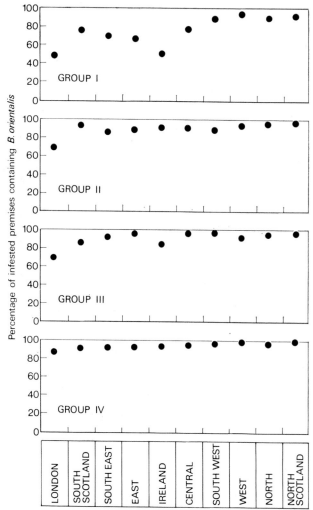

Fig. 144. b. Percentage of infested premises containing *B. orientalis* in geographical areas. Premises grouped in order of decreasing incidence of *B. germanica*. Areas ranked in order of decreasing incidence of *B. germanica* relative to *B. orientalis*.

Infestations in cities and large towns

Reference has been made in the previous section to the probable influence of data from urban areas on the ratio of German to Oriental Cockroaches in different parts of the country. To examine this further, an analysis has been made of the incidence of the two species in the most commonly infested properties, (restaurants and hotels), in cities and large towns in different areas. Two of these are London and Glasgow, two are holiday

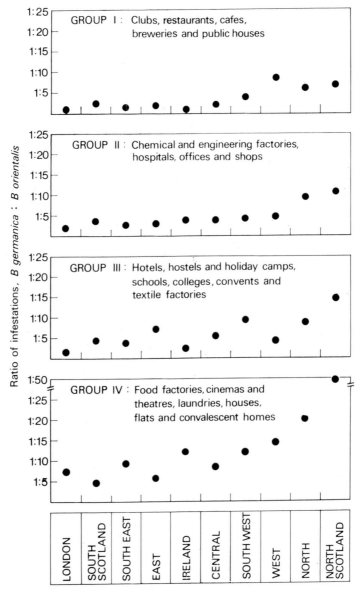

Fig. 145. Ratio of infestations of *B. germanica* to *B. orientalis* in geographical areas. Premises grouped in order of decreasing incidence of *B.germanica*. Areas ranked in order of decreasing incidence of *B. germanica* relative to *B. orientalis*.

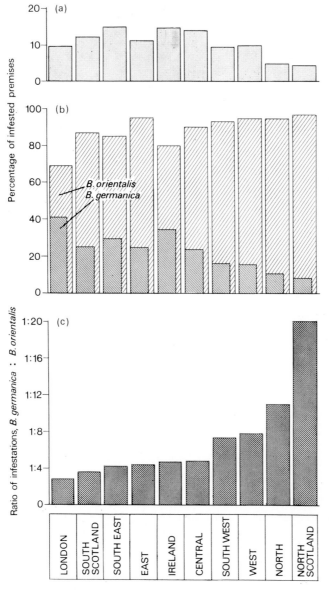

Fig. 146. Mean infestation rates (for all premises) in geographical areas, ranked in order of decreasing incidence of *B. germanica* relative to *B. orientalis*. (a) Percentage of infested premises in which both species occur, (b) percentage of infested premises containing *B. germanica* and *B. orientalis*, (c) ratio of incidence of the two species.

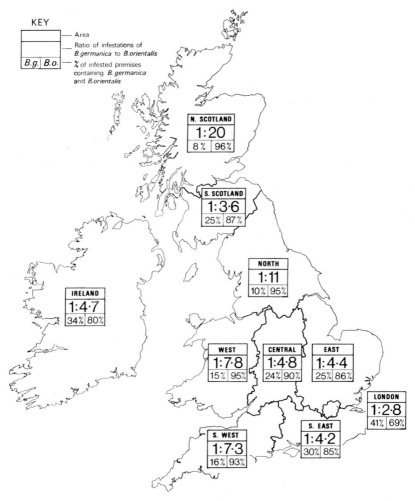

Fig. 147. The geographical distribution of *B. germanica* and *B. orientalis* in infested premises in Britain based on a survey of 4,004 premises. About 10% of premises contain both species.

towns in the 'South-East' (Bournemouth and Brighton), and two are in the 'North', Manchester, an industrial town, and Blackpool, a coastal resort.

The analysis (Table XLIV) shows considerable variation in the incidence of the two species in urban communities even when these are relatively close, e.g. London and Brighton (60 miles) and Manchester and Blackpool (50 miles). It also shows that in two towns, which are both coastal resorts,

Bournemouth in the 'South-East' and Blackpool in the 'North', there is even greater variation. In fact, the ratios for the six towns, whilst being somewhat lower than those for the areas to which they belong, show the same pattern of distribution of *B. germanica* relative to *B. orientalis* as has been obtained for the geographical areas. It will be appreciated that in obtaining the ratios for towns, restaurants and hotels only have been considered, thereby avoiding heterogeneity in the samples.

TABLE XLIV

INCIDENCE OF GERMAN AND ORIENTAL COCKROACHES IN CITIES AND TOWNS IN DIFFERENT PARTS OF THE COUNTRY

Town	Restaurants		Hotels		Area ratio (all properties)
	Infestations of both species	Ratio B.g. : B.o.	Infestations of both species	Ratio B.g. : B.o.	
London	110	1 : 0·6	14	1 : 1·0	'London' 1 : 2·8
Glasgow	37	1 : 1·6	11	1 : 1·2	'S. Scotland' 1 : 3·6
Bournemouth	27	1 : 1·1	76	1 : 1·7	'S. East' 1 : 4·2
Brighton	23	1 : 1·9	15	1 : 2·8	
Manchester	28	1 : 4·6	*	*	'North' 1 : 11
Blackpool	19	1 : 18·0	24	1 : 11·0	

* Insufficient data.

Other species

Fourteen infestations were recorded of *P. americana* and one of *S. supellectilium*. To the overseas reader these numbers may seem exceptionally small, but in reality one infestation of the American Cockroach in Britain per 300 of the more common cockroaches is probably an over estimate of the true incidence of this species. This is because infestations of cockroaches other than *B. germanica* or *B. orientalis* are so rarely encountered that when found, the occasion is not readily forgotten. Hence the Service staff who reported the occurrences of *P. americana* probably reported all the findings of this species that they could recall during their entire servicing experience.

The 14 infestations of *P. americana* were divided between 'London' (five), the 'South-East' (three) and the 'North' (six). Twelve occurred in pre-war premises and two in post-war premises, which is in accordance with the proportion of old and new buildings infested by other species.

Three of the infestations occurred in hospitals; one in an X-ray unit, to which the insects had probably escaped from laboratories, and two where *P. americana* had become established in basements, ducts, kitchens, linen stores and a laundry. Five records of American Cockroaches involved factories: in the paper stores of a confectionery producer, the kitchens and canteen of a textile mill, and in the basement, boiler room, ducts and kitchens of a factory producing rubber products. In the rubber factory there was strong evidence to indicate that the insects were being introduced with raw materials direct from the docks.

Evidence of introduction was also seen at a factory processing paper and cardboard. Here the insects were found in the cores of large reels of paper recently arrived in the stores. In the fifth factory, a bakery, the cockroaches were imported in nuts and dried fruit held in the raw materials store.

Among the remaining six infestations, one occurred in a restaurant, again introduced with imported foods, one in the kitchen of a large hotel in an area where a crate of bananas had stood the previous day, and a third in a house where the insects were introduced with bananas bought from a local shop.

Another instance of *P. americana*, associated with bananas, occurred at a banana importers, the type of premises which acts as an intermediary in the distribution of the insect to other premises. The two remaining records of American Cockroaches involved a brewery, where the insects were found in a covered drain to a boiler house, and a college where *P. americana* had become established in the cellars of a science block. This infestation is suspected of originating from insects which had escaped from the Zoology department.

The one recorded instance of Brown-banded Cockroaches (*S. supellec-tilium*) occurred in London in the offices of a new building where the infestation was thought to have been established for at least a year before efforts were made to control it. The premises were centrally heated and the infestation became established in the ducts and offices. At the time of the infestation, some of the offices in this building were involved in the import of goods from the Continent.

Conclusions from the survey

This survey has confirmed much of the existing knowledge about the incidence of pest cockroaches in buildings in the British Isles, but for which statistics have not previously been obtained. It has added to this knowledge notably on the occurrence of German and Oriental Cockroaches in old and new buildings and on the geographical distribution of the two commonly occurring species. The salient conclusions obtained from the survey in which 4,004 premises were examined, all of which had contained cockroaches at some time, may be summarised as follows:

1. In the British Isles, infestations of *B. orientalis* outnumber *B. germanica* by 4 : 1. Both species occur together in about ten per cent of infested properties. Other species, mainly *P. americana*, occur in not more than 0.35 per cent of infested properties. This figure is probably an over-estimate.

2. The relative incidence of *B. germanica* and *B. orientalis* in different types of property varies considerably from 1 : 1·7 (in clubs and public halls) to 1·17 (in houses, flats and convalescent homes).

3. Premises which most favour the German Cockroach are clubs and public halls, restaurants and cafés, breweries and public houses. The high incidence of *B. germanica* in all these premises, where alcoholic beverages are consumed, provides strong circumstantial evidence in support of the beer crate as a means of spread of this species between properties.[435]

4. The number of infestations of *B. germanica*, relative to *B. orientalis*, in post-war buildings (1 : 2·2) is twice that in pre-war buildings (1 : 4·5). This increase is apparent in most types of property, but is greatest ($\times 3$) in those premises, mentioned above, most susceptible to infestation by the German Cockroach.

5. Whilst the incidence of *B. germanica* relative to *B. orientalis* is higher in new buildings than in old, care must be taken in interpreting this in-formation. It could be argued that the German Cockroach is spread more readily in trade than *B. orientalis* making new buildings more prone to infestation by the German species. Not until another survey is made, per-haps in five or ten years time, will it be possible to establish beyond doubt that the German Cockroach is increasing in abundance.

6. No correlation can be found between the relative incidence of the two commonly occurring species and the type of heating. Whilst a correlation between infestation and heat is well recognised, the 'presence' or 'absence' of central heating is probably not a sufficiently critical measure of the environment to demonstrate a relationship.

7. The paucity of reports of infestations of both species in non-centrally heated, post-war buildings (compared with centrally heated) is an indica-tion that a relationship between infestation and central heating exists, at least in newer types of building.

8. The growth of central heating would not appear to be responsible for the greater incidence of infestations of *B. germanica* in post-war properties.

9. About 16,000 observations were made of the positions within buildings where cockroaches are found. These confirm that in certain properties, (notably restaurants, cafés, hotels, dwellings, teaching establishments and hospitals), kitchens offer the preferred environment for *B. germanica*. The kitchen is also the preferred location of *B. germanica* in other properties where *B. orientalis* favours the basement, boiler room and heating ducts. The preferred place of the German Cockroach in clubs is the bar. Toilets and bathrooms tend to favour *B. orientalis*. The high incidence of cock-

roaches in toilets (in about 20 per cent of infested properties) emphasises the potential hazard of cockroaches in disease transmission.

10.   In all types of property, infestations of Oriental Cockroaches are found in a greater number of locations than those of the German Cockroach. Infestations of *B. orientalis* are most widespread in hospitals and those of *B. germanica* most widespread in hostels and holiday camps.

11.   Infestations of German Cockroaches occur in an equal number of locations in pre- and post-war properties. Those of Oriental Cockroaches are less widely distributed in post-war than in pre-war buildings.

12.   The incidence of *B. germanica* relative to *B. orientalis* is highest in London (ratio, 1 : 2·8), followed by south Scotland, principally Glasgow, (1 : 3·6) and the south-east of England (1 : 4·2). These values apply to the 'average premises'. The ratio of infestations, German : Oriental, increases from the south-east of England to the west and north and is highest in the north of Scotland (1 : 20).

13.   Premises in which German Cockroaches occur most often (i.e. clubs, restaurants, etc.) show a relatively small geographical variation in the incidence of this species, except in the extreme north and west. The greatest geographical variation in the ratio of *B. germanica* to *B. orientalis*, occurs among properties (food factories, cinemas, theatres, laundries and dwelling houses) in which *B. germanica* is relatively uncommon.

14.   The high incidence of *B. germanica* in London and Glasgow suggests that this species is favoured by conditions associated with densely populated areas. Nevertheless, variations do occur in the ratio of infestations, *B. germanica* : *B. orientalis* in identical types of property in large coastal towns (e.g. Bournemouth, Brighton and Blackpool).

15.   The origins of most infestations of 'exotic' species of cockroach can be traced to the import of infested goods from overseas (notably bananas), or to escapes from laboratory cultures.

ABOUT VOLUME II

INSECTICIDES AND COCKROACH CONTROL

A great variety of insecticides exists for cockroach control. Volume II is concerned with the development of the major groups of insecticides and their properties. A review is given of the information currently available on the mode of action of these compounds. Early simple remedies for 'getting rid of cockroaches' have now been replaced by the use of more sophisticated, modern, synthetic chemicals. Volume II is a practical and technical guide to all those concerned with pest species of cockroach and their eradication: the success of cockroach control depends on the treatment of all infested harbourages and recommendations for their detection in buildings are given. Methods of application of insecticides and the most suitable equipment for this purpose are described.

Attention is given to the formulation of insecticidal compounds in oil and water as well as dusts and lacquers; recommendations are provided for the use of each formulation. The application of insecticidal preparations with minimum hazard to man—the user and the public—as well as to domestic animals and wild life is exercising the attention of Government bodies and the pest control industry more than ever before. The labelling of pesticidal products, with precautionary measures and appropriate directions for use, is one of the subjects dealt with in a chapter on Safe Pest Control Practice.

Resistance to insecticides, notably by the German Cockroach, emphasises the need for the continued screening of new insecticidal compounds for cockroach control. The history is given of this problem since resistance was first detected in cockroaches in 1953, together with an analysis of environmental factors which most favour its development. Methods of trapping wild populations for detecting resistance in wild strains are described.

The evaluation of new insecticidal compounds for cockroach control involves special laboratory techniques for rearing and handling insects, together with test methods, involving the topical application of solutions, the preparation of test surfaces for appraising contact activity, and the subsequent statistical handling of data to compare the efficacy of different materials. Attention is drawn to the importance of the repellent action exhibited by some of the more recent insecticides which can be a disadvantage in the control of cockroaches in infested premises. In contrast, insect repellents for the treatment of containers and packing materials, to prevent the dissemination of cockroaches in trade, is an advantage which has yet to be exploited.

347

BIBLIOGRAPHY

1 REHN, J. A. G. (1945). Man's uninvited fellow-traveller—the cockroach. *Sci. Monthly*, **61** (4), 265–276.
2 MARLATT, C. L. (1908). *Cockroaches.* U.S. Dept. Agric. Div. Ent. Circ. No. 51.
3 BLATCHLEY, W. S. (1920). *Orthoptera of North-Eastern America.* Nature Pub. Co., Indianapolis, pp. 59–114.
4 ROTH, L. M. & WILLIS, E. R. (1960). The Biotic Associations of cockroaches. *Smithsonian Misc. Collect.*, **141** (4422), 470 pp.
5 RAU, P. (1940). The life history of the American cockroach *Periplaneta americana* Linn. (Orthop.: Blattidae). *Ent. News*, **51**, 121–124, 151–155, 186–188, 223–227, 273–278.
6 ROTH, L. M. & WILLIS, E. R. (1957). The Medical and Veterinary importance of Cockroaches. *Smithsonian Misc. Collect.*, **134** (10), 1–147.
7 SHIPLEY, A. E. (1916). *More Minor Horrors.* Smith, Elder & Co., London. 163 pp.
8 ANON. (1958). *The Cockroach.* Brit. Mus. (Nat. Hist.) Econ. Series No. 12, 26 pp.
9 SCHARRER, B. (1951). The Woodroach. *Sci. American*, **185** (6), 58–62.
10 TILLYARD, R. J. (1937). Kansas Permian Insects. Part 20, The cockroaches, or Order Blattaria. *Amer. J. Sci.*, **34**, 168–202, 249–276.
11 SELLARDS, E. H. (1904). A study of the structure of Paleozoic cockroaches, with descriptions of new forms from the Coal Measures. *Amer. J. Sci.*, **18**, 113–134, 213–227.
12 BRONGNIART, C. (1894). Les insectes de l'époque carbonifère. *C. R. Acad. Sci.*, t, **118**, p. 1128, Paris.
13 BOLTON, H. (1920). *A monograph of the fossil insects of the British Coal Measures.* Palaeontographical Soc., London (1922), **74**, 156 pp.
14 BROWN, R. W. (1957). Cockroach egg case from the Eocene of Wyoming. *J. Wash. Acad. Sci.*, **47** (10), 340–342.
15 HANDLIRSCH, A. (1908). *Die fossilen Insekten und die Phylogenie der rezenten Formen.* Leipzig. 1430 pp.
16 PRUVOST, P. (1919). *La faune continentale du terrain houiller du Nord et de Pas-de-Calais.* Gîtes minéraux, Serv. Cart. Géol. France.
17 LAURENTIAUX, D. (1951). Le problème des blattes Paléozoiques à ovipositeur externe. *Ann. Paleonte*, **37**, 187–196.
18 IMMS, A. D. (1931). *Recent Advances in Entomology.* Churchill, London, 431 pp.
19 SNYDER, T. E. (1948). *Our Enemy the Termite.* Constable & Co. Ltd., London. 257 pp.
20 RAU, P. (1941). Cockroaches: the forerunners of termites (Orthoptera: Blattidae): Isoptera. *Ent. News*, **52**, 156–259.
21 GOULD, G. E. & DEAY, H. O. (1940). *The biology of six species of cockroaches which inhabit buildings.* Bull. No. 451, Agric. Res. Sta., Purdue University.
22 REHN, J. W. H. (1951). Classification of the Blattaria as indicated by their wings (Orthoptera). *Mem. Amer. Ent. Soc.*, **14**, 1–134.
23 LINNAEUS, C. (1758). *Systema Naturae*, ed. X, I. pp. 424, 425.
24 LINNAEUS, C. (1767). *Systema Naturae*, ed. XII, I. pp. 687–689.
25 DE GEER, C. (1773). *Mémoires pour servir à l'histoire des Insectes.* III. pp. 399–554.

26 OLIVIER, A. G. (1789). *Encyclopédie méthodique, dictionnaire des Insectes, Orth.*, **4**, pp. 1–331.
27 LAMARCK, J. B. (1801). *Système des Animaux sans vertèbres*, pp. 201, 243.
28 LEACH, W. E. (1816). *New Edinburgh Encyclopaedia*, **8**, pp. 646–753.
29 LATREILLE, P. A. (1817). In Cuvier, *Le règne animal distribué d'apres son organisation, pour servir de base à l'histoire naturelle des animaux et d'introduction à l'anatomie comparée* **3**, pp. 365–384.
30 BURMEISTER, H. C. C. (1838). *Handbuch der Entomologie*, **2**, pt. 2a, pp. 459–756.
31 SERVILLE, J. G. A. (1839). *Histoire naturelle des insectes, Orthopteres*, xviii+777 pp. 14 pl.
32 SAUSSURE, H. DE (1864). *Mem. Hist. Nat. Mexique.* 3 memoire, pp. 16–28, 154–169.
33 BRUNNER VON WATTENWYL, K. (1865). *Nouveau système des Blattaires.* xi+426 pp.
34 VERHOEFF, K. W. (1903). Uber die Nerven des Metacephalsegmentes und die Insectenordung Oothecaria. *Zool. Anz.*, **26**, 20–31.
35 NAVAS, L. (1905). *Mem. R. Acad. Cienc. y Artes, Barcelona*, 3a epoca, V. num. 13, p. 21.
36 IMMS, A. D. (1925). *A General Textbook of Entomology.* Methuen, London. 886 pp.
37 IMMS, A. D. (1957). *A General Textbook of Entomology.* 9th Edition, Ed. by Richards & Davies, 886 pp.
38 PRINCIS, K. (1960). *Zur Systematik der Blattarien.* Eos. 36: 429–449.
39 MCKITTRICK, F. A. (1964). *Evolutionary Studies of cockroaches.* Memoir 389. Cornell Univ. Agric. Expt. Sta.
40 ROTH, L. M. (1967). The evolutionary significance of rotation of the ootheca in the Blattaria. *Psyche*, **74** (2), 85–103.
41 ROTH, L. M. & WILLIS, E. R. (1955). Water content of cockroach eggs during embryogenesis in relation to oviposition behaviour. *J. exp. Zool.*, **128** (3), 489–509.
42 ROTH, L. M. & WILLIS, E. R. (1954). *The Reproduction of Cockroaches.* Smithsonian Misc. Collect., **122** (12), 1–49.
43 HEBARD, M. (1917). The Blattidae of North America, north of the Mexican boundary. *Mem. Amer. Ent. Soc.*, No. 2, 1–284.
44 WILLIS, E. R., RISER, G. R. & ROTH, L. M. (1958). Observations on reproduction and development in cockroaches. *Ann. Ent. Soc. Amer.*, **51**, 53–69.
45 RAGGE, D. R. (1965). *Grasshoppers, crickets and cockroaches of the British Isles.* Warne & Co. Ltd., London. 299 pp.
46 HEBARD, M. (1943). The Dermaptera and Orthopterous families, Blattidae, Mantidae and Phasmidae of Texas. *Trans. Amer. Ent. Soc.*, **68**, 239–311.
47 MIALL, L. C. & DENNY, A. V. (1886). *The structure and life history of the cockroach (Periplaneta orientalis). An introduction to the study of insects.* Lovell Reeve & Co., London. 224 pp.
48 LUCAS, W. J. (1912). British Orthoptera in 1911. *Entomologist*, **45**, 114–117.
49 SHUYLER, H. R. (1956). Are German and Oriental roaches changing their habits? *Pest Control*, **24** (9), 9–10.
50 HERMS, W. B. (1926). *Hippelates* flies and certain other pests of the Coachella Valley, California. *J. econ. Ent.*, **19**, 692–695.
51 FELT, E. P. (1926). *21st Report of the Director of the State Museum and Science Dept.* New York State Mus. Bull. No. 267, 37–48.
52 LUCAS, H. (1849). Histoire naturelle des animaux articulés. Troisieme partie. Insects 527 pp. *Exploration scientifique de l'Algerie pendant les années* 1840, 1841, 1842. Paris.
53 TAKAHASI, R. (1924). Life-history of Blattidae. *Dobutsugaka Zasshi (Zool. Mag.), Tokyo*, **36** (427), 215–230.
54 PORTER, A. (1930). Cockroaches as vectors of hookworms on gold mines of the Witwatersand. *J. Med. Assoc. South Africa*, **4**, 18–20.

55 CHAMBERLIN, J. C. (1949). *Insects of agricultural and household importance in Alaska with suggestions for their control.* U.S. Dept. Agric. Alaska Agric. Exp. Sta., Circ. No. 9, 59 pp.

56 WOODRUFF, L. C. (1938a). Observations on roach reproduction. *J. Kansas Ent. Soc.,* 11 (3), 94–96.

57 HABER, V. R. (1919). Cockroach pests of Minnesota. *Univ. of Minn. Bull.,* 186, 16 pp.

58 RAU, P. (1944). A note on the period of incubation of eggs of the cockroach, *Blattella germanica* L. *Canad. Ent.,* 76 (10), 212.

59 GOULD, G. E. (1941). The effect of temperature upon the development of cockroaches. *Proc. Indiana Acad. Sci.,* 50, 242–248.

60 ROSS, H. H. (1929). The life history of the German cockroach. *Trans. Illinois State Acad. Sci.,* 21, 84–93.

61 GOULD, G. E. & DEAY, H. O. (1937). Notes on the bionomics of roaches inhabiting houses. *Proc. Indiana Acad. Sci.,* 47, 281–284.

62 POPE, P. (1953). Studies on the life histories of some Queensland Blattidae (Orthoptera). Part I. The domestic species. *Proc. Roy. Soc. Queensland,* 63 (2), 23–46.

63 VLASOV, IA. P. (1929). Biology of *Phlebotomus sergenti* Parrot. *Russek. Zhurn Trop. Med., Med. Vet. Parazitol,* 7, 688–692.

64 QADRI, M. A. H. (1938). The life-history and growth of the cockroach, *Blatta orientalis* L. *Bull. ent. Res.,* 29, 263–276.

65 RAU, P. (1924). The biology of the roach, *Blatta orientalis* Linn. *Trans. Acad. Sci. St. Louis,* 25, 57–79.

66 NIGAM, L. N. (1933). The life-history of a common cockroach (*Periplaneta americana*) Linnaeus. *Ind. J. Agric. Sci.,* 3, 530–543.

67 LUCAS, W. J. (1916). British Orthoptera in 1914. *Entomologist,* 49, 16–19.

68 LUCAS, W. J. (1918). British Orthoptera in 1917. *Entomologist,* 51, 229–231.

69 LUCAS, W. J. (1925). Notes on British Orthoptera (including Dermaptera) in 1924. *Entomologist,* 58, 81–86.

70 VERRIL, A. E. (1902). The Bermuda Islands: Their scenery, climate, productions, physiography, natural history and geology. *Trans. Connecticut Acad. Arts & Sci.,* 11, 413–956.

71 ANON. (1967). Up a tree for American roach control. *Pest Control,* 35 (12), p. 16.

72 HOWARD, L. O. (1912). *The Insect Book.* Doubleday, Page & Co., New York.

73 GRIFFITHS, J. T. & TAUBER, O. E. (1942). The nymphal development for the roach, *Periplaneta americana* L. *J. N.Y. Ent. Soc.,* 50, 263–272.

74 GOULD, G. E. & DEAY, H. O. (1938). The biology of the American cockroach. *Ann. Ent. Soc. Amer.,* 31, 489–498.

75 GIER, H. T. (1947). Growth rate in the cockroach *Periplaneta americana* (Linn.). *Ann. Ent. Soc. Amer.,* 40 (2), 303–317.

76 GRIFFITHS, J. T. & TAUBER, O. E. (1942). Fecundity, longevity and parthenogenesis of the American roach, *Periplaneta americana* L. *Physiol. Zool.,* 15, 196–209.

77 HABER, V. R. (1920). Oviposition by a cockroach, *Periplaneta americana* Linn. *Ent. News,* 31, 190–193.

78 SEIN, F. Jr. (1923). *Cucarachas.* Puerto Rico. Ins. Exp. Sta. Circ. 64, 12 pp.

79 FISCHER, O. VON (1927). Die Entwicklung von *Periplaneta americana*. *Mitt. Naturforschenden Ges. Bern,* pp. 5–7.

80 SHAW, E. (1925). New genera and species (mostly Australasian) of Blattidae with notes and some remarks on Tepper's types. *Proc. Linn. Soc. N.S.W.,* 50, 171–213.

81 FROGGATT, W. W. (1906). Domestic insects: Cockroaches. *Agric. Gaz. N.S.W.,* 17, 440–447.

82 PRATT, H. D. (1955). Cockroach identification. *Pest Control,* 23 (5), 9–12.

83 REHN, J. A. G. & HEBARD, M. (1927). The Orthoptera of the West Indies. No. I, Blattidae. *Amer. Mus. Nat. Hist.,* 54, 1–320.

84 REHN, J. A. G. (1910). On the Orthoptera of Bermuda. *Proc. Acad. Nat. Sci. Phil.*, **62**, 3–11.

85 BEATTY, H. A. (1944). Fauna of St. Croix, Virgin Islands. *J. agric. Univ. Puerto Rico*, **28**, 103–185.

86 MOULTON, J. C. (1912). 'Where Wallace Trod': being an account of an entomological trip to Mt. Serambu, Sarawak, Borneo. *Entomologist*, **45**, 213–217, 246–251.

87 HEBARD, M. (1915). Dermaptera and Orthoptera found in the vicinity of Miami, Florida, in March 1915. *Ent. News*, **26**, 397–408.

88 EDMUNDS, L. R. (1957). Observations on the biology and life history of the Brown Cockroach, *Periplaneta brunnea* Burmeister. *Proc. Ent. Soc. Wash.*, **59**, 283–286.

89 BUNTING, W. M. (1955). Orthoptera imported into Britain with bananas from Dominica (Leeward Isles). *Ent. mon. Mag.*, **91**, 134.

90 BUNTING, W. M. (1956). Preliminary notes on some Orthoptera imported with bananas from Dominica. *Ent. mon. Mag.*, **92**, 284–286.

91 BILLS, G. T. (1965). The occurrence of *Periplaneta brunnea* (Burm.) (Dictyoptera, Blattidae) in an International Airport in Britain. *J. Stored Prod. Res.*, **1**, 203–204.

92 BILLS, G. T. (1966). The second established colony of *Periplaneta brunnea* (Burm.) (Dictyoptera, Blattidae) in an airport in Britain. *Ent. mon. Mag.*, **102**, 130.

93 HAINES, T. W. & PALMER, E. C. (1955). Studies of distribution and habitat of cockroaches in South Western Georgia, 1952–53. *Amer. J. Trop. Med. & Hyg.*, **4**, 1131–1134.

94 FULTON, B. B. (1928). *Cockroach destruction in buildings*. Iowa agric. Expt. Sta. Circ. No. 112.

95 SAUSSURE, H. DE (1864). Orthopteres de l'Amerique Moyenne. *Mém. Hist. Nat. Mexique*, **4**, 108–110.

96 WHELAN, D. B. (1929). *Supella supellectilium* (Serville) as a household pest in Nebraska. *J. econ. Ent.*, **22** (2), 421.

97 BACK, E. A. (1937). *Cockroaches and their control*. Leaflet No. 144, U.S. Dept. of Agric., Wash.

98 BACK, E. A. (1937a). The increasing importance of the cockroach, *Supella supellectilium* Serv. as a pest in the United States. *Proc. Ent. Soc. Wash.*, **39**, 205–213.

99 SHAW, E. (1924). *Supella supellectilium* Serv., a cockroach not before recorded from Australia. *Queensland Nat.*, **4** (6), 115.

100 KEVAN, D. K. McE. & CHOPARD, L. (1954). Blattodea from Northern Kenya and Jubaland. *Ann. Mag. Nat. Hist.*, **7** (12), 166–187.

101 HAFEZ, M. & AFIFI, A. M. (1956). Biological studies on the furniture cockroach *Supella supellectilium* Serv. in Egypt (Orthoptera: Blattidae). *Bull. Ent. Soc. Egypt*, **40**, 365–396.

102 REHN, J. A. G. (1916). The Standford Expedition to Brazil, 1911. *Trans. Amer. Ent. Soc.*, **42**, 215–308.

103 ZIMMERMAN, E. C. (1943). New cockroach parasite from Honolulu. *Proc. Hawaiian Ent. Soc.*, **12**, 20.

104 LEVER, R. J. A. W. (1943). Entomological notes. *Agric. J. Fiji*, **14** (2), 40–44.

105 MALLIS, A. (1954). *Handbook of Pest Control*. 2nd Ed. MacNair-Dorland Co. Ltd., New York. 1068 pp.

106 ZAPPE, M. P. (1919). *Life-history and development of the greenhouse cockroach*. Connecticut agric. Expt. Sta. Ann. Rep. for 1918. Bull. 211, 311–313.

107 PALMER, R. (1928). Cockroaches introduced with bananas. *Entomologist*, **61**, 19.

108 GURNEY, A. B. (1953). Distribution, general bionomics and recognition characters of two cockroaches recently established in the United States. *Proc. U.S. Nat. Mus.*, **103** (3315), 39–56.

109 ILLINGWORTH, J. F. (1942). An outbreak of cockroaches, *Nauphoeta cinerea* (Olivier) in Hawaii. *Proc. Ent. Soc. Hawaii*, **11**, 169–170.

110 ANON. (1952). Items of interest. *Florida Ent.*, **35** (2), p. 77.

111 POPE, P. (1953a). Studies on the life histories of some Queensland Blattidae (Orthoptera). Part 2. Some native species. *Proc. Roy. Soc. Queensland*, **63** (3), 47–59.

112 MACKERRAS, M. J. & MACKERRAS, I. M. (1948). *Salmonella* infections in Australian cockroaches. *Aust. J. Sci.*, **10**, 115.

113 HARTMAN, H. B. & ROTH, L. M. (1967). Stridulation by the cockroach *Nauphoeta cinerea* during courtship behaviour. *J. inst. Physiol.*, **13**, 579–586.

114 TRUMAN, L. C. (1961). Lesson No. 6, Cockroaches. *Pest Control*, **29** (6), 21–28.

115 PIQUETT, P. G. & FALES, J. H. (1954). Life-history of *Blaberus giganteus* (L.). *J. econ. Ent.*, **46** (6), 1089–1090.

116 SEVERIN, H. C. (1953). An unusual infestation of wood cockroaches. *J. econ. Ent.*, **45** (6), 1079.

117 HEBARD, M. (1935). Studies in the Orthoptera in Arizona. Part I. New genera, species and geographical races. *Trans. Amer. Ent. Soc.*, **61**, 111–153.

118 RIHERD, P. T. (1953). The occurrence of *Blattella vaga* Hebard in Texas. *Proc. Ent. Soc. Wash.*, **55** (1), 39–40.

119 FLOCK, R. A. (1941). The field roach *Blattella vaga*. *J. econ. Ent.*, **34** (1), 121.

120 BALL, E. D., TINKHAM, E. R., FLOCK, R. & VORHIES, C. T. (1942). *The grasshoppers and other Orthoptera of Arizona.* Univ. Arizona Coll. Agri. Exp. Stat. Tech. Bull. No. 93, 257-373.

121 PALERMO, M. T. (1960). The cockroach twins. *Pest Control*, **28** (6), 12.

122 SMITH, M. E. & CHAO, H.-F. (1956). Outdoor roaches. *Pest Control*, **24** (9), 50.

123 CLEVELAND, L. R., HALL, S. R., SANDERS, E. P. & COLLIER, J. (1934). The wood-feeding roach, *Cryptocercus*, its protozoa, and the symbiosis between protozoa and roach. *Mem. Amer. Acad. Sci.*, **17**, 185–342.

124 WHEELER, W. M. (1900). A new myrmecophile from the mushroom gardens of the Texas leaf-cutting ant. *Amer. Nat.*, **34**, 851–862.

125 CHOPARD, L. (1950). Sur l'anatomie et le développement d'une blatte vivipare. Eighth Internat. Congress of Ent. Stockholm, 1948, 218–221.

126 REHN, J. W. (1950). A key to the Genera of North American Blattaria, including established adventives. *Ent. News*, **61** (3), 64–67.

127 REHN, J. A. G. (1931). African and Malagasy Blattidae (Orthoptera). Part I. *Proc. Acad. Nat. Sci. Philadelphia*, **83**, 305–387.

128 REHN, J. A. G. (1933). African and Malagasy Blattidae (Orthoptera). Part II. *Proc. Acad. Nat. Sci. Philadelphia*, **84**, 405–511.

129 REHN, J. A. G. (1937). African and Malagasy Blattidae (Orthoptera). Part III. *Proc. Acad. Nat. Sci. Philadelphia*, **89**, 17–123.

130 HEBARD, M. (1929). Studies in Malayan Blattidae (Orthoptera). *Proc. Acad. Nat. Sci. Philadelphia*, **81**, 1–109.

131 SCOTT, H. G. & BOROM, M. R. (1966). Cockroaches: Key to egg cases of common domestic species (pictorial key). *Pest Control*, **34** (6), 18.

132 RICHARDS, A. G. & ANDERSON, T. F. (1942). Electron microscope studies of insect cuticle, with a discussion of the application of electron optics to this problem. *J. Morph.*, **71**, 135–184.

133 DENNELL, R. & MALEK, S. R. A. (1956). The cuticle of the cockroach *Periplaneta americana*. VI. The composition of the cuticle as determined by quantitative analysis. *Proc. Roy. Soc.*, **145**, 249–258.

134 DENNELL, R. & MALEK, S. R. A. (1955). The cuticle of the cockroach *Periplaneta americana*. III. The hardening of the cuticle: impregnation preparatory to phenolic tanning. *Proc. Roy. Soc.*, (B.), **143** (912), 414–434.

135 RAMSEY, J. A. (1935). The evaporation of water from the cockroach. *J. exp. Biol.*, **12**, 373–383.

z

136 BEAMENT, J. W. L. (1951). Wax secretion in insects. *Nature Lond.*, **167** (4251), 652–653.

137 BEAMENT, J. W. L. (1945). The cuticular lipoids of insects. *J. exp. Biol.*, **21**, 115–131.

138 DENNELL, R. & MALEK, S. R. A. (1955a). The cuticle of the cockroach, *Periplaneta americana*. II. The epicuticle. *Proc. Roy. Soc.*, (B.), **143**, 239 (Part II).

139 GILBY, A. R. (1962). Absence of natural volatile solvents in cockroach grease. *Nature Lond.*, **195** (4842), 729.

140 BEAMENT, J. W. L. (1955). Wax secretion in the cockroach. *J. exp. Biol.*, **32** (3), 514–538.

141 WIGGLESWORTH, V. B. (1945). Transpiration through the cuticle of insects. *J. exp. Biol.*, **21**, 97–114.

142 WINSTON, P. W. (1967). Cuticular water pump in insects. *Nature Lond.*, **214**, 383–384.

143 STANISLAVSKIJ, B. (1926). To the question of hypodermis structure in *Periplaneta orientalis*. *Publications de la Faculté des Sciences de l'Universite Charles*, **56**.

144 KRAMER, S. & WIGGLESWORTH, V. B. (1950). The outer layers of the cuticle in the cockroach *Periplaneta americana* and the function of the Oenocytes. *Quart. J. micro. Sci.*, **91** (1), 63–71.

145 DUSHAM, E. H. (1918). The wax glands of the cockroach (*Blatta germanica*). *J. Morph.*, **31** (3), 563–581.

146 DUSHAM, E. H. (1918a). The dorsal pygidial glands of the female cockroach, *Blattella germanica*. *Canad. Ent.*, **50** (8), 278–280.

147 STOCK, A. & O'FARREL, A. F. (1954). Cercal spinning glands in the cockroach, *Blattella germanica*. *Aust. J. Sci.*, **17**, 64.

148 ROTH, L. M. & STAHL, W. H. (1956). Tergal and Cercal Secretion of *Blatta orientalis* L. *Science*, **123**, 798–799.

149 PRINGLE, J. W. S. (1938a). Proprioception in insects. I. A new type of mechanical receptor from the palps of the cockroach. *J. exp. Biol.*, **15**, 101–113.

150 PRINGLE, J. W. S. (1938b). Proprioception in insects. II. The action of the campaniform sensilla on the legs. *J. exp. Biol.*, **15**, 114–131.

151 FRINGS, H. & FRINGS, M. (1949). The loci of contact chemoreceptors in insects. *Amer. Mid. Nat.*, **41**, 602–658.

152 PUMPHREY, R. J. & RAWDON-SMITH, A. F. (1936a). Hearing in insects; the nature of the response of certain receptors in auditory stimuli. *Proc. Roy. Soc. Lond.*, (B.), **121**, 18–27.

153 PUMPHREY, R. J. & RAWDON-SMITH, A. F. (1936b). Sensitivity of insects to sound. *Nature Lond.*, **137**, 990.

154 RAU, P. (1940). Auditory perception in insects, with special reference to the cockroach. *Quart. Rev. Biol.*, **15** (2), 121–155.

155 RAU, P. (1945). Food preferences of the cockroach, *Blatta orientalis* Linn. *Ent. News*, **56** (10), 276–278.

156 HAFEZ, M. & AFIFI, A. M. (1956). Histology of the digestive tract of the furniture cockroach, *Supella supellectilium* Serv. *Bull. Soc. Ent. Egypt*, **40**, 397–414.

157 ROSS, H. H. (1930). Notes on the digestive and reproductive systems of the German cockroach. *Tran. Ill. Acad. Sci.*, **22**, 206–216.

158 DAY, M. F. (1951). The mechanism of secretion by the salivary gland of the cockroach, *Periplaneta americana* L. *Aust. J. Sci. Res.*, (B), **4**, 136–143.

159 WIGGLESWORTH, V. B. (1927a). Digestion in the cockroach. I. The hydrogen ion concentration in the alimentary canal. *Biochem. Jl.*, **21**, 791–796.

160 EIDMANN, H. (1922). Permeability of chitin in osmotic processes. *Biol. Z.*, **42**, 429–435.

161 ABBOTT, R. L. (1926). Contributions to the physiology of digestion in the Australian roach, *Periplaneta australasiae*. *J. exp. Zool.*, **43**, 219–253.

162 SANFORD, E. W. (1918). Experiments on the physiology of digestion in the Blattidae. *J. exp. Zool.*, **25**, 355–411.

163 EIDMANN, H. (1924). Untersuchungen über die Morphologie und Physiologie des Kaumagens von *Periplaneta orientalis* L. *Z. wiss. Zool.*, **122**, 281–307.

164 SCHLOTTKE, E. (1937). Distribution of digestive enzymes in gut and malpighian tubes: Carabidae. *Z. vergle. Physiol.*, **24**, 210–247.

165 WIGGLESWORTH, V. B. (1965). *The Principles of Insect Physiology*. Methuen, London. 741 pp.

166 CAMERON, E. (1961). *The Cockroach, Periplaneta americana* L. Heinemann, London.

167 KOLLER, G. (1948). Rhythmische Bewegung und hormonale Steuerung bei den Malpighischen Gefüssen der Insekten. *Biol. Z.*, **67**, 201–211.

168 DATTA, S. K. (1966). Ion regulation in the isolated hind-gut of the cockroach, *Byrsotria fumigata*. *Dissertation Abstracts* (B), **27** (6), 2181.

169 SNIPES, B. T. & TAUBER, O. E. (1937). Time required for food passage through the alimentary tract of the cockroach, *Periplaneta americana* Linn. *Ann. Ent. Soc. Amer.*, **30**, 277–284.

170 DAY, M. F. & POWNING, R. F. (1949). A study of the processes of digestion in certain insects. *Aust. J. Sci. Res.*, (B), **2**, 175–215.

171 WIGGLESWORTH, V. B. (1927b). Digestion in the cockroach. II. The digestion of carbohydrates. *Biochem. J.*, **21**, 797–811.

172 SWINGLE, H. S. (1925). Digestive enzymes of an insect. *Ohio J. Sci.*, **25**, 209–218.

173 SCHLOTTKE, E. (1937b). Digestive enzymes of insects. III. Enzyme content as a function of type of food. Tests with *Periplaneta orientalis* L. *Z. vergl. Physiol.*, **24**, 463–493.

174 EHRHARDT, P. & VOSS, Z. (1962). Beitrag zum Wirkungsspektrum Kohlenhydrats-paltender Fermente und ihre Verteilung im Verdauungstrakt der Schaben *Blaberus discoidalis* Sv. und *Leucophaea maderae* F. (Blattoidea). *J. ins. Physiol.*, **8**, 165–174.

175 BANKS, W. M. (1963). Carbohydrate digestion in the cockroach. *Science*, **141**, 1191–1192.

176 WIGGLESWORTH, V. B. (1928). Digestion in the cockroach. III. The digestion of proteins and fats. *Biochem. J.*, **22**, 150–161.

177 TRAGER, W. (1932). A cellulase from the symbiotic intestinal flagellates of termites and of the roach, *Cryptocercus punctulatus*. *Biochem. J.*, **26**, 1762–1771.

178 FISK, F. W. & RAO, B. R. (1964). Digestive carbohydrases in the Cuban burrowing cockroach. *Ann. Ent. Soc. Amer.*, **57**, 40–44.

179 WHARTON, D. R. A., WHARTON, M. L. & LOLA, J. E. (1965). Cellulase in the cockroach. *J. ins. Physiol.*, **11**, 947–959.

180 ALEXANDROWICZ, J. S. (1926). The innervation of the heart of the cockroach (*Periplaneta orientalis*). *J. Comp. Neurol.*, **41**, 291–310.

181 McINDOO, N. E. (1939). Segmental blood vessels of the American cockroach (*Periplaneta americana* (L.). *J. Morph.*, **65**, 323–351.

182 YEAGER, J. F. & HENDRICKSON, G. O. (1934). Circulation of blood in wings and wing pads of the cockroach *Periplaneta americana* Linn. *Ann. Ent. Soc. Amer.*, **27**, 257–272.

183 PRATT, J. J. Jr. (1950). A qualitative analysis of the free amino acids in insect blood. *Ann. Ent. Soc. Amer.*, **43**, 573–580.

184 AUCLAIR, J. L. (1959). The influence of dietary amino acids on the blood amino acids of the German cockroach, *Blattella germanica* (L.). *J. ins. Physiol.*, **3**, 127–131.

185 YEAGER, J. F. & TAUBER, O. E. (1932). Determination of total blood volume in the cockroach, *Periplaneta fuliginosa*, with special reference to method. *Ann. Ent. Soc. Amer.*, **25**, 315–327.

186 YEAGER, J. F. & MUNSON, S. C. (1950). Blood volume of the roach *Periplaneta americana* determined by several methods. *Arthropoda* (*Argentina*), **1**, 255–265.

187 WHEELER, R. E. (1963). Studies on the total haemocyte count and haemolymph

volume in *Periplaneta americana* (L.) with special reference to the last moulting cycle. *J. ins. Physiol.*, **9**, 223–235.

188 GUNN, D. L. (1931). Temperature and humidity relations of the cockroach. *Nature, Lond.*, **128** (3222), 186–187.

189 WHARTON, D. R. A., WHARTON, M. L. & LOLA, J. E. (1965). Blood volume and water content of the male American cockroach, *Periplaneta americana* L.— Methods and the influence of age and starvation. *J. ins. Physiol.*, **11**, 391–404.

190 TAUBER, O. E. (1937). The effect of ecdysis on the number of mitotically dividing cells in the haemolymph of the insect, *Blatta orientalis*. *Ann. Ent. Soc. Amer.*, **30** (1), 35–39.

191 COON, B. F. (1944). Effects of paralytic insecticides on heart pulsations and blood circulation in the American cockroach as determined with a fluorescein indicator. *J. econ. Ent.*, **37** (6), 785–789.

192 TAUBER, O. E. & SNIPES, B. T. (1936). Velocity of haemocyte circulation in the elytron of the cockroach, *Periplaneta americana* Linn. *Proc. Soc. Exp. Biol. Med. N.Y.*, **35** (2), 249–251.

193 YEAGER, J. F. & HAGER, A. (1934). On the rates of contraction of the isolated heart and malpighian tube of the insect, *Periplaneta orientalis*: Method. *Iowa State Col. Jnl. Sci.*, **8** (3), 391–395.

194 YEAGER, J. F. (1938). Mechanographic method of recording insect cardiac activity, with reference to effect of nicotine on isolated heart preparations of *Periplaneta americana*. *J. agric. Res.*, **56**, 267–276.

195 CAMERON, M. L. (1953). Secretion of an Orthodiphenol in the corpus cardiacum of the insect. *Nature, Lond.*, **172** (4373), 349–350.

196 SCHARRER, B. (1952). Neurosecretion. XI. The effects of nerve section on the intercerebralis-cardiacum-allatum system of the insect, *Leucophaea maderae*. *Biol. Bull.*, **102** (3), 261–272.

197 DAVEY, K. G. (1961). The mode of action of the heart accelerating factor from the corpus cardiacum of insects. *Gen. comp. Endrocrin.*, **1**, 24–29.

198 DAVEY, K. G. (1961a). Substances controlling the rate of beating of the heart of *Periplaneta*. *Nature, Lond.*, **192** (4799), 284.

199 DAVEY, K. G. (1962). The release by feeding of a pharmacologically active factor from the corpus cardiacum of *P. americana*. *J. ins. Physiol.*, **8**, 205–208.

200 RALPH, C. L. (1962). Heart accelerators and decelerations in the nervous system of *Periplaneta americana* (L.). *J. ins, Physiol.*, **8**, 431–439.

201 FRAENKEL, G. & HSAIO, C. (1962). Hormonal and nervous control of tanning in the fly. *Science*, **138**, 27–29.

202 FRAENKEL, G. & HSAIO, C. (1963). Tanning in the adult fly: a new function of neurosecretion by the brain. *Science*, **141**, 1057–1058.

203 MILLS, R. R., MATHUR, R. B. & GUERRA, A. A. (1965). Hormonal control of tanning in the American cockroach. *J. ins. Physiol.*, **11**, 1047–1053.

204 MILLS, R. R. (1965). Hormonal control of tanning in the American cockroach. II. Assay for the hormone and the effect of wound healing. *J. ins. Physiol.*, **11**, 1269–1275.

205 MILLS, R. R. (1966). Hormonal control of tanning in the American cockroach. III. Hormone stability and post-ecdysial changes in hormone titre. *J. ins. Physiol.*, **12**, 275–280.

206 HABER, V. R. (1926). The tracheal system of the German cockroach, *Blattella germanica* Linn. *Bull. Brooklyn Ent. Soc.*, **21** (3), 61–92.

207 GUNN, D. L. (1933). The temperature and humidity relations of the cockroach (*Blatta orientalis*). I. Desiccation. *J. exp. Biol.*, **10** (3), 274–285.

208 BARRON, E. S. G. & TAHMISIAN, T. N. (1948). The metabolism of cockroach muscle (*P. americana*). *J. Cell. Comp. Physiol.*, **32**, 57–76.

209 SAMUELS, A. (1956). The effect of sex and allatectomy on the oxygen consumption

of the thoracic musculature of the insect, *Leucophaea maderae. Biol. Bull.,
Woods Hole, Mass.*, **110**, 179–183.

210 SÄGESSER, H. (1960). Über die Wirkung der corpora allata auf den Sauerstoffver-
brauch bei der Schabe *Leucophaea maderae* (F.). *J. ins. Physiol.*, **5**, 264–285.

211 RALPH, C. L. & MATTA, R. J. (1965). Evidence for hormonal effects on metabolism
of cockroaches from studies of tissue homogenates. *J. ins. Physiol.*, **11**, 983–
991.

212 ENGELMANN, F. (1957). Die Steuerung der Ovarfunktion bei der ovoviviparen
Schabe *Leucophaea maderae* (Fabr.). *J. ins. Physiol.*, **1**, 257–278.

213 HARKER, J. E. (1960). Endocrine and nervous factors in insect circadian rhythms.
Cold Spr. Harb. Symp. Quant. Biol., **25**, 279–287.

214 PATTON, R. L., GARDNER, J. & ANDERSON, A. D. (1959). The excretory efficiency of
the American cockroach (*Periplaneta americana* L.). *J. ins. Physiol.*, **3**, 256–
261.

215 KILBY, B. A. (1963). The biochemistry of the insect fat body. *Advances in Insect
Physiology*, Academic Press, London, p. 111–174.

216 HENRY, S. M. & BLOCK, R. J. (1962). Amino acid synthesis, a rumen-like effect of
the intracellular symbionts of the German cockroach. *Federation Proc.*, **21**, 9.

217 GALLAGHER, M. R. (1962). *Vitamin synthesis by the symbionts in the fat body of the
cockroach, P. americana* (*Linnaeus*). Ph.D. Thesis, Fordham Univ.

218 HAYDAK, M. H. (1953). Influence of the protein level of the diet on the longevity of
cockroaches. *Ann. Ent. Soc. Amer.*, **46**, 547–560.

219 KELLER, H. (1950). Die Kultur der intrazellularen Symbioten von *Periplaneta
orientalis. Z. Naturforschg.*, **5B**, 269–273.

220 BODENSTEIN, D. (1953). Studies on the humoral mechanisms in growth and metamorphosis of the cockroach, *Periplaneta americana*. II. Humoral effects on
metabolism. *J. exp. Zool.*, **124** (1), 105–115.

221 VROMAN, H. E., KAPLANIS, J. N. & ROBBINS, W. E. (1965). Effect of allatectomy on
lipid biosynthesis and turnover in the female American cockroach, *P. americana*
L. *J. ins. Physiol.*, **11**, 897–904.

222 ROTH, L. M. & DATEO, G. P. Jr. (1964). Uric acid in the reproductive system of
males of the cockroach *Blattella germanica. Science*, **146**, 782–784.

223 ROTH, L. M. & DATEO, G. P. Jr. (1965). Uric acid storage and excretion by accessory sex glands of male cockroaches. *J. ins. Physiol.*, **11**, 1023–1029.

224 ROTH, L. M. & WILLIS, E. R. (1952). A study of cockroach behaviour. *Amer. Mid.
Nat.*, **47**, 65–129.

225 KHALIFA, A. (1950). Spermatophore production in *Blattella germanica* L. *Proc. R.
Ent. Soc.* (A), **25**, 53–61.

226 ROTH, L. M. (1967). Uricose glands in the accessory sex gland complex of male
Blattaria. *Ann. Ent. Soc. Amer.*, **60** (6), 1203–1211.

227 SHAW, J. & STOBBART, R. H. (1963). Osmotic and ionic regulation in insects. 315–
399. *Advances in insect physiology*. Ed. Beament, Treherne & Wigglesworth.
Acad. Press, London. 512 pp.

228 GILMOUR, D. (1965). *The Metabolism of Insects*. Oliver & Boyd, Edinburgh. 195 pp.

229 WILLEY, R. B. (1961). The morphology of the stomodeal nervous system in *Periplaneta americana* (L.) and other Blattaria. *J. Morph.*, **108** (2), 219–261.

230 WILLEY, R. B. & CHAPMAN, G. B. (1962). Fine structure of neurons within the pars
intercerebralis of the cockroach, *Blaberus craniifer. Gen. Comp. Endocrinol.*, **2**,
31–43.

231 BARTH, R. H. Jr. (1962). The endocrine control of mating behaviour in the cockroach *Byrsotria fumigata* (Guérin). *Gen. Comp. Endocrinol.*, **2**, 53–69.

232 SCHARRER, B. (1945). Experimental tumours after nerve section in an insect. *Proc.
Soc. exp. Biol. N.Y.*, **60**, 184–189.

233 SUTHERLAND, D. J. (1963). Experimentally induced tumours in *Periplaneta americana* L. *J. ins. Physiol.*, **9**, 131–135.

358　　BIBLIOGRAPHY

234 HARKER, J. E. (1957). Experimental production of mid-gut tumours in *Periplaneta americana* L. *J. exp. Biol.*, **35**, 251–259.

235 PUMPHREY, R. J. & RAWDON-SMITH, A. F. (1936). Synchronized action potentials in the cercal nerve of the cockroach (*Periplaneta americana*) in response to auditory stimuli. *J. Physiol.*, **87** (1), 4–5 P.

236 PUMPHREY, R. J. & RAWDON-SMITH, A. F. (1937). Synaptic transmission of impulses through the last abdominal ganglion of the cockroach. *Proc. Roy. Soc.* (B.), **122**, 106–118.

237 ROEDER K. D., KENNEDY, N. K. & SAMSON, E. A. (1947). Synaptic conduction to, giant fibres of the cockroach and the action of anticholinesterase. *J. Neurophysiology*, **10**, 1–10.

238 ROEDER, K. D. (1948). Organisation of the ascending giant fibre system in the cockroach (*Periplaneta americana*). *J. exp. Zool.*, **108** (2), 243–261.

239 HUGHES, G. M. (1965). *Neuronal pathways in the insect central nervous system.* 12th International Congress of Entomology, London, 1964 (*The Physiology of the Insect Central Nervous System*, edited by J. E. Treherne & J. W. L. Beament). pp. 79–112.

240 ROEDER, K. D., TOZIAN, L. & WEIANT, E. A. (1960). Endogenous nerve activity and behaviour in the mantis and cockroach. *J. ins. Physiol.*, **4**, 45–62.

241 MILBURN, N. S. & ROEDER, K. D. (1962). Control of efferent activity in the cockroach terminal abdominal ganglion by extracts of corpora cardiaca. *Gen. comp. Endocrinol.*, **2**, 70–76.

242 STREJČKOVÁ, A., SERVÍT, Z. & NOVÁK, V. J. A. (1965). Effect of neurohormone C_1 and D_1 on spontaneous electrical activity of the central nervous system of the cockroach. *J. ins. Physiol.*, **11**, 889–896.

243 KEARNS, C. W. (1952). Temperature and the action of DDT on the American roach. *J. econ. Ent.*, **45**, 484.

244 BEAMENT, J. W. L. (1958). A paralysing agent in the blood of cockroaches. *J. ins. Physiol.*, **2**, 199–214.

245 WIGGLESWORTH, V. B. (1960). The nutrition of the central nervous system in the cockroach, *Periplaneta americana* L. *J. exp. Biol.*, **37** (3), 500–512.

246 TREHERNE, J. E. (1960). The nutrition of the central nervous system in the cockroach, *Periplaneta americana* L. The exchange and metabolism of sugars. *J. exp. Biol.*, **37** (3), 513–533.

247 TREHERNE, J. E. & BEAMENT, J. W. L. (1965). *The Physiology of the Insect Central Nervous System.* Academic Press, London. 277 pp.

248 KARLSON, P. & BUTENANDT, A. (1959). Pheromones (Ectohormones) in insects. *Ann. Rev. Ent.*, **4**, 39–58.

249 GÖTZ, B. (1951). Die sexualduftstoffe an Lepidopteren. *Experientia*, **7**, 406–418.

250 JACOBSON, M., BEROZA, M. & JONES, W. A. (1960). Isolation, identification and synthesis of the sex attractant of Gypsy Moth. *Science*, **132**, 1011–1012.

251 JACOBSON, M., BEROZA, M. & YAMATOTO, R. T. (1963). Isolation and identification of the sex attractant of the American cockroach. *Science*, **139**, 48–49.

252 ROTH, L. M. (1967). *Male pheromones.* McGraw Hill Year Book, Science & Technology, p. 293–295.

253 WHARTON, M. L. & WHARTON, D. R. A. (1957). The production of sex attractant substance and of oothecae by the normal and irradiated American cockroach, *Periplaneta americana* L. *J. ins. Physiol.*, **1**, 229–239.

254 YAMATOTO, R. (1963). Collection of the sex attractant from female American cockroaches. *J. econ. Ent.*, **56** (1), 119–120.

255 JACOBSON, M. & SMALLS, L. A. (1966). Masking of the American cockroach sex attractant. *J. econ. Ent.*, **59** (2), 414–416.

256 ENGLEMANN, F. (1960). Mechanisms controlling reproduction in two viviparous cockroaches (Blattaria). *Ann. N.Y. Acad. Sci.*, **89**, 516–536.

257 BARTH, R. H. Jr. (1960). Hormonal control of sex attractant production in the Cuban cockroach. *Science*, **133**, 1598–1599.

258 WHARTON, D. R. A., MILLER, G. L. & WHARTON, M. L. (1954). The odorous attractant of the American cockroach, *Periplaneta americana* (L.). I. Quantitative aspects of the response to the attractant. *J. Gen. Physiol.*, **37** (4), 461–469.

259 SNODGRASS, R. E. (1937). The Male genitalia of Orthopteroid insects. Smithsonian Misc. Coll., **96** (5), 1–107.

260 ROTH, L. M. & BARTH, R. H. Jr. (1967). The sense organs employed by cockroaches in mating behaviour. *Behaviour*, **28**, 58–94.

261 NUTTING, W. L. (1953). Observations on the reproduction of the giant cockroach, *Blaberus craniifer* Burm. *Psyche*, **60**, 6–14.

262 HARTMAN, H. B. & ROTH, L. M. (1967). Stridulation by a cockroach during courtship behaviour. *Nature, Lond.*, **213** (5082), 1243–1244.

263 ROTH, L. M. (1962). Hypersexual activity induced in females of the cockroach, *Nauphoeta cinerea*. *Science*, **138**, 1267–1269.

264 ROTH, L. M. (1964). Control of reproduction in female cockroaches with special reference to *Nauphoeta cinerea*. I. First pre-oviposition period. *J. ins. Physiol.*, **10**, 915–945.

265 ROTH, L. M. & BARTH, R. H. (1964). The control of sexual receptivity in female cockroaches. *J. ins. Physiol.*, **10**, 965–975.

266 ROTH, L. M. (1964a). Control of reproduction in female cockroaches with special reference to *Nauphoeta cinerea*. II. Gestation and postparturition. *Psyche*, **71** (4), 198–243.

267 ENGELMANN, F. (1960a). Hormonal control of mating behaviour in an insect. *Experientia*, **16**, 69–70.

268 AMERSON, G. M. & HAYS, S. B. (1967). Gametogenesis in the German cockroach. *J. econ. Ent.*, **60** (2), 429–432.

269 ZABINSKI, J. (1933). Fonctionnement des différentes parties des appareils copulateurs chitines males et females de la blatta (*Periplaneta orientalis* L.). *C.R. Soc. Biol., Paris*, **112**, 598–602.

270 GUPTA, P. D. (1947). On the structure and formation of spermatophore in the cockroach, *Periplaneta americana* L. *Indian J. Ent.*, **8**, 79–84.

271 ROTH, L. M. & STAY, B. (1962). Oocyte development in *Blattella germanica* and *Blattella vaga* (Blattaria). *Ann. Ent. Soc. Amer.*, **55** (6), 633–642.

272 GIER, H. T. (1936). The morphology and behaviour of the intracellular bacteroids of roaches. *Biol. Bull.*, **71** (3), 433–452.

273 BLOCHMANN, F. (1888). Über das regelmässige Vorkommen von bakterienähnlichen, Gebilden in den Geweben und Eiern verschiedener Insecten. *Zeitschr. f. Biol.* **24**, 1–15.

274 LÜSCHER, M. & ENGELMANN, F. (1955). Über die Steuerung der Corpora allata-funktion bei der Schabe, *Leucophaea maderae*. *Rev. Suisse Zool.*, **62**, 649–657.

275 ENGELMANN, F. (1962). Further experiments on the regulation of the sexual cycle in females of *Leucophaea maderae* (Blattaria). *Gen. Comp. Endocrinol.*, **2**, 183–192.

276 SCHARRER, B. & HARNACK, M. VON (1958). Histophysiological studies on the corpus allatum of *Leucophaea maderae*. I. Normal life cycle in male and female adults. *Biol. Bull.*, **115**, 508–520.

277 GIRARDIE, A. (1962). Biometrical study of ovarian growth after extirpation and implantation of corpora allata in *Periplaneta americana*. *J. ins. Physiol.*, **8**, 199–204.

278 PARKER, B. M. & CAMPBELL, F. L. (1940). Relative susceptibility of the ootheca and adult female of the German cockroach to liquid household insecticides. *J. econ. Ent.*, **33** (4), 610–614.

279 ENGELMANN, F. (1959). The control of reproduction in *Diploptera punctata* (Blattaria). *Biol. Bull. Woods Hole*, **116**, 406–419.

280 ROTH, L. M. & STAY, B. (1959). Control of oocyte development in cockroaches. *Science*, **130**, 271–272.

281 ENGELMANN, F. (1964). Inhibition of egg maturation in a pregnant viviparous cockroach. *Nature, Lond.*, **202** (4933), 724–725.

282 ROTH, L. M. & WILLIS, E. R. (1956). Parthenogenesis in cockroaches. *Ann. Ent. Soc. Amer.*, **49**, 195–204.

283 HIGHNAM, K. C. (1962). Neurosecretory control of ovarian development in *Schistocerca gregaria*. *Quart. J. micr. Sci.*, **103**, 57–72.

284 HILL, L. (1962). Neurosecretory control of haemolymph protein concentration during the ovarian development in the desert locust. *J. ins. Physiol.*, **8**, 609–619.

285 RAO, B. R. & FISK, F. W. (1965). Trysin activity associated with reproductive development in cockroach. *J. ins. Physiol.*, **11**, 961–971.

286 STAY, B. & ROTH, L. M. (1962). The colleterial glands of cockroaches. *Ann. Ent. Soc. Amer.*, **55**, 124–130.

287 PRYOR, M. G. M. (1940). On the hardening of the ootheca of *Blatta orientalis*. *Proc. Roy. Soc.*, (B), **128**, 378–393.

288 PRYOR, M. G. M. (1940a). On the hardening of the cuticle of insects. *Proc. Roy. Soc.*, (B), **128**, 393–407.

289 PRYOR, M. G. M., RUSSELL, P. B. & TODD, A. R. (1946). Protocatechuic acid, the substance responsible for the hardening of the cockroach ootheca. *Biochem. J.*, **40**, 627–628.

290 BRUNET, P. C. J. & KENT, P. W. (1955). Mechanism of sclerotin formation: the participation of a Beta-glucoside. *Nature, Lond.*, **175** (4462), 819–820.

291 CAMPBELL, F. L. (1929). The detection and estimation of insect chitin; and the irrelation of 'chitinisation' to hardness and pigmentation of the cuticula of the American cockroach, *Periplaneta americana* L. *Ann. Ent. Soc. Amer.*, **22**, 401–426.

292 HAGAN, H. R. (1951). *Embryology of the viviparous insects*. (Chapter 12, 291–346.) The Ronald Press Co., New York, 472 pp.

293 ROTH, L. M. & WILLIS, E. R. (1957). An analysis of oviparity and viviparity in the Blattaria. *Trans. Amer. Ent. Soc.*, **83**, 221–238.

294 RAU, P. (1943). How the cockroach deposits its egg-case; A study in insect behaviour. *Ann. Ent. Soc. Amer.*, **36**, 221–226.

295 LAWSON, F. A. (1951). Structural features of the oothecae of certain species of cockroaches. *Ann. Ent. Soc. Amer.*, **44** (2), 269–285.

296 WOODRUFF, L. C. (1938). The normal growth rate of *Blattella germanica* L. *J. exp. Zool.*, **79**, 145–167.

297 ROTH, L. M. (1967). Water changes in cockroach oothecae in relation to the evolution of ovoviviparity and viviparity. *Ann. Ent. Soc. Amer.*, **60** (5), 928–946.

298 WHEELER, W. M. (1889). The embryology of *Blatta germanica* and *Doryphora decemlineata*. *J. Morphology*, **3**, 291–386.

299 FULLER, C. (1920). On the post-embryonic development of the antennae of termites. *Ann. Natal Govt. Mus.*, **4**, 235–295.

300 LÜSCHER, M. & ENGELMANN, F. (1960). Histologische und experimentelle Untersuchungen über die Auslösung der Metamorphose bei *Leucophaea maderae* (Orthoptera). *J. ins. Physiol.*, **5**, 240–258.

301 WOODRUFF, L. C. (1939). Linear growth ratios for *Blattella germanica* L. *J. exp. Zool.*, **81** (2), 287–298.

302 SEAMANS, L. & WOODRUFF, L. C. (1939). Some factors influencing the number of molts of the German roach. *J. Kansas Ent. Soc.*, **12** (3), 73–76.

303 WOODRUFF, L. C. (1937). Autospray and regeneration in the roach, *Blattella germanica* (Linnaeus). *J. Kansas Ent. Soc.*, **10** (1), 1–9.

304 LANDOWSKI, J. VON (1938). Effect of individual rearing and communal life on development and growth of nymphs of *Periplaneta orientalis* L. *Biol. Zentrabl.*, **58**, 512–515.

305 PETTIT, L. C. (1940). The effect of isolation on growth in the cockroach *Blattella germanica* L. (Orthoptera: Blattidae.) *Ent. News*, **51** (10), 293.

306 MELAMPY, R. M. & MAYNARD, L. A. (1937). Nutrition studies with the cockroach (*Blattella germanica*). *Physiol. Zool.*, **10**, 36–44.

307 NOLAND, J. L., LILLY, J. H. & BAUMANN, C. A. (1949). A laboratory method for rearing cockroaches, and its application to dietary studies on the German roach. *Ann. Ent. Soc. Amer.*, **42**, 63–70.

308 NOLAND, J. L. & BAUMANN, C. A. (1951). Protein requirements of the cockroach *Blattella germanica. Ann. Ent. Soc. Amer.*, **44**, 184–188.

309 SIEBURTH, J. F., BONSALL, M. G. & McLAREN, B. A. (1951). A simple biological assay method using the cockroach, *Periplaneta americana* Linn. for protein utilization. *Ann. Ent. Soc. Amer.*, **44**, 463–468.

310 GILMOUR, D. (1961). *Biochemistry of Insects.* Academy Press, London. 343 pp.

311 BROOKS, M. A. & RICHARDS, A. G. (1955). Intracellular symbiosis in cockroaches. I. Production of aposymbiotic cockroaches. *Biol. Bull.*, **109** (1), 22–39.

312 BOWERS, R. E. & McCAY, C. M. (1940). Insect life without vitamin A. *Science*, **92**, 291.

313 WOLLMAN, E., GIROUD, A. & RATSIMAMANGA, R. (1937), Synthesis of vitamin C in an orthoptera insect (*Blattella germanica*) reared aseptically *C. R. de la Soc. de biol.*, **124**, 434–435.

314 CLARK, A. J. & BLOCH, K. (1959). Conversion of Ergosterol to 22-Dehydrocholesterol in *Blattella germanica. J. Biol. Chem.*, **234**, 2589–2594—**10**.

315 CAMERON, E. (1957). On the parasites and predators of the cockroach. II. *Evania appendigaster* (L.) *Bull. ent. Res.*, **48**, 199–209.

316 EDMUNDS, L. R. (1952). Some notes on the habits and parasites of native wood cockroaches in Ohio (Orthoptera: Blattidae). *Ent. News*, **63** (6), 141–145.

317 EDMUNDS, L. R. (1953). Collecting and culturing of native wood roaches in Ohio, with some additional notes on their parasites. *Ent. News*, **64** (9), 225–230.

318 ROTH, L. M. & WILLIS, E. R. (1954). The biology of the cockroach egg parasite, *Tetrastichus hagenowii* (Hymenoptera: Eulophidae). *Trans. Amer. Ent. Soc.*, **80** (2), 53–72.

319 CAMERON, E. (1955). On the parasites and predators of the cockroach. I. *Tetrastichus hagenowii* (Ratz). *Bull. ent. Res.*, **46**, 137–147.

320 WILLIAMS, F. X. (1942). *Ampulex compressa* (Fabr.). A cockroach-hunting wasp introduced from New Caledonia into Hawaii. *Proc. Haw. Ent. Soc.*, **11** (2), 221–233.

321 RAU, P. (1937). A note on the nesting habits of the roach-hunting wasp, *Podium* (*Parapodium*) *carolina*, Rohwer (Hym.). *Ent. News*, **48**, 91–94.

322 SHELFORD, R. (1906). Studies of the Blattidae. VII. A new genus of symbiotic Blattidae. *Trans. Ent. Soc. London*, Part IV, 515–518.

323 PIMENTAL, D. (1958). Ecological and physiological requirements of cockroaches. *Pest Control*, **26** (6), 20, 22, 52.

324 BAKER, E. W., EVANS, T. M., GOULD, D. J., HULL, W. B. & KEEGAN, H. L. (1956). *A manual of parasitic mites of medical or economic importance.* Nat. Pest Control Assoc. Inc., New York. 170 pp.

325 FIELD, G., SAVAGE, L. B. & DUPLESSIS, R. J. (1966). Note on the cockroach mite *Pimeliaphilus cunliffei* (Acarina: Pterygosomidae) infesting Oriental, German and American cockroaches. *J. econ. Ent.*, **59** (6), 1532.

326 EISENER, T., McKITTRICK, F. & PAYNE, R. (1959). Defense sprays of roaches. *Pest Control*, **27** (6), 9, 11, 12, 44–45.

327 ROTH, L. M. & HARTMAN, H. B. (1967). Sound production and its evolutionary significance in the Blattaria. *Ann. Ent. Soc. Amer.*, **60** (4), 740–752.

328 WILLE, J. (1920). *Biologie und Bekämpfung der deutschen Schabe (Phyllodromia germanica L.).* Monog. zur angew. Ent. Beihefte, I. zur Zeits. f. angew. Ent., **7** (5), 1–140, Berlin.

329 BERTHOLD, R. & WILSON, B. R. (1967). Resting behaviour of the German cockroach, *Blattella germanica. Ann. Ent. Soc. Amer.*, **60** (2), 347–351.

330 ANON. (1953). The Tyler Project. *Texas Health Bull.*, **6** (3), 8–15; **6** (7), 12–15.

331 EADES, R. B., ZUBEN, F. J. VON, BENNETT, S. E. & WALKER, O. L. (1954). Studies on cockroaches in a municipal sewerage system. *Amer. J. Trop. Med. Hyg.*, **3** (6), 1092–1098.

332 SCHOOF, H. F. & SIVERLY, R. E. (1954). The occurrence and movement of *Periplaneta americana* (L.) within an urban sewerage system. *Amer. J. Med. Hyg.*, **3** (2), 367–371.

333 JACKSON, W. B. & MAIER, P. P. (1955). Dispersion of marked American cockroaches from sewer manholes in Phoenix, Arizona. *Amer. J. Trop. Med. Hyg.*, **4** (1), 141–146.

334 JACKSON, W. B. & MAIER, P. P. (1961). Additional studies of dispersion patterns of American cockroaches from sewer manholes in Phoenix, Arizona. *Ohio Jr. Sci.*, **61** (4), 220–226.

335 BÜNNING, E. (1959). Chapter 'Physiological mechanism and biological importance of the endogenous diurnal periodicity in plants and animals'. *Photoperiodism and related phenomena in plants and animals* (Edit. Withson, R. B.). Publication No. 55. Amer. Assoc. Adv. Sci., Washington D.C.

336 HALBERG, F. (1959). *Photoperiodism and related phenomena in plants and animals* (Edit. Withson, R. B.). Amer. Assoc. Adv. Sci., Washington. pp. 803–878.

337 HARKER, J. E. (1960)a. The effect of perturbations in the environmental cycle of the diurnal rhythm of activity of *Periplaneta americana* L. *J. exp. Biol.*, **37** (1), 154–163.

338 HARKER, J. E. (1956). Factors controlling the diurnal rhythm of activity in *Periplaneta americana. J. exp. Biol.*, **33** (1), 224–234.

339 ROBERTS, S. K. DEF. (1960). Circadian activity rhythm in cockroaches. I. The free-running rhythm in steady-state. *J. Cellular Comp. Physiol.*, **55** (1), 99–110.

340 SULLIVAN, W. N., SCHECHTER, M. S., DUTKY, S. R. & KELLER, J. C. (1962). Monitoring electrophysiological responses of cockroaches for space research. *J. econ. Ent.*, **55** (6), 985–989.

341 DUTKY, S. R., SCHECHTER, M. S. & SULLIVAN, W. N. (1963). *Monitoring electrophysiological and locomotor activity of insects to detect biological rhythms. Bio. Telemetry—The use of telemetry in animal behaviour and physiology in relation to ecological problems.* Edit. Slater, N.Y. 1963. Proc. of the Interdisciplinary Conf. N.Y., March 1962.

342 SCHECHTER, M. S., DUTKY, S. R. & SULLIVAN, W. N. (1963). Recording circadian rhythms with a capacity-sensing device. *J. econ. Ent.*, **56** (1), 76–79.

343 BÜNNING, E. (1958). Über den Temperatureinfluss auf die endogene Tagesrhythmik, besonders bei *Periplaneta americana. Biol. Zbl.*, **77**, 141–152.

344 GUNN, D. L. (1940). The daily rhythm of activity of the cockroach, *Blatta orientalis. J. exp. Biol.*, **17**, 267–277.

345 SCHARRER, B. (1941). Neurosecretion. II. Neurosecretory cells in the central nervous system of cockroaches. *J. Comp. Neurol.*, **74**, 93–108.

346 HARKER, J. E. (1955). Control of diurnal rhythms of activity in *Periplaneta americana* L. *Nature Lond.*, **175** (4460), 733.

347 HOYLE, G. (1955). Functioning of the insect ocellar nerve. *J. exp. Biol.*, **32** (2), 397–407.

348 HARKER, J. E. (1960b). Internal factors controlling the sub-oesophageal ganglion secretory cycle in *P. americana* L. *J. exp. Biol.*, **37** (1), 164–170.

349 MALLIS, A., ESTERLINE, W. E. & MILLER, A. C. (1961). Keeping German cockroaches out of beer cases. *Pest Control*, **29** (6), 32–35.

350 LAIRD, M. (1956). Wartime collections of insects from aircraft at Whenuapai. *N.Z. J. Sci. Tech.*, **38** (2), 76–84.

351 PORTER, J. E. (1958). Further notes on public health service quarantine entomology. *Florida Ent.*, **41** (1), 41–44.

352 REAGAN, E. P. (1966). Preventive Pest Control measures in Scientific Aspects of Pest Control. *Nat. Acad. Sci.*, Publ. 1402, pp. 185–192.

353 PEMBERTON, C. E. (1944). *Entomology.* Hawaiian Sugar Planters' Assoc. pp. 17–21.

354 ZWALUWENBURG, R. H. VAN (1946). Recent immigrant insects. *Hawaii Plant Rec.*, **50** (1), 11–17.

355 WHITFIELD, F. G. S. (1939). Air transport, insects and disease. *Bull. ent. Res.*, **30** (3), 365–442.

356 LAIRD, M. (1952). Insects collected from aircraft arriving in New Zealand during 1951. *J. Aviation Med.*, **23** (3), 280–285.

357 LAIRD, M. (1951). Insects collected from aircraft arriving in New Zealand from aborad. *Vict. Univ. Coll. (N.Z.) Zool. Publ.*, **1** (11), 1–30.

358 SHELFORD, R. (1912). The oothecae of Blattidae. *Ent. Rec.*, **24** (1), 283, 287.

359 MOFFETT, T. (1634). *Insectorum sive minimorum animalium theatrum.* 326 pp. Thomas Cotes, Londini. (Trans.: 1658, The theater of insects: or, lesser living creatures. 889–1130 pp. London.)

360 BLIGH, W. (1792). *His narrative of the voyage of Otaheite; with an account of the mutiny and of his boat journey to Timor.* 283 pp. Cover title: Bligh and the Bounty. Unabridged 1963 ed. of Bligh's narrative first published in 1792, New York.

361 CHAMISSO, A. VON (1829). Ein Zweifel und zwei Algen. *Verhandl. Ges. Naturf. Freunde, Berl.*, **1**, 173–180.

362 LEWIS, R. H. (1836). Notes made during a voyage from England to Van Diemen's Land, with a sketch of the entomology of the Cape of Good Hope. *Trans. Ent. Soc. London*, **1**, pp. lxxix–lxxxi.

363 EVANS, B. R. & PORTER, J. E. (1965). The incidence, importance and control of insects found in stored food and food handling areas of ships. *J. econ Ent.*, **58** (3), 479–481.

364 HOWE, R. W. & FREEMAN, J. A. (1955). Insect infestation of West African produce imported into Britain. *Bull. ent. Res.*, **46** (3), 643–668.

365 MELLANBY, K. (1939). Low temperature and insect activity. *Proc. Roy. Soc.*, (B), **127**, 473–487.

366 KNIPLING, E. B. & SULLIVAN, W. N. (1957). Insect mortality at low temperatures., *J. econ. Ent.*, **50** (3), 368–369.

367 GARDNER, A. E. (1954). *Blatta orientalis* out-of-doors. *Entomologist*, **87** (1095), 167.

368 LUCAS, W. J. (1922). Notes on British Orthoptera in 1921. *Entomologist*, **55**, 200–203.

369 SOLOMON, M. E. & ADAMSON, B. E. (1955). The powers of survival of storage and domestic pests under winter conditions in Britain. *Bull. ent. Res.*, **46** (2), 311–355.

370 GUNN, D. L. & NOTLEY, F. B. (1936). The temperature and humidity relations of the cockroach. IV. Thermal death-point. *J. exp. Biol.*, **13** (1), 28–34.

371 MELLANBY, K. (1932). The influence of atmospheric humidity on the thermal death point of a number of insects. *J. exp. Biol.*, **9** (2), 222–231.

372 GUNN, D. L. (1934). The temperature and humidity relations of the cockroach (*Blatta orientalis*). II. Temperature preference. *Z. vergl. Physiol.*, **20**, 617–625.

373 GUNN, D. L. & COSWAY, C. A. (1938). The temperature and humidity relations of the cockroach. *J. exp. Biol.*, **15**, 555–563.

374 GUNN, D. L. (1935). The temperature and humidity relations of the cockroach. III. A comparison of temperature preference, rates of desiccation and respiration of *Periplaneta americana, Blatta orientalis* and *Blattella germanica. J. exp. Biol.* **12** (3), 185–190.

375 NECHELES, H. (1927). Observations on the causes of night activity in some insects. *Chinese Jnl. Physiol.*, **1** (2), 143–156.

376 PACKCHANIAN, A. (1954). Altitude tolerance of normal and infected insects. *J. econ. Ent.*, **47** (2), 230–237.

377 PACKCHANIAN, A. & PINKERTON, M. (1955). Further studies on the effects of simulated altitude on eight additional species of arthropods. *Texas Rep. Biol. Med.*, **13**, 865–881.

378 SULLIVAN, W. N., DU CHANOIS, F. R. & HAYDEN, D. L. (1958). Insect survival in jet aircraft. *J. econ. Ent.*, **51** (2), 239–241.

379 THORNTON, B. C. & SULLIVAN, W. N. (1964). Effects of high vacuum on insect mortality. *J. econ. Ent.*, **57** (6), 852–854.

380 STARKWEATHER, R. J. & SULLIVAN, W. N. (1964). Insect tolerance to increased atmospheric pressures. *J. econ. Ent.*, **57** (5), 766–768.

381 SULLIVAN, W. N. & WESTLAKE, G. E. (1959). The effects of multiple gravity on the life cycle of an insect. *J. econ. Ent.*, **52** (4), 559–561.

382 SULLIVAN, W. N., SCHECHTER, M. S., FULTON, R. A., KELLER, J. C. & DUTKY, S. R. (1961). The survival of the Madeira cockroach in various atmospheres. *J. econ. Ent.*, **54** (4), 661–663.

383 WILLIS, E. R. & LEWIS, N. (1957). The longevity of starved cockroaches. *J. econ. Ent.*, **50** (4), 438–440.

384 ROTH, L. M. & WILLIS, E. R. (1955b). Water relations of cockroach oothecae. *J. econ. Ent.*, **48** (1), 33–36.

385 ROTH, L. M. & WILLIS, E. R. (1955a). Relations of water loss to hatching of eggs from detached oothecae of *Blattella germanica*. *J. econ. Ent.*, **48** (1), 57–60.

386 ANTONELLI, G. (1930). La blatta nella igiene domestica. *Rev. Soc. Ital. Igiene, Milan*, **52**, 132–142.

387 BEI-BIENKO, G. IA. (1950). Fauna of the U.S.S.R. Insects. Blattodea. (In Russian.) *Inst. Zool. Acad. Sci. U.R.S.S. Moscow*, n.s. **40**, 343 pp. (Trans. by Ruth Ericson.)

388 TEJERA, E. (1926). Les blattes envisagée comme agentes de dissemination des germes pathogènes. *C.R. Soc. Biologie*, **95**, 1382–1384.

389 ANON. (1939). Cockroaches. Diseases to humans. *New Guinea Agric. Gaz.*, **5**, 43–44. (Reprinted from Straits Times. 27 Dec. 1938.)

390 BONNET, D. D. (1948). Certain aspects of medical entomology in Hawaii. *Proc. Hawaiian Ent. Soc.*, **13**, 225–233.

391 ZUBEN, F. J. VON (1955). Cockroaches in municipal sewers. *Pest Control*, **23** (5), 14–16.

392 ANON. (1957). Oriental roaches from sewers. *Pest Control*, **25** (2), 26, 46.

393 DOW, R. P. (1955). A note on domestic cockroaches in South Texas. *J. econ. Ent.*, **48** (1), 106–107.

394 BITTER, R. S. & WILLIAMS, O. B. (1949). Enteric organisms from the American cockroach. *J. Infect. Dis.*, **85**, 87–90.

395 ZMEEV, G. IA. (1940). Certain points in the epidemiology of dysentery and its endemic foci in Central Asia connected with the cockroach *Shelfordella tartara* Sauss. (In Russian.) Second Conference on parasitological problems, November 1940, Leningrad. p. 35 Izd. Akad. Nauk. USSR. Moscow. (From *Rev. Appl. Ent.* 1946, Ser. B. **34**, 110.)

396 ANTONELLI, G. (1943). La blatta—veicolo di malattie infettive nei rurali. *Mutual. Rurale Fasciata*, **7**, 206–220.

397 MACKERRAS I. M. & MACKERRAS, M. J. (1949). An epidemic of infantile gastroenteritis in Queensland caused by *Salmonella bovis-morbificans* (Basenau). *J. Hygiene*, **47**, 166–181.

398 BREED, R. S., MURRAY, E. G. D. & HITCHENS, A. P. (1948). *Bergey's Manual of Determinative Bacteriology*, VIth Edition. Pub. Williams & Wilkins Co., Baltimore 1948.

399 WEDBERG, S. E., BRANDT, C. D. & HELMBOLDT, C. F. (1949). The passage of micro-organisms through the digestive tract of *Blaberus craniifer* mounted under controlled conditions. *J. Bact.*, **58**, 573–578.

400 JANSSEN, W. A. & WEDBERG, S. E. (1952). The common house roach, *Blattella germanica* Linn., as a potential vector of *Salmonella typhimurium* and *Salmonella typhosa. Amer. J. Trop. Med. Hyg.*, **1**, 337–343.

401 CAO, G. (1906). Nuove osservazioni sul passaggio dei microorganismi a traverso l'intestino di alcuni insetti. *Ann. Igiene Speriment.*, **16**, 339–368.

402 HERMS, W. B. (1939). *Medical Entomology.* 3rd Ed. (reprinted 1946), 582 pp. New York.

403 JETTMAR, H. M. (1935). Küchenschaben als Krankheitsübertsubertäger. *Wiener Klin. Wochenschr.*, **48**, 700–704.

404 SPINELLI, A. & REITANO, U. (1932). Ricerche sulle blatte, quali agenti di diffusione dei germi del colera, della febbre tifoide e della dissenteria bacillare. *Ann, d' Igiene*, **42**, 745–755.

405 SARTORY, A & CLERC, A. (1908). Flore intestinale de quelques Orthopteres. *C.R. Soc. Biol. Paris*, **64**, 544–545.

406 NICEWICZ, N., NICEWICZ, W. & KOWALIK, R. (1946). Description of micro-organisms supported on the bacteriological analysis in the alimentary tracts of the bed bug, house fly, and cockroach. (In Polish.) *Ann. Univ. M. Curie-Sklodowsha, Lublin*, **1**, 35–38 (English summary).

407 STEINHAUS, E. A. (1941). A study of the bacteria associated with thirty species of insects. *J. Bact.*, **42**, 757–790.

408 GRAFFER, M. & MERTENS, S. (1950). Le rôle des blattes dans la transmission des salmonelloses. *Ann. Inst. Pasteur*, **79**, 654–660.

409 HUNTER, W. (1906). The spread of plague infection by insects. *Centralb. Bakteriol., Parasitenk. Infekt.*, **40**, 43–55.

410 MOISER, B. (1945). Modes of transmission of Hansen's disease (leprosy). *Leprosy Rev.*, **16**, 63–66.

411 MOISER, B. (1946). Leprosy: A new outlook. *E. African Med. J.*, **23**, 295–300.

412 MOISER, B. (1946a). Transmission of Hansen's disease (leprosy). *Acta Med. Scandinav.*, **126**, 347–350.

413 ARIZUMI, S. (1943). On the potential transmission of *B. leprae* by certain insects. *Internat. J. Leprosy*, **2**, 470–472.

414 ARIZUMI, S. (1943a). On the potential transmission of *Bacillus leprae* by certain insects. (In Japanese.) *J. Med. Assoc. Formosa*, **33**, 634–661. English summary. pp. 54–55.

415 SYVERTON, J. T., FISCHER, R. G., SMITH, S. A., DOW, R. P. & SCHOOF, H. F. (1952). The cockroach as a natural extrahuman source of poliomyelitis virus. *Fed. Proc.*, **11**, 483.

416 HSIANG, C. M., POLLARD, M. & MICKS, D. W. (1952). The possible role of the cockroach in the dissemination of Poliomyelitis virus. *Texas Reports on Biol. Med.*, **10** (2), 329–335.

417 MORREL, C. C. (1911). Bacteriology of the cockroach. *Brit. Med. J.*, **2**, 1531–1532.

418 LONGFELLOW, R. C. (1913). The common house roach as a carrier of disease. *Amer. J. Publ. Hlth.*, **3**, 58–61.

419 BARBER, M. A. (1912). The susceptibility of cockroaches to plague bacilli innoculated into the body cavity. *Philippine J. Sci.*, **7**, 521–524.

420 MACFIE, J. W. S. (1922). Observations on the role of cockroaches in disease. *Ann. Trop. Med. Parasit.*, **16**, 441–448.

421 OLSON, T. A. & RUEGER, M. E. (1950). Experimental transmission of *Salmonella oranienburg* through cockroaches. *Pub. Hlth. Rep.*, **65**, 531–540.

422 MACKERRAS, I. M. & POPE, P. (1948). Experimental *Salmonella* infections in Australian cockroaches. *Exp. J. Biol. Med. Sci. Aust.*, **26**, 465–470.

423 JUNG, R. C. & SHAFFER, M. F. (1952). Survival of ingested *Salmonella* in the cockroach, *Periplaneta americana*. *Amer. J. Trop. Med. Hyg.*, **1**, 990–998.

424 ENGELMANN, RUTH (1903). Cockroaches as conveyors of typhoid infection. *Medicine, Detroit*, **9**, 431–435.

425 AKKERMAN, KLASSJE (1933). Researches on the behaviour of some pathogenic organisms in the intestinal canal of *Periplaneta americana* with reference to the possible epidemiological importance of this insect. *Acta Leidensia*, **8**, 80–120.

426 MORISCHITA, K. & TSUCHIMOCHI, K. (1926). Experimental observations on the dissemination of diseases by cockroaches in Formosa. (In Japanese.) *Taiwan Igakkai Zasshi, J. Med. Assoc. Formosa*. No. 255, pp. 566–569. English summary, pp. 2–6.

427 MCBURNEY, R. & DAVIS, H. (1930). Common cockroach as a host-carrier of *Bacillus typhosus* (preliminary report). *Trans. Med. Assoc. Alabama*, **63**, 307–325.

428 BERNTON, H. S. & BROWN, H. (1964). Insect Allergy. Preliminary studies of the cockroach. *J. Allergy*, **35**, 506–513.

429 BERNTON, H. S. & BROWN, H. (1967). Cockroach allergy. II. The relation of infestation to sensitisation. *S. Med. J.*, **60** (8), 852–855.

430 PATTON, W. S. (1931). *Insects, Ticks, Mites and Venomous Animals of Medical and Veterinary Importance*. H. R. Grubb Limited, Croydon. 740 pp.

431 MASTERS, C. (1960). Diseases carried by food service cockroaches. *Pest Control*, **28** (6), 22, 24.

432 WRIGHT, C. G. (1965a). Cockroach species in apartment projects in N. Carolina. *Pest Control*, **33** (6), 14–15.

433 WRIGHT, C. G. (1965b). Identification and occurrence of cockroaches in dwellings and business establishments in N. Carolina. *J. econ. Ent.*, **58** (5), 1032–1033.

434 GREEN, A. A. (1962). The trouble with cockroaches. *New Scientist*, **16** (308), 74–76.

435 DELONG, D. M. (1962). Beer cases and soft drink cartons as insect distributors. *Pest Control*, **30** (7), 14, 16, 18.

SUBJECT INDEX

(Figures in italics indicate pages on which illustrations, diagrams or graphs appear.)

Abdomen, 20–21
    modification of terminal segments, 184
abdominal segments,
    development, 227, *228*
    sagittal sections, *188*
    terminal, *98*, 184, *185*
absorptive cells, 124
accessory glands (mushroom gland),
    see also colleterial glands, 193, 194
    secretion and corpus allatum, 167
    storage excretion and, 158–159
acclimatisation, 280
acetylcholine, 168
Acheta domesticus, 34
acini, 121
Acrididae, 158
adults, identification key to, 96
aerogenoides, see *Paracolobactrum.*
air movement,
    effects of, 290
air travel, insect pests and, 269
aircraft
    cockroaches in, 270, 271, 272
    cockroaches taken from, in New
        Zealand, 272–3
    insects carried in, 270–271
    tests in jet, 292
alatarum, see *Blattarum.*
alimentary canal, 116–133, *118*
    speed of movement of food through,
        127, *128*
alkalescens, see *Shigella.*
allergy to cockroaches, 312-313
alveolar glands, 107
American Cockroach, see *Periplaneta
    americana.*
americana, see *Periplaneta.*
amino acids,
    effect of deficiency in diet, 239
amoebic dysentry, 309
amphibia, 243
Ampulex compressa, 245–246
amylase, 121, 122, 128
    relative activity of, 130
Anagasta kühniella, 258
Anaplecta sp., 275
Anaplectinae, 37
anatis, see *Salmonella.*
anatomy, lack of specialisation and, 16

Ancylostoma
    ceylanicum (Dog Hookworm), 310
    duodenale (Human Hookworm), 310
Anopheles mosquitoes, 272
antennae, 19
    chemo-reception and, 114
    courtship and, 179, 183
    growth of, 226
    regeneration of, 234, 235
ants, 12
Aphthoroblattina johnsoni, 21, 27
apodemes, 102
appendages,
    loss of, 139, 233–234
    regeneration of, 234–236
appendigaster, see *Evania.*
armarium, 124
arolium, 52, 251
Ascaris lumbricoides, 310
ascorbic acid, see vitamins.
aspartic acid, 240
atmospheric pressure, 293
atropos, see *Blaberus.*
Atta spp. (leafcutting ants), 94
    inquiline cockroaches and, 242
Attaphila fungicola,
    appearance, 94–95
    association with ants, 90, 93, 94, 242
auditory perception, 114–115
aureomycin, 240
aureus, see *Staphylococcus.*
australasiae, see *Periplaneta.*
Australian Cockroach, see *Periplaneta
    australasiae*

Bacteria, 243, 303
    cellulose digesting, 31
    disease outbreaks and isolation of,
        305–309
    pathogenic examples, 306–308
    persistance in excrement, 312
bacteroids, 155
    appearance of, 200–201
    entry into oocytes, 201–202
    fate of, 221–222
    ovaries and, 200
Bananas, cockroach introduction and,
    269, 344
Barbulanympha sp., 131, *131*

367

bats, 12, 51
bed bug, 11
biological clock, see also circadian
    rhythm, 258
birds, 243
bivitatta, Ischnoptera (=*Phyllodromia*),
    see *Blattella germanica*.
Blaberidae, 37
    abdominal segments, terminal, *188*
    brood sac, 187
    intersternal folds, 189
    ovipositor valves, 187, 188, 189
Blaberoidea, 35, 37
    phallomeres of, 185
Blaberus, 15, 74, 83–85
    appearance, 84
    atropos, 83
    biology, 84–85
    boliviensis, 83
    cellulase and, 132, 133
    craniifer (Giant Death's-head Cock-
        roach),
        bacteria and, 306
        biology, 84
        brain, anatomy of, 163
        cellulase content of intestinal
            tract, 132
        common name, 15
        distribution, 83
        enzyme system, 129
        habitat, 83
        life span, 84
        mating, 191
        moulting, 84
        nymphs, 84
        ootheca, 84
        pest status, 83
        Salmonella typhosa and, 312
        size, comparative, 61
        spermatophore, 196
        stomatogastric system, 165
    description of species, 83–85
    discoidalis, 83
        appearance, 84
        cellulase and, 132,
        distribution, 83
        enzymes and, 129
        habitat, 83
    false ovoviviparity and, 216
    giganteus
        adult, *84*
        biology, 83, 85
        cellulase and, 132
        moulting, 85
        nymphal development, 85
        stomatogastric system, 164
    habitat, normal, 74
    identification key, 96
    nymphs, 84–85
    ootheca, 84
'black beetle', see *Blatta orientalis*.
'black clock', see *Blatta orientalis*.

Blatta, 5, 32
    americana, see *Periplaneta*.
    australasiae, see *Periplaneta*.
    cinerea, see *Nauphoeta*.
    cubensis, see *Supella supellectilium*.
    germanica, see *Blattella*.
    kakerlac, see *Periplaneta americana*.
    orientalis (Oriental Cockroach, Black
        Beetle),
        abdominal segments, terminal, *185*
        abdominal sternites, terminal, *228*
        adult, *50, 51*
            life span, 52
        antennae, growth of, 227, *227*
        appearance, *20*, 52
        arolium, effect of lack of, 251
        auditory perception, 115
        bacteria and, 305, 306, 307, 308
        bacteroids and oocyte destruction,
            202
        biology, 52, 53
        Britain, in, 316, 318
        buildings,
            age of, and, 326
            favoured by, 326
            locations in, 331, 334, 335
        Carolina, in, 316
        central heating and, 330
        cerci, *115*, 226
        circadian rhythm and continuous
            light, 263–264
        cities and large towns and, 338,
            342, 343
        classification (of cockroaches), 31–37
        climbing ability, 251
        co-existence with man, 13
        cold-hardiness, 282
        colleterial glands and formation
            of oothecae, 211
        common names, 14, 15
        crop, cuticular lining of, 127
        dermal glands, 109
        description, 49–53
        desiccation, 288
            temperature range and, 283
        development period, 52
        development, seasonal variation in,
            242
        diploid number, 147
        distribution, 49
            British Isles, in, *317*
        early spread of, *43*
        eggs,
            incubation period of, 52
            unfertilised, hatching of, 214
            water content of, 221
        ejaculatory duct, 193–194
        environmental factors and, 290, 316
        enzymes in, 129
        fat body, lobe of, *156*
        females, unfertilised, 52
        flight and, 52, 251

Blatta orientalis—cont.
  food, 116
  genitalia, male,
    external, 184
    internal, 193, *193*
  geographical areas and infestations,
    336
  gut, *122*
  habitat, 49–52, 63
  haemocyte count, 139
  haemolymph, mitotically dividing
    cells in, 140
  hair sensillae, *115*
  heart of, 135
    rate of beating, 142
  hospitals and, 305
  humidity and, 288
  hypodermis, 108
  identification key, 96
  incidence, 337
    survey, in, 325, *328*, *329*, *332–333*,
      334–335, *342*
    toilets, in, 334
  infestation rates, *341*
  infestations, *340*
    central heating and, 330–331
    locations, *335*
    within buildings, 331–336
  infested premises, 339
  introduction,
    into the U.K., 268–269
    with coke, 268
  longevity on starvation diets, *295*
  malpighian tubules, 126
    contractions of and temperature,
      125
  mating, 190
  migration, 252–253
  moulting, 139
  movement of, 48–49, 254
  mushroom mite and, 247
  names in other countries, 14–15
  nymph, final moult, *229*
  nymphal development, 52
  nymphal growth, 225
  occurrence,
    frequency of on ships, 275, 277
    outdoors, 50
  ootheca, 38, 52, *100*, 198
    adult with, *51*
    carried by transport, 267
    deposition of, 217–218, 296
    formation of, *212*
    identification key, 99
    incubation period of, 52, 222
    production of, 213
    structure of, 218
    water content of, 221, 296–297
  origin of, 41, *43*, 49
  oviparity and, 214
  oxygen consumption, *149*
  oxygen requirements, 149–150

  parasitic wasps and, 243–264
  pest status, 50, 51
  phallic gland, 193, 194
  phallomeres, 185
  Pimeliaphilus cunliffei and, 247
  population density effects, *236*
  population size, effects of, 236–237
  'pronymph', 52
  protein requirements, 237–239
  proventriculus, *122*
    musculature of, 124
  pygidial glands, 110
  ratio of infestation, 337, *340*
  respiration, 149–150
    temperature and, 282
  Salmonella, and, 305
    typhosa and, 312
  season, influence of, 242
  seminal vesicles, 193
  sewers and, 303, 304
  sexes, differences between, 52
  size, comparative, *61*
  spermatophore, 194, 196
  starvation, water and, 295, *295*
  sternites, growth of terminal
    abdominal in female, 227
  summer diarrhoea and, 309
  survey in the U.K., 318–346
  survival below zero temperature,
    281
  survival outdoors and, 282
  temperature,
    high, effects of, 282–283
    low, effects of, 279–280
      recovery from, 280–281
    preferendum, 285, *285*, *286*
  tergal secretions, 110
  testes, 193
  typhoid and, 303
  vasa deferentia, 193
  vector capabilities, 311
  water loss and respiration rate, 289
  water loss and temperature, *283*, 284
  wax layer, 107
  wings, *22*
    growth of, 227
  pensylvanica, see *Parcoblatta*.
  surinamensis, see *Pycnoscelus*.
  wings, *22*
blattae, see *Syntomosphyrum*.
Blattaria, 33, 34, 35
  brief description of, 35
  classification of, *36*
  energy consumption, 150
  evolutionary development, *37*
  excretory system, 153
  Isoptera, relationship with, 131
  proventriculus of, 124
  subdivisions of, 35
Blattarum alatarum, 274
Blattella (=*Blatta*, =*Ectobius*, =*Phyllodromia*, =*Ischnoptera*),

Blattella—cont.
  choline, need for, 240
  endophallus, 194
  ootheca, retention of, 38
  sterols and, 240
  germanica (=*obliquata*, =*bivittata*.
      German Cockroach, Steam-fly).
    abdomen, *46*
    abdominal segments, terminal, *188*
    adult, *44*, *45*
    aircraft, records in, 271, 272
    alimentary canal, 117
      speed of movement of food through,
        127, *128*
    allergy and, 312–313
    amino acid deficiency effect, 239
    antennae and courtship, 179, 183
    appearance, 45
    bacteria and, 305, 306, 307, 308
    biology, 46–48
    blood, 137
    Britain, in, 315–318
    buildings,
      age of, and, 326–327
      favoured by, 326
      locations in, 331–336
    carbamate insecticides and, 299
    Carolina, in, 315
    central heating and, 330–331
    chemo-receptors, 114
    circadian rhythm, measurement of,
        261
    cities and large towns and, 339–343
    classification, 36, 37
    common names, 15
    comparison with *B. vaga*, 48, 88, 89
    copulation, use of genitalia in, 189
    copulatory behaviour, 189
    corpora allata and, 205
    courtship, *182*
    description, 42–48
    desiccation, 288
    development period, 47–48
    diet, effects of, 237
    diploid number, 197
    distribution, 42–43
      British Isles, in, *317*
    disturbance at night, 260
    early spread of, *43*
    eggs,
      desiccation of, 198
      unfertilised, development of, 214
      water content, 221
    embryological development, 221
    endophallus, 194
    environmental factors and, 290, 318
    enzymes in, 129
    flight and running, 48, 251
    food poisoning organisms, 311
    genitalia,
      male external, 185, *186*, 187
      male internal, *187*

  geographical areas and infestations,
      336
  growth curves, *233*
  habitat, 43, 44
  harbourages, 250–251, 278
  historical, 12–14
  hospitals and, 304–305
  identification key, 96
  incidence in
    ships, 273, 274, 275
    survey, 325, *328*, *329*, *332–333*,
        336, *342*
    toilets, 334
  infestation rates, *341*
  infestations, *340*
    central heating and, 330–331
    establishment of new, 277–279
    locations of, 331–335, *335*
  infested premises, *338*
  insecticides, resistance to, 304, 374
  insemination, 195–197
  introduction into the U.K., 268
  invertase and, 129
  jet aircraft and, 292
  longevity on starvation diets, *295*
  mating, *182*, 189
    secretion of uric acid and, 158
  migration, 252
  moults,
    loss of appendages and, 234
    number of, 231
    sclerotised parts and, *235*
  movement, involuntary, 267
  nymphs,
    growth of, *230*
    weight of, *241*
  oocyte,
    development and food, 200, 210
    growth, *204*
  ootheca, 46, 47, 48, *100*, 148
    adult with, *45*
    formation of, *204*
    hatching from, 223, *225*, 296
    hormone inhibition and, 204
    incubation period of, 47, 222
    indentification key, 99
    keel of, 218, *219*
    number of eggs per, 47
    premature detachtment, 298
    structure, 218
    two, end-to-end, 215
    water content, 221, 298
    weight loss, *299*
  origin of, 42, *43*
  oviparity and, 215
  ovipositional behaviour, 216
  oxygen requirements, 150
  pest status, 43–44
  Pimeliaphilus cunliffei and, 247
  poliomyelitis virus and, 309
  population size, effects of, 237
  protein requirements, 239

Blattella germanica—cont.
pygidial glands, 110, *110*
ratio of infestation, 337, *340*
regeneration of appendages, 234
Rhipidius spp. and, 270
Salmonella and, 305
typhosa and, 312
season, influence of, 242
seminal vesicles, 194
sex attractants, 179, 180, 181, 183, 184
sexes, differences between, 45
sexual behaviour, 181–184
ships and, 268, 269, 273, 274, 275, 276, 277
size,
increase, 232
comparative, *61*
spermathecal glands, 196
spermatogenesis, 194
spermatophore, 194, *195*, 196
starvation, water and, 294
survey in the U.K., 318–346
synonymy, 15
temperature,
high, effects of, 283–284
preferendum, 286, 291
testes, 193
uric acid and accessory glands, 158
utriculi,
breviores, 193
majores, 194
vasa deferentia, 193
vector capabilities, 311
vitamin requirements, 240
water and, 107, 294
water loss and,
respiration rate, 289
temperature, 107, *284*
wax secretory glands, 108, *109*
weight, increase in, 231, 232
vaga (Field Cockroach)
adult, *89*
appearance, 88
biology, 48, 89
comparison with *B. germanica*, 88
description, 88–89
distribution, 41, 88
eggs, 89
unfertilised, development of, 214
water content of, 47
habitat, 88
indentification key, 96
longevity on starvation diets, *295*
nymphs, 89
oocyte development and food, 210
ootheca, 89
adult with, *89*
number of eggs per, *47*
origin of, 88
oviparity and, 215
starvation and, 294

uric acid and accessory glands, 158
water content, 300
changes in, *297*
weight loss, age and, *300*
Blattellidae, 37
abdominal segments, terminal, *188*
male, external genitalia, 186
Blattellinae, 37
Blattidae, 28, 32, 35, 52
Blattoidea, 37
phallomeres, 185
blood, see also haemolymph,
cell count, 139
circulation,
HCN and, *142*
presystolic notch, 142
regulation by neuro-hormones, 142
speed of, 140–142
dorsal vessel, 135–136
volume, 138
changes in, 138
boliviensis, see *Blaberus.*
bolliana, see *Parcoblatta.*
'Bombay Canary', 15
booklice, 33
brain, 162-163, *163*
anatomy, of 162-163
nerve activity and, 173
neuro-endocrine functions, 163
segmentation of, 163
bredeney, see *Salmonella.*
Britain, changes in post-war, 316–318
'Brotaetare', 15
Brown Cockroach, see *Periplaneta brunnea.*
Brown-banded Cockroach, see *Supella supellectilium.*
brunnea, see *Periplaneta.*
buccal cavity, 120
bursicon, 145
activity after ecdysis, 147
concentration, *147*
level in blood, 146
tanning and, 147
Byrsotria fumigata (Cuban Burrowing Cockroach)
cellulase and, 132, 133
circadian rhythm and total darkness, 264
corpus allatum and, 167
false ovoviviparity and, 216
hind gut, 127
sex attractant, 180

caementarium, see *Sceliphron.*
canae, see *Methana.*
cannabalism, 139
Carausius morosus, 34
Carboniferous,
fossil records, 38
period, 19, 25
rocks, 22, 26, 27

cardiac cycle, *136*
cardina, see *Podium*.
cargoes infested, *276*
Carolina,
  cockroaches in three cities in, 316
caudal (proctodeal) system, 164
caves, species in, 83
cellulase content of intestinal tract, 132
cellulase, protozoan symbionts and, 31,
  130–133, *131*
centipedes, 243
central heating, effects of, 316, 318,
  324–325 330–331, 345
cerci, *115*
  auditory perception and, 115
  growth of, 226–227, *228*
  neuronal pathways and, 168
  shape of, 65, *115*
ceylanicum, see *Ancylostoma*.
characteristics of present-day cockroaches, 19–20
chemo-receptors, 114
  sex attractants and, 178–179
chill coma,
  recovery from, 280–281
  temperature, 280
chitin, 64
choline, 240
chorion, 200
chromosome numbers, 197
cibarium, 121
cinerea, see *Nauphoeta*.
Cinerous Cockroach, see *Nauphoeta
  cinerea*.
circadian rhythm, 111, 258
  changes in light and darkness, 263–264
  endocrine secretion and, 266
  influence of temerature and food,
    262–263
  measurement of, 261
  neurosecretory cycle and, 266
  suboesophageal ganglion and, 167
circulatory system, 134–137
circum-oesophageal commissures, 162
city and large town infestations, 340–343
classification, 31–37
climate, influence of, 41
climbing ability, 251
clypeus, 118
coagulocyte, see cystocyte.
cockroach control, 12, 347
  night inspection, 260–261
  pyrethrum sprays and, 260
cockroach mite, see *Pimeliaphilus
  cunliffei*.
cockroach odour, 247
cockroaches,
  anatomy, general, *20*
  associated with man, 40, 41
  attacking man, 13
  captivity, in, 16
  co-existence with man, 13

eaten by vertebrates, 246
fossil, *21*
historical, 12–14
hygiene and, 11, 13, 14
laboratory insects, 16
orthopteran-type insects, relationship
  with, 33–37
pest status, 11, 12
publications and, *17, 18*
scientific interest in, 16
sewers, latrines, cesspools, in, 303-304
space, in, 261, 292–294
coguereliana, see *Gromphadorina*.
cold death point, 281–282
Coleoptera, 32
coli, see *Escherichia*.
coliforme, see *Paracolobactrum*.
colleterial glands, 199
  formation of oothecae and, 211–212
  inhibition of secretory activity, 204
colonic sphincter, 131
colour, as a diagnostic feature, 42
comma, see *Vibrio*.
commissurus corporis allati, 166
commissurus corporis cardiaci, 166
common ancestry with termites, 29–31
common names, local names, and, 13–15
compressa, see *Ampulex*.
contact receptors, 111–113
copulation,
  genitalia, use of in, 189–190
  period of, 190
copulatory behaviour, 189–192
corpora allata,
  fat body and, 156
  food and oocyte development, 209–211
  functions of, 167
  growth, moulting and, 227, 228
  heart rate and, 144
  inhibition by brain, 206
  inhibition of, 208
  mating and, 192
  oocyte development and, 202–203, 210
  oocyte maturation and, 202–203
  oxygen consumption relationship, *152*
  removal and implantation effects,
    205–206
  reproductive behaviour and, 181
  respiratory effects of, 151–152
  sex attractants and, 180
  stomatogastric system and, 167
corpora cardiaca, 143
  extract of and heart beat, 143
  fat body and, 156
  function of, 167
  mating and, 192
  nerve activity and, 173
  stimulation of, 143–144
  stomatogastric system and, 167
courtship, *182, 183*
coxa, 252
craniifer, see *Blaberus*

crescentic sclerite, 186, 190
  use in copulation, 189
crickets, 19, 24, 32, 33
crop, 121, 123
cross fertilisation, 197
'Croton bug', see *Blattella germanica*.
cryptic habits, 22, 247
Cryptocercidae, 35, 36
Cryptocercus punctulatus, 35
  adult, *94*
  appearance, 93
  bacteroids and oocyte destruction,
    202
  biology, 93–94
  colon of, 131
  description, 93–94
  digestion of cellulose, 31, 94
  distribution, 93
  egg mass, *29*
  nymphs, 93–94
  ovulation, 199
  protozoan symbionts, 31, 93–94,
    130–132
  size, comparative, *61*
Cuban Borrowing Cockroach, see
  Byrsotria fumigata.
Cucaracha, 14
cunliffei (=*podapolipophagus*), see
  Pimeliaphilus.
Cursoria, 32
curvigera, see *Methana*.
cuticle (exoskeleton), 101–111, *102*
  alkali soluble constituents, 105
  cement layer, 109–110
  chemical composition, 104
  deposition of waste products in, 159
  excretory system and, 153
  glands,
    dermal, 107–108
    pygidial, 110–111
    unicellular, 102
  hypodermis, 107–109
  insecticide formulation and, 104
  laminae, 102
  lipid content, 107
  penetration of, 104
  pore canals, 102–104
  rate of growth and, 101
  section of, *102*, *103*
  structure of, 101–111
  tanning of, 145, 146, 147
  tergal secretions, 110–111
  thickness, 104–105
  water content, 104–105
  water soluble constituents, 105
  wax, chemical composition, 107
  wax content, function of, 105–106
  wax layer, 105–107
  wax secretion, 107–109
Cypress Cockroach see *Diploptera
  punctata*.
cystine, 240

cystocyte (coagulocyte), 140
cytoplasmic membrane, 108

Daily rhythm (see also circadian
  rhythm), 258–259
'Däne', 15
darkness, effects of changes in, 263–264
darwiniensis, see *Mastotermes*.
DDT, 174
defence sprays, 247–248
Dermaptera, 32
dermestid beetles, 246
desiccation, *287*
  different species and, 288–289
  eggs and, 38
deutocerebrum, 163
development, seasonal variation in,
  242
Dictuoptera, 32
Dictyoptera, 32, 33, 34, *34*
Dieldrin, effect on excretion, 153
diet,
  amino acid deficiency effects, 239–240
  effects of, 238–239
  materials used as, 237
  moulting and, 234
  protein requirements, 237–240
  vitamins, 240
digestion, 123
dihydroxyphenyl acetic acid, 230
Diploptera punctata (Cypress
    Cockroach),
  corpora allata and mating, 208
  defence spray, 248
  eggs, water content of, 221
  false viviparity, 216
  longevity on starvation diets, *295*
  oocyte development and food, 210
  ootheca, 213
  pygidial glands, 110
  wings, *22*
Diptera, 114
discoidalis, see *Blaberus*.
disease, 302–314
  experimental transmission of, 310
  gastroenteritis and food poisoning,
    310–311
  outbreaks and associated bacteria,
    305, 309
  transmission by cockroaches, 313–314
  typhoid, 311–312
distribution of cockroaches, see under
    individual species.
  geographical, in Britain, 320
disturbance sound, 248
Dorylaea rhombifolia, see *Neostylopyga*.
douvillei, see *Palaeoblatta*.
ductule-containing cells, 221
duodenale, see *Ancylostoma*.
Dusky Cockroach, see *Ectobius
    lapponicus*.
Dyar's Law, 231

Earwigs, 32
ecdysis, see moulting.
ecdyson, 145
　growth and moulting, 227
edible frog, 246
Ectobiinae, 37, 90, 92
Ectobius,
　germanicus, see *Blattella germanica.*
　lapponicus (Dusky Cockroach),
　　description, 90, 91
　　distribution in England and Wales,
　　　90
　　early records on ships, 274
　　oviparity and, 215
　livens, see *pallidus.*
　lividus, see *pallidus.*
　pallidus (=*livens*, =*lividus*. Tawny
　　Cockroach),
　　description, 90, 91
　　distribution in England and Wales,
　　　90
　　oviparity and, 215
　　wings, *91*
　panzeri (Lesser Cockroach),
　　description, 90, 91
　　distribution in England and Wales,
　　　90
　　oviparity and, 215
ectodermal invaginations, 101
ecuadorana, see *Nahublattella.*
egg(s), 28, 29
　case, see ootheca.
　chamber, 200
　deposition of, 28, 31, 38
　desiccation of, 28, 38, 198
　development of, 220, 221
　evolution towards internal incubation,
　　38–39
　internal incubation, 38
　parasites of, 243–246
　parasitism, and, 59
　sac, desiccation of, 38
　unfertilised, hatching of, 214
　water content, 221
ejaculatory duct, 193, 194
ejaculatory pouch, 194
electrophysical activity, monitoring
　apparatus, 261
embryo respiration, 218
embryological development, 220, 221
endocrine control and pericardial cells,
　143
endocrine glands, fat body and, 156–157
endocrine secretion, circadian rhythm
　and, 266
endocuticle, 101, 102
endophallus, 194
Endrin, effect on secretion, 154
Entamoeba histolytica, 310
enteric caeca, 125, 128, 132
enteric fever, 309
enteritidis, see *Salmonella.*

environment,
　air travel, 291–292
　physical factors influencing, 279
　preferred, 250
environmental factors, 290–291
enzyme(s)
　activity, sites and levels of, 129–130
　activity in gut, 208–209
　digestion and, 128–129
　oocyte maturation and, 208–209
　proteolytic, 129
　range of activity, 129
　secretion of, 128
　types in gut, 128
epicuticle, 101, 102
　waste products and, 159
Epilamprinae, 36
epiproct, 184
epithelial cells, 125
epithelial plug, 199
Escherichia coli, 306, 310
Eulophidae, 243
Eurycotis, 15
　floridana, 85
　　adult, *85*
　　appearance, 86
　　biology, 86
　　defence spray, 247
　　distribution, 85
　　eggs, 86
　　　unfertilised, development of, 214
　　flight, loss of, 251
　　habitat, 85
　　identification key, 97
　　longevity on starvation diets, *295*
　　mating, 191
　　moulting, 86
　　nymphal development, 86
　　odour, 86
　　ootheca, 86
　　　adult with, *85*
　　oviparity and, 215
　　parthenogenesis, 86
　　size, comparative, *61*
　　wings, *22*
Evania appendigaster, 243, *244*
Evaniidae, 243
evolutionary development, *37*
evolutionary link with termites, 28
Eye worm of poultry, see *Oxyspirura
　mansoni.*
eyes, 19–20
excretion,
　efficiency of, 153
　haemolymph and, 152
　storage, 154–156, 158–159
　temperature and rate of, *154*
excretory system, 151–159
　cuticle and storage, 159
　fat body and storage, 154–156
　male accessory glands and storage, 158
　malpighian tubules, 153–154

exocuticle, 101, 102
  waste products and, 159
exoskeleton, see cuticle.

False ovoviviparity, 38, 95, 214, 216
  types of, 216
false viviparity, 214, 216
fat body, *155*
  endocrine control of, 156–158
  enzyme systems in, 155
  excretion and, 153, 156
  intracellular bacteria and, 156
  lobe of, *156*
feeding, heart rate and, 143–145
femur, 252
fertilisation, 214
fervens, see *Atta*.
Field Cockroach, see *Blattella vaga*.
flagellates, see protozoa.
flavipenne, see *Podium*.
fleas, 11
flight,
  gliding, 251
  running and, 251
floridana, see *Eurycotis*.
follicular cells, 200
  bacteroids and, 202
follicular epithelium, 200, 202
  bacteroids and, 202
food, 115, 133
  absence of, 294–295
  oocyte maturation and, 209–211
  receptivity of female and, 192
food poisoning organisms, 310–311
Forficula, 32
fossil,
  cockroaches, *21*, 21–28
  records, 19, *27*
  remains, 19
'Franzose', 14
French Cockroach, see *Blatta
    orientalis*.
frogs, 246
fuliginosa, see *Periplaneta*.
fumigata, see *Byrsotria*.
fungicola, see *Attaphila*.

Galea, 119
ganglia, 162–163, 164
  abdominal, 164, 168
    nerves from, 164
  thoracic, 164, 170
    nerves from, 164
  frontal, 165
  hypocerebral, 165, 166
  ingluvial, 165
  prothoracic, 164
  reflex transmission within, 170
  segmental, 162
  suboesophageal, 162, 164, 165, 166,
    167, 168, 170
    regulating function, 167

  spontaneous nerve activity, 173
  terminal, *175*
gaseous environment, 294
gastroenteritis, 310–311
gastrula, 117
genital chamber, 39, 187
genital pouch, 24, 37, 38, 184, 187, 198
genitalia,
  external,
    female, 24, 37, 186–189, *190*
    male, 184–186, *186*, *187*, 190
  internal,
    female, *188*, 199
    male, *187*, *193*, 193–194
geographical areas,
  infestations of *B. germanica* and *B.
    orientalis* in, 336
geographical distribution in Britain, 320
geographical variation in incidence,
    336–340
geological range, 27
geological systems, 26
germ cells, chromosomes in, 197
German Cockroach, see *Blattella
    germanica*.
germanica, see *Blattella*.
germanicus, *Ectobius*, see *Blattella
    germanica*.
germarium, 199
  bacteroids and, 202
Giant Death's-head Cockroach, see
    Blaberus craniifer.
giganteus, see *Blaberus*.
gizzard, see proventriculus.
glial cells, 175, 176
glial lacunae, 175
glossa, 120
glutamic acid, 240
glycogen, 176
gonadrotrophic hormone, 167, 202
  inhibition of release of, 205
  moulting and oocyte maturation, 203
gonads,
  bacteroids and, 201
  reproductive behaviour and, 181
grasshoppers, 19, 24, 32
Gromphadorhina,
  coguereliana, 95
  laevigata, 95
    eggs, 95
    false ovoviviparity, 216
    ootheca, 95
    mating, 191
  portentosa, 95
    adult, *94*
growth, moulting and, 227–237
growth curves, *233*
Gryllidae, 158
Grylloblatta, *34*
Grylloblattodea, 33, *34*
Gryllotalpidae, 33
gustatory receptors, 114

gut,
 feeding behaviour and, 133
 fore, 117, 121–124, *122*
 parts of, 121
 hind, 117, 126–127
 parts of, 126
 mid, 117, 124–125, *122*
 epithelial lining, 124, 125
 nervous supply to, 117
 speed of movement of food through,
 127–128
 tracheal supply to, 117

Haemocoele, 117, 135
 haemolymph flow in, *135*
 respiratory system and, 147
haemocyte(s), 137, 138
 count, 139
 division of and haemolymph
 coagulation, 139–140
 injury and, 140
 types of, 138
haemolymph, 125, 134, 135, 136,
 137–138
 coagulability, 139–140
 coagulation and division of
 haemocytes, 140
 direction of movement, 135, *135*
 flow in wings and tegmen, *137*
 mitotically dividing cells in, *140*
 nervous system and, 174
 osmotic pressure and, 147
 plasma of, 137
 speed of circulation, 140–142, *141*
 transport of materials, 159
 volume and water content, 138, 139
hagenowi, see *Tetrastichus.*
harbourages, 250–251, 278
harpyoides, see *Hyptia.*
head, 19–20, 26, 119
heart, *118*, 134
 pulsation of, 136, *136*
heart beat
 control and cardio-accelerators, 145
 control and compensating mechanisms, 145
 corpora cardiaca extract and, 143
 HCN and, *142*
 homogenate of pericardial cells and,
 144
 rate, feeding and, 143
 stimulatory substance, 143
hedgehog, 246
helminths, 243
Hemimetabola (Exopterygota), 220
Hemiptera, 32, 114
Henschoutedenia spp., 269
Heptachlor, effect on excretion, 154
historical, 12–14
Holometabola (Endopterygota), 220
homes, accidental invaders of, 85–89
hookworms, see *Ancylostoma.*

hormones, 17
 distribution of cardio-accelerators,
 144
 homogenates, effect on heart beat, 114
 respiratory effects of, 151–152
hospital infestations, 304, 305
house fly, see *Musca domestica.*
humidity, response to, 287–288
Hymenoptera, 114
 inquiline cockroaches and, 242–243
 parasitic, 243–246
hypodermal cells, 101
hypodermis, 101, 107, 117
 wax secretion and, 107–109
hypopharynx, 114, 117, *120*
Hyptia,
 harpyoides, 243, *245*
 thoracica, 243
histolytica, see *Entamoeba*

Identification key
 adults, 96
 oothecae, 99
infestation(s),
 B. germanica/B. orientalis ratios, *338,*
 339, 340
 central heating and, 330–331
 establishment of new, 277–279
 locations within buildings, 331–335
 property age and, 326
 property types and, 326
 tracing origins of, 267–268
ignota, see *Periplaneta.*
ileum, 126
inquiline cockroaches, 242–243
insect control,
 sex attractants and, 178–179
 synthetic compounds and, 13
insecticide research, 17–18
insecticide resistance, 347
insecticides, 14, 104, 173–174, 374
 behaviour on heart, 141
 carbamate, 299
 DDT, 174
 Dieldrin, 154
 excretion and, 153
 resistance to, 292, 304
insemination, 195–197
intercalary ducts, 121
interference factor, 237
intermediary metabolism, 154
international dissemination, 268–269
intestinal round worms, 310
introduction in laundry baskets, 268
introduction with coke, 268
invertase, 128, 129, 130
 relative activity of, *130*
involuntary movement, 267, 268
irrorata, see *Panchlora.*
Ischnoptera bivittata, see *Blattella
 germanica.*
Isodrin, effects on excretion, 154

javanica, see *Panesthia*.
juvenile hormone, 227

kakerlac, Blatta, see *Periplaneta americana*.
'Kakkerlak', 15

Labial palps, 114
labium, 114, 117, *120*
labrum, 117, *120*
lacinia, 119
lactase, 128
    relative activity of, *130*
laevigata, see *Gromphadorina*.
lapponicus, see *Ectobius*.
lativalvis, see *Tachysphex*.
leaf insects, 32, 33
leaf-cutting ants, see *Atta* spp.
legs, 20
    articulation of, 252
    regeneration of, 234–236
    structure, *252*
Lepidoptera, 114, 179
leprae, see *Mycobacterium*.
Lesser Cockroach, see *Ectobius panzeri*.
Leucophaea maderae (Madeira Cockroach), 41
    abdominal segments, terminal, *188*
    adult, *79*
    appearance, 78
    atmospheric pressure, *293*
    biology, 79
    cellulase, and, 132, 133
    circadian rhythm and, 261, 264
    corpora allata and, 166–167
        moulting and, 227, 228
        oxygen consumption and, *152*
        stimulation of, 208
    description, 76–79
    distribution, 76–77
    early spread of, *77*
    enzymes and, 129
    Escherichia coli and, 310
    false ovoviviparity, 216
    flight, 78
    food, 78
    gaseous environment and, 294
    gonadotrophic hormone, inhibition of, 206
    habitat, 78
    identification key, 97
    introduction into U.S., 268
    locomotor activity, *262*
    mating, 79, 191, 192
    moulting, 79
    nervi corporis allati, 166
    nymphs, 78
    odour of, 78
    oocyte development, 203
        control of, *207*
        food and, 209–213
    oocyte growth, corpora allata and, *205*

origin of, 77, *77*
pest status, 78
receptivity of female, 192
recurrent nerve and, 167
respiratory effects of hormones, 151
sex attractant, 180
space, and 293
stridulation, 78, 114
wings, *22, 23*
lice, 11
light,
    effects of changes in, 263–264
    receptors, 111
lintneri, see *Tyrophagus*.
lipase, 128, 129
lipid, composition of, 157, 158
    content of cuticle, 107
Litopeltis sp., on ships, 275
livens, see *Ectobius*.
lividus, see *Ectobius*.
lizards, 246
Lobster Cockroach, see *Nauphoeta cinerea*.
locomotor activity, *262, 263, 265*
    neurosecretory cycle and, *267*
    rhythm, 260
    stages of, 259
locust(s), 24, 32, 33
    enzyme activity and oocyte maturation, 209
    fossilised, 28
    swarm behaviour, 253
longevity on starvation diets, *295*
low pressures, effects of, 292
Lower Eocene, 28
Lower Tertiary, 29
'lucifuga', 14
lumbricoides, see *Ascaris*.

Madeira Cockroach, see *Leucophaea maderae*.
maderae, see *Leucophaea*.
male accessory glands, 193, 194
    storage excretion and, 158–159
malpighian tubules, 125–126, 153–154
    contractions and temperature, and, *125*
    excretory system and, 153
    peristaltic movement, 126
maltase, 128, 129, 130
    relative activity of, *130*
mandibles, 117, 118, *120*
mansoni, see *Oxyspirura*.
Mantidae, 158
mantids, 19, 32, 34, 35
Mantis, 32
    religiosa, 34
Mantodea, *34*, 34, 35
marginalis, see *Methana*.
Mastotermes darwiniensis, 29, 30
    egg mass, *29*
    wing folding, *25, 30*

mating, 178, 179, 182, 198, 191
  endocrine control of, 180, 181
  factors involved in, 178
  storage and excretion of uric acid,
    158–159
maxillae, 118, *120*
maxillary palps, 112, 113, 114, 119
  musculature of, 112, *112*
mealworm, see *Tenebrio.*
megacephala, see *Pheidole.*
melanin pigment, 101
mentum, 120
mesenteron, see ventriculus.
metabolism,
  aureomycin, and, 240
  protein and hormone control, 157
Methana,
  canae, 93
  curvigera, 92
  marginalis, 93
methionine, 240
mice, 246
migration, 51, *253*
  mass, 252–254
  sewage drain pipes and, 253
migratory instinct, 252
'mill beetle', see *Blatta orientalis,*
mites, 243
  cultures and, 247
mobility quotient, 261
modification, areas of, 24
mongoose, 246
montevideo, see *Salmonella.*
morbificans, see *Salmonella.*
mortality from low temperature, 281
moult(s),
  embryonic, 223
  number of and diet, 234
  number of and loss of appendages,
    233–234
  oocyte maturation and, 203
  sclerotised parts and, *235*
moulting (ecdysis), 16, 139–140, 145
  cell debris and, 139
  ecdyson and, 145
  growth and, 227–231
mouth parts, 112, 114, 117–121, *120*
movement (see also involuntary
    movement), 249–277
  distance of, 254–255
  Phoenix investigation and, 254
mud-daubing wasp, see *Sceliphron
    caementarium.*
murine typhus, 11
Musca domestica (House Fly), 293
  atmospheric pressure and, *293*
muscle, excitation through nerves, 168
mushroom gland, see accessory glands.
mushroom mite, see *Tyrophagus
    lintneri.*
mycetocytes, 154, 155, 202
Mycobacterium leprae, 308, 310

Nahublattella ecuadorana, 275
natural enemies, 243–246
Nauphoeta (= *Blatta*) *cinerea* (Lobster
    Cockroach, Cinerous Cockroach),
  adult, *81*
  appearance, 81
  bacteria and, 307
  biology, 81–82
  defence sound, 248
  description, 79–82
  distribution, 78–80
  early spread of, *77*
  false ovoviviparity, 82, 216
  food, 81, 211
  habitat, 80–81
  identification key, 96
  introduction into the U.S., 268
  longevity on starvation diets, *295*
  nymphs, 82
  oocyte development and food, 209–
    211
  ootheca, 82
    internal incubation of, 192
  origin of, 79
  pest status, 79
  Pheidole megacephala and, 247
  receptivity of female, 192
  sex attractant, 192
  starvation, water and, 294
  stridulation, 81, 114–115, 191
  trypsin and development of ovary,
    209
  vector capabilities, 311
  wings, *23*
Neoconocephalus palustris, 34
Neostylopyga (= *Dorylaea*) *rhombifolia,*
  adult, *81*
  appearance, 83
  biology, 83
  defence spray, 247
  description, 82–83
  distribution, 82–83
  habits, 83
  identification key, 96
  incidence in ships' holds, 274–275
  longevity on starvation diets, *295*
  nymphs, 83
  ootheca, 83
  origin, 83
  oviparity, and, 215
  parthenogenetic eggs, 83, 214
nerve activity,
  brain and, 173
  corpora cardiaca and, 173
  endogenous or spontaneous, 171–173
  neuro-hormones and, 173
  reflex arc, 168
  spontaneous, 168
  types of, 168
nerve cord severence,
  different positions, at, 208
  oocyte development and, 206–207

nerve impulses,
  conduction of, 167, 168
  oscilloscope traces, *172*
nerve tissue, units of, 160–162
nerve toxins, 173–174
nervi corporis allati, 166
  inhibition of corpora allata and, 206
nervi corporis cardiaci, 166
nervous system, 160
  autonomic, 160
  cardio-accelerator hormones and, *144*
  central (somatic system), *118*, 160,
    162
  evasion response and, *169, 170*
  haemolymph and, 176
  inhibitory centres, 173
  peripheral, 160
  reflexes, *171*
  simplified diagram of, *161*
  supply of nutrients to, 174–177
  sympathetic (visceral system), 160,
    164–165
nervus connectivus, 165
neural lamella, 164, 175
neuro-endocrine secretion, mating
  and, 180
neuroglia, 164
neuro-hormones,
  heart beat control and, 145
  nerve activity and, 173
  regulation of circulation, 142
  transport of, 145–147
neuronal pathways, 168–171
neurone, 160, 162
  association, 162, 163, 164
  motor, (efferent), 162–164
  reflex arc, 170
  sensory, (afferent), 162–163
  types of, 162
neuropile, 162, 164
neurosecretory cells,
  circadian rhythm and, 266
  tanning hormones and, 145
neurosecretory cycle,
  changes in, 266–267
  reset mechanism, 266–267
  stages of, 266
night activity, 258–260, *259*
nurse cells, 194, 199
Nyctibora sp. on ships, 275
Nyctiborinae, 37
nymph(s)
  antennae, growth of, 226, *227*
  cerci, growth of, 226–227
  development, weight increase, *232*
  development, variation in, *226*, 241
  diet, effects of, 237
  final moult, *229*
  growth of, *230*
    characteristics of, 225
  hatching from ootheca, 223–224
  increase in size, 232–233

increase in weight, 231
individual and communal rearing,
  236–237
loss of appendages, 233–234
moulting, 227–231
number of moults, 233–234
oogenesis in, 198
post-embryological development,
  224
predator of, 246
protein requirements, 237–239
regeneration of appendages, 234–236
seasonal variations in development,
  240–242
terminal abdominal sternites, growth
  of, 227
vitamins and, 240
weight of, *241*
wings, growth of, 227

obliquata, Blatta, see *Blattella
  germanica*.
occurrence, frequency of in ships,
  275, 277
ocelli, 111
  diurnal rhythm and, 264, *265*
oenocytes, 101, 108, 154
  function of, 108
oesophageal invagination, 124
oesophageal nerve, 165
oesophagus, 121, 162
oocytes,
  allatectomised cockroaches and,
    157
  bacteroid entry into, 201–202
  control of development, 202–203,
    207
  corpus allatum and, 167
    growth and, *205*
  development, inhibition of, 206,
    207
  development and corpora allata,
    205–206
  development of, 199
  growth of, *203, 204*
  maturation, moulting and, 203
  maturation and enzyme activity in
    gut, 208–209
  maturation and food, 209–211
  maturation and mating, 208
  primary, 199
  receptivity, of female 192
  respiration and, 151
  secondary, 199
  trypsin relationship, *210*
oogenesis, 200
oogonia, 200
ootheca(e), 21, 24, 28, 37, *100*, 187
  artificial, severance of nerve cord and,
    206–207
  carried by transport, 267, 268
  deposition of, 217–218

ootheca(e)—cont.
    dermestid beetles and, 246
    development in pest species, 296
    effects of humidity and removal of
        keels, 298
    formation, *204, 212*
        colleterial glands and, 211–212
    fossil, 28
    hatching from, 223–224, *224, 225,*
        295–296
        time, *222*
        temperature and, *223*
    hormone inhibition and, 204–206
    humidity, weight loss and, 299
    identification key, 99
    incubation period, 222–224
    internal incubation, 38–39, 215
    keel of, 218, *219*
    loss of water from, 296–301
    mite infestations and, 247
    oviparity and, 214
    oviparous habit of dropping, 38
    parasites of, 243–246
    production of, 213
        in *P. americana*, 209
    retention of, 38
    retraction of, 38
    rotation of, 37, 38, 215, 216
    structural features, 218–219
    tanning agent, 211
    water content, 221, 296, *300*
        changes in, *297*
    weight loss and humidity, *299*
        age and, *300*
Oothecaria, 32
oranienberg, see *Salmonella.*
Oriental Cockroach, see *Blatta*
    orientalis.
orientalis, see *Blatta.*
origin of cockroaches, 19, 41
ortho-dihydroxy phenol, 211
Orthoptera, 32, 33, *34*
outdoor species, 90–95
    Australia, 91–93
    Britain, 90–92
    United States, 93–95
ovarian cells, bacteroids and, 201–202
ovarioles, 199, 201, *201*, 202
    bacteroids, and, 201–202, *201*
    development of, 200
    panoistic, 199
ovary(ies), 199–200
    bacteroids, associated with, 200
    mycetocytes and, 202
oviducts, 199
oviparity, 214–216
oviposition, types of, 214–216
ovipositional habits, 39
ovipositor, 24
    fossilised, 28
ovipositor valves, ovulation and, 213
ovivora, see *Syntomosphyrum.*

ovoviviparity, 216
ovulation, 213
oxidative metabolism, 150
oxygen consumption, *149*
    corpora allata relationship and, *152*
Oxyspirura mansoni (Eye worm of
    poultry), 310

Palaeoblatta douvillei, 26
Palaeoblattidae, 26, 28
Palaeozoic era, 26, 28
Palaeozoic ferns, 28
pallidus, see *Ectobius.*
panama, see *Salmonella.*
Panchlora,
    irrorata, 275
    spp., 269
Panesthia javanica, protozoan symbionts
    in, 131
panzeri, see *Ectobius.*
Paracolobactrum,
    aerogenoides, 307
    coliforme, 307
paradysenteriae, see *Shigella.*
paraglossa, 120
paraprocts, 184
parasites of, cockroaches, 243–247,
    270
parasitic worms, 309
parasitism, 243
Parcoblatta (=Blatta. Wood
    Cockroach), 15, 85, 93
    bacteroids and, 201
    bolliana, 86, 93, 303
        size, comparative, *61*
    development, 242
    flight, 251
    identification key, 96
    occurrence, frequency of on ships,
        275
    oviparity and, 215
    parasitic wasps and, 243, 244
    pensylvanica,
        appearance, 87
        auditory perception, 115
        biology, 87
        description, 86–87
        distribution, 86
        habitat, 86–87
        infestation of, 86
        moults, 87
        nymphs, 86–87
        ootheca, 86
            keel of, 218, *219*
        origin of, 86
        parasitic wasps and, 243, 246
        sewers and, 303
        size, comparative, 61
        temperature, effect on, 87
pars intercerebralis, 145
parthenogenesis, 214
Pasteurella pestis (Plague), *308*, 310

pathogenic bacteria, 14, 306–308
pathogens, 303
pericardial cells,
  endocrine control and, 143
  heart rate and, 145
perineural cells, 175
Periplaneta (=*Blatta*), 15, 38
  americana (=*kakkerlac*. American
    Cockroach, 'Bombay Canary'), 15,
    40, 41, 42
  abdominal sternites, 57
    terminal, *98*
  adult, *56, 57*
  air movement and, 290
  aircraft, records in, 272, 292
  alimentary canal, 116–133, *118*
  antennae, growth pattern of, 226
  appearance, 55
  attacking man, 13
  auditory perception, 114–115
  bacteria and, 305, 306, 307, 308,
    309
  bacteroids and, 200, 222
  bananas, introduction with, 269
  biology, 56, 58, 59, 60
  blood (see also haemolymph),
    circulation, HCN and, *142*
    circulation in wings, 136–137
    segmental vessels and, 135, 136
    speed of circulation of, 140–142
    volume, 138
  brain,
    anatomy of, 163
    regulating function of, 167
  Britain, in, 315, 316
  bursicon concentration, *147*
  Carolina, in, 315, 316
  cardiac cycle *136*
  cardio-accelerator hormone and,
    144
  cellulase and, 132
  central nervous system, *118*
  cerci, 65, 114
  chemo-receptors, 114
  circadian rhythm, 258, 261, 262
  comparison with other *Periplaneta*
    spp., 60, 62, 63, 64, 65–66, 67
  contact receptors, 111–113
  copulatory behaviour, 189
  corpora cardiaca, and 167
  cuticle, 102, 104, 105, 107, 159
    section of, *102, 103*
  dermal glands, 109–110
  description, 53–60
  desiccation, 283, 288
  development, seasonal variation in,
    240–241
  development period, 58, 59
  diploid number, 197
  distribution, 53
    in Britain, *54*
  early spread of, *43*

egg,
  laying, 31, 213
  unfertilised, hatching of, 214
  water content of, 221
  environmental factors and, 290
  excretion, temperature and rate,
    154
  excretory system, efficiency of, 153
  fat body and, *155*, 156, 157
  food, 294
  gastroenteritis, and, 309
  habitat, 54–55
  haemocyte count, 139
  haemolymph,
    coagulation of, 140
    flow in tegmen and bindwing, *137*
    speed of circulation, *141*
  harbourages, 278
  head, *119*
  heart, *118*, 135
    beat, HCN and, *142*
    frequency and amplitude of beat,
      140
    rate and food, 143
  identification key, 97
  incidence in,
    ships, 272, 274, 275
    survey, 325, 343
  indoors, 54, 55
  insecticides, behaviour on heart, 141
  insemination, 196
  introduction into the U.S., 268
  jet aircraft, and 292
  leg structure, *252*
  locomotor activity, 259, 260, *263*,
    265
  longevity on starvation diets, *295*
  malpighian tubules, 126
  mating, 190–191
  maxillary palps. 112, *112*
  migration, 252
  moulting, 59
  mouthparts, *120*
  movement,
    distance of, 254–255
    involuntary, 268
    of food through gut, 127
  names, 15, 41
  nerve activity, endogenous or
    spontaneous, 171
    toxin, manufacture of, 174
  neurosecretory cycle and, 266
  nerve impulses, *172*
  night activity, *259*
  nymph(s)
    abdomen, 66
    antennae, 66
    cuticle, 104
    development, 55, *226*
    first stage, 66
    mesothorax, 66
    stages, 55

Periplaneta Americana—cont.
  weight increase, 232
  occurence, frequency of on ships,
    275, 277
  oocytes, 200
    growth of, *203*
    nymphal development and, 203
  ootheca, 55, 60, 65, *100*, 213
    adult with, *47*
    deposition of, 217
    effects of humidity and removal
      of keels, 298
    identification key, 99
    incubation period, 222
    keel of, 219
    production of, 209
    structure, 218
  origin of, *43*, 53
  ovaries, 199
  ovariole, *201*
    bacteroids and, *201*
  oviparity and, 214
  ovulation and, 213
  oxygen requirements and uptake,
    150
  parasitic wasps and, 243, 244, 245
  parthenogenesis, 60, 214
  peristalsis, 167
  pest status, 53
  phallic gland, 193, 194
  phallomeres, 185
  Pimeliaphilus cunliffei and, 247
  poliomyelitis virus and, 309
  population size, effects of, 237
  pore canals, 102–103, *103*
  pronotal pattern, *98*
  proprioceptors, 114
  protein requirements, 237–239
  recurrent nerve and, 167
  reproductive organs, female internal,
    199
  respiration and, 151
  Rhizoglyphus tarsalis and, 247
  salivary gland, *123*
  Salmonella and, 305
    oranienberg in intestinal tract
      of, 309
    panama in intestinal tract of, 309
    typhosa and, 309
  sensillae, 114
  sewers, latrines, cesspools, and,
    254, 303, 304
  sex attractants, 178, 179–180, 181
  sexes, difference between, 55
  ships and, 273, 274, 275, 277
  size,
    comparative, *61*
    increase, 233
  spermatophore, 194–195
  starvation, water, and, 294, 295
  stomatogastric system, 165, *166*
  stomodeal nervous system, *165*

  summer diarrhoea and, 309
  survey in the U.K., 325, 343, 344
  tanning, *146*
    hormone, 146
  temperature,
    circadian rhythm and, 262
    high, effects of, 283–284
    preferendum, 286–287, *286*
  tergite, longitudinal section of, *102*
  trochanter, *113*
  vector capabilities, 305, 309, 310
  volatile attractant, 179–180
  water,
    content, 138
    loss and respiration rate, *289*
    loss and temperature, *283*, 284
  wax layer, 106, 107
  weight and sex, 232
  wings, *23*
  worms carried by, 310
australasiae (Australian Cockroach),
    40, 41
  abdominal segments, terminal, *98*
  adult, *62*, *63*
    life span, 64
  aircraft, recorded in, 271
  appearance, 63–64
  bacteria and, 308
  biology, 64
  crop, 124
  description, 60–64
  diploid number, 197
  distribution, 60–61
  eggs, unfertilised, hatching of, 64, 214
  enteric caeca, 125
  food poisoning organisms and, 311
  habitat, 62–63
  identification key, 97,
  incidence in ships, 275, 277
  introduction into the U.S., 268
  movement,
    involuntary, 268
    of food through gut, 127
  names, 15, 41
  nymphs, 64
  ootheca, *100*
    adult with, *63*
    identification key, 99
  origin of, 53
  parasitic wasps and, 243, 244, 245
  pest status, 60, 61
  pronotal pattern, *98*
  reproductive activity, 64
  Salmonella typhosa and, 312
  sewers and, 303
  size, comparative, *61*
  vector capabilities, 311
  ventriculus, 125
brunnea (Brown Cockroach), 40
  abdominal segments, terminal, *98*
  adult, *65*
    life span, 66

Periplaneta brunnea—cont.
appearance, 66
biology, 66
Britain, in, 68, 273
cerci, 65
comparison with other species of
Periplaneta, 55, 64, 67
description, 64–66
distribution, 64–66
eggs, unfertilised, hatching of, 66
flight, 65
habitat, 64
identification key, 97
incidence in ships, 277
infestation at London Airport, 273
nymph(s), 66
ootheca, 66, *100*
identification key, 99
origin of, 64
parthenogenesis, 66
pest status, 64
pronotal pattern, *98*
sewers and, 304
size, comparative, *61*
fuliginosa (Smoky-brown Cockroach),
abdominal segments, terminal, *98*
appearance, 67
biology, 67
blood volume, 138
description, 66–67
distribution, 66
haemocyte count, 139
identification key, 97
occurence, frequency of on ships,
277
ootheca, *100*
identification key, 99
parasitic wasps and, 224
privies and, 304
pronotal pattern, *98*
sewers and, 303
size, comparison, *61*
ignota, vector capabilities, 311
orientalis, see *Blatta orientalis*.
peritoneal coat, 199
peritrophic membrane, 124
Permian system, 29
fossil records, 38
pest control industry, 14
pest species, seasonal variation and
development, 242
pest status, 39, 40, 49, 51, 53, 55, 60,
85
pestis, see *Pasteurella*.
phagocytes, 138, 139
phagocytosis, 138, 139
phallic gland, 193, 194
phallomeres, 185–186
pharynx, 114, 117
Phasma, 32
Phasmida, 32, *34*
brief description of, 33

Phasmidae, 158
Pheidole megacephala, 247
phenylalanine, 240
pheromones, 178, 179
Phoenix experiments, 254, 255, 256,
257, 304
Phyllodromia bivittata (=*germanica*),
see *Blattella germanica*.
Pimeliaphilus cunliffei (=*podapolipophagus*,
Cockroach mite), 247
plague, 11, 310
Plectopterinae, 37
podapolipophagus (=*cunliffei*), see
Pimeliaphilus.
Podium, 243, 246
cardina, 246
flavipenne, 246
rufipes, 246
poliomyelitis virus, 309
Polybia pygmaea, cockroaches in the
nest of, 242
polybiarum, see *Sphecophila*.
Polyphagidae, 35, 37
polyphenol, 211
Polyzosteria, 30
population density effects, *236*
population pressure, effects of, 237, 256
pore canals, 108
portentosa, see *Gromphadorhina*.
post-embryological development, 224
post-war building, *B. germanica*, *B.
orientalis*, and, 327
potential disease carriers, 11, 254
predation, 243
predators, 246
defence mechanism against, 247–248
prementum, 120
'Preusze', 14
primitive families, 35
primitive germ cells, bacteroids and, 202
primordial germ cells, see spermatogonia.
proctiger, 184
proctodeal system, see caudal system.
pronotal patterns, *98*
pronotum, 26
proprioceptors, 113–114
protease, 128, 129
protein level, influences in diet, 238, 239
protein requirements, 237–239
protocatechuic acid, 211
protocerebrum, 163
inhibition of corpora allata and, 206
Protozoa, 31, 94, 303, 309
protozoan symbionts and cellulase,
130–132
proventriculus (gizzard), *122*, 124
musculature, 124
Przibram's Rule, 231
Pseudomonas aeruginosa, 306
Pteromalidae, 244
publications, increase of, *17*, *18*
punctata, see *Diploptera*.

punctulatus, see *Cryptocercus*.
Pycnoblattina, 29, 30
  wings, *30*
Pycnoscelus (=*Blatta*), 15
  surinamensis (Surinam Cockroach),
    adult, *75*
    aircraft in New Zealand, in, 272
    appearance, 75–76
    biology, 76
    description, 74–76
    distribution, 74
    eggs, 76
    false ovoviviparity, 76, 216
    gestation period, 207
    habitat, 75
    identification key, 97
    longevity on starvation diets, *295*
    natural environment, 75
    nymph, last stage, *75*
    oocyte development,
      food and, 210
      inhibition of, 207
    ootheca, 76
    origin of, 74
    Oxyspirura mansoni, and, 310
    parthenogenesis, 74, 76, 214
    pest status, 74
    starvation, water and, 295
pygidial glands, 110–111, *110*
pygmaea, see *Polybia*.
pyloric sphincter, 126
pyrethrum sprays, 260

Quarantine, 269, 270
quinone, 211

Rats and cockroaches, 17
rearing, effects of individual and
  communal, 236–237
receptivity of female, factors affecting,
  192
receptor organs, 111–115, 206, 208
rectum, 126, 127
reflex arc, 170
reflexes, 170–171
regeneration of appendages, 234–236
reproduction, 178–219
reproductive organs,
  external, see genitalia, external.
  internal, female,, *188*, 199–200
  internal, male, *187*, *193* 193–194
reptiles, 243
respiratory system, 147–152
  difference between species, 149–150
  gaseous exchange, 149
  hormones and, 151–152
  reproductive cycle and, 151
  temperature and, 149–150, 282–283
  tissue respiration, 150–151
  tracheal system, 147–148
rest, behaviour at, 250–251, *250*

retrocerebral complex, 166
Rhizoglyphus tarsalis, *247*
Rhodnius, oocyte development in, 202
rhombifolia, see *Neostylopyga*.
rhythmical peristalsis, 127
rickettsial organisms, 11
rodent diseases, 11
rufipes, see *Podium*.
running, flight and, 251
Russian Cockroach, see *Blatta
  orientalis*.

Salivarium, 121
salivary glands, 121, *123*
salivary secretion, 31, 121
Salmonella, 305, 309, 311, 312
  anatis, 307
  bredeney, 306, 309
  enteritidis, 311
  montevideo, 311
  morbificans, 307, 309
  oranienberg, 306, 309, 311
  panama, 309
  schottmuelleri, 306, 309
  typhimurium, 307, 311
  typhosa, 307, 309, 311, 312
  vector capability, experiments and,
    311
Saltatoria, 32
Sceliphron caementarium (Mud-daubing
    Wasp), 246
schottmeulleri, see *Salmonella*.
'Schwabe', 14
scleroprotein, 211
sclerotin, 211, 230
scorpions, 243
season, influence of, 242, 258
seminal vesicles, 194
sensillae
  campaniform, 113
  hair, 115, *115*
  ovoid, 114
sensory receptors, 162
setae, 111
sewers, cockroaches in, 254, *255*,
    303–305
sex attractants, 178–181
  endocrine control, of, 180–181
  insect control and, 178
'Shad roach', 15, 51
Shigella,
  alkalescens, 308
  paradysenteriae, 308, 309
  sonnei, 309
'shiner,' 15
ships,
  cockroaches and, 273–277
  early records of cockroaches on, 274
  incidence in food areas on, 274
  incidence in holds, 274, 275, 277
shrews, 246
Silurian sandstone, 26

size,
    comparative, *61*
    increase in, 232–233
slave trade, cockroaches and, 268
Smoky-brown Cockroach, see *Peri-
    planeta fuliginosa.*
somatic system, see nervous system.
sonnei, see *Shigella.*
'Spanier', 15
specialisation, lack of, 21–23
species,
    closely associated with man, 42–73
    occasionally associated with man,
        74–85
    special interest, of, 95
    spread of, 41
Sphecophila polybiarum, inquiline
    habits of, 242
spermathecae, 196, 199
spermathecal glands, 196, 199
spermatids, 194
spermatocytes, 194
spermatogenesis, 194
spermatogonia (primordial germ cells),
    194, 199
spermatophore, 195
    structure and formation, 195, *195*
    uric acid and, 158, 159
spermatozoa, 196
spiders, 243
spines, see setae.
spiracles, 148, 149
spiracular nervous system, 164
Spotted Mediterranean roach, see
    Ectobius pallidus.
Staphylococcus spp., 306, 310
starvation, water and, 294
starvation diets, *295*
'steam-bug', see *Blattella germanica.*
'steam-fly', see *Blattella germanica.*
sternites, growth of terminal abdominal
    in female, 227
sterols and, 240
stick insects, 32, 33
stomatogastric (stomodeal) system,
    121, 165–166, *165, 166*
    frontal connectives, 165
    frontal ganglion, 165
    function of, 167–168
    nervus connectivus, 165
    recurrent nerve, 165
    suboesophageal ganglion, 165
stomodeal system, see stomatogastric
    system.
storage excretion, fat body, and, 153,
    154–156
stretch receptors, 206, 208
stridulation, 114
submentum, 120
suboesophageal ganglion, 162, 163,
    163, 164, 165
    circadian rhythm and, 265, 266

inhibition of corpora allata and,
    206
nerves from, 162
sub-social behaviour, 31
summer diarrhoea, 309
Supella (=*Blatta*), 15
    supellectilium (Brown-banded
        Cockroach), 37
    abdominal sternites, terminal, 228
    adult, *70,* 71
    aircraft, records in, 271
    alimentary canal, 116, 117
    appearance, 71–72
    biology, 72–73
    Britain, in, 68, 343, 344
    Carolina, in, 316
    cerci, growth of, 226–227
    description of, 67–73
    development, 73
    distribution, 67, 68, *69*
    eggs, development of unfertilised,
        214
        ootheca, number in, *72*
    food poisoning organisms and,
        311
    flight, 70
    habitat, 54, 68–71
    incidence in survey, 325
    indentification key, 96
    introduction into the U.S., 268
    life span, 73
    light, attraction to, 251
    longevity on starvation diets, *295*
    nymph(s), 72
        development, *241*
        growth rate of, 73
    ootheca, 72, *100*
        adult with, *71*
        deposition of, 298
        eggs, number in, *72*
        emergence from, 223
        incubation period of, 222
        indentification key, 99
        keel, *219*
        structure of, 218
        water content of, 297
    origin of, 67
    oviparity and, 214
    ovulation, 199
    pest status, 68, 78
    poliomyelitis virus and, 309
    season, influence of, 241
    size, comparative, *61*
    spread in the U.S., 268
    starvation, water and, 294
    vector capabilities, 311
    wings, *23*
supellectilium, see *Supella.*
supraoesophageal ganglion, 162
Surinam Cockroach, see *Pycnoscelus
    surinamensis.*
surinamensis, see *Pycnoscelus.*

survey of pest Cockroaches in the
   British Isles, 315–345
   central heating and, 324, 325
   conclusions of, 344–346
   geographical distribution, 320
   heating, 324, 325
   incidence of species, 325, 334,
      336–340
   infested properties,
      cities and large towns, in, 340–343
      numbers, distribution and types,
         322, 326
      pre- and post-war, 323
   locations within buildings, 331–325
   property, age, distribution and type,
      323–324
   report form, *319*
   sample, 320
   sampling areas, *321*
survival outdoors, 282
swarm behaviour, 253
symbiosis, 90, 94
synapse(s), 162, 164, 168, 169
Syntomosphyrum,
   blattae, 244
   ovivora, 244

Tachysphex lativalvis, 243, 246
Taenia saginata (Beef Tapeworm), 310
tanning of the cuticle, 145, 146, *146,*
   147
tapeworm, see *Taenia saginata.*
tarsalis, see *Rhizoglyphus.*
tarsus, 252
   regeneration of, 234
Tawny Cockroach, see *Ectobius
   lapponicus.*
tegmina (=forewings), 20, 24, 26
   haemolymph flow in, *137*
temperature,
   chill-coma, 280, 281
   high, effects of, 282, 284
   humidity requirements and, 277, 278,
      279
   influence of food and, 262–263
   low, effects of, 279–280
      recovery from, 280
   preferendum, 285, *285,* 286, 290
      different species, of, 286, *286*
   upper lethal, 282–283
   zero, death and survival below, 281
Tenebrio (mealworm), tanning and, 146
tentorium, 102
termites, 12, 19, 28, 29–31, 35
   common ancestry with cockroaches,
      29–31
   fossil, 29, 30
   swarm behaviour in, 253
testes, 193, 194
   mycetocytes and, 201
Tetrastichus hagenowi, 243, 244, *245*
Tettigoniidae, 158

thoracica, see *Hyptia.*
thorax, the, 20
threonine, 240
tibia, 20, 252
toilets, latrines and cesspools,
      incidence in, 303–305, 334
toxins, manufacture of own, 174
tracheae, 147
tracheal supply, *148,* 148
tracheoles, 147, 149
Tribolium, on ships, 274
trichiura, see *Trichuris.*
Trichonympha, 131
Trichuris trichiura (Human Whipworm),
   310
tritocerebrum, 163
trochanter, *113,* 252
trophallaxis, 110
trophocytes, 154
trypsin, oocyte maturation and, 209,
   210
tunica propria, 199
Tyler Project, 254, 255, 256, 303, 305
tympanic organs, 114
typhimurium, see *Salmonella.*
typhoid, 303, 309, 312
typhosa, see *Salmonella.*
typhus, 11
Tyrophagus lintneri (Mushroom Mite),
   247
tyrosine, 240

Urate cells, 154, 156
urates, 156, 157
   insemination and, 195
uric acid, 156
   accessory glands and, 158
   storage excretion, 158
uricose glands, 153
utriculi breviores, 194
utriculi majores, 158, 192, 194

vaga, see *Blattella.*
vasa deferentia, 193
vector capabilities of different
      species, 311
ventriculus (mesenteron), 124
vestibulum, 187
   ovulation and, 214
Vibrio comma, 310
viruses, 303, 309
vitamins, 240
vitellarium, 199
vitelline membrane, 202
viviparity, definition of, 216
voluntary movement, 249–250

Wasps, parasitic, 243–246
waste products
   deposition in cuticle, 159
   storage in fat body, 154–156
   storage in male accessory glands, 158

'Water Bug', 15, 304
water
    absence of, 294–5
    content of haemolymph, 138–139
    loss and respiration rate, 289, *289*
    loss and temperature, 107, *283*, 284
    oothecae, and, 296
wax, cuticular, 107–109
wax glands, *109*
weight, increase in, 231–232
whipworm, see *Trichuris trichiura.*
wings, 20, *22*, *23*, 24, *25*, 26
    folding of, 24, *25*, 29, 30
    fore, see tegmina.

fossil, 28, *30*
growth of, 227
haemolymph circulation in, 136–137
hind, 20, 24, 29
venation, *22*, 24, 28, *30*, 32
Wood Cockroaches, see *Parcoblatta* spp.
wood inhabiting cockroaches, 31
woodboring cockroach, see
    Cryptocercus punctulatus.

'Yankee Settler', 15

Zootermopsis, 31
zymogenic cells, 121

AUTHOR INDEX

(The figures indicate the reference number in the bibliography. Text page numbers are given in parentheses. A name given in this index may not be the first mentioned in the bibliography or text if a co-author.)

Abbott, R. L., 161 (124, 127)
Adamson, B. E., 369 (382)
Afifi, A. M., 101, 156, (70, 73, 117, 227, 228)
Akkerman, K., 425
Alexandrowicz, J. S., 180 (135)
Amerson, G. M., 268 (194, 200)
Anderson, A. D., 214 (154)
Anderson, T. F., 132 (102, 103, 104)
Anon, 8, 71, 110, 330, 389, 392
Antonelli, G., 386, 396 (303)
Arizumi, S., 413, 414
Auclair, J. L., 184

Back, E. A., 97, 98 (68)
Baker, E. W., 324 (247)
Ball, E. D., 120 (88)
Banks, W. M., 175 (128)
Barber, M. A., 419 (310)
Barron, E. S. G., 208
Barth, R. H. Jr., 231, 257, 260, 265 (180)
Baumann, C. A., 307, 308 (237, 238)
Beament, J. W. L., 136, 137, 140, 244, 247 (106, 107, 174, 177)
Beatty, H. A., 85
Bei-Bienko, G. Ia., 387
Bennett, S. E., 331 (303, 309)
Bernton, H. S., 428, 429 (313)
Beroza, M., 250, 251
Berthold, R., 329
Bills, G. T., 91, 92 (273)
Bitter, R. S., 394 (309)
Blatchley, W. S., 3 (12, 26)
Bligh, W., 360 (274)
Bloch, K., 314
Blochmann, F., 273
Block, R. J., 216 (155)
Bodenstein, D., 220
Bolton, H., 13 (27, 28)
Bonnet, D. D., 390
Bonsall, M. G., 309 (238)
Borom, M. R., 131
Bowers, R. E., 312
Brandt, C. D., 399 (311)
Breed, R. S., 398
Brongniart, C., 12 (24)
Brooks, M. A., 311 (240)
Brown, H., 428, 429 (313)
Brown, R. W., 14 (28)

Brunet, P. C. J., 290 (211)
Brunner von Wattenwyl, K., 33 (32)
Bünning, E., 335, 343 (262)
Bunting, W. M., 89, 90 (16)
Burmeister, H. C. C., 30 (32, 53)
Butenandt, A., 248

Cameron, E., 166, 315, 319 (10, 243, 244)
Cameron, M. L., 195 (143)
Campbell, F. L., 278, 291
Cao, G., 401
Caudell, (13)
Chamberlin, J. C., 55
Chamisso, A. von, 361 (274)
Chao, H.-F., 122
Chapman, G. B., 230 (163)
Chopard, L., 100, 125 (70, 95, 216)
Clark, A. J., 314
Clerc, A., 405
Cleveland, L. R., 123 (94, 131)
Collier, J., 123 (94, 131)
Coon, B. F., 191 (141, 142)
Cosway, C. A., 373 (288, 291)

Dateo, G. P. Jr., 222, 223, (158)
Datta, S. K., 168 (127)
Davey, K. G., 197, 198, 199 (143, 144)
Davis, H., 427 (312)
Day, M. F., 158, 170 (121, 123, 128)
Deay, H. O., 21, 61, 74 (31, 54, 59, 60, 213, 222, 241, 252, 255)
De Geer, C., 25 (32, 53)
DeLong, D. M., 435
Dennell, R., 133, 134, 138 (104, 105, 106, 107)
Denny, A. V., 47 (9, 43)
Dow, R. P., 393, 415 (309)
Du Chanois, F. R., 378 (292)
Duplessis, R. J., 325 (247)
Dusham, E. H., 145, 146 (108, 110)
Dutky, S. R., 340, 341, 342, 382 (261, 262, 263, 264, 294)

Eades, R. B., 331 (303, 309)
Edmunds, L. R., 88, 316, 317 (243)
Ehrhardt, P., 174 (128, 132)
Eidmann, H., 160, 163 (124)
Eisener, T., 326

Engelmann, F., 212, 256, 267, 274, 275, 279, 281, 300 (180, 192, 202, 205, 206, 207, 208, 312)
Engelmann, R., 424 (312)
Esterline, W. E., 349 (267)
Evans, B. R., 363 (274, 275)
Evans, T. M., 324 (247)

Fales, J. H., 115
Felt, E. P., 51
Field, G., 325 (247)
Fischer, O. von, 79
Fischer, R. G., 415 (309)
Fisk, F. W., 178, 285 (209, 210)
Flock, R. A., 119, 120 (88)
Fraenkel, G., 201, 202 (145)
Freeman, J. A., 364 (275)
Frings, H., 151 (114)
Frings, M., 151 (114)
Froggatt, W. W., 81 (60)
Fuller, C., 299 (226)
Fulton, B. B., 94
Fulton, R. A., 382 (294)

Gallagher, M. R., 217
Gardner, A. E., 367 (282)
Gardner, J., 214 (154)
Gier, H. T., 75, 272 (60, 156, 200, 201, 222, 226, 232, 233)
Gilby, A. R., 139 (106)
Gilmour, D., 228, 310 (159)
Girardie, A., 277 (203)
Giroud, A., 313 (240)
Götz, B., 249
Gould, D. J., 324 (247)
Gould, G. E., 21, 59, 61, 74 (31, 47, 51, 52, 54, 56, 59, 60, 67, 87, 213, 222, 241, 252, 255)
Graffer, M., 408 (314)
Green, A. A., 434 (318)
Griffiths, J. T., 73, 76 (60, 196, 209, 237)
Guerra, A. A., 203
Gunn, D. L., 188, 207, 344, 370, 372, 373, 374 (149, 282, 283, 284, 285, 286, 287, 288, 289, 291)
Gupta, P. D., 270 (195)
Gurney, A. B., 108 (78, 91)

Haber, V. R., 57, 77, 206 (46, 148, 217, 290)
Hafez, M., 101, 156 (70, 73, 115, 227, 228)
Hagan, H. R., 292 (216, 221)
Hager, A., 193
Haines, T. W., 93 (305)
Halberg, F., 336 (258)
Hall, S. R., 123 (94, 131)
Handlirsch, A., 15
Harker, J. E., 213, 234, 337, 338, 346, 348 (259, 260, 261, 263, 264, 265, 266, 267)
Harnack, M. von, 276
Hartman, H. B., 113, 262, 327 (191, 248)

Haydak, M. H., 218 (158, 238, 239)
Hayden, D. L., 378 (292)
Hays, S. B., 268 (194, 200)
Hebard, M., 43, 46, 83, 87, 117, 130 (41, 49, 51, 61, 88, 95, 98)
Helmboldt, C. F., 399 (311)
Hendrickson, G. O., 182 (137)
Henry, S. M., 216 (155)
Herrman, (309)
Herms, W. B., 50, 402
Highnam, K. C., 283
Hill, L., 284
Hitchens, A. P., 398
Hohn, (309)
Howard, L. O., 72
Howe, R. W., 364
Hoyle, G., 347 (265)
Hsaio, C., 201, 202 (145)
Hsiang, C. M., 416
Hughes, G. M., 239 (170, 171, 177)
Hull, W. B., 324 (247)
Hunter, W., 409

Illingworth, J. F., 109 (81)
Imms, A. D., 18, 36, 37 (29, 32)

Jackson, W. B., 333, 334 (255, 256, 257, 258, 304)
Jacobson, M., 250, 251, 255
Janssen, W. A., 400 (311)
Jettmar, H. M., 403
Jones, W. A., 250
Jung, R. C., 423 (311)

Kaplanis, J. N., 221 (157)
Karlson, P., 248
Kearns, C. W., 243 (174)
Keegan, H. L., 324 (247)
Keller, H., 219 (156)
Keller, J. C., 340, 382 (261, 294)
Kennedy, N. K., 237 (169)
Kent, P. W., 290 (211)
Kevan, D. K. McE., 100 (70)
Khalifa, A., 225 (158, 190, 195, 196)
Kilby, B. A., 215 (159)
Knipling, E. B., 366 (292)
Koller, G., 167 (125)
Kowalik, R., 406
Kramer, S., 144 (102, 108, 109)

Laird, M., 350, 356, 357 (269, 272)
Lamarck, J. B., 27 (32)
Landowski, J. von, 304 (236, 237)
Latreille, P. A., 29 (32)
Laurentiaux, D., 17 (28)
Lawson, F. A., 295 (218, 219)
Leach, W. E., 28 (32)
Leclerque, J., (295)
Lever, R. J. A. W., 104
Lewis, N., 383 (294, 295)
Lewis, R. H., 362 (274)
Ley, Lt.-Col. (302)

Lilly, J. H., 307 (237, 238)
Linnaeus, C., 23, 24 (32, 43, 49)
Lola, J. E., 179, 189 (132, 133, 138)
Longfellow, R. C., 418
Lucas, H., 52
Lucas, W. J., 48, 67, 68, 69, 368 (282)
Lüscher, M., 274, 300 (202, 206)

Macfie, J. W. S., 420 (310, 312)
Mackerras, I. M., 112, 397, 422 (311)
Mackerras, M. J., 112, 397
Maier, P. P., 333, 334 (255, 256, 257, 258, 304)
Malek, S. R. A., 133, 134, 138 (104, 105, 106, 107)
Mallis, A., 105, 349 (71, 267)
Marlatt, C. L., 2 (12, 267)
Masters, C., 431
Mathur, R. B., 203
Matta, R. J., 211 (151)
Maynard, L. A., 306 (237, 241)
McBurney, R., 427 (312)
McCay, C. M., 312
McIndoo, N. E., 181 (136)
McKittrick, F. A., 39, 326 (35, 36, 37, 38, 39, 122, 124, 188)
McLaren, B. A., 309 (238)
Melampy, R. M., 306 (237, 241)
Mellanby, K., 365, 371 (279, 280, 281, 284)
Mertens, S., 408 (314)
Miall, L. C., 47 (9, 43)
Micks, D. W., 416
Milburn, N. S., 241 (173)
Miller, A. C., 349 (267)
Miller, G. L., 258
Mills, R. R., 203, 204, 205 (146, 147)
Moffett, T., 359 (274)
Moiser, B., 410, 411, 412
Morischita, K., 426
Morrel, C. C., 417
Moulton, J. C., 86
Munson, S. C., 186
Murray, E. G. D., 398

Navas, L., 35 (32)
Necheles, H., 375 (290, 291)
Nicewicz, N., 406
Nicewicz, W., 406
Nigam, L. N., 66 (58, 294)
Noland J. L., 307, 308 (237, 238)
Notley, F. B., 370 (284)
Novák, V. J. A., 242 (173)
Nutting, W. L., 261

O'Farrel, A. F., 147 (110)
Olivier, A. G., 26 (32)
Olson, T. A., 421 (311)

Packchanian, A., 376, 377 (292)
Palermo, M. T., 121 (88)
Palmer, E. C., 93 (305)
Palmer, R., 107
Parker, B. M., 278

Patton, R. L., 214 (154)
Patton, W. S., 430
Payne, R., 326
Pemberton, C. E., 353
Pettit, L. C., 305 (237)
Pimental, D., 323 (278)
Pinkerton, M., 377
Piquett, P. G., 115
Pollard, M., 416
Pope, P., 62, 111, 422 (91, 93, 311)
Porter, A., 54
Porter, J. E., 351, 363 (274, 275)
Powning, R. F., 170 (128)
Pratt, H. D., 82
Pratt, J. J. Jr., 183
Princis, K., 38 (35)
Pringle, J. W. S., 149, 150 (112, 113, 114)
Pruvost, P., 16
Pryor, M. G. M., 287, 288, 289 (211, 230)
Pumphrey, R. J., 152, 153, 235, 236 (115, 169)

Qadri, M. A. H., 64 (193, 225, 226, 227, 228)

Ragge, D. R., 45 (41, 54, 68, 90, 92, 317, 340)
Ralph, C. L., 200, 211 (145, 151)
Ramsey, J. A., 135 (283, 290)
Rao, B. R., 178, 285 (209, 210)
Ratsimamanga, R., 313 (240)
Rau, P., 5, 20, 58, 65, 154, 155, 294, 321 (13, 16, 47, 53, 87, 110, 115, 116, 191, 217, 242, 246, 247)
Rawdon-Smith, A. F., 152, 153, 235, 236 (115, 169)
Reagan, E. P., 352 (269)
Rehn, J. A. G., 1, 83, 84, 102, 127, 128, 129 (11, 41, 49, 53, 77, 80, 83, 95)
Rehn, J. W., 22, 126 (35, 95)
Reitano, U., 404 (312)
Richards, A. G., 132, 311 (102, 103, 104, 240)
Riherd, P. T., 118 (88)
Riser, G. R., 44 (42, 48, 53, 56, 66, 72, 79, 83, 89, 237)
Robbins, W. E., 221 (157)
Roberts, S. K. de F., 339 (261, 264)
Roeder, K. D., 237, 238, 240, 241 (169, 171, 172, 173)
Ross, H. H., 60, 157 (48, 117)
Roth, L. M., 4, 6, 40, 41, 42, 44, 113, 148, 222, 223, 224, 226, 252, 260, 262, 263, 264, 265, 266, 271, 280, 282, 286, 293, 297, 318, 327, 384, 385 (10, 13, 38, 41, 42, 48, 53, 56, 66, 72, 79, 83, 89, 110, 158, 179, 181, 183, 184, 191, 192, 204, 206, 208, 210, 211, 215, 216, 237, 243, 244, 248, 252, 253, 274, 296, 297, 298, 299, 300, 302, 306, 307, 308, 313)

Rueger, M. E., 421 (311)
Russell, P. B., 289

Sägesser, H., 210 (151, 152)
Samson, E. A., 237 (169)
Samuels, A., 209 (151)
Sanders, E. P., 123 (94, 131)
Sanford, E. W., 162 (124, 129)
Sartory, A., 405
Saussure, H. de, 32, 95 (32, 67)
Savage, L. B., 325 (247)
Scharrer, B., 9, 196, 232, 276, 345 (16, 17, 79, 264)
Schechter, M. S., 340, 341, 342, 382 (261, 262, 263, 264, 294)
Schlottke, E., 164, 173 (128)
Schoof, H. F., 332, 415 (256, 304, 309)
Scott, H. G., 131
Scudder, S. H., (26, 31)
Seamans, L., 302 (234, 235)
Sein, F. Jr., 78
Sellards, E. H., 11 (24, 26, 28)
Serville, J. G. A., 31 (32, 66)
Servít, Z., 242 (173)
Severin, H. C., 116 (86)
Shaffer, M. F., 423 (311)
Shaw, E., 80, 99
Shaw, J., 227 (159)
Shelford, R., 322, 358 (273)
Shipley, A. E., 7 (14)
Shuyler, H. R., 49
Sieburth, J. F., 309 (238)
Siverly, R. E., 332 (256, 304)
Smalls, L. A., 255
Smith, M. E., 122
Smith, S. A., 415 (309)
Snipes, B. T., 169, 192
Snodgrass, R. E., 259 (185, 186, 187, 193)
Snyder, T. E., 19 (31)
Solomon, M. E., 369 (382)
Spinelli, A., 404 (312)
Stahl, W. H., 148 (110)
Stanislavskij, B., 143 (109, 110)
Starkweather, R. J., 380 (293)
Stay, B., 271, 280, 286 (204, 206, 208, 210)
Steinhaus, E. A., 407
Stobbart, R. H., 227 (150)
Stock, A., 147 (110)
Strejčková, A., 242 (173)
Sullivan, W. N., 340, 341, 342, 366, 378, 379, 380, 381, 382, (261, 262, 263, 264, 292, 293, 294)
Sutherland, D. J., 233
Swingle, H. S., 172 (128, 129)
Syverton, J. T., 415 (309)

Tahmisian, T. N., 208
Takahasi, R., 53
Tauber, O. E., 73, 76, 169, 185, 190, 192 (60, 139, 140, 196, 209, 237)

Tejera, E., 388
Thornton, B. C., 379 (293)
Tillyard, R. J., 10 (19)
Tinkham, E. R., 120 (88)
Todd, A. R., 289
Tozian, L., 240 (171, 172, 173)
Trager, W., 177
Treherne, J. E., 246, 247 (176, 177)
Truman, L. C., 114
Tsuchimochi, K., 426

Verhoeff, K. W., 34 (32)
Verril, A. E., 70
Vlasov, Ia, P., 63
Vorhies, C. T., 120 (88)
Voss, Z., 174 (128, 132)
Vroman, H. E., 221 (157)

Walker, O. L., 331 (303, 309)
Wedberg, S. C., 399, 400 (311)
Weiant, E. A., 240 (171, 172, 173)
Westlake, G. E., 381
Wharton, D. R. A., 179, 189, 253, 258 (132, 133, 138)
Wharton, M. L., 179, 189, 253, 258 (132, 133, 138)
Wheeler, R. E., 187 (138, 139)
Wheeler, W. M., 124, 298 (221)
Whelan, D. B., 96 (68)
Whitfield, F. G. S., 355 (271)
Wigglesworth, V. B., 141, 144, 159, 165, 171, 176, 245 (102, 107, 108, 109, 128, 129, 130, 138, 174, 175, 231, 281)
Wille, J., 328 (251, 260, 261)
Willey, R. B., 229, 230 (163, 164, 165, 166)
Williams, F. X., 320 (245)
Williams, O. B., 394 (309)
Willis, E. R., 4, 6, 41, 42, 44, 224, 282, 293, 318, 383, 384, 385 (13, 38, 41, 42, 48, 53, 56, 66, 72, 79, 83, 89, 179, 181, 183, 184, 216, 237, 243, 244, 252, 253, 274, 294, 295, 296, 297, 298, 299, 300, 302, 306–308, 313)
Wilson, B. R., 329
Winston, P. W., 142 (108)
Wollman, E., 313 (240)
Woodruff, L. C., 56, 296, 301, 302, 303 (48, 230, 231, 233, 234, 235, 236)
Wright, C. G., 432, 433 (316)

Yamatoto, R., 251, 254 (180)
Yeager, J. F., 182, 185, 186, 193, 194 (136, 137)

Zabinski, J., 269
Zappe, M. P., 106
Zimmerman, E. C., 103
Zmeev, G. Ia., 395
Zuben, F. J. von, 331, 391 (303, 309)
Zwaluwenburg, R. H. van, 354